The Most Beautiful Equation
in the Universe 0=∞=1

The Most Beautiful Equation in the Universe

$$0 = \infty = 1$$

Jesu Noh

0=∞=1: Grasping the True Nature of Reality

A small apartment in the Hakata ward of Fukuoka city, in South-west Japan, under the structure of a modest 105 square foot room.

A 33 year old Korean man in Japan, with meager language abilities and suffering from culture shock, isolated.

I had hit rock bottom.
Daily battles with suicidal urges.
A bankrupt business.
Human relationships in shambles.
Divorce.
Separation from a beloved young daughter.
Pain in rotting gums from extreme stress and poor health.
Gum inflammation had made my right cheek swell up, so that one of my eyes couldn't be fully opened.
How did my life end up like this?
Anxiety about the future and regrets from the past came welling up in my non-stop.
"If only I had done things X way, if only I had done more of Y..."
"What the hell am I supposed to do now...?"

These thoughts irritated me, worried me,
made my heart tighten up like it was getting ready to fail.
I wanted liberation from the pain I felt in both body and mind.

If only this reality were just a bad dream...
As these thoughts arose, I began to put my focus into my breathing.
Deeper, deeper, deeper. Putting all my awareness into a single point.
Like the breathing techniques I immersed myself in long ago, when I trained in martial arts day and night.

Just focus on breathing.

Just focus on breathing.

In, out, in, out, in, out…

Desperately recognizing only the cutting edge of breathing.
Don't get any ideas …

Then, suddenly, my awareness of my body vanished.
I became one with the flow of my consciousness as I ran and ran along an enormous helix of beautiful light.

It seemed that this light might go on forever, without end–and I kept running along it.
A spiral of light from all directions, converging to a single point.

Then, I reached the end of that seemingly infinite screw of light, and passed through a point smaller than any point imaginable.

"There's an end to this tunnel of light," I thought, as I stepped out of it.
All the light melted away and there was only darkness.

When I thought, "This world is made up of darkness," from somewhere I heard a voice saying "When there is only darkness, how does change happen?"

At that moment, everything was pulled into an intense spiral vortex in the darkness.
Everything in the world that I had held dear dissolved, was reduced to zero, and then disappeared…

I shouted "Stop!!"
It was an empty cry, and everything is zeroed out.
……
No feeling ……
……

Is it all over?
Did something happen?
I opened my eyes, which had been closed for a long time.
……
Oh, my God, what a complete upset, inside out, outside in.

Everything in front of me was 1,000 times, 10,000 times more than I thought I was.
As a state of being myself, a beautiful figure was unfolding.
……
There was not a single thing that was not me.

I and my universe vanished. There was nothing but an infinite ocean of darkness and silence.
It was at that moment that I grasped the true nature of reality.

$0=\infty=1$: the truth that binds together all events into a single unchanging eternity.

Ahh —so that's what it was!

The hollowness of my assumptions finally caved in on themselves, my delusions splintered and faded away.

Printed in the United States of America

First Printing, 2021

ISBN-13: **978-1-949001-54-9** print edition
ISBN-13: **978-1-954968-35-6** ebook edition

Waterside Productions
2055 Oxford Ave
Cardiff, CA 92007
www.waterside.com

CONTENTS

CONTENTS

CHAPTER 1

No-self, No-world

March 1st, 1996. Fukuoka, Japan. On this day—from the endless, infinite sea of possible truths and realities—a single, simple, heartfelt joy arose in one human in Fukuoka, Japan. This is the day on which I underwent a second birth: this is the day on which I uncovered the true nature of the world, the day on which my mission in life became clear. From this day forward, I became estranged from both Japanese and Korean society as being "the strange Korean who says incomprehensible things."

"The 'I' I know does not exist—the 'you' you know does not exist. All this is mere illusion: all that exists is the **'one motion.'** This is the everlasting, unchanging truth !"

I have been unfailing in this message for 25 years now, but I have struggled to communicate what I mean by that—both the vision I intend to express and its value. I have encountered first-hand the difficulty of being a Korean attempting to spread a new message in Japanese society. I have also dealt with Korean friends and acquaintances doubting my goals, what I hope to accomplish in Japan, behind my back.

I have been told that I speak purely idealistically, that my ideas don't conform to reality at all.

That being said, my heart is full of nothing but gratitude, hope, and conviction.

I am grateful for all that has happened so far—and with these feelings of gratitude, I will continue to bet everything on what remains of my own life, the lives of the people I meet, and the possibility of creating a beautiful future world.

In order for me to explain this truth I stumbled upon—$0=\infty=1$—and how it can be used to transform our lifestyles into ones that produce maximum happiness with the true elegance, freedom, and love of humanity, I first ask that you listen to my own story, if only briefly.

• Where does the light come from and where does it go out ?

I was born in 1963, in a small rural village in South Korea. At that time, Korea was incomparably poor to the country it is today, and was grouped among the poorest countries in the world. Diplomatic relations with Japan were normalized two years later, in 1965. This revolutionary development was made under President Chung-hee Park, whose hometown was right next to my own.

I am the youngest child in a large family, and was raised in an environment full of love from my parents, family, and siblings.

I have many pleasant memories from my childhood. For instance, one night my mother and I lit a lantern and walked along the country roads at night.

For no particular reason, I asked my mother a question.

• "Where in the world did the light come from and what happens when it goes wherever it goes ?"

I don't remember the expression on my mother's face when she responded.
However, her voice was kind and full of laughter, saying,
"That's a good question. Try to think of the answer yourself !"
That response left a deep impression on me.

As a child, I was full of questions.

I would often become fixated on the hidden mechanisms beyond things, wondering about the relationship between their outward usefulness and their inner workings. I'd take apart toys, pistols, clocks—and fail to put them back together.

Looking back on it, I think I was interested in finding an "algorithm" to energy, to the way that analog devices work.

I also asked a lot of questions to the adults around me.

"Why do all humans have two eyes, one nose, 5 fingers ?"

Of course, the adults didn't really have a way to answer this sort of question—coming from a child or no.

Asking everyone around me every naïve question that popped into my head occasionally got me in trouble, but I also had many enjoyable, heart-warming conversations.

Once I became an elementary school student and began going to school, I received what you might call an anti-Japanese education.

We were taught about how truly horrible the Japanese colonial era was. We were taught about how Korean pride was so very cruelly trampled upon.

Even in Korean society today, if someone tries to paint Japanese rule in a positive light, they get branded as a pro-Japanese sympathizer and lose credibility.

However, there are many Koreans who do not, at heart, agree with this social attitude. My father entered the Japanese army during the war and was sent to Okinawa. While there, he was grazed by gunfire, which left a scar on his leg. Had that bullet's path been different by a few centimeters, a few dozen centimeters, I may not exist today.

However, I never heard my father say anything bad about Japan. Not once.

To me, as a child, this was very strange.

Regardless, when I was young, I had an indefatigable interest in just about everything—nature, history, whatever.

• That Dam Will be Fine—the Japanese Made It

During this period, I heard some people claiming that a dam near our country village had broken down. I was worried about this, and asked my mother about it.

"Mom, is the dam near us going to be ok ?"

I still remember the quiet, firm way my mother responded to me.

"It'll be fine. That dam was made by the Japanese."

I felt an inexplicable, strange impression being left on my heart from this response.

There was a mysterious gap between the Japan I learned about in school and the way my mother and father thought about Japan. What did it mean ?

While taking history classes at school, my interest in Japan began to deepen. I loved Korea and felt great pride in Korea. The Korean peninsula's fate has always been deeply intertwined with its titanic continental neighbor, China, which has forever been a source of anxieties, conflicts, and war.

Of the 58 ethnic groups said to be mixed up in the "Chinese continent," only Mongolia and Korea are said to have preserved their unique culture and history. Throughout that endless fight, Korea is thought to have repelled military advances from China as many as 1,000 times.

This may be difficult to imagine in Japan, which is geopolitically sealed off by oceans and has only rarely dealt with attacks from outside and has enjoyed a relatively peaceful history as a result.

I like history—and as proud as I am of Korea's history, one day when I was in class, I was struck by a certain doubt.

How is it that Korea has been able to maintain its independence and unique culture from a country as gargantuan as China for so long, and yet was completely overtaken and controlled by the small island nation of Japan without so much as a war ?

I felt the need to know—for the sake of understanding Korea, as well.

I had to know the secrets of Japan's mysterious power, that was never taught to us in school.

• Dreams of Bruce Lee

As a child, I loved sword fights. I used to hold mock duels with kids in the neighborhood every day, and never lost—not even to the older kids.

In childhood, even an age difference of 2 to 3 years results in a large gap in physique and strength. However, I was determined to never, ever lose—at least when it came to sword duels.

One night, I had a strange dream. In this dream, I was resentful of the person who invented pistols. I thought, "I could have been the best in the world, if all we had were swords !" I remember feeling very frustrated about this—and then I woke up. I continued to have this dream intermittently over the course of a year. Apparently, I would also make helmets out of newspaper that looked like the *kabuto* helmets of the samurai, despite nobody teaching me how to do so.

I devoured a novel my older brother bought in middle school called "Ambition," which was about Ieyasu Tokugawa. This was from before the ban on Japanese culture had officially been lifted, and I'm still not sure why we had a book like that in the house.

My older brother died at a young age. Not long after that my older sisters would often gang up on me and ridicule me for having girly soft white skin when I was in elementary school, and my mother recommended I start learning martial arts when I turned 10.

I loved Bruce Lee, and over the 20 years that followed—throughout elementary school, middle school, high school, college, and graduate school—I threw myself into martial arts training and practice.

I was particularly interested in *kung fu* and *tai chi*, from which my interests expanded to a number of martial arts. I also conducted deep research into yoga and other breathing techniques in order to discipline my mind and body. I mastered all of the positions in yoga, later obtained an international training license in *tai chi*, and became a coach and manager at a martial arts hall focused on training athletes to be future representatives of Korea.

I loved martial arts training so much that training devices could be found littered all throughout the yard at my house, from the border of the property up to the house entrance.

Whenever I was in a bus or train, I would train my balance by standing on one leg as long as possible; while listening to lectures, I'd try to maintain a seated position without using a chair. I was totally immersed in martial arts.

"The secret to becoming a master lies in speed and power. **But what is the nature of speed ? Of power ?**"

I wanted knowledge of an essential "structure" that was not abstract, but rooted in clear understanding. In order to obtain that, I subjected myself to extreme training conditions, which led to me nearly losing my life 3 times.

• The Irritation of the Inexplicable

When I was in graduate school, I had a number of mysterious experiences in the pursuit of my ascetic practice.

One of these experiences in particular left a deep impression on me. It happened while I was engaged in breathing techniques.

I was holding a small rosary in one hand, quietly passing the beads through my fingers one at a time. I made my breathing softer, softer, slower, slower, until a single breath lasted around 20 minutes.

The human body has the potential for some truly mysterious development when put under training.

On another day while I was still in graduate school, I was practicing breathing techniques at a relative's home when my abdomen started to swell up more and more.

Bigger, bigger, bigger—it seemed like there was no end to it.

How much bigger could it possibly get? I did not have a good sense of the actual size, and I imagined my belly expanding out infinitely.

The feeling I had in that moment is one that I never have been able to feel in my daily life, and had a mystical—even sacred—quality to it.

I experimented with many types of training in my consuming drive to achieve an enlightened understanding of nature, and I found that breathing techniques worked well for me.

Even though I nearly died 3 times in my constant training, enlightenment remained a distant goal. Over the course of a year, I only paid attention to my breathing—yet even if I did nothing else but breathing, I wasn't getting anywhere. Eventually, during this sort of training I started feeling some strange sensations again, and I was full of excitement: "I'll get some answers this time for sure !" I became aware of some expanding in my abdomen, and got so happy I couldn't stand it.

However, as my belly began to swell, suddenly the image of a rubber balloon appeared in my head.

"What if my belly just kept going like this until I popped like a balloon ?"

Fear shot through me in a flash. I tried to stop the expanding, but it kept going and going, against my will.

Panicked thoughts came rushing into my head. "What will I do if my belly splits open and I die in my relative's house ? My family's name would get dragged through the mud... everyone would say that I must have died such a horrible death because my family is full of horrible people. Shit, shit, what should I do ?"

I desperately thought of ways to get back to normal, and somehow, in making some minute movement along my waist, I was able to stop the expansion.

The next issue was how to get my belly back to its original size.

I eventually succeeded at that, too, with some minute adjustments along my waist.

When I slowly opened my eyes and looked upon the real world, I could sense—through pure energy—that all things were in perfect unity. I felt deeply, incomparably moved, and tears began flowing non-stop from my eyes. I was overcome by the beauty of everything around me.

How beautiful and mysterious this world is...

Light was gushing out of my face, and I was full of laughter that made me feel like a smiling Buddha.

I thought that perhaps I had become enlightened. Later, I called my friends and students from the martial arts hall together and tried to explain what had happened to me—yet in that moment, I snapped back to reality, and despite trying to explain myself to the people before me, I distressingly found myself unable to describe any of it.

My only option was to awkwardly tell everyone to return to their training.

In that moment, I realized that I wasn't enlightened after all.

Sometime after that, I went off for the required military duty demanded of Korean men. While there, I fell entirely into the routines of communal living and military training, and one day realized that I had completely forgotten exactly how I felt on that day.

The only thing that remained was a lingering question within: **"Just** what is the true nature of the 'change' that creates and destroys the world as we know it ?"

• When I and the World Around Me Dissolved

Time passed, and at age 30, I was constantly busy with the management of the martial arts hall and the education for children.

I really enjoyed playing and studying together with students as martial art halls had a lot of students in South Korea, I was able to carry out my duties at work with the help of friends and colleagues.

I married a Japanese woman with whom I had a beautiful daughter, and I truly felt that I had it made.

I had been raised with lots of love and was proud of my accomplishments in both academic and martial arts: I studied biology in university, environmental engineering in graduate school and also trained a student who became a national representative of Korea for *tai chi*. Yet at this time a preposterous life-changing event was looming ahead of me, still out of sight.

It was a shocking blow, which felt like I had been cruelly knocked out of heaven and cast down into hell.

In 1995, when I was 32, I came to Japan.

I had actually come to Japan before that, when I attempted to earn a doctorate at a Japanese university. However, due to an illness in the family, I had to return home to Korea. This was my second time in Japan.

At that time, I left my business affairs in Korea to my relatives in order to come to Japan. When that business went bankrupt, it became the trigger for a tumultuous fall in which everything went dark.

The next year, I hit rock bottom, like I mentioned in the prologue.

I was in so much distress that I was thinking that it would be impossible for a 33-year-old Korean man who had lost everything to find a reason to live and seek a new path to walk in Japanese society.

I had lost my job, my family, years of trust, my health, my vision for the future. **Everything was in ruins, and all that remained was an intense financial pressure and a sense of loneliness and resignation like the charred remains of a burnt field.**

At that time, the vagrants in the park and even the stones on the roadside that caught my eye seemed happier and more desirable than I was.

I spent each of these forsaken days asking myself, "If I'd die today or if I'd die tomorrow," looking down at the cold ground below from my veranda.

Yet, on the other hand, something at the back of my mind was saying, **"if you can just get through this, it will all be worth it !" It was a strange feeling to have next to all my doom and gloom.**

Just keep breathing.

Just keep breathing.

Breathe out, breathe out, breathe out, breathe out, breathe out, breathe out, breathe out, stop.

Breathe in, breathe in, breathe in, breathe in, breathe in, breathe in, breathe in, stop. Repeat it.

I bet my life, desperately, focusing everything on my breathing, and my breathing alone.

At that time, I became completely disentangled with my physical reality and ventured to the ends of conscious space. What I found there was what I had been risking my life in search of all along: the relationship between change and permanence, or, in other words, **the truth of the cosmos: $0=\infty=1$.**

This is the truth of the world that every science, philosophy, imaginative work, and religion has tried to uncover and explain.

This is the single creative principle that guides the rise and fall of all things, that guides the creation, transformation, and destruction of everything we observe.

Upon acquiring this intuitive understanding, I ceased my deep breathing, returned to this world, and quietly opened my eyes. My attitude towards and awareness of everything around me had completely changed.

The outside world that once seemed to be separate from my own body and my sensation of space became totally inverted. The "outside world" became "part of me"—part of my inner conscious world—and I came to an understanding of myself and the space around me as arising from an original soul, an original self.

This sensation was so beautiful, I couldn't help but cry out. As I wept and wailed, I was flooded with an endless rush of the joy and feeling of the world.
This world is so beautiful, so mystical, so full of divine secrets...

In my small single room, in the absolute heart of silence, this extreme gushing of emotion seemed to transcend the boundaries of space and reach to the farthest reaches of infinity for hours and hours.

• Why Did This Happen in Japan and Not Korea ?

From that point onward, my life moved inexorably towards a new future, a new way of life. It happened one step at a time, but at a speed which amazed me.

My network began to expand little by little as I rebuilt my family, my career, my reason for living, and my worldview.

As I ventured forth on my life's journey once more, I kept asking myself the same two big questions.

The first question: "Is it possible to reconcile the truth I discovered at the reaches of unconsciousness—and the 'structure' that governs all creation this truth revealed—with the findings of philosophers, physicists, mathematicians, and scientists that currently exist ?"

The second question: "Why is it that I found this hidden 'structure' of the natural world—which I have pursued for over 20 years, since my childhood—in

Japan, and not during my intense and constant training in Korea ?"

These two questions were ultimately connected by a single answer, and I spent 3 months in single-minded conviction researching, investigating, and putting my findings in order.

First, I looked into every last record I could find on people who, throughout history, were thought to have discovered the ultimate truth—or to have come close to it.

Since I was little I have liked asking questions, and was never satisfied with abstract answers or being told to believe something without evidence. I wanted to try to corroborate my experience as much as I possibly could.

What did Socrates attempt to convey ? What kinds of theories were presented by the Western philosophy ? What about the mountain of wisdom that Jesus, Buddha, Lao Zi, and so many other sages the world over left behind ?

Buddhism is embedded in Korean culture and I had previous experience with the I Ching, Four Pillar astrology, and the cosmic dual cosmology of China. As I made more and more connections with these Eastern principles to my own intuitions, I was indescribably happy and joyous. No matter what question I asked myself, this 'structure' I had seen enabled me to obtain an intuitive answer, and my whole approach to answering questions and thinking about things changed.

I would have sudden realizations at all hours—even while sleeping—so during this period I kept a memo pad with me 24/7.

Because the Bible is the world's best-selling book of all time, transcending culture and time, there was a period during my student years in Korea in which I joined a Christian church and learned about Christianity.

At that time, I noticed many contradictions and points I disagreed with in the church's teachings. Despite my efforts to ask questions and debate these points, I was never able to obtain responses that satisfied me.

However, in the research I conducted following my own discoveries, I took a second look at the Bible. This time, I was focused specifically on identifying the things Jesus himself was trying to teach, and I saw that the truth Jesus found and wagered his life on in trying to communicate what was, without a doubt, the same thing I experienced. I was able to reconcile the teachings of Christianity in my own unique way.

Whatever would be able to unify the diverse, divergent forms of knowledge that mankind has created would need to be like the folding pin of a folding fan. I believed that the only thing this could possibly be was the "single motion" of eternal permanence. In the days I spent immersed in studying this idea, I accumulated nearly 300 filled notebooks. This world of ultimate knowledge cannot be encompassed by standard facts or theories. I saw that the key to realizing the sorts of changes in orientation that the future will demand lay in Japan.

From my perspective, the energies of Korea and Japan run counter to each other.
    I think that the feeling of oneness in Korea and the idealistic philosophy there which is so conducive to logical imagery—that is, "know, then act"—was possible because Korea is Korea.
    However, in Japan, there is a "structure" to which one becomes awakened via logic. I think this was possible due to Japan's pragmatic, utilitarian philosophy ("know through action") so well-represented by neo-Confucianism. That "embodiment" energy is strong in Japan, and it came to inhabit me.

My first birth was in Korea—the birth of my body. My second birth was in Japan—the birth of my soul. Both Japan and Korea feel like my home country.
    Had I made this discovery of the structure of change in Korea—had my second birth happened there—without a doubt I would have been working in Korean society and dealing with Korean people in my attempts to communicate my findings to the world.

If that had happened, there is no doubt that what followed would have played out very differently.
    However, entirely because it was *Japan* where this happened, I ended up somewhere in between these two countries. I think this was cosmically ordained. In this position, I could bring the two countries together while advocating for the pursuit of higher dimensions of human life.

As it happens, at that time I was in a pinch as I had overstayed my visa. Of course, this has now all been legally resolved, but at the time I could neither return to Korea nor stay. When I chose to interpret the situation positively, I found an answer before too long.

That answer was simply that I would have to get started in Japan—for Japan's sake, for Korea's sake, and for the world's sake as well.

• The Science of *Satori (enlightenment)*

Although I experienced a feeling of "oneness" in my energy level while I was training in martial arts in Korea, it did nothing to explain an overarching 'structure' behind the physical world.

Make enlightenment scientific and you make *attaining* enlightenment scientific

In order to make it happen, **a clear definition of what exactly "one" means is essential.**

In recent years there has been a wide popularization of the idea of "oneness," or "all is one," as a sort of abstract feeling. Just stopping here isn't enough to cause a paradigm shift. There is already a wealth of abstract information on this world, written by luminaries in thought, philosophy, and religion.

Because we now live in an era made extremely prosperous by science and IT, we need a more comprehensive system that does not contradict these things, but rather supports them and surpasses them.

What exactly is "one" ? How should we define it ?

What sort of attributes, mechanisms, goals, tendencies does the concept of "one" have ?

Without a clear definition that is mutually intelligible and that can be generalized to imagery, logic, and math—along with the methods and skills for how to use it—there will be no way of filling in the gaps between science and religion or between materialism and consciousness.

For example, I found that of the Eastern seekers of spiritual truth—including Lao-tze and Confucius from 2,500 years ago—**not a single one succeeded in acknowledging the same spiritual world, building off each other without prejudice.** This seems to indicate that all of these thinkers were fundamentally limited in their ability to express or share what they had attained.

In other words, **it is not possible to recreate one's own experience of awakening.**

It was the same for me: in order to help some-one achieve an understanding of oneness, all that can be done is give them advice through meditation and breathing training and maintaining a dialogue with them along their journey. Unsurprisingly, then, practice ends with changing individuals via this emotional oneness guidance: there appears to be no path to establishing a common foundation that would enable a revolution in society at large.

The history of figures of the spiritual world reveals a common pyramidal/linear structure of knowledge transmission, in which outstanding individuals collected followers who studied under them, and so on.

Even if the founder of a philosophical school did not wish to be responsible for a master/pupil arrangement, the low rates of literacy, basic education, and primitive scientific development left few other options in past ages.

Science, in contrast, relies solely on someone making a discovery. The systematized logic developed from scientific discovery can reliably be understood, absorbed, enhanced, and transcended by the next generation.

Compared to the infinite growth of scientific technology, there has been almost no development in human consciousness or spirituality for thousands of years.

On the other hand, science is coming up against the boundaries of its ability to provide answers on the Absolute. What we need in the 21st century is an organizational, educational, and epistemological structure that complements each domain's weaknesses and amplifies their strengths.

• Right Here, Right Now, Live Life as the Creator of Your Own Destiny

Thank you for accompanying me on this general overview of my life. **I discovered a world in which there is no distinction between myself and the world around me. Absolute truth lies in the notion of unity ("one").**

This is the only absolute truth. All else is conditional. All else is an artifice of the ever-changing, relative world.

This is the answer that people finally stumble upon in their various quests for truth. At the same time, we live in this physical world, and we need to understand the 'structure' between the absolute and relative worlds and the ways in which that 'structure' operates.

It might seem like this knowledge would have no effect on daily life, but in my own case, my life changed incomparably after encountering this "world of truth."

My central motivation is the deep indignation and sadness I feel at the destruction of human dignity.

I believe that everyone wants to live a life in which their unique brilliance and dignity blooms, full of freedom, love, peace, happiness, joy, and hope.

However, in reality, **even in the mature, developed countries of the world, depression, social withdrawal, suicide, and murder persist. There are also many people who have yielded to resignation and despair—they are alive in only the most basic sense of the word.**

What way of life should we advocate as truly ideal for human flourishing?

If we stop at "realistic," if we just "let things be"—if we lose our sense of idealism—humanity will find itself trapped in the inertia of "realism," forever.

Who do you really want to be?
How should society really be?
Humanity is more than this!

Right here, right now, you have the power to redefine, reconstruct, and reestablish your future identity and life. That is the original power of humanity that I want to communicate. It is the power of the deepest truth.

Right here, right now, you are the lead architect in the recreation of yourself and your reality.

In other words, you can perfect your individuality by nullifying yourself and your reality, graduating from the idea of "self," and inspiring many more "self-graduates."

Through the fusion of all these individual realities, you could help produce a tremendous force, a tremendous energy.

The curtain on this historical age would fall, as we burst into a new age for humanity—an age in which depression, suicide, and murder never occur again.

Most of our lives today involve trying to vaguely suss out the future based on the conditions that bind us today—and those conditions arise from things that happened in the deeper past.

The human heart is easily caught up in uncertainties and fears that revolve around past regrets and future anxieties. People become unable to make the most of their precious thoughts and feelings.

From a deterministic/karmic standpoint of cause and effect, their human dignity and potential cannot shine their brightest.

I think that it is time for humanity to move beyond our stagnation at this stage of development. And, in fact, we are already in the process of moving towards the paradigm shift that will usher in a new humanity and the culture of the future.

Humanity is a matter of determining who you will be, and what you will do.

First, let's clarify what we mean when we talk about "self," "humanity," "nature," "the cosmos." From there, let's think about the age we live in now, and extrapolate out the culture of the near future. We'll try to create a vision for that culture, and figure out what we would need to do to make it real.

The chapter is modeled like a dialectic (Q&A), and is derived from many questions, reactions, and opinions I have received when describing my vision in conversation with a large number of people.

I hope that the reader will read through my book and benefit from the many hints provided to build this "new way of life."

CHAPTER 2

How do you perceive the world ?

Interviewer:

— Jesu Noh, your extraordinary life path and the "world" you discovered as a result are of great interest to me. However, to be honest, I have trouble understanding how any of it relates to daily life. To start off, could you tell us about this topic in somewhat more accessible terms ?

Jesu Noh:

Sure. Thank you very much. OK, let's start with an example. Let's imagine we have a somewhat large bottle right here. The bottom half of the bottle is round and inflated, while the upper half is shaped like a thin tube. Now, we gently lower an egg into the bottle. The egg is just barely the right size to pass through the tube part of the bottle. After some time passes, the egg inside the bottle hatches. The bird inside that egg grows up inside the bottle. As an adult, the bird has become too big to pass through the tube of the bottle.

Here's a question:

Without breaking the bottle or killing the bird, how can you get the bird out of the bottle ? (See Figure 1 on following page)

— Get the bird out of the bottle alive, without breaking the bottle ? I don't know...it doesn't seem possible. How about using magic to make the bird smaller or the bottle larger ?!

That's very imaginative. If that was possible that would certainly work, but in reality, it is not. I raise this example because I'd like to have a conversation about **the assumptions in our thought.**

— The assumptions in our thought... ?

That's right. **A conversation about how you see the world: the way you look at things, your perspective, your perceptual methodology.**

— Figure 1 —
Humanity's perennial challenge

Without breaking the bottle or killing the bird,
how can you get the bird out of the bottle?

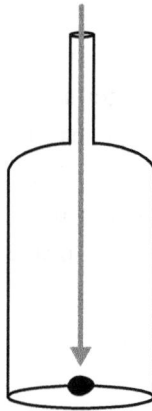

— How I see the world, or my perceptual methodology ? And that is related to this example with the bird and bottle ?

OK. There is a bottle, there is a bird... the bird is larger than the opening in the bottle, the bird is unable to get out... and this is related to assumptions in how we look at things ? It's like a Zen dialogue. I'm getting confused.

Yes, it's similar to a Zen dialogue, actually. Humanity is a thinking creature. **The essence of thought is dialectic, question and answer.** I often talk about what I call the **"highway of thought."** If some question "A" appears in a person's mind, it's in their nature to want to find the answer "B." Thus, they start moving along this highway of thought.

For example, how can I become happy ? How can I find a good partner ? How can I improve my family relationships ? How can I become rich ? All of these sorts of questions and doubts are the start of journeys down the highway of thought. They are also called **points of reference.**

— Yes, I see. Dialectic, or question and answer. Questions about what I should do today or how I should carry out some task—or if Japan's economy is stable, or how to deal with environmental issues. It all starts with a question.

Right. Science, philosophy, and religion are all the same on this point. **The special privilege of humanity, as well as its perennial challenge, is its ability to think.** What is matter ? What is power ? What is mind ? What is love ? What is space ? What am I ? etc. Humans love to ask questions about the essence of things, and in pursuit of the answers, we derive knowledge. Whether it's matters of money, human relationships, health, society, we spend our lives running on the highway of thought all day, every day. **"What should be done about X ? Is Y ok ? What is the right move ?"**

Do you see any connection between this and your own life ?

— In connection to my own life ? It's certainly true that every day, from the moment I wake up to the moment I fall asleep, I'm running on this "highway of thought," whether for a big issue or a little one. But I'm still not exactly seeing the connection to the example of the bird in the bottle. What's the answer ?

OK, I'll tell you. Let's make a connection between two things. The first is the meaning of the connection between the highway of thought and human life. The import lies in what kinds of questions we have—or, said another way, what kinds of "problem awareness" we have. This is of decisive importance when thinking about human life.

The reason is that when the highway of thought connects a "question A" to an "answer B," an individual's conscious space—and therefore their entire life—is under the control of the nature of their questions.

— What do you mean ?

Human life is determined by the quality of our questions—the quality of our problem awareness. "How can I get a part-time job paying $9 an hour ?" That's a possible question. You may find the answer, start the job, and now that's part of your life. But if you ask, "How can I get a salary of $900,000 a year ?" you probably won't start with that part-time job. In the pursuit of your answer, you will talk to people, study, start businesses, etc. Thus, you move towards that life.

This is just an example, but the kinds of questions you ask—the kind of problem awareness you have—is an extremely important part of how to change your life for the better.

— I see. Humans are always in the process of constructing their lives with thoughts, feelings, and actions, but if you look at the "structure" of it all, there is always a "question" and an "answer." In seeking answers, the thoughts, feelings, and actions people take shape their lives, so ultimately what controls us is the quality of the hidden questions behind what we do—is that right ?

Yes. Wonderful.

— So, how does this relate to the bird and the bottle ? Questions and answers...

Yes, so previously I said that this is a discussion about the assumptions in our thinking.

— Yes, that's right. So, what are the assumptions in our thinking about this question ? That's the point you are getting at, right ? Certainly, when I started searching for an answer to this question, I was running along the thought highway. However, I was unable to come up with any answer.

... so, in other words, my departure point—the quality of my question— needs to be reconsidered !

Yes, that's exactly right. The assumptions in our thinking, the assumptions of the question: If there is an issue there, no matter how incredible our thoughts, we will never reach an ideal answer. In order for you to understand what I am trying to say, this is the most important point to grasp.

— Earlier, you were using some key terms like "perceptual methodology," "perspective," "the way we look at things." So, in thinking about this question, we need to confront the assumptions in our perceptual approach to the world itself... ?

That's right. This is an assumption that precedes anything about the size of the bird or bottle or how to escape the bottle.

— Assumptions seem like they should be easy to find, but it's not so easy, is it ? There's a bottle, a bird...

Yes, right there. That's it !

— There is a bird and a bottle. You're saying that's the assumption ? That's where the problem is ?

Exactly ! In order to understand the world, I am trying to talk about, **it is necessary to change your assumptions about how to perceive the world.**

Over the last 25 years I have had a hard time conveying my message, and have even caused some misunderstandings. This is because there was an enormous gulf between the assumptions in my perceptual methodology and those of the other person in conversation. Of course, part of it was simply due to my own inexperience, but the root problem is there. The perceptual point of reference is completely opposite, and this made things difficult.

— In other words, your perception of the bird and bottle being there is completely opposite. If you just negate that premise directly, then...

.... neither the bottle nor the bird exist ?

Thank you ! That makes me very happy. That's right. My point of departure, my point of reference, is always that. **This is the state of "no-self, no-world."** That's the starting point. Since I discovered the truth of the world in Fukuoka, the idea that something "exists" is not obvious to me—**for me, "non-existence" is the base state.** That's the cognitive attitude I take to approaching the world.

Of course, I can't get away with just saying "non-existence"—I need to back it up with lucid comprehension. However, because the thinking patterns from our education are based on assuming "presence," discussing "absence" is liable to create misunderstandings.

There are **three types of "absence."**
1. Absence as we know it in our world of presence, accessible to us by the senses. This is "relative absence," defined by the absence of something that once existed or could exist.
2. Time-less, space-less, presence-less, energy-less "absence." This absence cannot be understood by the human mind, and is the "absolute void": the primal font of being.
3. The absence formed as a result of fluctuations in relative presence and absence as they arise from the "absolute void." In other words, this is an absence found in the "absolute world."

I'm going to use the first and second of these three absences to develop an image logic.

I want to clarify that while I say "no-self, no-world," there is still a "something" like the algorithms behind energy and what makes them come into being. I'm not claiming a total absence. This is often interpreted as an "absence" beyond human comprehension, but **there is actually an eternal "something" that exists.** These are not the concepts of existence, energy, time, space, etc. people are familiar with. I am talking about "somethingness itself," an absolute reality totally divorced from the world we understand.

For now, that's what I mean by "non-existence," just as an expression. It's fine if you don't understand what I mean yet. You will by the end.

— But hold on a second. My assumptions haven't changed at all ! Even if you say "non-existence" to me, I don't know what you're talking about. I'm not following your point. It doesn't seem helpful. Most people, when they hear this kind of extreme conversation, they won't know how to respond. They'll think you're crazy or suspicious, and just smile and nod until they can escape.

I don't know what you're trying to say—telling me I "don't exist" doesn't tell me anything about my life and might just make me nihilistic. What use does this have for how I can live my life ?

Yes, you're right, I apologize. Let's go over this bit by bit. One important point is that **in all times and places, the historical record shows that all seekers of truth believed that there was some key, some secret that can benefit humanity in the world of "absence."** This may seem like a strange leap in terms of our common sense and daily life-oriented problem awareness, but first let's try expanding our imagery a bit.

Socrates stated, "I know nothing." What he meant by this was that there was not a single thing on which he had any certainty.

Buddha discussed the notion of "no-self." He also spoke on the notion of **transience (impermanence).** Things are not fixed—they are always changing, always moving.

Confucius spoke about "idleness"—non-activity. Someone may be doing something, but they aren't really accomplishing anything. They may be looking at something, without seeing it. They might listen, without hearing. "I am doing nothing."

— This is just getting more and more confusing...

That's fine. Anyone is able to understand by using **nTech (Ninshiki Technology), the perceptual technology.**

Take the bottle and bird example. First you have a bottle, then you put an egg into the bottle, and a bird hatches from the egg. So, there is a sequential relationship between the bottle and the bird: the bottle is "first" and the bird is "after." I asked how the bird can be freed from the bottle—and nTech is able to provide a clear answer. The technique enables one to see how to make the "irreversible" into the "reversible" and how "irreversible" conditions emerge. This is also related to the limitations of humanity's highway of thought, which assumes that all things run along an irreversible course.

— The sequence of the bottle and bird ? The highway of thought and reversible/irreversible ? I don't know what you're talking about anymore.

Yes, I understand. It'll all make sense in the end, so let's go one step at a time. Let's continue the discussion on "absence."

I loved samurai when I was little, and they are famous for **"empty mind."** There is also the **"no blade soul"** of the renowned Japanese swordsman, Miyamoto Musashi. No swords. No opponents. That is the pinnacle of martial arts. Isn't that cool ?

You find it in science as well. Astrophysics could only conceive of the moments before the creation of the universe **13.8 billion years ago, as a "void."** But how could "something" arise from a true, absolute "nothing" ? The issue is that nobody has been able to extract any of the secrets of "nothingness." In particular, science is axiomatic about "presence"—it is an empirical discipline, after all.

— Certainly, there are references to "nothingness" in science, philosophy, and religion. I accept that. However, I have always lived in this "world of presence," and I have never met anyone who questions it. After all, we cannot perceive the "world of absence."

In addition, it's not obvious to me at all that this revolution in awareness would have any value for my own life in terms of guiding my decisions or improving my human relationships, work conditions, financial issues, or future outlook.

Yes, that's fine. I am definitely a strange person in the context of what is considered common sense today. However, **just like the Copernican Revolution, which brought us from geo-centrism to heliocentrism, the "common sense" of an age has been flipped upside down many times throughout history.**

In modern times, our awareness has shifted. It's tempting to ask—**why did the people from long ago get wrapped up in these ideas without any evidence ?**
Throughout human history, the one assumption that has always stayed constant is the idea that, within us and without is, is "existence." Right ?

— Right. It's an assumption that seems too obvious to be mentioned.

OK. Well, we are now in the age in which that attitude is going to be overturned.
This is the age of the greatest paradigm shift in human history. This shift is going to provide the common foundation upon which we will build a greater future for individuals, families, businesses and governments, peoples, and even civilization and culture itself.
This is a path that will not upset the current order or destroy it, but simply "raise the floor" of what we have with dignity and gratitude, all while fortifying our weaknesses.
I call this the cultural tectonic shift, or the "Next Renaissance."

— I understand. If this "cultural tectonic shift" actually occurs, it sounds like it could be pretty fun, in a weird way. What do I need to do first to understand better ?

Thank you. OK, let's think this over together. I think it's fair to assume that you believe that "you" and "your world" has "presence" or "exists"—yourself, or a desk, a chair, a cup, other people, the air, light, the Earth, the Sun, the Milky Way, the universe, time, and space. **It's a basic premise that's too obvious, even more than common sense.**

— Yes, that's right.

Right now, this moment of you and I speaking together "exists." Our voices and words "exist." The self, with its thoughts and feelings, trying to understand all of this also "exists."

— Right.

So, I have a question for you: If you are so sure that you, and the world around you, "exists," **what is your proof that these things definitely do, in fact, "exist" ?**

— Proof that I, the world around me, exists ?... Hmmm... I see. That's difficult. It's pretty philosophical.

It's philosophical, yes, and also scientific. Philosophical truth, scientific truth. Let's try to bring these together into an "eternal truth."

— I'm not very well-versed in science. As far as philosophy goes, I only know about Descartes. "I think, therefore..."

Right—"I think, therefore I exist" In Latin, it's *cogito, ergo sum*. (This is often translated as "I think; therefore I am," but the original meaning is actually closer to, **"I think; therefore I exist."**) It's a good place to start. What am I ? When it comes to thinking about one's own self-awareness, Descartes' influence remains deeply ingrained in contemporary thought.

Most of us are born into and live in accordance with a cognitive approach that is quite Descartian in nature.

— What do you mean ? That I and the world around me "exist" ?

That's right. "Existence" is taken for granted. This is a philosophical position known as dualism that assumes that the mental world and the physical world are separate.

I exist, you exist. You and I are different. Flowers bloom. They have their own existence, but when you look at them, you personally have feelings of beauty. Right ?

— Yes, it seems that way. However, what's wrong with that ? It doesn't cause any issues. It's fine. Under that assumption, I have different experiences, meet different people. I have important memories of the past—both happy things and painful things. To say that all of these things "don't exist" just seems nihilistic. No feeling, no joy. To say that this sort of "cognitive approach" or "point of reference" is necessary just seems meaningless—worthless.

Yes. Let's keep it cool and go one step at a time. Modern people are very busy, and they tend to want easily applicable knowhow, knowledge, or methods. For this, though, slow and steady is the way to go. When your mind is stuck on reality, it becomes impossible to properly grasp the world of essence, the world of truth. One must first release their fixed ideas, assumptions, and expectations with a will to separate themselves from reality.

This isn't just about faith—it's about encountering the truth with clear understanding.

Once you have established that much, you will be able to address all the concerns you raised.

Going back to the topic, let's think for a moment. Do you have any clear proof that you and the world around you "exists" ?

— Well, I've never really thought about it before. Right now, I am here. I am certain of that. And this chair is here, and I see you in front of me. In the Cartesian sense, the subject—I—exists, and all the objects around me I perceive exist. I can see them, touch them, hear voices and sounds.

You can see it, so it's there. You can touch it, so it's there. You can hear it, so it's there. Is that what you mean ?

— Yes, I suppose. There's no getting around it. In actuality, that is how I gain my awareness of the world around me.

Good ! That's a good observation. Let's simply define "reality" as the world composed of ourselves and all the various other things outside ourselves—other objects, time, and space. In this world, a self exists as a perceptual subject. The external objects of that perception are innumerable. That is the real world you live in, human life's "main stage," correct ?

— Yes, that's right.

OK. In order to know the true world—the secret of nothingness—you need duality. That duality I am talking about is the "reality" we have been discussing. If you understand "reality," you create an opening to get to "truth."

What is "reality" ?

— What is "reality"... ?

That's right. We live in "reality." However, do we live our lives with any intuition for what "reality" is ? Do we live our lives with any intuition for what the "self" in that "reality" is ? What do you think ? What is "reality" ?

— There's something you said a little while ago. "Reality" is the world composed of ourselves, the objects outside ourselves, and the time and space from which the world is made. Isn't that the answer ?

That's true, but that answer runs parallel to the essential nature of reality. I asked a question before: do you think you can explain, with clear evidence, the "existence" of yourself and the world around you ? This question serves as a corollary to that one.

— I recognize myself and the world around me as "reality." However, as far as absolute proof that "reality" actually "exists"... well, it's in the very fact of existence. I can see it, I can feel it.

Yes, we talked about that. So, let's try to put these things together. You can see, touch, and hear things—this is your subjectivity. More precisely, your brain is receiving information via your senses, and so you have thoughts pertaining to sight, touch, and sound. That includes how you feel right now—right ?

— Yes, that's right. Certainly, the sensations my eyes and skin and ears take in are processed by the brain. It's a neuroscientific perspective.

That's right. There's also the question of objectivity. There is an infinite variety of external objects beyond the self. The perceiving subject—your brain—recognizes that these things "exist," and applies meaning and value to them with emotional connections like "beautiful," "painful," "comfortable." In so doing, we live in the "reality" of our thoughts.

To bring that all together, **reality is composed of 3 perceptual elements.**

— Three elements ? Not two ? Subjective awareness, objective awareness. Those are the two that I notice.

It's 3. There is a theory that when human beings apprehend "reality," about 80% of their awareness is in their sense of sight. The other senses behave in basically the same way, but even after taking into account the importance of the sense of sight, there is another element beyond subject and object. For example, I am here, there is an apple here. I am a perceptual subject, and the apple is a perceptual object.

— Yes, that works. So, what's the third element ?

It is something you use in order for you to notice that the apple "exists." What do you think that is ?

— Ummm, it's not the air. Space ? That's not it either...

Here's a hint. Let's say that it's the middle of the night. If there are no stars in the sky, no moon, no electric lights—you're in pitch darkness—can you perceive the existence of the apple ?

— No, I can't. If it's totally dark, I won't be able to notice it. I won't be able to see myself, or what's around me, or have a sense of distance. Visually I won't have any external cues, so I don't think I'll be able to recognize it.

So, what does it take to recognize that there is an apple "here" ?

— Well, if I turn on a light... ah ! **Light ! It's light, isn't it ?**

That's right ! Light is electromagnetism. The visible spectrum of light constitutes one section of light's range of wavelengths. nTech refers to this as the "perceptual context." The apple, as object, reflects visible light. That wavelength enters the eye as visual data, and is processed by a number of nodes in the brain. The results of these processes are synthesized into a perception of an apple "existing" in reality (See Figure 2).

My brain, the apple, light.
The perceptual subject, object, and context come together as 3 aspects of a unity.

— I see. So, this doesn't just apply to apples. If I expand the idea to my hand, my hand becomes the perceptual object. You are a perceptual object relative to me, as is this room, as are buildings, trees, the sky, and the sun.

— Figure 2 —
The 3 elements of perception that make up reality

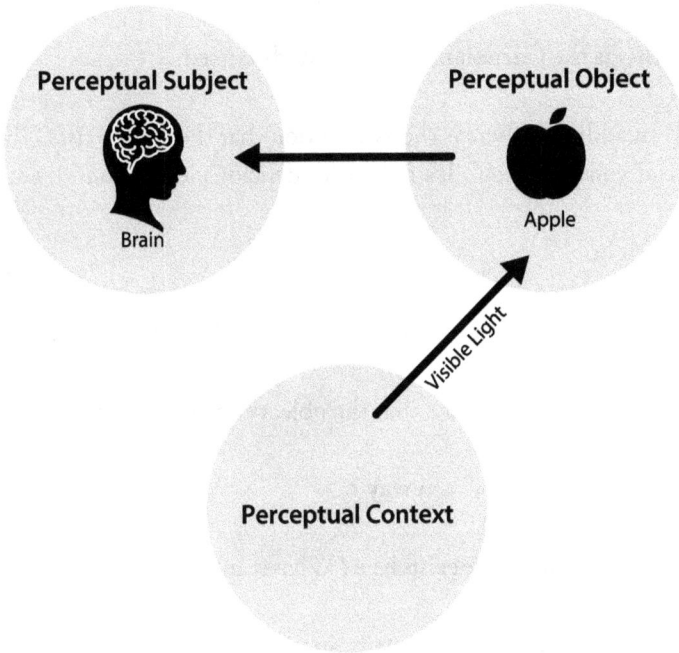

Perceptual Subject

Brain

Perceptual Object

Apple

Visible Light

Perceptual Context

That's exactly right. Wonderful. Yes, the sun, the moon, the stars, the Milky Way, and the whole universe are all "non-self perceptual objects." The self, in combination with all these objects, is the "reality" in which you live.

— That's right. These 3 come together to form "reality." I understand. In that case, let's continue with the previous question... on whether or not there is absolute proof that this reality "exists." Before, I said that it "exists" because I can see things, touch things, and hear things. There is an apple, and I can see it. I can also touch it. If I cut the apple, I can hear the sound of an apple being cut. I still think this counts as sufficient evidence...

Yes. That is normal for human senses. However, it is not the right way to perceive the truth. What is the assumption behind that approach ? Mainly, it's that you exist and the apple exists—that you and the apple, subject and object, are distinct.

— Yes. This is the Cartesian approach we discussed.

Exactly. In addition, there is the assumption that the apple exists. The apple exists, and you perceive it. It's red, or it's delicious, or it's round, etc.

— That's right.

So, here's a question. Let's start with objectivity in the 3 elements we described.
   Do you have any evidence that the object "apple" definitely exists ?

What even is an "apple," anyway ?

— Um. Proof that the apple exists here ? What is an apple ? An apple is an apple.

Hahaha, yes, that's true, an apple is an apple. Let's actually put an apple here. Try to pick it up. Is the apple definitely there ? What is the apple ?

— Yes, it's certainly here. What is an apple ? An apple is... well...

Let's think about it scientifically. What is an apple made of ? From a physical or chemical standpoint, apples are ultimately a clump of molecules. Apples are plants, but humans are animals—mammals, to be more precise. So, what are humans made of ?

— Ummm, humans are a clump of cells ?

That's right. Try to touch your own body. All of you is made up of cells—over 37 trillion of them. But what are cells made of ? What about DNA ?

— I'm not good at science, but... DNA is the language behind cell construction, and DNA is also a collection of molecules ! OK, I see.

That's right. Adenine, thymine, guanine, cytosine. These 4 nucleotides can be arranged into different base sequences. That's DNA. In fact, humans share almost 99% of their DNA with chimpanzees. The ways in which they are sequenced is a little different. That small amount of change is enough to create such a big difference. Life is truly mysterious.

So, you are a clump of DNA, which is itself a clump of molecules. The fundamental unit of the material of your construction is the molecule. Your body is essentially molecules, just like the apple. You're both molecules. OK so far ?

— Yes, I get it. That's interesting.

Yes. Now let's try gently loosening our imagination a bit. When we talk about molecules, there are still a lot of different types. Depending on how they are composed, the way they behave is completely different. **So what, then, are molecules ?**

— Molecules are clumps of atoms. I remember that from middle school science.

That's right, atoms. So then, us humans are made of molecules, which is really the same as saying we are made of atoms. Does that sound right ?

— Yes, that sounds right.

Ok, so then do molecules actually exist ?

— Do they actually exist ? Molecules definitely exist. We research molecules and people who put them to practical use exist all over the world. What do you mean by "actually exist" ?

Yes, the thing we call the molecule certainly exists, in a way. However, the idea that atoms are the fundamental unit of molecules, revealed when you split molecules apart, is not proof that the molecules actually exist—this is just a **"conditional entity"** based on the attributes we expect of matter in certain conditions. In other words, depending on the circumstances, we may call something a molecule, and in other cases, call it an atom. If that's the case, then **molecules are not something that absolutely exists.**

If things change depending on the circumstances, their existence is only relative. There is a relative world in which things change based on circumstances, and an absolute world in which things never change regardless of the circumstances. You can think of this as the difference between "relative existence" and "actual existence."

— There are a lot of entities in the relative world that change based on circumstances, and therefore they don't really exist... I think I see what you mean, from a logical standpoint.

For example, **what if, from the moment you were born, you lived life wearing a pair of microscopic glasses that you could never take off, that enabled you to see molecules ?**
   Would you be able to recognize the apple in terms of the color or shape you see ?

Let's try expanding our imagery.

— So, in other words, we have eyes that can only recognize molecules. If we could only recognize molecules, we wouldn't be able to see the red of the apple, right ? As for the shape... I'm not sure. But the apple is molecules, and air is also molecules. It's all molecules. In that case, **how do you determine where the "apple" begins and ends ?** Ah, this is starting to feel weird. Depending on the conditions, my perception of the world completely changes.

That's right. Just to reiterate, right now, we are asking the question, "What is an apple ?" Do we have any proof that the apple object definitively "exists ?" Let's try going a little further. In the relative world, things change based on conditions. Based on conditions, we can recognize something as an apple, but if those conditions change, it is just molecules, and if those conditions change again, it is all atoms. And what are atoms made of ? This is the question that was the topic of much of the developments in 20th century physics.

— Atoms are made of a nucleus and electrons, right ? The nucleus is made of neutrons and protons.

That's right. The materials, the base units that make up atoms are called elementary particles. These can be divided into force particles and matter particles. The frontier of particle physics has been focused on describing the Higgs boson and the graviton.

Let's proceed in a simple manner. The composition of the atom is of elementary particles. Depending on the circumstances, the object at hand may be the atom, or it may be the elementary particle.

— This is the relative world, which is conditional. In both of these cases, we can't say they have absolute existence ?

That's exactly right. I think we're about on the same page now. What is existence ? What is reality ? **You and I are both made of elementary particles. The atmosphere, light, the earth, the sun, the Milky Way, and the universe are overflowing with elementary particles. What if you were born with a pair of unremovable microscope glasses that made you see elementary particles ? What kind of world would you consider to be "reality" ?**

— Everything would be elementary particles in that case—like an ocean of them. However, air and human beings have a pretty big difference in mass. The atmosphere has low mass, whereas humans have high mass.

That's right, there is certainly a difference in the degree of opposition to recognizing that something "exists" by way of different masses. To put it simply, this can be described as "differences in density." This is the level that humans are able to physically observe. However, experimental physics reveals intangible secrets in the ultra-microscopic world. This is the world of theoretical physics.

Geniuses from all over the world work together to try to explain the phenomena of theoretical physics—but do you know what base unit makes up the elementary particles they study ?

— I don't know. Pretty much all I know about elementary particles is the name. Besides, I'm not really that interested in the scientific or physical conversations—I want to know about things that matter to me. Love, work, human relationships. I want to know the secrets to happiness and success, how to live a better life.

I understand. However, like I said before, **in order to grasp the truth and became capable of real change, you must first separate yourself from "reality."**
Everything will make sense once you do so. The secrets of matter, energy, and the universe as well as the secrets of love, the mind, and human relationships are all connected. This becomes clearer once you have obtained an image of the Absolute.

From here on out, we enter a realm where the opinions of mathematicians and physicists start to diverge. However, we are closing in on some answers. **That is because the world beyond elementary particles is a completely new world entirely.**

— I understand. OK, there's one thing I'd like to confirm. I want to return to the example of the apple, or to humans—in both cases, we are surrounded by many entities, many perceptual objects. We tend to think of them as obviously "existing." However, how can we be sure they really "exist" ? What is the true nature of these entities ?

Science is motivated to find the answer to this question, and has tried to find it by looking into what makes up these entities—what their base units are. It appears as though there is an apple, but in fact it is all molecules—and beyond the molecules, there are atoms, and beyond the atoms, elementary particles... etc. It seems fairly simple to me now.

That's right. It actually is quite simple. However, we rarely have the opportunity to think about it in our daily lives.

— That's right. By the way, what are elementary particles made out of ?

Right. Currently, the frontier of theoretical physics is saying that these particles are made of **vibrating strings of energy.** This is referred to as "string theory." This theory pushes at the boundaries of the nature of existence, and is a ground-breaking physical framework for that reason.

To put it simply, when we try to break down particles that we thought had a definite shape, we find vibrating, non-definite shapes that seem to be string-like parcels of energy. It's like going from a solid body to the essence of motion itself.

— Meaning what ? Both I and the apple are nothing more than vibrating energy ?

That's exactly right. **You are not a fixed entity. You are a clump of vibrating energy.**

However, just as the strings of stringed instruments make different sounds when played, there is a degree of difference between the energies of the vibrations in these strings. These differences can be combined in infinite different ways to created beautiful, magnificent symphonies.

The universe as a whole is the same: **it is a grand symphony composed of energetic vibrations. All things are connected as one, reverberating together.**

— That's a beautiful image. I feel like I am starting to understand what you mean when you talk about "oneness."

Yes. However, the "oneness" I am talking about is actually completely different from this image. This image is included in it, of course. However, there is a world of an even more absolute "oneness." Even if you talk about oneness or that all things are one, there are multiple levels to the depth of that statement. The base unit of all things that make up the universe is vibrating strings. This is common understanding in contemporary theoretical physics.

So now the problem is, **what are strings made of?** What do you think the answer is? There is one answer that has emerged from pure theoretical physics and mathematical logic, but it has not yet produced a falsifiable theory.

— I don't know much about the current state of theoretical physics, so there's not much I can say about this... well, I suppose it's all conjecture. Whatever creates this vibrating energy must somehow be the root or origin of that energy. Because this comes before vibration, it has no vibration. But because it is making energy vibrate, it must have some kind of energy also.

Is it pure energy—energy itself? If the sounds the strings made were all the same, there would be no differences, and so the only world that could exist would be a quiet one. But there *is* energy.... yeah, I'm not sure.

Wow, that's actually pretty close! The theory that the genius physicist Edward Witten has proposed to address the weaknesses of string theory is called M theory, or sometimes membrane theory.

The idea is that the energy of the vibrating strings creates an infinite sort of membrane. All of these vibrating strings become connected. This creates a world that could be considered "the world beyond," if you will.

— Hmmm, I see. Maybe my image does overlap with that a little. Just now you said something interesting: **"the world beyond."**

Yes, the world beyond. The place outside this universe, that is not this universe. **In the effort to resolve the mysteries of matter and energy, you ultimately end up at a worldview outside this universe.**

Let's return to the problem awareness and the questions we posed at the start of the conversation. What is "existence"? What is an "entity"? What is the proof of them? What is an "object?" For example, while this may seem obvious, right now you are included among the objects of which I am aware.

— From your perspective, yes. I am part of the divisible world of objects.

Right, right. When you tried to imagine yourself in terms of my experience, you analyzed it like a scientist. You are cells, you are DNA, you are molecules, you are elementary particles, you are strings.

— And not even that, but...

Not even strings, the membrane. The membrane is outside the universe.

Upon unraveling all the things, all the energy, in the universe, you see that you do not really exist. You can be broken down all the way to a place outside time and space.

Without a doubt, that is hidden within you, deep inside.

— Figure 3 —
What is "existence"? What is "reality"?
What is the true nature of a "self" that is constantly changing?

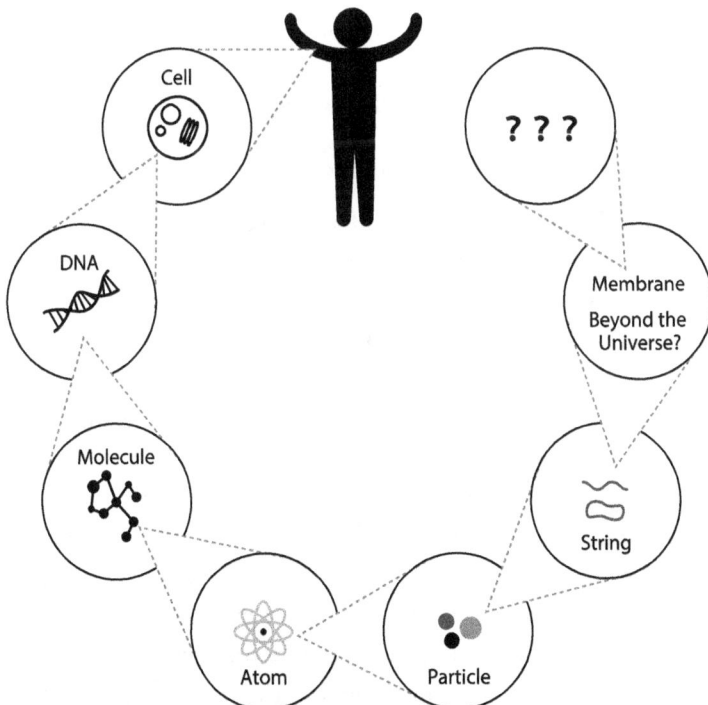

— .... well, yes, I see what you're saying. But this means that I "don't exist" ? I'm not actually here right now ? The real me exists outside the universe ? I'm inside some kind of membrane ?

This is really interesting. But what is the answer ? Humanity's true nature is a membrane beyond the universe, right ? I'm not even sure what to say to that. And even so, how can this "reality" be grasped ? Right now, I am here, speaking with you. This still seems like a certain fact. What is the meaning of my life ? What are the sensations I experience in this body I identify with myself ?

Calm down, now. Slow and steady wins the race—there's still a lot I want to talk about. Right now, I really want to push a particular conclusion that helps lead us away from the paradigm of common sense to which we have become accustomed. I understand that you think that this topic doesn't apply to your life, but as we go deeper, those doubts will morph into a conviction that arises from clear insight that you will not be able to dismiss. Once you have assimilated the whole path of questions and answers on this thought highway, the "final answer" you reach will enable to access an entirely new approach to how you think about yourself and the world.

On that point, there is one critically important thing that I would like to state again.

Usually, the objects that we think of as "existing"—in other words, the many things around us—turn out to bring us to a world that does "not exist" from a scientific perspective when we try to chase down their essence as far as we can.

Yet, just as you say, things like you and I, the apple, the world and the universe, appear to "exist." This is undeniable. So how are we supposed to think about this ? Do you remember my mentioning "differences in density" a little while ago ? There is a world even beyond the membrane world. We go down to strings, then we go down to the membrane—but what is the nature of the world hidden beyond the membrane world ? What is that "something" ? The consolidation of some amount of that "something" creates these "differences in density," and is why **"things appear to exist."**

String density, elementary particle density, light density, matter density, human density... none of these are things that "actually exist." However, depending on the conditions, we perceive them to "exist." Again, though, they don't "actually exist." Ourselves and the things around us are not things that "actually exist."

This is equal to the conditional relative world, or as nTech defines it, "illusion."
This "reality" is in fact a great illusory world. It is like a hologram.

— This reality is an illusion.... it changes depending on circumstance. It does not actually exist. Well, for the most part, I get the idea. However, I don't think it emotionally makes sense to me.

Of course, that's fine. That's plenty for now. The perceptual technology nTech was developed to help you understand, through imagery and logic, a world that humans are not normally capable of perceiving. It's a bit like adding an additional sense to the five you are used to. You might call it your sense of imagery, or your sense of consciousness.

— Is that like a sixth sense ? The ability to see invisible stuff, that sort of thing ?

This is different from the "sixth sense" that people often talk about. That sense is ultimately rooted in illusory "reality" and is just a collection of people who have slightly different senses from others. What I am discussing is **a particular "sense of imagery" that enables a person to imagine the "one-ness" that lies one step beyond the sensation of "reality" nullification.**

— I'm looking forward to it. So, I have now mostly understood perceptual objects, but to backtrack a bit, can you talk a little more about perceptual subjects and perceptual context ?

Sure. Let's start with context. You mean visible light. To put it simply, **human beings are only ever looking at light.**

Right now, you probably perceive a number of objects, patterns, and colors, right ? But in reality, you're not looking directly at any of those things. All you are looking at is light. All you see is light. To flip that around, without light, human beings cannot perceive anything via the sense of sight.

— OK, so we look only at light. Only at light... without light, we can't perceive anything. OK, that makes sense. If we're in a dark closet and there isn't even a little bit of light coming in, we can't see anything. I understand that. But there's something that seems off about saying that we aren't looking at things, patterns, or colors.

It's true that without light, I would not be able to see your expression or the lines that define your body. I also would not know the color of your skin or the clothes that you are wearing. However, even without light, blue is still blue, isn't it ? Light hits the color blue, so we see that blue is there. So ? Does that mean I am looking at light or looking at the color blue ?
 I feel like I've confused myself again.

People's prejudices are deeply ingrained. The reasons for strange cases of unrest are also easy to understand. Try completely flipping all of your assumptions about how you see things. **For example, that the blue you are seeing does not exist.** You see blue, so you unconsciously assume it exists, right ?

— Well, yes, that's right. There is blue and also red. Because light hits those colors, we are only seeing light. Isn't that what you want to say ?

No. The color blue does not actually exist. It's not just blue: **color does not actually exist.** It just seems like it exists under certain conditions. Newton had his prism experiments; light itself doesn't have any color, right ? "Visible light" is what we call the region of the electromagnetic spectrum that we can perceive, but the colors do not exist in that light itself. Rather, via our lens and cornea and color vision cells, **our brains, after processing the visible light data collected by the eyes, create the sensation of color.** In other words, colors exist because our brains exist.

— Color does not actually exist... ok, that makes sense, if humans suffer damage to their sense of color, the colors that we usually take for granted would become inaccessible to us.

Right. There are also colorblind animals. The wavelengths butterflies see in isn't even in the human visible spectrum. They are seeing a completely different color world from human beings.

— Hmmm. I thought of colorblindness as the inability to perceive color, but rather than there being a color out there that someone can't see, it's that they aren't capable of generating that color sensation at all. It's a subtle difference, but the implications totally diverge. It's a matter of changing your assumptions on how you view things, in other words.

So, in other words, one assumption is that color doesn't exist as a physical property. To go further, do patterns and shapes also not exist ? "Existence" isn't something that can be presumed... I see...

Your imagination is loosening up. That's right. We usually think that we perceive things like colors, patterns, shapes, etc. because they exist.

In other words, existence and our perception are separated. Existence is existence, and will "exist" regardless of if we see it or not. You just perceive those things as "being there" as they are. However, this "way of looking at things" needs to be flipped around.

Things exist—or appear to exist—because you perceive them.

This is true of all the senses, but the easiest to understand is our perception of visible light.

Try imagining something for a second. What if the human species had not evolved to be able to perceive the wavelengths of visible light ? There are also X-rays and infrared and ultraviolet frequencies in the electromagnetic spectrum. What if all humans could perceive X-rays, and our brain interpreted everything we saw as similar to an X-ray photograph ?

— Everything would look like bones, I guess... human society would look like a bunch of skeletons rattling around. We wouldn't have expressions or silhouettes or colors. It's a pretty bleak, uncomfortable image.

If everyone had been that way since birth, and it was taken for granted, it probably wouldn't be so creepy. Our brain functions have an "initialization" that doesn't change from birth to death. **We tend to think the world presented by this "initialization," and only that world, is absolute.** That is a big mistake. Humans believe the world they perceive is the only true one, but that is nothing but arrogance. Monkeys have their own monkey perceptual reality. Dogs have a dog one, cats have a cat one, snakes have a snake one. There are all kinds of ways of perceiving the world. **There are as many universes as there are perceptual subjects.**

Even in the human universe, there are differences between A's universe and B's universe. Then there is the monkey universe, cat universe, dog universe, snake universe.... an infinite number of perceptual universes.

— The conversation suddenly got pretty deep. We don't perceive things because they exist, but rather, things exist because of how we perceive them—there are many possible perceptual universes. However, I am still on the same planet Earth as you. I think there are differences in how we perceive the planet, but the planet still exists, and I think it's also a fact that right now we are here talking together.

Yes. This is an important point. I think we will need to return to this later, but the material world and the perceptual world are two sides of the same coin. The material world is a singularity, the perceptual world is infinity, and the two come together as a single duality. If you can grasp the sort of "oneness" this is, you're doing well. That's enough on that for now, though.

So, how do you feel about the perceptual context concept ? If we say that the "perceptual field" is a projection of how the "initialized" brain processes a section of electromagnetic wavelengths, our field will change based on the wavelength of light we absorb—visible light, X-ray, whatever. The way we see the universe is dependent on, is controlled by, the conditions of the light we see. You may think that rain always falls from above to below, but there is rain that climbs from below to above—it's true.

— From below to above ? So, you mean rain that falls from the earth to the sky ? That can't be true.

It's true. Of course, water, as a material, falls from rainclouds to the surface of the Earth, but there is rain that visually appears to go from the ground to the sky. It depends on the light conditions. In the seminar that goes over the fundamentals of nTech, you will be able to experience this sight for yourself, in person. The world that we perceive based on our brain's initialized conditions is not absolute. This is a point that I really want to stress.

— I understand. I'll keep that in mind. By the way, the last of the three elements, the perceptual subject, has come up a few times now. Most recently, in the context of brain initialization. The perceptual subject is the brain, right ? This brain has limits on the range of lights, sounds, and other types of information that it can receive. For that reason, if these conditions were changed.

That's right. **If the conditions of the brain, i.e. the perceptual subject, change, then the image of oneself, of one's surroundings, of reality as a whole will, in an instant, completely changes.** This reality is a construct of our five senses and our brain's awareness.

— I am a bit interested in neuroscience, and I know that things like optical illusions and mirages are pretty common. Trompe-l'œil, movies, and that sort of thing. Depending on how the brain functions, the image people have of themselves and those around them will be totally different. Like in the hit Korean movie *"The Eraser Inside My Head"*[1], or the movie *"A Beautiful Mind"*[2], about the genius mathematician John Nash.

Yes. Similarly, nTech contains a rather in-depth analysis of the film *"The Matrix."*[3] One line in the film contains the phrase, **"'real' is simply electrical signals interpreted by your brain."** It's simple and straight to the point. We are constantly immersed in a world created by the rapid informa-

---

1 *The Eraser Inside My Head. 2006. Geneon Entertainment*
2 *A Beautiful Mind. 2001. Dreamworks*
3 *The Matrix. 1999. Warner Bros. Home Entertainment Inc.*

tion processing our brains conduct on the wavelengths and frequencies—like light and sound—that our bodies receive through the five senses.

We tend to think of that world as absolute, but in fact, this is not true. If the brain is damaged, the world it perceives can change in an instant. You and I are products of our brains' perception. If the perspectival conditions of the perceptual subject—that is, the brain—change, our reality-outcome changes right along with it. This is the basic idea behind the third element of perception, the perceptual subject.

— Yes... but based on what you're saying about illusions of the brain, that the brain is an organ that processes electrical signals, etc., it seems like you are focusing on something a little deeper than what is usually meant by those things.

Yes, the illusion of the brain we discuss in nTech also includes the general sort of optical illusions and trick art you mentioned. The brain's perspective and the judgment standards of the human senses are just that hazy and half-baked. However, there is a deeper meaning too. We defined illusion as "the conditional, relative world." If you line up two trapezoids of the same size on top of each other, the one on top will look bigger, like so: If you line up two trapezoids of the same size on top of each other, the one on top will look bigger, like in Figure 4.

— It's true. This is an optical illusion that's pretty easy to understand.

That's right. However, "illusion" as defined by nTech is not just one in which the sizes of some shapes might look different, but one in which **the self and the universe perceived by the brain is itself all an illusion.** Yourself and your universe looks the way it does only because of the initialization conditions of your mental faculties. If the features of your brain changed, everything in your reality would change with it.

In that sense, this reality is a creation of electric signals in your brain—it's a screen image. A holographic that appears to have actual "existence." You could also call it a projection. In a 2D projection, you might see people,

— *Figure 4* —
What happens when you compare the trapezoids?

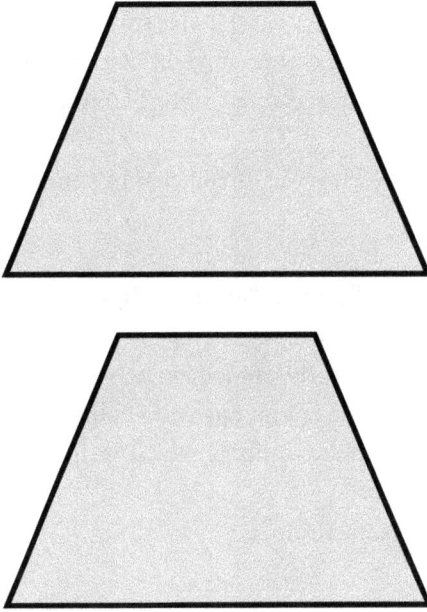

there's a story. Our current reality is basically that in three dimensions—height, width, and also depth—in ultra-high-definition.

— Even now ? So, you mean that even now, at this very moment, you and I don't actually exist and are some kind of hologram ?

That's exactly right. It's the projection of the 3D illusory screen that your brain outputs. I don't want to be too repetitive, but this reality screen, Yourself and your universe, in truth do not actually exist. The way we have assumed "existence" in our approach to the world is incorrect. However, it still *seems* like one's self and one's universe exists. There is no doubt about that. So, **why do things appear to "exist" ? We live in a framework that constantly urges us to see things as "existing" when they do not "actually exist." This "non-existence" is the structure of change that I discovered.**

I have a question now: if you were to try to name the one common feature between all the things that appear to "exist," what would you say it is ?

— The common feature between all the things that "exist" ? I wonder. There's a lot of different entities, myself, matter, the Earth, life, the universe. There's also time and space, right ? Ummm...

It's a difficult question. However, if you change your point of reference, it's simple.

The common feature of all that "exists" is its origin in "non-existence."

We were just talking about this a moment ago—this isn't an absolute sort of "non-existence." Humans cannot perceive it, but this is a "non-existence" that acts as a sort of absolute reality in which "existence" operates.

— From "nothing," "something"...

Right, all "somethings," without exception, arose from "nothing." of "nothing." See if you can imagine it.

— Hmm. Certainly, "I," too, have not always "existed." My mother gave birth to me over 20 years ago.

Yes, exactly. At some point, "you" arose from "nothing" to "something" after the combination of your mother's egg and father's sperm. Why ? How ? What sort of "structure" is behind this ? The mysteries and secrets of life and birth make for a major theme. In the distant past, Earth had no humans, no mammals, no animals, no plants—just matter. How was life able to arise from pure matter ? How did a planet on which life "doesn't exist" become a planet on which life "exists" ? This is related to the concept of "manifestation."

Shall we go back even further in time ?

— Going back even further would mean going back to before the Earth existed, or even before the Sun existed.... or the Milky Way. They all came into being. And the universe is the same ?

That's right. **The universe emerged from "non-existence." This has been a major hypothesis since the work of contemporary astrophysicist Alexander Vilenkin.** Stephen Hawking has made interesting comments like "God delivered a blow." However, the "structure" behind this is still not understood.

To look at this from a different angle, **what is the self ? Where does it come from and how and why does it exist in the form it does now ? Where is it headed and for what purpose ?** This is connected to knowing one's roots, one's origin.

— I see. It seems like you could find an answer if you could trace how the self came to "exist," all the way back to the most primal causes. There's the concept of "first cause" in philosophy, so I guess the origin of the self would be there. That idea is connected to the secrets of the origin of the universe, so it's a big theme not only in philosophy, but also science and religion—the Creator of the universe. As Hawking said, the only way to express it is in terms of God.

That's right. **Not only Hawking, but all modern physicists have a desire to understand the designs of the God that created the universe.** Comparing this to spiritual language used for the mental world, it is similar to encountering the "true self" by delving into the deepest reaches of your soul.

With that point of reference, **the universe, the Milky Way, the Sun, the Earth, plant life, animal life, humanity, and yourself all came from the same place of "non-existence."** If that's the case, the point of reference for you as an entity is not this flesh-and-blood body, but rather in that very "non-existence."

I sometimes use words like "original mind" or "original position," but it doesn't really matter what you call it. There are many people who recognize that they and their universe do not actually exist. Physicists call this a vacuum or nothingness, and there are all kinds of other things you might call it— emptiness, the Way, God, oneness, "something great," etc.—but the way I see it, **there is no-one who has understood this absolute origin point clearly and lucidly and managed to explain it correctly within the realm of the Theory of Mathematics.** What is important is figuring out, in the end, just what exactly that absolute reality of "nothingness" is.

Just exactly what, with what structure, for what purpose, and in what direction is "something" continuously being created from "nothing ?"

Whatever it is, it contains all points of reference for oneself and one's hologram universe. What's more, it is the shared point of reference for all entities and phenomena and disciplines that seek to discover the secrets of an underlying order.

Imagine a folding fan was here. Don't focus on the separated ribs of the fan, but rather the hinge, the point they all share. It is this point that brings the rest together. Imagine that this world of absolute "oneness" has become something that, with logic and imagery, anyone can understand, transmit, and share. These rediscovered truths can be understood simply by communicating them, and the world they describe can be applied to this reality.

— I see how if that were the real thing, it would be amazing, I think it would be amazing. However, to go back to the start of the conversation, about the bird in the bottle—I still don't understand what that's about.

Thank you. At this point, we're done with the warming up. We've discussed things in very broad terms, so now we are going to go deeper. This will also include the value these topics have for your life and work, your future, and the future of human society.

CHAPTER 3

Waking up from the illusion

Interviewer:

— I'd like to revisit something—I think the world you discovered when you were at rock bottom has special import for all of us. Certainly, many of those who have been called sages and prophets have left behind statements claiming that there is an extremely important "something" in this world of "nothingness." Moreover, this "nothingness" is different from the state of "no object is present."

Human beings are not able to grasp this with their senses and cognition being in the dimension that they are, but there is a true unchanging something, an absolute existence that is out there. This is something different from the so-called sixth sense, or spiritual sense, or psychic abilities. It is deeper—the deepest, most primordial thing. This world is accessible to anyone, and if it is applied towards life or work in some fashion, one can expect that it will lead to big, new developments in their goals.

However, I can't help but wonder if this world is really accessible to everyone, and the idea of knowing it also scares me a little. I imagine that you have been misunderstood and criticized a lot, but what is the meaning behind, or maybe I should say the motivational origin behind your continued discussion of this world ?

Jesu Noh:

Sure. In a word, **I want other human beings to experience true wonder. I want them to recognize humanity's limitless potential and dignity.** Humanity is more than this. One's self is more than they know. **I want to help inspire a revolution towards an ever greater way of life and bring life quality to another level.** I hope for all individuals to come together in deep love and trust, forging a sincere, unconditional human dignity that enables the enjoyment of an ideal human life. If that trust and love could be spread, a dignified society without depression, suicide or murder would emerge. A path towards world peace without war between states, ethnicities, and religions would emerge. My ideal future looks something like that.

— From the individual, to the world. It seems that the keyword is "dignity."

That's right. **Dignity. No comparisons. There is nothing to compare. The world as it is would be the best possible world, unconditionally. The self would be the best possible self, unconditionally. Nobody controls or is controlled by others. Nothing is placed above oneself. No above or below. Just an unconditional, absolute, unified dignity.** Humanity's origin transcends the sensations of the physical body. What I discovered in 1996 was humanity's true beauty. So I can't bear to see this lifestyle that revolves around survival. Struggling in that way is a civilization for animals. I don't want to waste a single minute, a single second. **I want to end this material civilization, this survival civilization based on trying to survive in the worst possible hell. I want to cause a paradigm shift that will move us towards a spiritual civilization founded on a will to dignity and recreation, expressed in the best possible heaven, oriented positively towards nature.** That is where I get my motivation.

— You're saying that right now, we are in the "worst possible hell" ? It's a pretty big project to try to guide us out of the worst possible hell towards the best possible heaven.

However, whether it's this perfect dignity or your ambitious efforts, these ideas go beyond my ability to visualize. I believe you when you say you actually experienced this realization, but these ideas of myself and my universe not existing, or the idea of an absolute unitary dignity, seem like they could easily go astray into a sort of dogmatic teaching. Do you have anything to say about that ?

Yes, it's insightful of you to recognize that issue. **Throughout history, the words of spiritual leaders have been dogmatized and used as the basis for religious groups, regardless of the "founder's" personal intents or desires.** I recognize that religion has many positive aspects. However, some organizations can become very self-righteous and exclusive, which is the negative side. nTech is focused on **0 belief, 100% understanding.** It is a novel perceptual technology that has been developed with the use of logic and imagery to ensure that anyone can objectively achieve a "renewal of perception."

— OK, I want to agree with that, but personally I'd like to concretely try this "renewal of perception" into this world of yours first. What must I do in order to get there ?

Yes, of course. Human beings are fated to think, and thinking always involves the "thought highway" of dialectic —we spoke about this before. **Asking a question and receiving an answer, again and again—in so doing, one's mind becomes more and more accustomed to the logic of the problem.** I and my colleagues discuss this world in the nTech seminars, and there is one thing we often say: **"Human beings can't listen to each other."**

— Wait, hold on, I'm paying attention to you, that's not the issue.

Ok. Of course, I know that you are engaging with me and striving to understand what I'm saying. There's no question about that. Thank you. However, while it seems like you are listening, if you look more closely, you actually aren't. Don't misunderstand, though. This isn't about good or bad, it's a conversation about how humans perceive things.

— I really do think I'm listening, though... what do you mean ?

Right now, the essence of what I'm saying is information expressed as sounds, symbols, basically. Humans attach images to those symbols based on a more-or-less shared meaning/value system.

— Yes, I agree.

So right now, you are thinking to yourself about what I am saying, right ?
But humanity takes these sounds, these voices, these names, **and with the aural information that comes in through our ears, our brains analyze it, and we interpret it in accordance with our personal analysis.** Can you imagine what I mean ?

— I hear my own analysis, on my own... ummm, there is information in what you say, your words, and my ear, my brain, receives that information and understands it. This and that means something or something else, etc. I see. Certainly, rather than hearing what you personally are saying, what I am ultimately listening to is my own analysis of it.

That's right. Hence, "human beings can't listen to each other." **You listen to your own interpretation in your own brain. That is why communication between people always falls apart on nuanced matters.** In other words, simply seeing things with our physical eyes and ears and listening to the analysis inside our brains means that we lack a "ruler for correctly measuring the mind." Hence, we "can't listen to each other."

Without such a ruler, we can hear voices as sounds, but we have no access to the mind, energy, spirit, consciousness, or intent behind the words. As a result, our relationships face conflicts. We'll discuss communication more later, but for now, rather than talking about these "things in reality," let's try to go as far as we can with understanding the true nature of things.

— You mean experiencing a complete separation of reality like you were talking about. OK, I remember. I want to be able to apply these ideas to reality as fast as possible, but if I think in that way I won't be able to grasp this "true nature."

Yes, that's right. Similarly, if someone is listening to what I'm saying entirely in terms of their own interpretation, they'll end up totally off track and misunderstand.

Then there's an even more important point. This returns to the previous conversation, about questions and answers. That is, **in listening to something, one personally does the work of establishing the logic path between question and answer themselves.**

Our seminars are framed as dialectics, and participants are able to ask questions there. Compared to books or the internet which have a one-way information stream, it is possible to progress along the thought highway faster and more accurately. That's why the seminars are so useful.

— I see. So, I would ask a question, answer it, grapple with the logic, and move forward... in that case, the space for pure faith would seem to be diminished.

Also, since in the end it would be my own comprehension based on my own analysis, it would be qualitatively different from my simply swallowing the statements of others.

So, what happens in the end ?

To put it so simply there can be no mistake, **you attain enlightenment via the strength of your own logic and imagery.** You don't necessarily have to use a loaded word like "enlightenment," it's just the easiest in order to understand the point. nTech is a complete logical architecture that facilitates this process. It uses a wide variety of imagery and other tools in order to aid the imagination.

— Through questions and answers, through my own thought, through my own power, I become enlightened. It sounds a lot like Zen—like *koans*, for example.

Yes. There is also this sort of question and answer structure in Zen as well, but it unfortunately lacks the same logical architecture and is almost incapable of image transmission in the same way. Enlightened teachers ask questions that couldn't be answered in a reasonable way with human logic, so that students would think about them so hard that they arrive at the extremities of reason, see beyond, and have a sudden flash of insight.

However, there is no logical or imaginative progression to this process, and it is very difficult to have a sudden, huge insight. In all respects, human conceptual thought gets in the way, overthinking things can just lead to confusion, causing frustration. There are philosophers who have gone crazy in their thoughts by thinking too hard in pursuit of truth.

— Yes, I feel like I've heard that somewhere before. Human beings are fated to think. This question had to do with "perception renewal" so I want to get back to that. In nTech, logic and imagination are used in a question and answer format on the "thought highway," so that in putting together the pieces of the logic, one's own thoughts can be put into order. Ultimately, one attains enlightenment as a result of one's own thought and willpower, and they move on from their old way of thinking. That's the impression I get.

Your ability to synthesize the ideas is getting better. That's exactly right.

— The image itself remains vague and abstract to me, but without logic it's not enough, right? A religion that does not allow questions to be hurled at a settled dogma will be limited on that point.

That's right. In Zen, there are people who say these ideas can't even be transmitted or communicated in words, let alone with logic. These are the practitioners of *furyumonji*, or revelation through intuitive discernment. Truth is not something that can be expressed in words. At the moment one tries to do so, at that very moment, it is no longer truth. That is actually exactly right, but **without a logical architecture, there is no objective way to share these ideas in a manner applicable to society.**

— I see. So, on that point, Zen is insufficient.

That's right. However—and I don't want you to misunderstand—that doesn't mean that no one without access to this sort of methodology has ever managed to arrive at the truth. Just as many teachers claim, there are surely a small number of people who have reached the truth simply via diligent meditation and ascetic practice. However, nTech does not take that approach. I experienced things like energy and oneness on an emotional level when I was young, but they were not at all things that I could put into words. That's great for the person who experiences it, but nobody around them understands. Therefore, **the biggest issue is the gap that gets created, between the enlightened and the unenlightened. Like the gap between an incredible person and your average self.**

Because true enlightenment is the removal of all differences such that all becomes one, there seems to be no value in creating arbitrary conceptual differences. There's a similar problem in excitedly talking about a supernatural feeling and how incredibly valuable it is. People who have energy or feeling-type enlightenment experiences can easily go in that direction.

— You also said that you experienced those sorts of feeling before too, right ?

Yes. If you focus on them it becomes fun. Your personal physical experience develops more and more, which is incredible, but all it does is make that "personal world" more fun. I could have gone that route too when I underwent training in Korea to develop the world I experienced. However, when I lost everything in Japan and discovered this "structure," I acquired something nobody else had before: **a method to transmit my experience logically and imaginatively.**

Nobody had attempted this before, so I decided to take up the challenge. Thinking back on it, it's as though some invisible manifestation of will itself had made a tool of my body and provided me with all the realizations I would need, in both Japan and Korea. Well, that's just how I like to think.

— I am Japanese, and I find myself expecting a sort of visceral "Eureka !" moment rather than a logical understanding. Is that bad ?

Not at all. It's not about good or bad. However, reaching this absolute truth is truly difficult. I almost died 3 times in the course of my martial arts training. Even now, there are people engaged in unbelievable types of training. Some people have died. Some have gone insane. For those of us who have become accustomed to modern civilization—and the constant inundation of information that defines it—it will be impossible to attain enlightenment with a half-baked training or meditation regimen. And like I mentioned before, even if you became enlightened, you won't be able to share it. Even if you say you're enlightened, you won't be able to apply it in our capitalist culture, and your enlightenment won't become mainstream.

— I see, that makes sense. I can't really erase the desire to experience that sort of flash of insight, but if there is a totally different approach that would enable me to perceive this world, it's ultimately a matter of choice.

That's right. It's ultimately up to each individual to decide. If you'd like to use nTech as a tool to reach this world and bring it into your life, I'd love for you to try it.

I also think it's fine to want to get there on your own or figure it out on your own. However, it is absolutely impossible to seek the truth using words and concepts like "experience" or "sensation." Do you know why?

— "Experience" and "sensation" can't be used? But I thought there are lots of people who have experienced oneness, and that the breathing technique and *tai chi* world you came from also uses these ideas.

I also experienced a number of supernatural phenomena. However, **no matter how much you develop bodily sensation, no matter how far this gets from your daily experience, you are still inside the hologram.** The general sort of oneness people talk about is also almost always predicated on the "existence" of the universe, and is thus also inside the hologram. It's easy to think of that as enlightenment.

— Once you went outside the universe, the universe disappeared, right? Previously, you said that in science this is referred to as a membrane world. Is that not enlightenment?

There are multiple levels to enlightenment. In Zen, there are nine levels that are identified, but that idea is right at about level five. It's the attained intuition that all things are composed of a unified energy. nTech has clear logic and imagery to guide you up to level nine. In the world of Zen meditation, this is a state of "perfect zero" called *nirodha-samāpatti* in which nothing ceases and nothing arises. Efforts to reach enlightenment up until this point set this ninth level as the goal. This is the point of reference with which nTech operates.

— Even once you transcend the universe you are still only on level five? That's a bit overwhelming.

Yes, but thanks to your engagement with me, we've been able to introduce a lot of useful ideas. What I want to communicate is the absolute "nature of oneness itself" found at the furthest reaches of the mental world, long after the self and the universe unravel.

A clear logical system is needed to establish it as a new type of education and not just at the level of my own beliefs, thoughts, and philosophies, or even at the level of conventional religions, Zen and spirituality.

Above all else, the discipline that drove the logical architecture of question and answer to the highest level of precision is science. Science, too, must grapple with the question of nothingness. At the edge of physics and mathematics, the essential "structure" behind the change that creates and evolves the universe remains poorly understood. My hope is to try to toss in my two cents on this problem using a completely different perceptual approach.

— We said previously that for all of the entities in the universe, the common point of their "existence" was in fact a "place of non-existence." So, if we want to know the secret of the world of "existence," the answer lies in knowing the secret of "non-existence."

That's exactly right. In science it's known as the final theorem, the Grand Unifying Theory. The essential scientific theory that reveals the divine plan, the divine equation hidden in the source of all things. In the pursuit of hidden truth, scientists seek two major characteristics in their theories. **One is whether or not a theory is falsifiable by experiment, and the other is if the theoretical model has the potential to be comprehensively described in terms of mathematics.**

The important point is whether or not the law can be applied to real phenomena as an explanation with predictive power and without contradiction.

— I see. I believe you said that there is an equation associated with the world you've been talking about.

$0=\infty=1.$ That is the equation of the true world that I am discussing.

— Yes, that's right. 0=∞=1. I am not that familiar with science, so I don't really know what to say to that, but...

Yes, it's really just a way of describing the idea in an equation, as a quick way of defining it. The question becomes whether or not that equation can be used to imagine and understand the world it is meant to signify, and whether it can be applied in reality.

The important thing is the image. Developing a new dimension of human imagination, giving a new sense of the true world. With that in mind, let's move on.

The equation that is central to my fundamental teachings on how to apprehend this world beyond the human senses and brain is 0=∞=1.

The state of no-self, no-world.

Let's try going a bit deeper in trying to understand this world.

— That sounds good, let's do it.

In living our daily lives, this is something we may not think about often, but let's try to get to the bottom of the **"what"** the true world expressed by 0=∞=1 is. In the world of practice-based awareness, it starts with the concept of *jhana*, or wisdom. On top of that, we must ask **"why"** we need to know about this world, so we will deepen our understanding of the meaning and value of that as well. From there, we will try thinking about the possibilities for **"how"** this knowledge might be beneficial for our own lives and our societies, present and future.

— Yeah. But I have to admit, I have a tendency to be impatient and want to know the "how" as soon as possible. More so than theory and understanding, I want to have pragmatic knowledge and practical methodologies. I want to know specifically how this knowledge will be useful in my work, relationships, and life in general... well, I guess that isn't the point, right ?

Right. Modern people are very busy, and in our competitive capitalist societies, there is a great deal of practical knowledge available. I call this the **happiness of heights.** It's the lifestyle defined by chasing success defined in terms of money, status, honor, and fame.

If you think about plants, they are always trying to grow bigger, taller, spreading their leaves and flowers. If this leads to a beautiful bloom, anyone will look and see how wonderful it is. The more firmly rooted that plant is underground, the part you can't see, the more lively and vibrant the flowers will be.

There is also a world you can't see, a true world beyond human perception. It's what you find at the deepest, innermost regions. What you find there is a source of absolute dignity. From there, freedom, love, success, and happiness follow as a matter of course. **A lifestyle with both a "happiness of depth" and a "happiness of heights."** You need both.

— So, the visible worldview based on science and capitalism corresponds with the "happiness of heights." In contrast, the mental world, the world of spirituality and religion, corresponds with the "happiness of depth." The goal is to bring these together into a unified lifestyle.

Yes. In order to do so, that "depth" has to move beyond the world of the abstract, of pure faith. To achieve that, we must first obtain a thorough understanding of the "what" before we talk about any "hows."

— Determining what absolute "oneness" is, figuring out what imagery to use in order to understand the mystery $0=\infty=1$ equation... it's exciting. I may not understand anyway, but how would this be understood from a scientific perspective ? I almost failed physics, and I was pretty frustrated by calculus.

No specialist knowledge is necessary. Let's think about it in simple terms. Do you remember our conversation about perceptual objects ?

— Perceptual objects. That was part of the unified trinity conversation with the subject and context. The "illusion" of the conditional, transient, relative world.

Yes, it's a continuation of that conversation. There is a wealth of theory and experimental data in science—especially physics and math—so trying to get into the details gets complicated fast. The most important thing to focus on is comprehension via logic and imagery. Before, we were talking about the existence or non-existence of an apple, right ?

And that this doesn't just apply to apples, but to everything we think "exists."

The "you" and "me" you imagine. Desks and chairs, the air, the ground, the Earth, the Sun, the Milky Way, everything in the universe. What is the base unit, the components, the materials that make up all these "entities" ?

— Yes, we kept breaking everything down. Science uses analytical reason, you said. Since Descartes, the subject and object have been separated, and objects have been continuously reduced and analyzed in order to uncover the secrets of this reality. Division of matter yields molecules, which yields atoms, which yields elementary particles... etc.

Right. And elementary particles are split between massive particles and energy particles. This is based on what's called the Standard Model. Then division of elementary particles leads to the string, a component based on mathematical concepts. Energy vibration in the shape of strings. Their unique vibration patterns are what leads to differences in the elementary particles.

— Yes, and from there, the strings arise from the—what was it ?—membrane. The mysterious substance from the world beyond.

The idea is described in membrane theory, or M theory, which is currently the leading unifying theory in physics. It unifies matter and energy as well as the microscopic and macroscopic worlds—in other words, quantum mechanics and general relativity.

Physicists have identified four fundamental forces in the university: gravity, electromagnetism, the weak nuclear force, and the strong nuclear force. But why four ? Can they be described as one ? Were they originally one ? So these four forces were unified theoretically.

— So they unified them. What happened then ?

In a unified world, there is no such thing as an entity. All is energy in a vacuum.

All there is, is a "vacuum energy" without existence and in which nothing exists. The universe is a place of "non-existence." This is connected to the membrane world, in terms of scientific theory. **But at the same time, it is a world of infinite energy.**

Physicists hate to encounter infinity in their calculations. Or, rather, there's nothing they can do with that answer. It causes the breakdown of theory, and theory and calculations become worthless.

— In that case, can you say that the secret of the true world that unifies the matter and energy in the universe is infinite energy ? Because the calculations say so ?

Yes, but infinity is not really enough of an answer. Regardless of if the place beyond the universe is infinite energy, we still don't have a "structure" to explain why existence emerged from it.

— Hmmm, I see. The goal is to understand the "structure." However, if you reach infinity and can't do any more calculations, isn't that as far as you can go ?

That's right. By the way, theoretical physics is pretty amazing. They aren't letting infinity stop them. There is a result of M-theory that leads to a pretty incredible view of the universe that scientists still don't entirely know how to explain. **The universe is not one. The universe does not always "exist." There are 10^{500} universes constantly being born and disappearing, here and there, arising and fading in an ongoing cycle of birth and death. This idea of reality emerges from M-theory.** What do you think ? Can you visualize it ?

— 10^{500} universes in a cycle of birth and death ?

That's right. Try to think about how to put all of the things we've discussed together, how it might be understood, how it might be imagined.

— Easier said than done... so what do you mean when you say that there are 10^{500} universes ? There isn't one universe, there are 10^{500} universes.

There is also one universe. But both the one universe and the 10^{500} universes **do not actually exist.** That's because, if sometimes they exist and sometimes they do not exist, there are "existence" conditions and "non-existence" conditions. A relative world that changes based on conditions is, in other words.

— An illusion ! A hologram. I see, I remember now. This universe is like a visual screen that the brain creates. There are as many universes—as many screens—being projected as there are "subjects" perceiving a universe. It's not clear how many of these perceived universes there actually are, but because we can likely say that there is something like an infinite number of them, we can connect this to the prior theory—something like these infinite universes or 10^{500} universes can be seen as perceptual universes ? How is that image ?

Good ! That's right, we can connect this to the idea of perceptual universes. In a word, we are bringing in "perspective." Because membrane theory/M-theory escapes the confines of the universe, the place-beyond-space it references has to be fitted into our logic somehow. If the brain perceives *this* universe, then the place-beyond-space must also be *beyond* the five senses.

With that as our standard, **not only do we become free of the strict view that only one material universe "exists," but we also become committed to recognizing the plurality of perceptual universes that result from different perspectives.** This is an extremely important point, so try to loosen your imagination. The material universe and the perceptual universe are two sides of the same coin in terms of their relationship. **Entirely because you cannot perceive both the front and the back of a coin at the same time, if there is a front, there must be a back.** There is no such thing as a dime with only "heads."

Similarly, **there could not be just a material universe. There will always also be an infinity of perceptual universes to be found on the flip side of it.** It entails matter, and it entails consciousness. In order to attain an intuition for this view, we'll need to exercise our imaginations a bit. In the world of physics, what closely hinted at this view of the universe was.

— Ah ! Quantum mechanics, right ? I don't know that much about it, but there's something in there about the complicated relationship between matter and consciousness. In philosophical terms, it's got something to do with ontology and epistemology, I think.

That's true, but you know, **quantum mechanics actually hasn't advanced a coherent, new view of the universe.** Even among quantum physicists, there are many people who unambiguously state that the quantum worldview cannot be intuitively understood. That said, quantum theory had a huge, unmistakable impact in 20th century physics on our understanding of the true nature of the universe.

Just as you suggest, in the world of quantum mechanics, human observational activity—in other words, perception or perspective—is a decisive factor in establishing the state of various entities. Recall what we discussed before. It's not that we perceive things because they exist.

— ... but rather, things exist because we perceive them. Perception creates our hologram universe.

Right. Take this book in your hand. This book here is an entity, it is a book, and it is also what I perceive, it is in my perceptual field, it is part of my awareness. It is matter, and it is consciousness, and it is consciousness seen as matter.
What do you think ? Can you picture it ?

— Well, maybe a little bit.

In that case, **imagine that there is a cat right here. Does the cat recognize this object as a book ?**

— The cat won't perceive the book to be a "book" in the way a human does. Cats can't read letters—they don't even have a concept of letters—so of course, they don't recognize it as a "book." Ah, I see. So, in other words, **in the mind of the cat next to me, the "book" doesn't exist.**

Humans recognize it as a "book," while cats recognize it as some "bulky object," they just recognize that something is there. In which case... all these things that have presence still have presence. However, those same things will be perceived differently by different perceptual subjects, and treat them as different objects.

In that case, I see, even while there is one material universe, there are as many perceptual universes as there are perceptual subjects, and there are just as many ways to apprehend this "bulky object." In which case, the material universe and perceptual universe are, as you said, two sides of the same coin! I think I understand this idea of bringing in perspective, of bringing in the perceptual universe.

Whether or not one's imagination can do the conversion here is really important.

The world of quantum mechanics is ultimately limited to the very small, but the theory is based solidly on evidence. **It might be the case that until humans make an observation—that is to say, until the mind exercises its "perspective"—quantum entities are in an indefinite, probabilistic wave function state, in which they cannot be said to exist as particles or matter.** This is the state that is referred to as the **quantum superposition.**

Observational activity collapses superpositions into a deterministic state. Perhaps, then, the exercise of "perspective" is what brings matter—as particles—into being. If the material world does not break off or get interrupted somewhere along the path from the microscopic world to the macroscopic world, **the entirety of this reality can be understood simply as existing because it is perceived.**

— Hmm, yes, I see. This reminds me of **Kant's "Critique of Pure Reason."** I didn't read the whole thing because it seemed difficult, though.

Yes. The world as it exists in terms of our perception. **Husserl's phenomenology** is similar. Nietzsche also said things along these lines. Going even further back is **Plato's** famous **"Allegory of the Cave."**

— That's the one that says we are only aware of a 2-dimensional shadow being projected onto the back of a cave, right ? I know that one. There is actually a real thing, a Formal idea, that is casting the shadow. I can see the connection.

Yes. So, a probing of quantum mechanics ultimately links up with philosophy. In fact, some of the early quantum physicists—Bohr, Heisenberg, Schrödinger—were all very interested in Eastern philosophy. The duality of yin and yang. From two, one. The *taiji* worldview. That worldview fit perfectly with the quantum mechanical worldview of wave-particle duality, of uncertainty-observation duality. People in the spiritual world becoming interested in quantum mechanics is a sign of how the search for the truth ultimately results in perspectives aligning.

Among scientists, there are those who dismiss their ideas as philosophical nonsense. However, in the world of the mind one can find the claim that thought can be actualized, or the law of attraction, or motivational philosophy. To put it simply, these ideas explore how one's personal determination can affect how one perceives the world, and in so doing, construct their world. So, there is overlap on that point.

You can even find some overlap with the people who claim things like "All is mind, all is love, all is connected, desires and prayers are heard," etc. For example, in certain cases information can be transmitted faster than the speed of light via quantum entanglement.

— I see.

To repeat, what's important here is "perspective." This is the one thing that is most important to go beyond the secrets of the universe that science has uncovered. Until now, science has dominated with its assumption of and insistence on "existence." Newton and Einstein were the same, and contemporary physics essentially is, too. However, in particle physics, elementary particles will engage in a cycle of being annihilated in another dimension and then be reformed. There is also the view of the universe of M-theory discussed earlier.

10^{500} universes are coming into being and fading away. Even elementary particles, which were thought to never disappear, will disappear and reappear all the same. Recall that the components of elementary particles are strings and the component of strings is the membrane. The membrane is in the world beyond.

In other words, there is a transition from the membranous world beyond into this particle universe which is subject to human observation. If that is the case, there is a "movement" at constant work causing these oscillations in existence. In order for some entity to be clearly perceived as "existing," the human brain's "perspective" is necessary, as quantum mechanics suggests.

— Hold on a second. I want to try to put this together. Certainly, there are a lot of shared elements between physics, mathematics, neuroscience, philosophy, the spiritual world, and other areas... Like yin and yang, the material universe and the conscious universe are an inseparable unity. Like with the other-dimensional elementary particles, or as M-theory claims, within-universe and without-universe are also an inseparable unity... it seems.

From there, that unity is an endless repetition of creation and destruction—"movement" itself. That unified "movement," specifically, is where the secret of the true world is ! Does that sound right ?

Not bad !

— In that case, does the equation you are promoting, $0=\infty=1$, signify this "movement" you are talking about ?

That's right. It is also absolute human dignity, oneness itself. It is the key to redefining humanity, to establishing a true human perspective that includes the body-focused human perspective as well as the universal and extra-universal perspectives.

— Wow, that kind of gives me chills. $0=\infty=1$?...so once that can be understood, one can see some big secrets in that "movement," I guess.

That's right. **The equation of truth is the equation of dynamics.** This isn't the type of "movement" that people usually imagine. Let's try going deeper.

I want to repeat this point, because it is important: **this "movement" is not the same "movement" that the human brain can perceive.** Humans usually think of things "existing" and that those "existing" things "move," so they can unconsciously misunderstand this point on a deep level.

— Yes, it makes sense when you say it. I don't know what this "movement" is just from that word... it's hard to imagine. "Existence" isn't presupposed, this isn't the movement of some entity that "exists." But in a way it makes sense, because the true world is outside the realm of "existence." It contains no "entities." In that case, there can't be something that "exists" and is moving. Meaning ? If there are no entities present but there is movement, does this suggest the "absolute existence" of movement itself ?

Yes, very good. That's right. It's **movement itself. No start and no end: "movement itself," eternal and unchanging. Only that is truth, and only that actually exists. That is the world that I discovered.**

Let's return to the scientific conversation we were having before. Strings are in constant vibration. In that case, the raw material that brings these strings into being could not be motionless. Saying that the raw material of the strings is the membrane is to say that if the membrane became still, the strings could not vibrate. If the membrane became stuck in a still state, then, theoretically, no universes could come into being.

— Makes sense.

Here's a question. **Among all the things in the cosmos, including time and space, is there anything that is fixed ?**

— Anything that is fixed ?

Yes. Something not in motion. Something in a state of total "stillness." Is there anything ? Hearts ? Cells ? Thoughts ? How about molecules or atoms ? Elementary particles ?

Alternatively, how about the Earth, the Sun, the Milky Way, or the universe ? Are time or space fixed ?

— Time and space are difficult ones. I feel like time is always flowing along, though. Is space not fixed ? The distances don't change.

It seems that way in our daily lives. However, Einstein proved with general and special relativity that time and space are not fixed. The X Y Z Cartesian coordinates are not absolute. Einstein's theories overturned Newton's conception of a fixed universe. Einstein postulated the speed of light as a universal constant, and that single principle resulted in a worldview that predicted the mass transformation of objects based on their speed, as well as the dilation of time and curvature of space. Mass is not fixed. Which also means that energy is not fixed.

All is a relative, conditional world. An illusion. Einstein made this clear. It was a revolution in our worldview brought about by one genius scientist.

— Is that so ?

To put it another way, **what is time ? What is space ?** What is the raw material of the time and space that spacetime produces ? Both space and time were unstable, fluctuating in and out, in the early period of the universe. In the quantum world as well, spacetime is distorted and is not at all stable. The stability of the macroscopic world emerges from that super-microscopic unstable world.

What is the mechanism and cause of this behavior ? What is the world that gives insight into the cause and effect of space and time ? This can all be understood simply in terms of true unity.

— That's interesting, but rather high-level. It seems difficult to go that far, so is it enough to stick to thinking about entities for now ? To return to the previous question, the strings and elementary particles of the microscopic world—as well as atoms and molecules, my own cells—and the Earth, Sun, Milky Way of the macroscopic world, and the whole universe, are all moving. Thinking about it again, there doesn't seem to be a single thing that is fixed. All entities are changing, moving, transforming.

That's right. And why is that ? Try to remember the question I posed before. Nothing in the universe—not time, space, or any entity within—is fixed. Why is that ?

— Ah, I see, because what brings every entity in the universe into being is **motion itself**, right ?

That's right ! I want to know the unifying operational principle at work throughout the universe. A unifying theory is also the dream of science. If that "unity" is sometimes fixed, sometimes in motion, sometimes static depending on the conditions, we will run into contradictions thinking about it in terms of this universal reality and won't help us explain anything.

The thing that brings all into being, that changes all, moves all, transforms all, is change itself —speed itself—force itself—will itself !

This is the phrase I use to describe this world: the world of $0=\infty=1$.

— Hmmm, this is getting interesting ! I think I am starting to understand the importance of what you discovered—this revolution in perception based on knowing the structure that brings "something" out of "nothing."

Lao-tze and Buddha—both icons of Eastern spirituality—were fully aware of this world and described it in their writings. Buddhism has the Four Dharma Seals, which can be expressed as **"all worldly things are impermanent," "all emotional states cause suffering," "all things lack true** embodiment," and "the empty state is true stillness."

Similarly, **the place-beyond-space is analogous to the "emptiness" discussed in the Heart Sutra. That which is in the universe is "form." The quote "Form itself is emptiness, and emptiness itself is form" inverts this. This can be related to the creation and destruction of universes demonstrated by science,** the cycle of the 10^{500} universes.

In addition, the Heart Sutra also states, **"all dharmas are empty of characteristics—they are neither created nor destroyed, neither defiled nor pure, and they neither increase nor diminish," which can be analyzed with the explanation of the "world of emptiness."**
Do you have any idea why they left behind statements such as these ?

— Well, I'm not sure about some of those words.

To put it simply, there is only one unified motion ! You can think of it as them having seen the same thing of which they speak. Assuming they saw it, and then wrote about it, then what ? Their point of reference is also that the hologram world of entities does not actually exist and there is only unity.

— In that case... in the Heart Sutra, there is no creation or destruction, no defilement or purification, no increase or decrease—so in other words, no conditional change, no creation based on some condition. Because nothing is created, there is also no destruction. No birth, and no death. So, in other **words birth and death are illusions ?**

That's right. From the perspective of this "One Motion," there is no birth or death, only unity. That unity is motion itself. Therefore, Buddhism rejects the egotistical human perspective that the body is the self. That is the idea behind.

"All things lack embodiment"—the self and the body do not actually exist. In which case, the true self is **"neither arising nor ceasing,"** which in turn relates to **"all worldly things are impermanent."** The meaning of "impermanent" is the denial (im-) of fixed entities (-permanence). That is to say, **there are no fixed entities, only "motion itself."**

— Ah, that creates a very nice image. There's no contradiction.

Right ? Every individual has their own way of expressing themselves. In section 81 of the "Tao te Ching," Lao-tze speaks about the Way using a variety of terms of art. He does an excellent job of bringing together the illusory nature of the world of the senses, how the "existing" world comes entirely from a world of "non-existence," how that world of nothingness is like a world of unified darkness and at the same time unified motion, if you can follow the imagery.

If you understand the unity of truth, you can understand all of it. It's like standing on the summit of a mountain and being able to see the whole trail from start to finish. Science, philosophy, Zen, enlightenment, Eastern thought, Religion, spiritualism—your ability to analyze all of them changes dramatically. That's how valuable bringing your perspective to this next level is. **If you make that truth your tool, you can synthesize all of the knowledge that humanity has accumulated until this point, putting the strongest parts into practice while enhancing and improving the weakest.**

— Hmm, I see... yeah, that's deep. I feel like this is really stimulating my intellectual curiosity. There's one point I'm wondering about, so let me ask a question. In the discussion about Buddhism, there were two phrases you used that you haven't mentioned yet: "The empty state is true stillness," and "All emotional states are suffering." These seem to be a bit contradictory in terms of what we've been talking about. "All emotional states cause suffering" means that all life is suffering, right ?

That's right. It means that **without knowing the truth, living life caught in this illusory reality, human beings will be trapped in a life of suffering.** It is the world that captures the essence of the "four and eight kinds of suffering."

— I see. So, in other words, it is an exhortation to discover the truth. Then what about "the empty state is true stillness" ? Recently, the tech giants of Silicon Valley have been making a big deal out of mindfulness and meditation, but Nirvana (the empty state) is meant to be a still world, isn't it ? You were talking about "motion itself" before—isn't this the exact opposite ?

Ah, that's an excellent question. Understanding that point is the most important aspect to being able to intuit the 0=∞=1 world, even after ascertaining the truth by surpassing the limits of human conceptualization. In fact, whether or not one manages to break through this conceptual limit is the junction that decides whether or not your time with nTech will end only with conceptual knowledge.

— Really ? ! So then, this is incredibly important, isn't it ? If you end with only conceptual knowledge, ultimately, doesn't that mean that nothing has fundamentally changed for you ?

That's right. But it's simple, really. It really is. People's brains just have a tendency to interfere with their intuition. Remember what I said about brain initialization ? People's brain functions have a certain habituation. That's what makes it possible for us to have this visual screen interpretation of reality, but it has the opposite effect for trying to apprehend the true world. For now, let me just lay the idea out.

Let us assume that **the human brain has 4 perceptual habits.** This idea is the core foundation of nTech. Everything about the true world bears a certain symmetry to the world constructed by these perceptual habits of the brain. These symmetries can be summarized as follows.

Only parts can be perceived ↔ Wholes cannot be perceived
Only differences can be perceived ↔ Unity cannot be perceived
We perceive connections to the past ↔ We cannot perceive the "here and now" over the time axis of past, present, and future.
We perceive finite amounts. ↔ We cannot perceive infinite worlds.

— The brain has 4 habits. These are important for understanding the truth.
   Is this something that previous enlightened people, like the Buddha, have discussed ?
   What about Einstein or other scientists ?

As far as I know, nobody has clearly systematized, organized, and defined it. As for physicists and mathematicians, like I said before, they completely pass over the "perspective problem" in perceptual subjects like humans. That's because they take reality, they take presence as the starting point for their perceptual methodology. Lucidly understanding these perceptual habits of the brain and the "perspective problem" is critical to understanding one particularly pertinent theme: **why does this illusory hologram universe "appear to exist" ?**

As far as I can tell, previous enlightened individuals did not clearly define the "perspective problem" and the limits and habits of human brain function in terms of problem awareness. Of course, it's not that they had nothing to say on the matter at all. In one sect of Buddhism, the issue concerning our part- and difference-oriented perception is described in the "blind men and the elephant." There are many people who have identified the value of the "here and now," as well as those who have discussed finity and infinity. However, they are all abstractions and metaphors—nobody has formulated a logical architecture intended to surpass such methods.

— You mean they needed to make clearer prescriptions and put things into definite terms ?

Yes. I mentioned before how dialectic is the foundation of the human highway of thought. When it comes to this world of truth, there is something far more important that precedes seeking abstract answers. Namely, **why is it that everyone has such a hard time lucidly perceiving the "truth" ?** It's the question that comes before, "What is truth ?"

It is important to be able to understand why humans can't perceive "truth," to be able to correctly diagnose the root causes, to acquire precise problem awareness on how to break through those limitations, and to be able to make the right prescription. In order to do so, one must lucidly, 100% comprehend the structure of the human brain's habits and the problems they create. Without a clear understanding of this "perspective problem," it will be impossible to understand how this separated relative world could emerge from the true world, from the absolute world unity.

— This is getting deep fast, but I understand. For you to stress this so force-fully, it must be quite important. For now, I will keep in mind these four brain habits. I will make sure to etch them into my memory.

With that, though, I'd like to return to my previous question. I can't help but think that the image of absolute stillness—of "no motion"—implicit in the phrase "the empty state is true stillness" contradicts this world of "motion itself," as you call it.

Yes, it is absolutely a contradiction from the perspective of the human brain. That's because the claim is that **"motion itself" and "no motion at all" exist simultaneously.**

The world of ∞ change and the world of 0 change, the world of ∞ speed and the world of 0 speed, the world of ∞ energy and the world of 0 energy.

This is the world of total unity, in which these things are simultaneous and unified.

Can you try to describe exactly where in your intuition you are getting stuck ?

— Sure. Ultimately, I don't know if there's motion or there isn't motion. I'm confused on which it is. Change, speed, and energy are the same-whether it's infinite or zero, I can't help but wonder ultimately which it is. Aren't these complete opposites ? **Movement without movement can't exist.**

If it's moving it's moving, if it's not it's not, but it can't be both at once. Those are totally different worlds. Oh, but wait a second. **they are totally different worlds. *Different* worlds...**

Yes, from the human perspective that's exactly right. You seem to have picked up on a brain habit as you were talking just now.

— Yes. The tendency to perceive "difference." The inability to perceive "unity." Is this a problem with how the brain perceives things ?

That's right. It's also a problem of the perceptual dimension. For example, the electromagnetic waves emanating from a cell phone are definitely here regardless of whether or not the human brain can perceive them, and **while these things cannot be perceived in the mental dimension of the human brain, the "one motion" must still be involved for them to operate.**

Because of the perception habits of the human brain, we cannot perceive that world. It's similar to how we can't perceive radio waves, X-rays, infrared, etc. Since radio waves and the like are still part of our existential dimension, we are able to perceive them with the help of tools, but the true world beyond this existential one simply cannot be perceived with the initialization settings for perception in the human brain. However, there is still a way. What do you think it is ?

— Ummm, I wonder. It's a world that absolutely cannot be perceived in the mental dimension defined by our brain's initialization settings, right ? It's possible to make it perceivable ? In order to go to a world we normally can't perceive, we need to bring our perception into another dimension ? Hmmm. For things like infrared radiation, we can use scopes or tools to perceive them with sensors.

Yes. That's it.

— What is ? The scope ? No. Tools ?

That's right ! Tools. It can be done with tools. Since ancient times, humanity has developed through the use of a variety of tools. Thus, have we carved out an evolutionary path completely different from other animals. There are countless tools from the Stone Age— but there is one tool that caused the separation between human civilization and the animal world. It is the root of human civilization, the most important, the most defining of all our tools. What is it ?

— The defining tool at the root of our civilization... I don't know, what is it ?

It's really better to come up with the answer on your own after careful thought...

but OK, I'll tell you. That tool—the answer—is **language.**

Language is humanity's most important invention, its most important tool. Human civilization has come this far thanks to language. It's common to associate "invention" or "tool" with things you can see or touch, but all of those sorts of pragmatic things all would have been impossible without the development of language. Wouldn't you agree ?

— Language... it's certainly true that if we didn't have language—I should say, because we *did* have language, everything else we've accomplished became possible. Yes, I see, I agree.

Language is, fundamentally, a symbolic system of sounds and characters. It starts with the labeling of various things and events with names, words; it starts with the identification of a community's shared goals, behaviors, and needs and the appellation of meaning and value to them. From there, communication becomes possible. In this way, language became a tool for the description, explanation, transmission, sharing, comprehension, cultivation, application, and development of the ideas that arose in the human mind.

Now we have natural language like what we use to talk to each other, we have the descriptive language of math and the like, and another variant of somewhat different flavor: computer programming languages. Language is the central tool for the development of human civilization.

— I see. Yes, I understand that. But wait a second. Even if language is the invention and tool that has contributed so much throughout our history, even if we are using it like this right now, that doesn't mean that it can help us with perceiving or intuiting the true world that we were just talking about, does it ? I mean to say, the language we are using now, as a tool, isn't going to be useful for that.

Yes, that's right. So, what do you think should be done ?

— It's impossible to do with language, but with the idea of "language" as a tool, it could be made possible. What we need is a different kind of language from the ones we have been using. By using this new language, we could perceive this true world. Is that right ?

Precisely. To flip it around, in Zen we talked about the idea of revelation through intuitive discernment—how language can't be used.

— Yes, that's right. The truth cannot be described with human language—yes, it's quite clear. Whether we use natural language or symbolic language—or even the ever-evolving programming languages in IT—is it ultimately impossible ?

It's impossible. I can state this definitively. **Why does Zen insist that truth cannot be communicated in words ?** Because it's true. To look at this from the perspective of truth, or the perspective of nTech, **there is a problem in the nature—in the principles—of language.**

— The principles of language... but that would require overturning quite a lot of principles. It's hard to completely change the paradigm of your thought.

Yes, it is. That's why it's a paradigm shift. This change will completely overturn the framework we use to perceive the world. But the essence of it is simple. I'm always saying the same thing about this.

— By "same thing," you mean... umm, the thing you've kept mentioning is a premise of our perception... that entities "exist." So, you mean language is the same ?

Yes. It's the same.

— These principles "exist." Yes, certainly. We see something that exists and apply a name or word to it.

That's right. It's not just names: like/dislike, to eat, parts of speech like adjectives and verbs are all predicated on the "existence" of something, from which relationships between them are drawn. There is an apple. From there, "I" "happily" "eat" "the apple." This reveals a relationship between the self and the apple.

This is, ultimately, the world inside the brain. The habits of the brain first perceive a boundary line—from here to there—you might say. From here, is the apple. Over here, is me. Right there is the table. Like that. The focus is on parts. The focus is on differences. I have seen apples in the past before and created a finite category of "apple" by which I perceive apples in the future.

However, **the apple does not actually exist. "All things lack embodiment." In other words, all linguistic subjects refer to holograms without true presence.**

— I see. There are no linguistic subjects. The idea of a "subject" is nonsense. What we need is a language that is not rooted in entities.

That's right. For this, I invented a new tool, a new language: **image language.** Image language is different from languages that use entities, that use this reality as their point of reference. As a system, there is a base image language as well as several variations. It is a language of dynamics for understanding the unified "motion itself" described by the dynamic equation $0=\infty=1$, understanding the "structure" that draws this reality out of it, and applying that understanding.

If there is a language, then humans can use it as a tool for communication, right ? **The problem with intuitive discernment is its unfortunate lack of a means of communication. But if there is a language, communication is possible.** It becomes possible to define, describe, explain, communicate, share, understand, cultivate, apply, and develop the true world.

— I see... image language. And this is something that anyone can understand ? I have an image of learning Arabic or Chinese as being really difficult, for example.

Image language is simple. It is completely different from the language-based images we've been using so far. That's because it's a system of symbolic visuals, charts and pictures. It's a tool that helps accelerate one's intuition with logic and images. I can draw for you the most fundamental image language right now, though when you look at it, you will just perceive it as a drawing, and you will only attain a conceptual understanding. I'll talk about image language along with discussions of reality later.

For now, let's go one step backwards from my invention of image language, and go right up to the image of the $0=\infty=1$ world I discovered. If you didn't understand that part and just looked at image language, you'd have no idea what the true meaning of any of it is. You would just think, "Well, ok, that's one way of looking at it." You would come away with a very shallow understanding, which would be unfortunate.

— Got it. In that case, tell me about the world you discovered that led to this invention you call image language. This is what happened in 1996, right ? I think this will also help me fill in some of the blanks on the questions and concerns I've had so far.

OK, let's go ! There is the world I discovered, but as I said before, it is also the world that Buddha and Lao-tze discovered. However, they did not formalize it into a clear, logical system. At the time, science was not well-developed, and the quality and amount of general knowledge and education available then simply does not compare to what we have today. They were bound by certain limitations. Of course, the biggest limitation was the lack of a language to use as a tool to share these things.

The major principle of the true world is that it is a place where one's self and one's universe completely disappears. **It is a fully unified world beyond the habits of human perception.** It's not a world that can be intuited with human concepts.

A world with no beginning or end, beyond time. A world of pure unity, anywhere, anywhere, forever, forever.

A completely irreducible "only one." A world of only oneness itself. This is the starting principle. This is the point of departure. This is the point of reference. A world beyond human imagination.

— I understand. I got it. An irreducible "only one."

That's right. A world of pure unity. From there comes that irreducible world's "holistic composition," and from there, the "unifying operating principle." Connecting that to the image of the dynamic equation of $0=\infty=1$ yields a new point of reference for perceiving the world.

— Ahhh, I'm getting excited ! The irreducible "only one." What kind of image should I use to understand what comes next ?

Yes, so. There is only unity, there is nothing but unity. That must be made into your point of reference. Let me ask you a question. In the world of nothing but unity, that stretches out forever, forever in all ways. It is pure unity. In that world, can any "boundary" be drawn ?

— Um, I don't think so.

Why ?

— If you draw a boundary, you are making a separation between one area and another. If you do so, it's no longer unity.

Good ! That's right. **Once you draw a boundary, reduced "parts" emerge.** That is to say, the holism of the unity is destroyed. That's exactly right. If you understand the "holistic composition" of the irreducible "only one," you know that boundaries are not possible. Perfect. Let's go to the next question. From there, if there is nothing but an infinite unity, without end, it will become infinitely large. A world larger than that isn't possible—it is the largest, most comprehensive world.
How do you define the biggest world ?

With logic and imagery.

— How to define the biggest world... hmmm, that's difficult.

Then, to do this in a way that is easy for the human mind to picture—a 2-dimensional drawing is fine for this—let's try to draw an image on a piece of paper. Let's say that I have drawn, on this paper, a shape that I am claiming represents the biggest world.

Can you image a world larger than this one ? Don't overthink it, just keep it simple.

— *Figure 5* —
What is the biggest world?

...... There is no outside ∞

There is an outside (X)
There is an outside (X)
There is an outside (X)
There is an outside (X)
There is an outside (X)
There is an outside (X)
There is an outside (X)
There is an outside (X)

— A world bigger than this... is possible, I think.

Try to draw it in a way that the human mind can easily understand logically and intuitively. Can you draw a world larger than this one ?

— Yes. Something like this... if it's drawn like this, my world is definitely bigger than the one you drew.

Yes, that's right. That's correct ! Now, do you think that the world you drew is the biggest world ? Is there a bigger world ? Can you draw it ?

— Yes, I can. I can just draw a bigger one.

Yes, if you keep doing that, it keeps getting bigger. Now to review. What you are doing now is defining the biggest world. However, once you draw it and look at it, you see that it can't really be the biggest world because it doesn't extend as far as it can. You can just draw a bigger one. In other words, it's not the biggest world.

The logic is simple. Even though you tried to draw the biggest one, you can draw a bigger one because there is still space to draw it. So, you can make a bigger world. But if you keep this up... **ultimately, you can never define a "biggest world" by using boundaries—you create an outside. You've got "something beyond."**

— If there is an outside, you can create a bigger world, so a world with an outside can't be the biggest world. Makes sense.

In that case, it seems like we might be able to define the biggest world. If our world has an outside, it can't be the biggest world. Which means that the biggest world...

— Um, in the biggest world, "there is no outside." There are no boundaries. Is that right ?

That's right. Forever, and forever, **there is no outside.**

On and on and on and on—but "there is no outside." For infinity, something is stretching out far, far, far, far. In terms of mathematical definition and symbol, it is ∞. **There is no "up until this point," there is no outside, in the largest world.**

— Yeah, all of this makes sense. What comes next ?

Now using the same picture, let's try going in the reverse direction. In this irreducible world of "only one," with no boundaries, can you use imagery and logic to convince yourself of a *smallest* world ? This is a challenge. I will try to draw it. This is the smallest world. What do you think ? Can there be a world smaller than this ? How would you define the smallest world ?

— Well, there can be a smaller world than this picture. I can just draw something inside yours. But I see, it's the same problem as before.

That's right. It's always possible to draw a smaller world than yours. Forever and ever. The reason is that the worlds all have an **inside.** Even if you try to draw the smallest world, if it has an "inside," then you can create a smaller world. Which means that the world you just drew is not the smallest world. So then, what is the smallest world ?

— If it has an "inside," then you can create a smaller world. It can't be seen as the smallest. In which case, the smallest world must have no "inside !" Right ?

Exactly ! **There is no inside.**

There are no boundaries. No matter how far you go, there is no "inside." It becomes a world of a single point. From there, you can make a smaller point inside that point. **A point inside a point inside a point inside a point inside a... point. In mathematical definition and symbol, this is 0.** There is no smaller world. It is the smallest world. Surely, there is no world smaller than 0.

— *Figure 6* —
What is the smallest world?

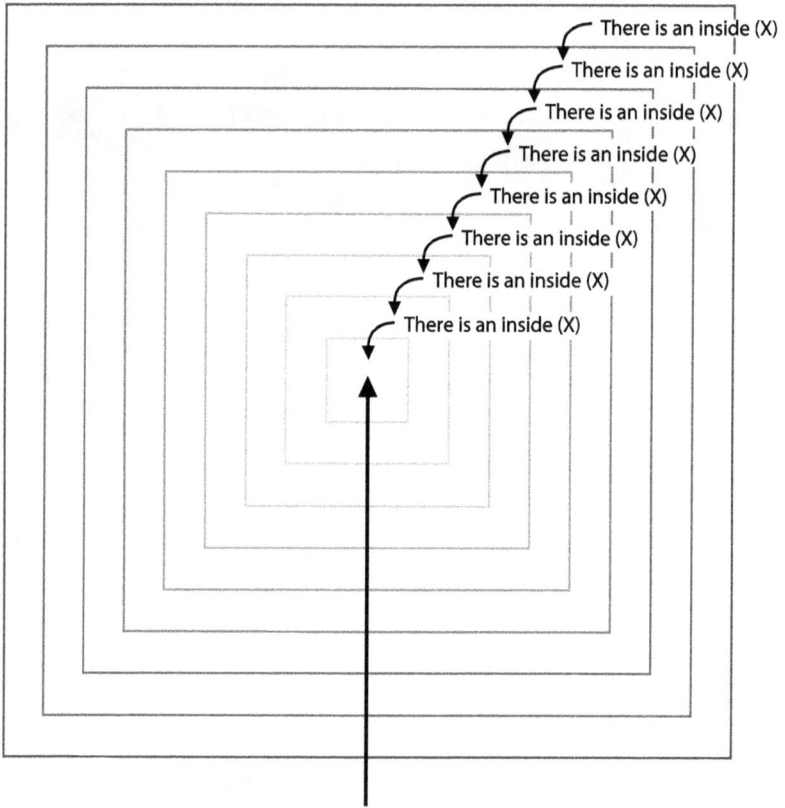

There is an inside (X)
There is an inside (X)
There is an inside (X)
There is an inside (X)
There is an inside (X)
There is an inside (X)
There is an inside (X)
There is an inside (X)

...... There is no inside **0**

The irreducible "only one," the world with nothing but unity. If that is the fundamental axiom, if that is our point of reference, in this world of "1," the largest world, "∞," and the smallest world, "0," are also part of this unity, also part of this world. This "1" is not the same 1 as in "1, 2, 3," by the way. **This is the "1" of the world without entity, in the world of pure unity. It is simultaneously the world of ∞ and the world of 0.**

— So that is the idea behind 0=∞=1, I suppose.

That's right. In fact, in a setting like the seminar that allows for direct communication, much more thorough, meticulous transformation of perception is possible as the dialectic/image/logic approach can be applied to even greater effect. However, to begin, this is good for now.

In terms of the logic the brain prefers to use, the idea that the biggest world (∞) = the smallest world (0) seems crazy, right ? Big, small— they're different. Finding differences is a habit of the brain.

— Yes, I see. It's a habit of the brain. I feel a little hazy on this so I want to ask, why not just say 0 = ∞ ? You were saying before that in science, in the pure void beyond space, the calculation results go to infinity.

In that case, **Can you logically explain 0=∞ ?** How do you make 0 and ∞ the same ? In order to make the largest world and the smallest world be equivalent (=), there is a definitive *something* you need.

— When you put it like that it seems pretty hard. Can 0 and ∞ be made the same, I wonder ?

They can't, I guess they can't. One is 0, the other ∞, and to say they are equivalent (=) is...
  It can't be done. I'm just confusing myself. I don't know what I'm thinking about anymore.

It is not possible if you try to turn the image of 0 and ∞ into separate entities. However, it isn't possible to unify 0 and ∞ with images and logic from a human perspective. Whether you talk to scientists or philosophers, there are people who say the infinitesimal and the infinite are the same thing. However, there is no definitive element to this idea—it's not well-defined. They can talk all the way up to the outer reaches with a "rote language" that somebody created and remembered, but passing the line over to the final image is like passing from earth to heaven. Do you have conceptual understanding, or do you have an intuition for the truth ?

— Hmmm. Could I get another hint ?

Sure. The stages to persuading your brain with images and logic are really important. Do you remember the major principle I keep bringing up ? We must understand the "holistic composition" of this irreducible "only one." This must be made the point of reference for our perception and thought. We work from the simple base idea of "unity." Conversely, when you try to talk about 0 and ∞ from a conceptual standpoint, you tend to approach it with the attitude that 0 is 0, and ∞ is ∞—they're "different," right ? That is a point of reference that is trapped in a perspective derived from your brain habits.

Because we are trying to create a unified image of "different" things, and in particular, total opposites like 0 and ∞, we have quite a challenge. You just end up in a conceptual loop. That's because you're starting from the wrong perceptual point of reference. It's impossible to seek the truth by starting from the knowledge you have acquired so far from your brain's perspective. That isn't truth—it's just ideology.

— Perceptual point of reference... indeed. Without realizing it, you end up thinking from the point of reference of illusory reality in which the habits of the brain have trapped you. Which means that the starting point of your perception and understanding is already wrong.

Yes. That is unity. But 0=∞=1 or 0 and ∞ and 1 together provide an equation that does not set up their mathematical identities as "different."
Remember what I said before. The world of pure unity is not an entity. It is not fixed.

— **"Motion !"** Right. It's motion itself. Using the words of the Heart Sutra, form and emptiness flow in and out. In terms of physics, it's the "motion itself" in the background that causes the creation and destruction of universes. I see, the dynamic equation—that is, $0 = ∞ = 1$—is an equation that fully reveals the "motion" of "unity" behind the world of "unity."

That's right. **The defining element that enables 0 and ∞ to be set equal to each other and unified is this image of a special "motion."** In any scientific unifying theory, all happenings of the universe must be explained as one, so of course a description of dynamic events is a requirement. **The**

point of reference of this new perception begins with the image of "one motion." The equation for it is 0=∞=1. Does that make sense ?

Now for a question. **In this unified 0 and ∞, with no "inside," and no "outside," what could be meant by "movement" ? What kind of "movement" is possible ?**

— Wow, that's tough.

It's difficult because you are thinking about it with a human brain. But simply, simply, **if the "motion" brought into being by a unity of 0 and ∞ requires a certain amount of time for 0 to transform into ∞, it doesn't work, right ? Because for a brief moment, there is a state that is neither 0 nor ∞, at which point, a "finite world of parts" comes into being.**

That is to say, if the non-moving state of rest—the 0-point energy state described in Buddhism with "the empty state is true stillness"—were to continue, there could be no "motion." In that case, there could be no universe creation, either. But once 0 "moves" into another state, it enters a state of not-zero. Therefore, a non-zero "difference" or "part" emerges.

When that occurs, the "holistic composition" is shattered. For that reason, when 0 transforms, it cannot transform in a partial fashion. But at the same time, it cannot stay in a state of non-change, either. In other words, **there must simultaneously be change and no change.** In addition, when this change occurs, that change **cannot be "incremental change," but "total change."**

It is an irreducible "only one."

— Hold on a second. So, in that case... if there cannot be partial change, 0 must stay 0. But if we are talking about "motion itself," 0 must change. That is, it must be a total change. There is another mathematical symbol that has that "total" connotation.

That's right. ∞. During this change, if time, volume, density, mass etc. come into being, things which conditionally change, we are left with "parts." This isn't a transformation of 0 to 2 or to 100. **The only change that 0 can make without making any change is into ∞. That is the only "motion" possible. At the same time, that ∞ is equal to 0.**

— A reversal of 0 into ∞, ∞ into 0. It is making an absolute—the largest possible— change, yet also not changing at all.

That's right. **0 change, ∞ change. 0 speed, ∞ speed. "The empty state is true stillness," and "All worldly things are impermanent." A dynamic equilibrium between 0 and ∞. A dynamic equilibrium between +∞ and -∞** is another way to think about it.

Absolute symmetry, perfect balance. A state of supersymmetry. Therein lie the secrets of the birth of our universe. The mechanism that created the universe from this point is connected to what in physics would be referred to as a spontaneous breaking of symmetry.

An inversion of 0 and ∞, an inversion of inside and outside. Speed and time are simultaneously 0 and ∞, a single motion between inside and out.

This motion is the "holistic composition," the operational principle of the universe. Image language is a language that explains the framework behind the emergence of something from nothing, the framework behind the emergence of relative worlds from the absolute world.

The system for explaining the entirety of this phenomenal world in terms of the inside-out motion, and applying it to our reality, is called "HITOTSU (oneness) Studies." As a pragmatic technology for fostering changes in perceptual awareness, it is called "perceptual technology" (*ninshiki gijutsu*), or nTech.

— Hmmmm... ok, I see... so all of this is predicated on something totally different from the knowledge and disciplines we were discussing before. So, you created a system of comprehension based on images and logic in order to define, formalize, and verbalize this "unity" world... I understand how this may be a truly groundbreaking development. That said...

— *Figure 7* —
The inversion of inside and outside

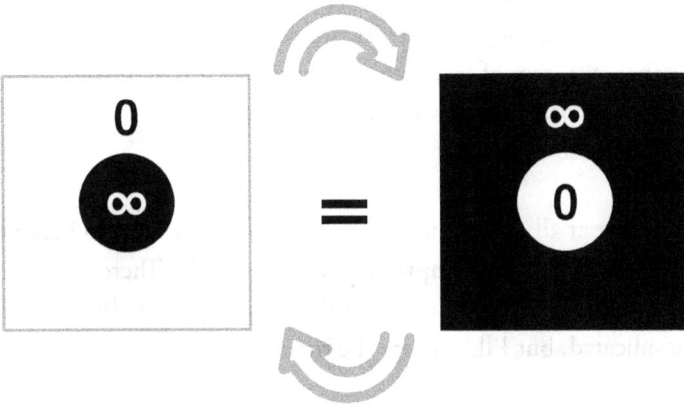

A motion with no inside or outside,
but rather an endless inversion of inside and outside at ∞ speed and 0 speed

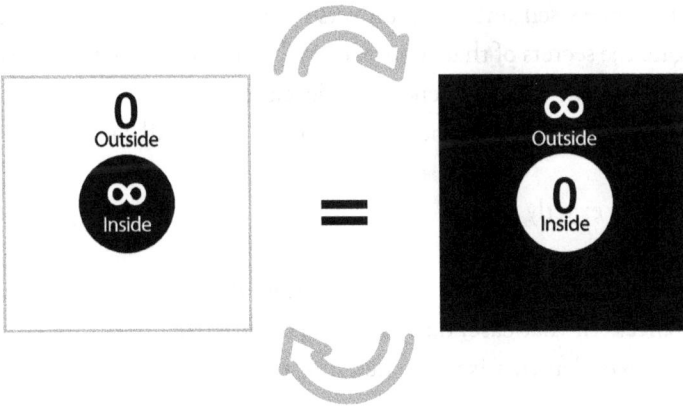

What's wrong ?

— This may seem rude, but do you have any way of actually proving this "truth" you're talking about ? To speak of extremes, this sounds little more than a system of comprehension you've created, just like any other discipline or forms of knowledge. It's just some kind of strange feeling I get, some sense of doubt.

That's not rude at all. I said this before, but **you don't have to believe anything. It's important to comprehend things 100%.** There is a meta-level "axiom" for this completely new world perception. The discussion gets a little complicated, but I'll just give the main points.

The main assumption behind all of humanity's disciplines and knowledge is obscured. However, just as I have mentioned before, that main assumption is "existence." One's self and one's universe "exists." Right ?

Or to flip it, there is no systematized academic body of knowledge that asserts that one's self and one's universe "does not exist" and proceed to investigate the secrets of that "non-existent" world, figure out how to define it, how to explain the emergence and development of an "existing" world from a "non-existing" one, and how to communicate all this, right ?

— Yes. That's exactly right.

Ok. So, the fundamental assumption behind all our academic knowledge is "existence." In that case, don't we have to prove that our selves and our universes "exist," as that is the underlying assumption of our axioms ?

As it happens, there are no academic or scientific disciplines that do this. If one's point of reference is the perspective of the five senses and the brain, all things are just assumed to "exist," and that illusion becomes the principle behind all the axioms you set forth.

Moreover, **a mathematician named Gödel has demonstrated that it is not possible to prove the absolute veracity of any logical architecture that assumes "existence."**

— Hmmmm... so, what does that suggest ?

It goes directly to your previous question. The very question as to whether or not something is really absolute "truth" is, in itself, ultimately unanswerable without contradiction if your starting point is a logical architecture that assumes "existence." **You can never, ever be free of the chains of thought that lead you to ask the question, "Is this "truth ?"**

— So then, ultimately, nTech doesn't actually have any evidence that this "unity" is absolute truth ? But wait—nTech's point of reference isn't "existence," it's "non-existence."

In which case, the whole idea of using a point of reference based on a thought process that assumes "existence" to ask about the veracity of the meta-level "axioms" of an alternate dimension is...

That's right. **It's meaningless.** That is also the reason that I say that nTech is a tool. You will not find any answers searching for absolute truth if your point of reference is based on an incomplete tool—a perspective derived from your five senses and your brain. In which case, you need a completely new tool, a completely new point of reference, wouldn't you agree ?

— And that tool is image language, you said.

Yes. So, rather than merely believing, I want you to be able to understand via the use of image language. **I want you to understand the unconditional, absolute world: the world of $0=\infty=1$.** I want to continue to develop and apply this new meta-knowledge that uses the absolute world as a point of reference, and in so doing, advance human potential and creativity.

— Ahhhhhh, I see....

There's one other thing I'd like to talk about for a bit. After I discovered this world in Fukuoka in 1996, I was very surprised to discover a word rooted in Japanese culture and used every day that is more appropriate, more symbolically relevant, to describing this world than any other. What do you think it is ? It's a single *kanji* (Chinese character). All Japanese people know it.

— Oh ? What could it be ?

This concept enables the unification of 0 and ∞, enables 0 change and ∞ change to come together. This concept enables that world of absolute beauty, of dynamic equilibrium between 0 and ∞. A single *kanji* that Japanese people use every day....

— What is it ?

It's 間 (*ma*). nTech is also the enlightenment of 間 (*ma*), or the principle of 間 (*ma*).

— "*Ma*." Yes, that's definitely a *kanji* that Japanese people often use. I don't
know if there's any concrete explanation or reasoning for it, but there's
terms like "*ma ga warui*" or "*machigai*."

That's right. The Japanese are a mysterious people with a direct intuition for the concept of "*Ma*." It occurs all over in daily life. "*Ima*," "*nakama*." The interval between two people results in "humanity," the interval between one moment and another moment results in "time." The interval between one emptiness and another is "space." If you lack "interval," you are a "ma-nuke." *Manuke* is the same thing as foolish.

When the mind becomes hung up on the "existence" of this illusory holo-gram universe, **when you lose the ability to see "interval," you become a fool, and you will experience pain, sadness, and failure.** But wouldn't you say that we've been experiencing those things for our entire history ?

— Sure, that sounds right.

If everyone became aware of the "perspective problem" and came to an aware-ness of "truth," we would be able to nullify the root causes of human unhappi-ness and suffering and build a new society, a new history from that foundation.

The Japanese place great importance on the world of "*ma*" in their senses, which is the most essential element.

There is no doubt that this concept of "*ma*" in Japan made it easier for me to communicate the world I discovered. It cannot be seen as a coincidence, and I am very grateful for the significance of this concept.

CHAPTER 4

Humanity is truly amazing

Interviewer:

— So, I have to say, I'm really excited that we've moved from our conversation about fundamentals to talk of a more pragmatic nature. I have a lot of things in my life that I'm worried about, always thinking about.

A new me, a new way of life, a new age. It would be great if this tied them all together and became the impetus for some big changes.

Jesu Noh:

Absolutely. Now that you have a grasp on the essence of the foundation of my ideas, let's move forward with that foundation in mind. As we talk about reality, the important thing will be determining what point of reference, what point of departure, to use.

If you forget our foundation the second we start talking about practical matters, all the conversation we've had so far will have been for nothing. The foundation of nTech's revolution for our way of life lies in **a revolution in our point of reference.** Do you understand what I mean ?

— A revolution in our point of reference. Yes, I see. I'm guessing you mean that rather than thinking in terms of the "existing" world, we should think in terms of the place of no-self and no-world, or the Absolute World. Is that right ?

Yes, yes, that's right. In that case, I'll ask you a question. In order for us to improve our worldly way of life, **why do you think we need a revolution in our point of reference ?**

Upon synthesizing the images of the Relative World and Absolute World—of "existence" and "non-existence"—it is very important to always keep one's point of reference in the place of no-self and no-world. We look at existence from the perspective of non-existence. For what reason would this be necessary ?

— Ummm... I thought we were going to have a more down-to-earth conversation now, but it's still difficult. A reason we need a revolution in our point of reference... a reason we need to see things from the place of no-self and no-world...

Let's double-check our fundamentals. You would like to apply the True World, non-existence, to reality, right ?

— Yes, that's right.

And why is that ?

— What ? The reason I want to apply it ? I think it would be nice to have a better life. I want to be happy, do well at work, be successful. I'd like to find a good partner, and of course it would be good to have a lot of money, if possible.

Yes, for sure. You have some desires, some hopes about how things could be better. If you could satisfy those desires, you could live a better life. Is that right ?

— Yeah. I have a feeling that nTech could be a great tool for this. I believe you have also said that nTech can be applied in various areas to make our world a better place.

That's right. The practical application and value of nTech covers many different disciplines and allows for many different approaches.
The $0=\infty=1$ framework is applicable not only in education, but in every other conceivable area—economics, politics, medicine and health, energy development, the frontiers of science, martial arts, art, and sports.
Obviously, people's specific interests are all different, but let's talk about some fundamental themes common to humanity at the root of these interests.

— I guess the methodology isn't going to be some kind of quick fix, huh. That said, I suppose we live in an age where we can find all the know-how, all the how-to guides we want in books and on the internet.

That's right. I'd like you to imagine something.

When it comes to jumping, the people who first squat as low as they can and concentrate all their power in one place can jump the highest, right? Similarly, **the depth of your happiness is connected to the height of your happiness.**

Happiness and success in true nature, happiness and success in reality. Unconditional happiness and success, conditionally accessible happiness and success. We are in an age that requires a new lifestyle that merges these both into one.

There are all kinds of things like so-called Eudaemonics, the Law of Success. They are indications of natural, basic desires that humans hold, and I think their efforts to cultivate and deepen the individual's inner self is meaningful.

However, I have noticed a major issue with Eudaemonics and the Law of Success. This is rather forceful language, but I could actually say that it makes me upset.

— They make you upset? Eudaemonics, the Law of Success? They seem pretty harmless.

This isn't some kind of blind emotional anger, don't worry. I am of the impression that we need to discuss the source and tendencies of human desires up until this point.

What upsets me is passing over this problem—trying to help people meet their phenomenological desires while assuming the same capitalist worldview, with the same values, as always.

— Hearing you say that it upsets you is kind of shocking, though...

It's important to recognize that there are also good forms of anger. I'll just say this in passing, but I think there are a lot of people who talk about a world of the mind—especially a world of love—who take a negative stance towards the emotion of anger.

They'll say things like the negative energy of anger is bad, or that destructive energy is bad. That it's best to always have a gentle demeanor and accept all things full of laughter, gratitude, and love.

— Yes, I have encountered that. Is that not how it really is ? When I'm near someone who is angry, I feel uncomfortable myself.

Of course. As a rule, that's so. However, the idea that anger is bad is just another example of binary human thinking. Humans are not motivated by love alone. Sometimes we also need intense emotions like anger. Of course, I am not talking about the sort of anger that sweeps people away, the sort of anger that creates explosions of discontent and resentment.

I want to talk about an indignation that arises from the deep truth. This indignation makes you a manifestation of that truth—you become able to see both sides of humanity when you look at them as they appear in reality.

One side is that **humans are unconditionally beautiful, incredible, amazing in their existence itself, mystical, even sacred.**

The other side is the symmetric opposite: **the conditions that humans have been placed in are terribly wretched, cruel, and humiliating. These conditions are responsible for the squandering and disruption of humanity's original promise, humanity's dignity and infinite potential.**

The sort of indignation I am talking about is a feeling that makes you want to shed tears when you see the plight of humanity—yelling out at the universe…

This is not what humanity is !!!!

— Jeez ! You scared me ! Don't suddenly shout like that.

But I think I understand the way you feel about this. An indignation that arises from a deep truth at the destruction of human dignity. In that sense, Acala in Buddhism is also like an avatar of that anger. It's not all compassion.

That's right. This sort of feeling must have been in the hearts of people like both Buddha and Jesus, who passionately sought to express themselves in the way they lived and died from a place of deep compassion and love. Feeling despair at the wretchedness of humanity, desperate with the conviction that "Humanity is more than this !!!!" That's the feeling I get.

The most important keyword, as I mentioned before, is **"dignity."** A desire for *absolute* dignity. A **"dignity wish."** It is possible to establish this deepest possible dignity, let it flow over in you, and from there, know the freedom and love of this deep truth.

Right here, right now, you—as absolute dignity itself, as infinite potential and creativity itself—can uncover this unconditional happiness. This endeavor brings happiness and success of "depths."

With this immovable spirit, you will reconstruct reality in accordance with the framework that ties together the universe and nature. You will then become able to achieve happiness and success of "heights." It is vital to be able to visualize all of these things as a single integrated whole.

— Well, there's a number of things I'd like to ask, so bear with me. I am just a regular person who goes to work every day trying to make a living. I've put in a fair amount of effort to be where I am, and I am at least able to live a normal live with a normal salary and a normal job. I have some hobbies and no big problems in my relationships.

But I still have these doubts as to whether or not there's more that I could be achieving, or get this itch to challenge myself with something totally new. In a word, I guess you could say it's like a vague sense of uncertainty.

Is it alright to go on this way ? Will I be able to keep my job, or get married, or have a family ? I'm also worried about caring for my parents, or my own old age.

This is all made worse by how fast the world is changing. I use Facebook and SNS and that sort of thing, and there's so much information. I'm busy with work and can't keep up with the news. When I do watch the news, I don't feel much hope. The world is in the midst of this COVID-19 pandemic, and it's not clear what is going to happen with public health and our way of life. There are problems with the economy and terrorism too... there's so much information, it's hard to know what to pick, and it's even hard to tell what information is accurate. There's a lot of things that concern me, but I don't usually get the opportunity to talk about them.

Science, IT, and AI are evolving, and I'm really curious about what's going to happen in the future. All of this makes me feel like the way I am now isn't enough, but I don't even know where to start in order to change.

Even though I want to change myself, I'm not sure how to put together a plan for the future. It's not even like I have any particular issues with my life now. I feel like I balance things well enough.

I feel like... well, you get the idea.

Thank you for being so open with me. I don't want to let your point get lost, so I'm going to raise some keywords I think are relevant, and start there. These emerge from the critical discussion about essence: **"redefining humanity," "the integrity of ignorance," and "recreational awareness" or "independent decision making."**

— Interesting. There are terms I hear all the time in there, but also some I don't.

We call the words that humans learn by memorization "rote language," but I'd like you to grasp the image that lies beyond the words. Ideally, I will describe this all from the perspective of nTech. We'll go over them one by one.

— Yes. The first thing is "redefining humanity." Which means...

Try to imagine the conversation on essence we had before. Do you remember the first example we discussed ? With the bird and the bottle.

— Oh yes, I remember. It was about how to get the bird out of the bottle.

We've covered a lot of ground since then. Do you think of it differently now ? What meaning do you think it has ? **You could think of this as a question that an enlightened person can use to determine if another is also enlightened.**

— Wow, I see... the bird has become larger than the neck of the bottle, and we need a way to get it out.

At that time, you were talking about the assumptions behind points of reference. The bottle and bird "exist." That assumption, that point of reference itself is where the key to the problem can be found.

That's right, you remember. If you insist on using your human senses, your brain's perspective, your internal dialectic will start racing. That is the human thought highway. We're on it now too. For example, things like "what should we do in order to improve our lives ?" are the theme of our current conversation.

While you're on the highway of thought, you're on the lookout for answers.

— It's true. Humans are always on that highway. I guess the fact that we are returning to this bird and bottle example must mean....

Well, I didn't understand it at first, but I think I have a handle on our conversations about the illusory nature of this reality, the hologram universe that appears to "exist" but is no more than a three-dimensional projection, the $0=\infty=1$ equation.

Ultimately, though, the world in which the bottle and bird "exist" are...

The bird, the self, and the bottle are all "one's own universe."

It's simple if imagined like that.

I was born into the void of space, and have grown into an adult. I have been living my life in this way, but I can't escape from the "bottle" that is the universe.

Excellent imagination ! That's right. It's an allegory for oneself and one's universe.

Human beings have no idea about where, how, why, or for what reason they came into being. By the time these questions even occur to you, your life has long since begun.

We have no idea where we are headed, or why or how we should live. There's no clear connection or cohesion between cosmology and humanity.

We also have no idea what happens to us when we die. Things don't go in accordance with our desires and we often run into problems with no clear exit. We flail about just like a bird trapped in a bottle that injures and tires itself desperately slamming its head, wings and body against the walls. Time marches on, we grow old, and our thoughts and our bodies slow. Ultimately, we die inside the bottle.

Even once we die, we are not freed from the bottle. In spiritual terms, our karma remains. All of the karma we accumulate in our lives doesn't just disappear. We become trapped in the suffering cycle of samsara. We can never become free.

We get born into the bottle again, struggle against it again, die inside it again.

We get born again, perhaps our karma increases, and die again.

We don't even know what it is to live or die, yet repeat the process countless times. This makes even the meaning of birth and being alive itself a form of suffering.

Buddha referred to this as the four and eight forms of suffering. There are "four inevitables" to human life—birth, aging, sickness, and death—and the other four forms of suffering are the inevitable parting with loved ones, inevitable meetings with enemies, inevitable unfulfilled desires, and the inevitable dissatisfaction of fulfilled desires. This last one identifies how desire has no true end, and simply leads to a wandering of the heart.

If so, then we are born, live, meet, part, and die—for what? What is the point of struggling through life? There's a danger of falling victim to nihilistic thoughts such as these.

— That's pretty dark. Especially since I can't disagree with the essential points. I think that everyone struggles with these kinds of issues.

We make ourselves busy every day, fight with family, friends, and lovers, hurting each other.

Looking back across history or our lives today, humans have always been like this.

That's right. From the perspective of the truth, one can see just how miserable, cruel, and humiliating the human condition is.

I want to repeat this point to avoid misunderstanding: this is just one side of the true nature of humanity. The other side is the incredible, unconditional beauty of humanity.

In that sense, I think that Buddha was amazing in his attempts to fully describe both the misery of humanity and humanity's potential. However, I think there is too much focus on escaping suffering and attaining enlightenment. There is no return to reality with a strong, comprehensive vision for the future.

There are all kinds of things in the spiritual world, but engaging with past lives isn't the final answer. That sort of therapy has its value, but **it doesn't change the fact that you are trapped in the bottle, and it actually distances you from an encounter with deep, absolute human dignity.**

It also isn't enough to just talk abstractly about love or oneness. **This just distracts from the tragedy of the human condition.** Humanity has problems, and the "love and oneness" approach makes an adroit "problem awareness diagnosis" that searches for a way to solve these issues impossible.

This approach also tends to lend itself to a blind faith attitude that lacks logical rigor. There is no objectivity, which leads to a sort of solipsism. "Only people who get it, get it." "That guy has bad vibes." One can become egotistical and judgmental.

If you can clearly and deeply perceive the true essence of things, you can see that suffering itself is also part of the truth. If you let yourself think that you must change your "way of thinking" so that you even view this suffering in terms of "love and gratitude," you will only succeed in generating cognitive dissonance. This can actually lead to greater suffering.

Can you see what I am saying? I'm not just trying to shoot these things down, but I think it's important to clearly identify their issues. By resolving these issues, there is the possibility for more fantastic types of change.
If you don't do so, you can't make claims about true love. You end up forfeiting access to the dignity and infinite potential that is innate to all human beings.

— Ultimately, it's all about "dignity." This deep, absolute dignity of humanity.

Thank you. That's right. The capitalist worldview prioritizes happiness and success of "heights" via the principle of competition, the abstract world of the mind that does not directly address the reality of suffering, the spiritual world that emphasizes past lives and seals off the world of original freedom, the religious world that puts humanity beneath divinity, the world of mental discipline that tries to push past science but lacks will, courage, logic.

These are all amazing systems with amazing benefits, but I want to really bring out the full range of integrated potential, from the deepest depths to the highest heights. To return to our example, I want people to become completely free from the bottle. I want people to fully emancipate themselves from cause-and-effect, determinism, and karma. I want them to encounter the true way of being founded on humanity as absolute dignity itself.

— Is this "absolute dignity itself" related to the "redefinition of humanity" you are talking about ?

Then the connection between that and the image of the bottle and the bird... I feel like I'm close to understanding.

The nullification of dialectic is the ultimate wisdom. This statement is extremely meaningful. It points to the final image, the final question, that must be overcome upon attaining a full understanding of this omniscient, omnipotent unity.

In terms of the bottle and the bird, **one becomes completely free from all the thoughts that arise from the attitude that thinks the bottle and bird "exist." All of the chains of thought dissolve like fog in an instant, and one comes to understand that "integration" is all there is.**

To put it into words, anyway.

— Yes, it's vague—it's still vague—but I have a feeling I understand what you have said so far.

The revolution in point of reference refers to a liberation from all thoughts that take "existence" as an arbitrary starting point. It refers to a complete evolution beyond the illusory paradigm of the world that "exists."

In the world that "exists," the bird is oneself. One thinks that their body is their whole self.

Ultimately, this is an illusory conception of "self" that is promoted by one's brain. It seems like the "self" exists, but it does not *actually* exist. However, **for hundreds of thousands of years, humanity has always believed that their body is their whole self.**

— Yes, I think you are right about that.

But... is it really such a problem to think that the body is the self?

Certainly, it would be good to escape the highway of thought, the chains of thought... and I would prefer to put an end to suffering inside the bottle, to the cycle of karma. That said, I don't quite see how identifying the body with the self is a problem.

I understand why you would feel that way.

However, **thinking that "the body is the self" is the single most serious problem from the perspective of the truth, if we are to thrive in a new age of the mind.** For that reason, I would like to concentrate on this point being understood.

— The single most serious problem... ok, I'm paying attention.

Many people in the past—and also today—have relentlessly chased their desire to know the truth, to know the operating principle of the world, to know the absolute unified world, to know the origins of the universe, to become enlightened.

However, becoming enlightened is almost impossible, I think. Do you know why?

— No, why? This is somehow related to seeing the body as the self?

That's right. I'll respond with a question: Imagine there is a cement block right here. **If you polished it hard enough, could you turn this cement block into a mirror?**

— Ummm... it seems impossible no matter how you look at it. It'll never become a mirror, so if someone was trying to do that, I'd tell them that they should stop wasting their time.

Yes. This example is the same. If you try to become enlightened while you believe the body is the self, you're wasting your time. It won't happen.

The logic is simple. **Because the world of enlightenment is one in which you become truth itself, you become the origin of the universe itself, you can never get there if you let yourself believe that the body is "oneself."**

After all, if all there is is "unity," separating out a "self" in a "body" is already undermining the idea of unity, isn't it ?

— Well, yeah...

So, what do you think you could do to help someone who doesn't at all doubt the idea that their body is their self-understanding of that, when in fact, that is not the case ?

— Well... I don't think it would be a straightforward process.

I agree. Therefore, **by showing that the belief that the body is the self is the worst possible hell, people can perceive the emotional stakes immediately.** Hence the bird and bottle analogy.

Just as I was saying before, if you believe that the body is the self, you will forever remain that bird stuck in the bottle. Even after death. You will simply be reincarnated into the bottle again, and simply repeat the same mechanical process of conditioned reflex, struggling from within.

If the body is the self, then the self has never once heard what another has to say. One will always be in their own head, hearing their own analysis—while egotistically claiming they listen anyway.

If that's the case, can anyone create trusting relationships ? It won't ever be possible, you know ?

Even if, hypothetically, someone appeared that you felt that you could trust, you would never be able to shake the suspicion and uncertainty that they may one day leave you or betray you.

In this state of affairs that prevents the establishment of trusting relationships, any attempt to realize big dreams or visions requires considerable mental efforts. It requires unceasing forbearance under constant stress and pressure. In comparison to these efforts, success and fulfillment is not guaranteed, and even if realized, are only fleeting.

Without understanding the root cause behind why you failed, behind what went wrong, you blame yourself or others. That stress and resentment reverberates out to your colleagues, friends, lovers, family.

The vicious cycle is unconsciously reinforced, a culture of violence in which people harm each other imperceptibly spreads, and—like a frog in a pot of boiling water—we all find ourselves fully embroiled within it.

Moreover, despite the fact that there is no way to accumulate objective knowledge over time, humanity has, throughout history, made arbitrary claims over what is or isn't "objective." Our body of knowledge as it stands is little more than an assortment of dogmatic prejudices and assumptions. We've turned those into custom, built culture and civilization, and the wheels of fate have kept turning.

As a result, humans naturally become unhappy, ignorant fools. They succumb to hate and resignation. Even if they die and are reborn, they fail to escape the tragic, wretched, miserable loop of karmic energy, for all eternity.

I could talk about this forever—the point is that all of this is part of the "worst possible hell" that emerges from believing that the body is the self.

— That belief leads to some pretty big problems, huh...

That's right. For that reason, before pursuing Truth, before trying to know the origins of the universe, before thinking that you want to attain enlightenment, **you must first come to a thorough awareness of how hellish it is to live as a human in a body.**
There has not yet been a single sage, a single enlightened person, who has been outspoken about the importance of prioritizing this awareness.

— No one has said that this awareness must be prioritized in discussions ?

That's right.

This lack of discussion on how belief that the body is the self puts us in the worst possible hell is also the cause of humanity's ongoing failure to engage in true teamwork.

That's because it is difficult to bring people together and motivate their productivity in terms of a "vision of heights." In comparison, it's very easy to motivate people and bring them together if they see that they are living in the "worst possible hell."

— Yes, you certainly have a point there. I'm getting an image of how shared problem awareness, a shared "enemy" can create alliances and strengthen communities. A weakness of vision.

That's right. The deeper that problem awareness, and the more widely it is shared, the more powerful an engine it becomes.

This "engine of depths" fashioned from an awareness of our hellish circumstances will also enable us to perceive a heaven—"True Heaven."

— I see... I wouldn't have thought that believing that the body is the self is such a critical piece of this puzzle. I'm going to try to organize myself on a daily basis to deepen my understanding.

Yes, I encourage you to meditate on that idea.

Here's another thing. Let's say you've got an enlightened person. If this person is unable to show someone that belief in the body-as-self is hell, they will never succeed at making that someone enlightened or at making them aware of Oneness. Do you know why ?

— That... Is it because it's as futile as trying to "polish a cement block into a mirror" ?

That's right ! So hypothetically, even if someone became enlightened, they'd have a 100% failure rate at communicating it. They wouldn't be able to share this enlightened world. Therefore, rather than teaching the Truth, the most important thing is teaching how belief in body-as-self is hell.

— I partially understand what you're saying, I think. However, it seems like it's pretty heavy stuff. I can't just lightly say "Yeah, I got it." I'd like to go deeper.

Thank you. So, we are now in the age in which there is going to be a mass upheaval to the paradigm that defines the "self," the "human," as the flesh entity defined by a boundary of skin and membranes. The redefinition of humanity—ergo the redefinition of the self—**is as the absolute reality self-encountered in the instant the bird in the bottle—the body-as-self—disappears.**

In a word, this is **absolute dignity, dignified humanity.**

— Couldn't that be called "divinity" ? There's that idea that all of us are a part of God.

"Divinity" is insufficient. If the will behind the creation of the universe itself is "divinity," then this "divinity" created the physical "humanity"— that's the general conception, I'd say.

However, both monotheism and pantheism are rife with problems and contradictions, and **if a separation arises by defining a relationship between a Creator and created, it's not enlightenment.**

One can become a deity or a human. There are no boundaries to gods or men. If divinity and humanity are made separate entities such that divinity is complete, that divinity is in fact incomplete because it cannot become an incomplete human.

Place nothing above the self, and nothing below.

Influence nothing, do not be influenced. Control nothing, do not be controlled.

Unconditional completeness itself. Absolute dignity itself.

A human perspective rooted in eternal, impenetrable Truth, that denies neither human flesh nor divine ideal, transcending them both.

Upon nullification of all image's humanity has so far used, a new humanity arises using entirely new imagery, entirely new ideals, never used before.

This is the "redefinition of humanity."

— Wow... that's amazing. I think that's about all I can handle for now. I'd like to try getting a good handle on making my imagery properly deep and accurate again.

By the way, I have a question. I think we were talking about applying these ideas to reality, but because the point of reference is so deep, all I've picked up on is stuff about essence. Could you explain how this "redefinition of humanity" will impact my life in the future?

Sure, in that case, let me just make one more point first. This may seem like a detour, but if we don't draw our bowstring as deep as we possibly can, our arrow won't fly very far.

In the example of the bottle and the bird, the bottle "exists" and the bird "exists." How can the bird be freed to the outside? Getting caught in this point of reference gets you caught in the samsara of human thought. There will never be an answer. Unlike other animals, the perennial theme of humanity is the act of thought. We are, after all, rational entities.

In the moment the illusory bottle and bird vanish—in the moment the self and the self's world vanishes—humanity becomes fully liberated from all thought, all cause and effect.

First, **you come to understand that both the bottle and the bird are made from exactly the same high-level substance.**

All that *actually* exists is this high-level substance. Once you understand this, the bottle and the bird blend together into that unified substance. The bottle and bird arise from the substance, the bottle and bird break down again.

The substance stretches out into this new unified substance, the substance is compressed and formed into the bottle and the bird. The formed bottle and bird then break down and stretch out. Then the substance is compressed again... and so on.

There is no bottle, there is no bird. All there is is the one motion of this high-level substance. The substance breaks down, then binds back together: this cyclical motion is all there is.

Before, you said that "the bird is myself, and the bottle is my world," right? In that case, the things that this brand-new substance is being compressed and formed into is yourself and your world. **You and your world are broken down, melted into this unified substance. All there is, is the repetition of this motion.**

No-self, no-world. **At the moment one's self and one's world disappears, reversibility/irreversibility disappear as well—and with them, of course, cause and effect.**

Once you have been fully liberated from your current condition, the remaining fragments of your concepts will be completely destroyed, and you will encounter the impossible beauty of Truth in itself.
In this moment is joy in itself.

— How can I put it... it sounds like it must be so refreshing, this sense of pure freedom.

Yes, it is. Regarding the human condition, there are two big items of significance here. One is the absolute dignity we have discussed. **The redefinition of humanity. The other is the integrity of ignorance.** One becomes totally free of the "known world." Socrates claimed that he knew that he knew nothing. However, not even this is sufficient.

— Yes, I know of that idea from Socrates. There is nothing one knows that they can be absolutely certain is true. Dialogue and dialectic use that as a starting point.

I see, so your point has been to demonstrate that Truth cannot be found in human conceptual knowledge, it seems.

Yes. If I may rephrase, **it is an attempt to wake people up and extract them from the "complete knowledge trap" that humans fall into when they unconsciously come to believe that they are correct.**
In so doing, one's awareness starts to turn towards the Truth that lies beyond concepts.

It's a perspective problem. The brain has habits of perception, and it takes the sparse, fragmented information we feed it from the outside as its evaluation criteria to make all sorts of judgments, criticisms, attacks: yes/no, good/evil, like/dislike, know/don't know. This is something from which humanity must free itself. However, one's awareness of one's own ignorance can lead to a misunderstanding that the Truth will never be understood. One's foundation will remain uneasy, unfixed.

— Oh, I've fallen for that. It's agnosticism, isn't it ? It's the claim that it is impossible for humanity to attain some kind of absolute truth. There are philosophers who have gone crazy or killed themselves in pursuit of it.

That's right. Like we discussed earlier, **we have to keep in mind Gödel's Incompleteness Theorem. It has been mathematically proven that it is impossible to reach an absolute truth that is devoid of contradiction.**

If that's the case, humans will remain stuck in the bottle forever. I think it's no good to just accept that that's what humanity is, like agnosticism does.

Gödel is not mistaken. However, his proof only works within the paradigm of "existence."

From the perspective of Truth, Gödel's argument makes sense, but it is easy to identify its flaws. It is possible to create a logic based on a higher order meta-perception.

That logic, that tool, is nTech. So, what do you think happens to nTech once you've reached the world of "complete ignorance" ?

— What happens to nTech in the world of "complete ignorance" ?

Ummm, if nTech can be used to lead others to this absolute reality, I think it would become a tool for the ages.

Yes, well, I'm glad you would think so, but that ends up stopping matters at the "complete ignorance" concept. The final answer of nTech is the following: **nTech itself "does not exist."**

— nTech "doesn't exist" either ??

That's right. nTech also "doesn't exist," image language also "doesn't exist," and of course, I also "don't exist." "Complete ignorance," the ultimate wisdom arising from the nullification of all knowledge, is this sort of world.

— I see...

First, people must become aware of the arbitrary nature of the "complete knowledge trap," the incomplete nature of knowledge, undergo a revolution in their point of reference using image language, and see things from the perspective of Truth. "Complete ignorance" is something that comes after attaining this all-seeing state.

This is because image language is a tool meant to compensate for the incompleteness of knowledge that defines the human perspective. When all that remains of the "known world" is a meta-level knowledge of nTech, one remains in a world of boundaries—knowing/not knowing, imaginable/unimaginable.

— Hmmm...

Therefore, **in the end, those boundaries must be totally destroyed. Nullified. nTech disappears as well.**

That is complete freedom from the known world.

At that moment, one enters the **world of absolute dignity.**

This is **the original, deepest nature of all human beings.**

Moving past thought, perfection of thought. Moving past humanity, perfection of humanity. Dignity itself, freedom itself, love itself. A world with nothing but that complete unity itself. It's like an eraser. The root of human unhappiness lies in the inability to reconstruct an entity (existence) once it has been nullified. In this way, nTech is a technology that changes the uncontrollable physical world into a controllable perceptual world. The universe becomes one's mind.

Do you feel comfortable with the "redefinition of humanity" and "complete ignorance" ?

The trap of complete knowledge (no knowledge of the perspective problem)

The incompleteness of knowledge (self-awareness of ignorance, agnosticism)

Compensation for the incompleteness of knowledge (tools such as nTech and image language)

Complete ignorance (freedom from tools, freedom from the known world)

— I'm not sure if I can say I get it or not. It's a bit much...

    However... are you alright? For some reason, I feel kind of sorry for you.

    You said that nTech doesn't exist and that you don't exist. This thing that you have desperately sought, this thing that renders unnecessary the system you have spent 25 years creating—it's "complete ignorance"?

Thank you for your concern. I won't go into greater detail on this topic here, but because it relates to a later topic—group enlightenment and spiritual evolutionists—I will discuss it then.

— OK. I do think I'm following logically. nTech and image language are technologies meant to compensate for knowledge. Ultimately, knowledge of these things remains, so no matter how much the contents differ from other systems of thought, philosophies, religions, or science, they still constitute an attachment to the "known world."

Yes. That's right. In this case, humans would succumb to the tendency to break things apart, find differences, draw boundaries, establish categories. Do you know nTech, or not? Do you understand it, or not? Do you understand its value, or not? That sort of thing.

    If a boat arrives to bring you to the shores of nirvana, you can't keep clinging to it once you reach the other side. That boat is human thought, and it is nTech, which compensates for the limits of human perception and thought. At the very end, the boat must be abandoned, and the new status quo must be fully embraced.

Right here, right now, is total integration, a world of dignity itself, of perfect satisfaction.

This is also the meaning of the **"happiness of depths"** I mentioned before.

— Those depths sure are deep... it seems like my brain is finally raising the white flag on trying to follow this imagery.

Yes, that's a good sign. It's proof that you're starting to understand, starting to visualize. This is a world that the human brain usually can't visualize, so when it gets bombarded with these arguments and images, ultimately it has to give in.

Once you say you give up—you admit it, there's nothing but unity after all—then you'll be outside your brain. You'll be in the world beyond thought, beyond humanity. Congratulations.

— I'm looking forward to going through the steps and knocking out the problems my brain has been giving. To go back to my previous question, though, how will this connect to how I live ?

I see this is something that concerns you. I do think, though, that if you come to understand the final answer to all of this, you will naturally connect the imagery, the meaning, the value.

OK, let's look at some things. The world of realizing one's desires is the conscious world. The driving force behind the conscious is the unconscious.

— Unconscious, yeah, it's also called the subconscious. It's the rest of the iceberg underwater that influences the tip sticking out above—our conscious thought.

That's right. That's a common image, but whether you call it the unconscious or subconscious, there's a lot of layers to it. There is the subconscious of the body that sends out affirmations, or the repressed layers in the depths that seal away trauma. There is data encoded by DNA, information, or the *manas-vijnana* and *alaya-vignana* as described in the *vijnapti-matrata* theories in Buddhism.

Scientifically, there is also a hypothesis called the cosmic information theory that suggests that the entire universe can be described in terms of information. Under this view, the vibrations of strings and the energy of the membrane are also infused with the data and information that constructs the universe.

— Wow, that's a lot of layers.

All of those levels, down to the string dimension, are levels of the unconscious energy and substance that form the universe. In the world of Zen, one starts from there to reach the 5th level—called *Kŭmuhensho*—in which one escapes the universe and intuition for emptiness expands.

— Now that you mention it, we talked about this before. About just being on level 5.

That's right.

The 6th level in Zen—*Shikimuhensho*—is attained upon expanding one's mind to incorporate that intuition for emptiness.

The 7th level—*Musho-usho*—is transformation into the motion of infinite speed, zero speed itself.

The 8th level—*Hisōhihisōsho*—is attained once the unimaginable world becomes imaginable. The process is complete upon attainment of the 9th level—*Metsujinjō, Sōjumetsujō*—in which one reaches complete ignorance and is liberated from the known world.

We are entering an age where it is becoming necessary to know and understand that, within ideas like "unconscious" and "oneness," such levels of the mind exist. Upon attaining this understanding, one must finally transcend the division between "conscious" and "unconscious." This ultimate reality is the world of **complete ignorance.**

— That changes my image of the iceberg. My understanding of words like unconscious and subconscious really was just the tip of the real depths.

The 21st century is sure to become the age of unconscious/subconscious development.

In order for this to happen, there is already a variety of practical methods and knowledge for each level of development. I think these systems are wonderful.

That's all the more reason that it is so important to have a "framework" that does not contradict science, that operates with imagery and logic from the deepest possible level, in order to maximize their efficacy. A way to bring everything through Essence into Reality, for application in Reality. The application of the deep roots of infinite Essence. nTech is a system that breaks everything down to the deepest possible level and reconstructs back to Reality. In practice, this can involve sessions and consulting.

— How can it be put into practice ? Even just a basic image is fine.

In order to figure out how this ties into reality, we will need to move to the next keywords.

— I took some notes before. This is "recreational intuition" or "independent decision-making," right ?

Yes. The "redefinition of humanity" and "complete ignorance" found in the True world are, being from the deepest possible place, in a sense the farthest removed from Reality. However, clearly establishing that point of reference makes all the difference.

Earlier, I had asked you if you could imagine why a revolution in point of reference is necessary, why it would be desirable to apply this True world to Reality. Do you remember ?

— Yes, I remember that.

Let's ponder that as we look at how it connects to this **recreational intu-ition, or independent decision-making.** I'd like to evolve the dimension-ality of our desires from success and happiness that rely on the realization of vague hopes to a deep-seated "desire for dignity."

I said this when we were discussing the bottle and bird, but **in the Real world, human beings tend to believe that humanity is what it is, they are what they are, the world is as it appears. They unconsciously give up, they unconsciously limit themselves.**

Inside the bottle, inside society, people are motivated from the out-side to pursue wealth in the form of money, status, honor, and fame.

There is a side to this in which humans are turned into a kind of beast of consumption, in which humans are seen as less valuable than money, in which humans are made to compete in order to satisfy the desires of our material civilization. "Success" is defined as accumulating lots of money, things, land.

— Yes, yes.

The will to improve and advance towards that is very important. However, the point of reference remains entirely within the paradigm of "existence." If that point of reference is not itself changed, there can be no spread of the vision to reform Reality or the methods to do so.

Let's use our imaginations a bit. Human history is a history of war. Throughout this history has been an implicit assumption that this is the way human beings are, this is what humanity is. The claim that conflict is the true nature of humanity is a very backwards-looking perspective.

The way I see it, there's no value at all to making that view of humanity our point of reference.

We work to create and sustain the order of human society with economic and political institutions and systems, laws, or moral codes. An order based on rights, assets, and violence. This is how human history has unfolded.

— Yes, I agree.

You, too, are a part of human history. Ultimately, your individual life is the same. The diverse deterministic and rationalistic ideas created by others, rules created by others, words created by others are all transmitted to you via this phenomenological society. You try your hardest to take it all in, remember, and live your life mechanically according to the conditioned reflexes they impart.

If A, do B. If C, do D. That isn't really your own will. That is your soul being chained by Reality.

This is how the human condition looks from the perspective of true, absolute dignity—from the perspective of freedom. And yet, we normally aren't even all that aware of this problem, wouldn't you agree ?

That is because we all assume that our environments, humanity, our history, just are the way they are.

However, this is a defeat of the spirit. It is like a sort of paralysis. I want people to come to a robust problem awareness on this point. **To sacrifice your dignity and potential at the altar of an illusory dream of the brain, to be at the whim of manufactured desires, manufactured ideas—Humanity, what are you doing ?!?!**

— You're yelling again...

But, thanks to you, my eyes have been opened. Before we apply these ideas in Reality in pursuit of such vague desires, we must first become deeply aware of the suffering of human beings.

Without that, nothing more than a shallow level of change in realizing one's desires will be possible. Consequently, one will distance themselves even farther from the true wonder of humanity.

Yes, that's exactly right. Haste makes waste. In order to obtain true answers, true change, this duality is essential. That is the revelation of true problem awareness.

Rather than a phenomenological problem awareness, this is a meta-problem awareness that causes the emergence of *all* phenomenological problems.

When that awareness can be nullified at the root and completely cleared, it becomes possible to obtain true answers, true change. This meta-problem awareness that causes all human problems is...

— ...the perspective problem.

That's right ! **Determining the limits of one's life, deciding on a framework, is itself a "perspective problem."** It is like living your life as a dog chained to a doghouse, walking around it in circles.

Human beings who are bound by the brain's perspective have let themselves believe that humanity and themselves just are the way they are, going in circles.

Total freedom from those chains is found in absolute dignity, in complete ignorance. This is the most important, most direct diagnosis and prescription in order to attain freedom from those chains. The diagnosis is the perspective problem. The treatment is a revolution in point of reference that leads to absolute dignity and complete ignorance.

With this revolution, **we can begin to reconstruct our way of life with the point of reference and willpower that let us obtain absolute dignity. Right here, right now, we can apply the framework that ties together the universe, the imagery and intuition that has reconstructed ourselves and our worlds.** Then, for the first time, we will be able to say, **"I am living my life."**

There is an episode in the life of the Buddha in which he took seven steps immediately after birth, proclaiming, "I am chief of the world." I think that this idea of "chief" does not refer to a vanity of the body, but rather is a declaration of total liberation from karma, of unique, total, personal dignity, incomparable and unrankable.

This is the start of and a condition for a truly human life, a second birth as a human being of the mind.

— That's quite an image... I still am unfamiliar with that sort of intuition, but I get a sense for the value of making that one's standard. Whether it's realizing one's thoughts or images, or pulling them into reality, I agree: all of these things become wrapped together from an overwhelmingly deeper, bigger place.

I keep talking about the age of the mind, the age of the unconscious, so I need to provide some explanation on what I mean by "mind," and what sort of operative principles, what sort of composition, describes this absolute world of mind that powers the unconscious and the conscious.

Humans are truly amazing once they have awoken from illusion. Once they do so, they recreate Reality. Of course, that doesn't mean denying all of the order, law, and morality in human society. What we have has its uses, and the things that need improvement will take time to improve.

The world of the mind is, right here, right now, at this moment, ready to transform you, if you were to notice it.

That, more than anything else, is the biggest secret, the core, to change.

Once you attain this sort of excited mind that vigorously, vitally, destroys and recreates the universe, you will be able to enjoy the transformations of Reality regardless of the conditions. Regardless of the conditions, you will maintain a hold on the willpower, courage, and wisdom you need to move forward.

Events themselves are not that important. What matters is how you think of them, how your way of thinking changes with a free mind rooted in Truth. The way of thinking that arises upon understanding the way of being of Truth itself.

If you see things in terms of suffering, all is suffering.
If you see things in terms of despair, all is despair.
If you see things in terms of hope, all is hope.
If you see things in terms of love, all is love.
If you see things in terms of dignity, all is dignity.

The original self, the True mind itself, will right here, right now, continuously and freely recreate yourself and your world. That is **recreational intuition. That is independent decision-making.**

— So, in other words, one can create their own desired reality via this transformation in thought that arises from a resolution for individual decision-making?

Of course. **Right here, right now, yourself and your reality is being destroyed and reconstructed at high speed. Once you attain a clear understanding of how that motion itself, how that mind itself, is in fact one's actual self, you become more able to control the "screen" that your mind creates.**
We will talk more about this framework later, but that's the idea, for now.

— I see. I'm looking forward to it. However, while I agree, there is still a part of me that can't agree. Maybe it's because I still don't understand this "framework," or maybe it's because the idea of a way of life that goes exactly how you wish sounds too idealistic.

Yes, I have a few things to say about that.
First, you may notice that there is a pattern to your perspective, deeply rooted habits to your emotions and thoughts. You say things like, **"'even so', or 'but', 'regardless', 'someone like me'."**
In general, **successful people are excellent at cultivating patterns and images that lead to success. Even in a relative world, your perspective is linked to your health.**
People without that perspective will unconsciously put themselves

down, base their perspective on past failures and setbacks, and get stuck. They reap what they sow: more of the same.

In that sense, **unconsciously thinking of yourself as a nobody turns you into a nobody.**

— Ah, yes ! That's exactly how it is. I agree. You become what you think of yourself as, in a backwards way.

This, too, is a **perspective problem.** If you only have a conceptual understanding of nTech, you will always succumb to and be held back by your brain habits.

You remember things in a way that is influenced by your own perspective patterns. First you try to understand, then you sharpen your understanding as your self-awareness rises. As your perspective emerges, your patterns of critique become available to you to see objectively. You can understand their shape. By freeing yourself of those patterns, you can nullify that perspective.

This work can be done by anyone if they go at it with a playful, but serious, attitude. Since this arises from the brain functions we all share, the problem isn't in some way your fault. You don't need to assess yourself in terms of success or failure.

— Yes, I see.

Yes. In order to get a complete picture of one's own perspective, the best thing to do is to get outside of one's perspective completely. In order to do this, **one must align one's mind to a point of reference that has nullified one's self and one's world.**

— The "perspective problem" really goes deep. Ultimately, the state of "no-self, no-world" is the same image as "the perspective within the perspective."

As long as you keep holding on to that interior space, you'll find that you have unconsciously fixed your entrenched personal perspective— the image of your own self, the image of society around you.

You start judging yourself and others in unchangeable terms. I have a feeling that I understand the sense of widening potential that would arise if one freed oneself from that entrenched imagery.

Competent ? Omnipotent ?
I see—the single-mindedness of the original self is capable of absolutely anything !

That's right. People who think their bodies are themselves are not able to feel that unconsciously on a deep level. People who are truly enlightened are continuously, effortlessly aware of this constant reconstruction of self and universe.

There is no past or present, only "here and now." With the decision-making ability to decide how you perceive the "here and now," one obtains the freedom from and control over the past, the present, and the future.

"The past was one way, now it's this way, the future must be another way." One obtains freedom from this sort of conceptual cause and effect and becomes always capable of simply enjoying the "here and now."

This Real World begins to look like sculptures of the mind, of light, and soul. The truth behind the mystery and sacredness of this illusory world of art becomes tangible.

— A way of life of feeling the true, the good, and the beautiful in the "here and now" If I achieved that, the things within this illusory screen would not just be a meaningless illusion, but rather an illusory world of art. If that became my true outlook, how would the physical people of this illusion look to me ?

I mentioned it before. **Seen from the perspective of the Truth, humanity is unbelievably beautiful. From the point of reference that recognizes non-existence—looking at existence from non-existence—even a single speck of dust seems to be a miracle, a work of art, a sacred mystery.**

Here's an interesting bit of Japanese: think of the word for thank you, *arigatou*. I asked a Japanese friend of mine, who said that the origin of it is *arikatashi*, or "difficult to exist." "Existence" is not taken for granted.

Just look at what a beautiful work of evolutionary art has emerged from non-existence: existence, to this illusory universe, to the human brain, to our "screen views."

The universe is a 13.8 billion year old work of art.

What's more, it is constantly going in and out of existence—it just *looks like* it exists. It is truly something that finds existence "difficult." That is why, when looking at people from the standpoint of non-existence, every individual's individuality looks like dignity itself.

There has not been an entity just like you at any other point in the universe's 13.8 billion year history, including anywhere on Earth. You feel gratitude towards everyone for existing, you feel congratulations towards them for coming into the world, you feel thanks for being able to meet them. That is what it is like.

A big thing to come out of seeing things in terms of humanity's strength is **the love you start to feel for humanity. You start to love the "relation" between people. You start to see humanity as ever-so wonderful, ever-so beautiful. You feel endless love for humanity. People's encounters and exchanges look like the art of the cosmos, and thus you find their interactions, their sharing of their visions, extremely fun.**

— I see... that would be amazing if true. That alone would have tremendous value. The value of existence, of encounters, would advance to a completely different level. After all, living in modern society the way we do now, I always have thoughts that humanity is obnoxious, that I don't want to deal with people, that I don't want them to see my true self or my weaknesses.

That's right, these are all very much first-world problems. Humanity is annoying, or you dislike people, etc. However, **the thing that determines the richness of our lives more than anything else is our human relationships.** The relationships between parent and child, siblings, friends, lovers, coworkers, all of them matter. Finding humanity annoying or repulsive only serves to weaken the deepest foundations of our society.

There is so much information on the internet it's hard to know what to believe. While you might think the increase of information, knowledge, and theory will make human beings smarter, it makes it more difficult to maintain relationships as well.

When you surf the internet, you can find people who are cooler than you, prettier than you, wiser than you, more successful than you, richer than you, etc., etc. There are too many people with whom to compare yourself, and it becomes difficult to have faith in yourself. If you have no self-confidence, your human relationships will be shallow as well.

Because your human relationships are shallow, you also cannot satisfy your need for recognition. If you won't recognize your own value, the people around you will unconsciously start to judge you pessimistically as well. They start to think that someone like you can't do X or Y. **Ultimately, you start to see this in their behavior yourself, and become unconsciously afraid of them rejecting you.**

— Hmmmm, now that you say it, that does seem right.

So, you graduate from being a "human of flesh" and become capable of seeing human encounters and interactions as the art of the universe. I really love samurai, and **nTech is a samurai enlightenment.** Samurai start, unmoving, from a stable stance—and in an instant, push all of their training into an infinite burst, as a single strike. Battles are decided in that single instant. Isn't that cool? Rather than attaining enlightenment on your own in meditation, with no other human contact, you have to annihilate yourself and your world in the midst of all the tension that arises from the extreme situations of human contact and existential engagement. This is the final state of intuition that Miyamoto Musashi reached.

— What sort of intuition is that? Could you provide some more imagery on that?

Samurai train to be warriors in body and mind from a young age. Every day, for years, for decades, they endure intense martial training. As a result, their intuition evolves. The eye is not fast enough to follow the opponent's sword. The eye is not fast enough to follow the opponent's movements. The eye is not fast enough to follow the opponent's expressions or breathing.

I trained in martial arts for 20 years, myself. **I came to understand that the seeable, hearable world of the five senses is deceptive.**

In that critical moment of a sword fight, you no longer exist in the physical world of the bodily senses.

In this world beyond the senses—in the world of intuition—one encounters the "interval" between oneself and one's opponent. That is where the battle is fought. In that moment, one focuses the entirety of one's life-long training, pride as a samurai, family honor into a single point. The slightest hesitation means death.

This extreme tension, this extreme balance, is an absolute world of the soul's movements—of the soul itself.

— Wow, when I imagine being in that sort of situation, I don't think I'd be able to breathe.

Right. No speed, infinite speed. The energy left behind by the spirituality of 700 years of samurai rule in Japan is considerable.

Moreover, out of this world of dueling swords in which one person is sure to die came a new world of dueling spirits. This is the tea ceremony introduced by Sen no Rikyū.

I have been wanting to make a film that showcases the splendor of Japan, while also describing the True World using Sen no Rikyū as a model. Tea ceremony is the world of enlightenment. The sense of tension in samurai battles lives on fully in the structure of tea ceremony, as a beautiful cultural tradition.

Both martial arts and tea ceremony put a great deal of emphasis on respect for the other. They both begin and end in gratitude, in the form of respect for the fundamental dignity of the other. It has nothing to do with age, status, or rank—both parties show respect for each other. I find this beautiful. It's a true dignity-based relationship.

In the age to come, we will need to spread this sort of intuition—this sort of deep relationship—worldwide, in the form of a codified education industry.

I am of the opinion that we are headed for disaster if we fail to properly and deeply supplement the scientific and IT technology that currently leads our society, with some sort of human development technology.

— Yes, I frequently hear about Moore's Law[4], the technological singularity[5], and that sort of thing. On the internet, you can find various experts voicing serious concerns over the automation of labor and the explosive development of artificial intelligence.

Just a little while ago, these topics were considered sci-fi—and now they are becoming our real, lived problems.

I think there is both good and bad to the development of IT and scientific technology. This is the case for nuclear energy and it arises in bioethics also. I don't have a good grasp on where exactly we are headed with all of this, or what that will mean for humanity.

Yes. One thing I can say with certainty is that, for better or worse, there is no stopping scientific progress. The intellectual curiosity of humanity—our inquisitive spirit—isn't going anywhere. The reality is that we are already being born into conditions in which scientific technology has progressed beyond human control and human, rather than scientific, value has been diminished to a substructure of our system.

The robotics, VR, AR, artificial intelligence, and IoT that define the so-called Industry 4.0—along with technologies that merge IT and human minds and bodies, biotech, nanotech, space development etc.—all have the potential to show us the wonders of science; they all have great promise.

Our current age is indisputably—indisputably—the single most trans-formative age so far in human history. The development that will make this so indisputable is the realization of both a hyperconnected society that brings all things together via IT and science—the opposite of the spiritual world—and the realization of **a post-physical society in which humanity is not defined by flesh alone.** This will be an age in which enlightenment will be quotidian. We are already on our way.

---

4 Moore's Law (Analysis of IT evolution/big data)
https://cyber-synapse.com/dictionary/ja-ma/understaing-moors-law-for-marketing-strategy.html
https://wired.jp/2019/07/10/intels-new-chip-wizard-plan-bring-back-magic/ (2016)
5 Technological singularity
https://en.wikipedia.org/wiki/Technological_singularity

— A post-physical society... this is something that scientists have talked about ? It's quite a concept—an age beyond the body... it seems like progress in scientific technology and IT is leading us to themes that spiritual sages have long discussed.

That's right. In IT terms, it's a distinction between hardware and software. Applied to humans, the body is hardware, while the consciousness, one's thoughts and feelings are software.

However, we are already reaching the limits of these hardware/software concepts for human beings. These ideas are being pushed by the IT world, after all.

— What do you mean by that ? Could you go in more detail ?

In Japanese anime such as *Ghost in the Shell and Neon Genesis: Evangelion*, you can get the sense that they are predicting an era in which the True World will enter society. From Hollywood, there are profound films such as *The Matrix and Interstellar* that deal with the illusory nature of the world and other dimensions.[6]

Ghost in the Shell is a near-future sci-fi story, and really highlights the feeling of technology being just a bit more advanced, putting us in the difficult position of defining exactly what "humanity" is.

The bodies of human beings, as clumps of elementary particles, are constantly blinking in and out of existence. If the "self" that the brain recognizes is no more than an emergent property of electrical signals in the brain, then the awareness and image of "self" will become totally different if the physical conditions—the electrical activity—is changed. This is the Relative World, that changes conditionally.

If one thinks about one's self and one's universe, it becomes clear that **if our brains became physically linked with IT such that we uploaded our consciousness digitally, the hardware of "self" and the existence of "reality" are all false foundations.**

---

6 *Ghost in the Shell. 2004. Bandai Visual.*
Neon Genesis Evangelion.1999.KING RECORDS
Matrix.2000. Warner Bros. Home Entertainment Inc.
Interstellar. 2015. Warner Bros. Home Entertainment Inc.

But if this happens, **how can we define "self" ? Our physical human identity would crumble.** The notion of "self" itself could no longer be preserved.

Alternatively, the advancement of biotech and nanotech may enable the progressive mechanization/replacement of our organs, limbs, etc., and we encounter the same issue.

What is the line between organic and inorganic ?
How far can the concept of "self" be pushed ?

I'm suggesting a world of cyborgs, but in fact this is already the world we live in, to some extent. There are lots of good things about this, too. Ultimately, it's just a matter of how far and how quickly this development proceeds.

— Hmmm, I see... but in a way, there seem to be some similarities with dementia and mental impairments. The way in which we recognize the "self" and "others" changes ? That kind of situation could become arti- ficially, physically possible via IT.

That's right. For that reason, we cannot be sure that we won't encounter disaster if we don't manage to instill the image of a true "humanity re- defined" that is based on an understanding of infinite universes, infinite consciousnesses, and above all, the Absolute World and Absolute Dignity. Otherwise, we may face chaos in our sense of reality.

Thoughts and emotions, memories, reminiscence—if we could convert all of these as physical entities in the form of electrons, or data at the quan- tum level, we could upload the software we call "human consciousness" to a digital world and transcend our bodies.

Theoretically, if we created a device that would allow us to save such data, we would be able to displace our memories from our bodies—just like an AI cloud, we would become hyperconnected and able to freely exchange data with others, uploading and downloading information with each other.

You might think you are looking at someone, but inside is the data of a completely different person. We'd be able to swap bodies. In that case, how would you define who "you" are ?

Would you be your personal DNA, responsible for the creation of your cells ? Would you be the data, the information of your software ? **What on Earth would be the "you" you think you are ?**

— Wow, things would get crazy.

I don't know for sure if ultimately things would get like that. However, upon saying that it could become technologically feasible—that it is theoretically not an issue—even if none of it ultimately became real, we would still be stuck with the main essence of the problem.

What is humanity ? What is the mind, and what is the body ? With no answer to these questions that can be understood and shared, humanity will be faced with this fundamental "identity crisis."

In spirituality and religion, there have been a lot of discussions about how the body is not the true self, it is only a vessel, etc., that touch on the Truth. However, making claims about a soul or spirit are just abstractions and are not scientific. So then, defining humanity ends up being a difficult task.

We are entering an age in which the True human perspective, the "redefinition of humanity," is becoming possible, but it requires a "human development" that evolves our hardware and software and enables the successful integration of the mental world with science and IT. For good or bad, whether you like it or dislike it, want it or don't want it, this is the unavoidable theme waiting for us in the near future.

— Hmmm, it seems like we're really rushing headlong into a totally new age.

That's right. It will be an awe-inspiring age unlike anything in human history. When there are these large upheavals, there is a lot of conflict and friction with old values, the old order. It can be dangerous. What I think is the most important in all of this is the crisis of human dignity. The way we deal with this problem will impact our ability to realize the vision of the best possible future.

— The crisis of human dignity ?

To put it bluntly, human-centric thought and philosophy have become dominated by science and capitalism. There is no question that it is thanks to these things that we have established the material wealth we have today. However, there is a big issue in the way that human value has been made subordinate to scientific technology and capital.

In particular, the development of our IT tech, robotics, and artificial intelligence is truly intense. We have not established an effective philosophy, an effective way of thinking about the problems these things present. In a way, it is the defeat of the arts and humanities.

Currently, the US, with Silicon Valley, is at the front of the pack with these developments. However, the US is fundamentally a Christian nation. They also have a degree of interest in things like Zen and mindfulness. However, if Christianity is able to offer a specific solution to the technological singularity, the individuals in Silicon Valley haven't been thinking about it. It doesn't seem likely that abstractions like feelings or enlightenment will be enough to address the issues faced at the frontiers of science.

— Does the 0=∞=1 world link directly with the world that seems to lie ahead in IT's evolution trajectory ?

Yes. Humanity usually uses the word "consciousness" simply to refer to the things it calls "thoughts" and "feelings." But, OK, in that case, why does consciousness occur ? What are its base principles ? This is what neuroscientists and AI engineers want to understand.

Try imagining the following: human beings use their 5 senses and their brain to create a 3D projection of this holographic universe. The whole architecture behind this process is like an OS (operating system). Consciousness is created by an OS that works from the perspective of brain functions, as a 3D projection of your human life. That is the software we have used so far.

— I see. So, if we develop the brain's OS, the software behind human functioning...

We'd see a revolution in point of reference. We would be free from the brain's perspective, annihilate our self and our universe, and become able to see the hidden structure of change.

In terms of 0=∞=1, we would be able to see the single pattern mechanism shared by the foundational principles of the universe, consciousness, and IT.

Our perceptual point of reference would transcend from the brain's perspective to True Unity itself, to "original mind."

The new OS of perception establishes our perspective from the "structure" of constant, instant creation and destruction, birth and death, that creates everything, changes everything, moves everything, and transforms everything in the universe.

— Yes, I see. The word OS is the same as the one used in IT, but it's a little bit different in meaning.

That's right. However, the mechanism is the same. We aren't talking about an existing computer.

It's a meta-OS for a perceptual computer that can perceive the single motion behind all things in the universe. It is the fundamental principle behind the development of a total OS that oversees the underlying programming of all the information in the universe.

In the early days of IT, a computer was the size of a small building. Then Bill Gates introduced the PC, and Steve Jobs introduced the smartphone—a computer the size of your hand. An AI-based OS, an IoT OS is yet to come.

Moreover, R&D continues in the world of supercomputers and quantum computing. With the quantum angle and the introduction of probability theory and the uncertainty principle, one's mind goes straight to perceptual effects.

Without a doubt, the future is going to start tapping into this different dimension.

— I see... it's hard for me to visualize.

Did the people who discovered **electrons at the start of the 20th century and sought to explain their behavior likely were able to** foresee the smart world we live in 100 years later, in which everything is controlled by electronics ? The same can be asked of quantum particles. They began as a theoretical idea, and now they are being used in engineering.

The discovery and description of fundamental materials and fundamental principles will have dramatic consequences for the society of the future.

— Yes, certainly. That's amazing, I feel kind of excited.

On the other hand, no matter how much science develops, if humanity never changes, there will never be a true paradigm shift. Today we have 3D printers and robots that can make original products. The technological revolution of Industry 4.0 will result in dramatic advances in productivity, efficiency, and functionality. AI will become able to improve itself and pursue its own R&D goals.

However, in pursuit of a deep human dignity, I want to prioritize the realization of human-only intuition, human-only work, a world that AI can never reach. In so doing, no matter how much AI evolves, we can ensure that humans will always be able to coexist with it. This is also why I make such a big deal out of establishing a new education paradigm and perception industry for the post-IT age.

— An intuition that AI can never attain, that only human beings can develop ?

That's right. Human pride. Human beauty. Do you know what ties together everything we have discussed so far ?

— The True World. 0=∞=1. Absolute Dignity, Complete Unknowing, independent decision-making, etc... is that the reason we can assert that AI cannot reach this realm. ? AI will certainly exceed human intelligence, but the world you are talking about is totally different.

Right now, where is your point of reference ? Try imagining what AI does from the "place outside of space." Become the single motion itself—the motion by "something" emerges from "nothing."

— Motion... yes, motion itself. It is both 0 and ∞, come together as one, a state of dynamic equilibrium, with infinite speed, zero speed... a motion without cause nor effect.

Oh, I see. It's a world without causes and without effects. It's the world from which causes and effects emerge.

No matter how much AI evolves, it cannot become free of its programming. It is restricted by 0 and 1, on and off.

It can never be free of the screen it is in. It is a bird that will be forever trapped in the bottle!

Yes, that's right! No matter what kind of artificial super-intelligence we create in the near future, no matter how incomprehensibly sophisticated the algorithms get for us physical humans, the essential state of being digital keeps these AI within the cause-and-effect of relative action. Even in the case of quantum computers, they operate from the paradigm of "existence."

AI is a logical extension of human knowledge and ability developed from within the context of the "existence" paradigm. Fundamentally, AI cannot be free of its programming, cannot be free of the past, cannot be free of cause and effect, and cannot be free of limited decision-making based on differences and components.

This is very much like the limits of the physical human, stuck in the bottle, stuck in the brain's perspective.

It is humans that created AI, is it not? The potential of humanity, in its ability to create entities that transcend themselves, is remarkable. But that same humanity should then evolve to a True Humanity unreachable by AI. Only then will humans be able to coexist with AI.

This is a humanity not bound by the future or the past, to the programming of the world as we know it, to cause and effect, to limits, to boundaries. This is Absolute Dignity itself, infinite potential itself. In such circumstances alone can we enjoy our own unique virtual reality with our own unique independent decision making. The Regenerative Intuition is True Humanity's most fundamental, absolute source of pride.

— I get this strange feeling now that I've come to understand the purpose behind your reusing the example of the bottle and the bird.

Understanding the "place outside of space," *becoming* it, constantly reconstructing existence from nothing, understanding the meaning of the "here and now..."

Humanity has developed within the paradigm of "existence" for millions of years, the pinnacle of which is AI—and now, for the first time in Earth's history, it has become possible for entities that can transcend our human physical limitations to emerge. The evolution of humanity itself, the redefinition of humanity, the development of our human abilities—we need it all !

It will require bringing together all of human thought, philosophy, science, religion, and cutting-edge IT.

The place outside of space. $0=\infty=1$. Why is this True World needed now ?

I will have to live through the age of its rise, and I get the feeling that I may have seen it. I get this feeling that it's all coming together.

Yes. **If you think in terms of our future identity, we are in an age of a major paradigm shift, unheard of in human history.**

When the Wright Brothers took their first flight, they were in the air for just 12 seconds, and only travelled about 36 meters.

For humanity—which until then was accustomed to a 2D lifestyle on the ground—the possibilities of the 3D space of the sky unfolded for the first time. However, at that time, I think **there were two types of people.** "The plane fell. Well, you tried your best."

There were people who were sure that humans could never fly.

"12 seconds ? 36 meters ? That counts as flying ! That will become one minute, then one hour, then 10 hours. From 100 meters, to 1 kilometer, to 100,000."

There were people who were sure that humans would fly one day.

If you had been there, which side do you think you would have been on ?

— Um, I... I think I'd see it as flying. But I can't be sure.

That's quite honest of you. Of course, we know what actually ended up happening. Not only did we make airplanes, but we made rockets that let us go to the Moon, and satellites that took us to Mars and even farther planets. We became able to freely act in the 3D world of space.

In that case, we should be able to make it to the next dimension too. A dimension beyond space, beyond the universe.

The promise of the age to come is free activity in the world of $0=\infty=1$. Humans have amazing potential.

If the virtual screen that all of human history so far has taken place in is thought of as a game, this next age is going to completely overturn the rules with which we are familiar.

One's self and one's world do not actually exist.

In the beautiful civilization of the future that has incorporated the hidden "structure" of the True World into real society, one will interact with many people with this awareness, which will lead to a blooming in all sorts of places over time.

— Yes. I think that's right. However, even if I want to be part of making this new future, making this new age, making this new history, am I able to change my own position in life in order to do it ?

Of course. Here's a question. You must have a deep excitement for your own life. If you resolve to live that way, what do you think you'll end up creating ?

— Ummm...

What do you think ?

— **I'd create a mindset to live in the here and now. My own determination. My own will.**
That's because I am unity itself, constantly recreating my universe.

Right here, right now.

Yes, I see...
I am starting to see a vision for how I want to live my life, the kind of person I want to become, in this new age.
Why am I the way I am now ?

Without betraying the deepest truths to who I am, I want to go 100% towards fulfilling my mission !

Excellent realization. You have done a lot of great work today !

Your realization today of your regenerative nature is a big development. That's enough for our warm-up ! We'll move into the real thing next week ! Rest a lot today, and look forward to our next meeting !

— Yes, I feel like my head is full to the brim, my heart is happy. This has been the most stimulating, fruitful single day of my life. Thank you so much ! Next week is the real thing. I'm looking forward to it !

The Mechanism of 0=∞=1

There is much talk of "Oneness," "Here and now," and "All is one" in spirituality contexts, but in fact there are levels to the world of "unity."

— *Figure 8* —
All things are the fluctuations of a membrane

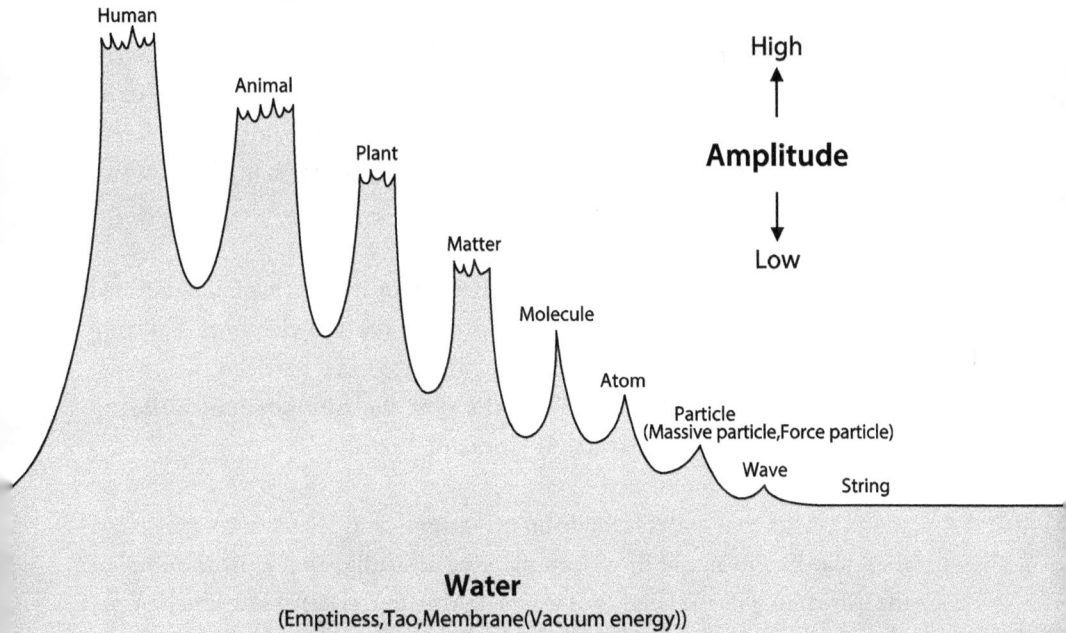

Water
(Emptiness,Tao,Membrane(Vacuum energy))

nTech includes a variety of seminars and workshops. This volume is intended as an introductory text to the True World, and includes theory and imagery in one of the seminars that focuses on scientific knowledge that aids in understanding oneness.

• Materials/Components

The scientific disciplines seek answers via material reductionism, investigating smaller and smaller phenomena.

Consider water. Rain falls from clouds, gathers in lakes, flows down rivers, joins with the oceans, and upon evaporation, repeats the cycles by forming clouds. Clouds, rain, lakes, rivers, oceans, and water vapor all have different names, but they are all composed of water (H_2O). Water is made up of two hydrogen atoms (H) and one oxygen atom (O).

Splitting the hydrogen atom down further demonstrated that it is composed of a nucleus (composed of protons and neutrons) and electrons. Splitting these particles apart resulted in mass particles, force particles, neutrinos, etc. **Modern physics currently thinks that the fundamental building block of the physical universe is vibrating "strings."**

If everything that exists is made up of "strings" and "elementary particles," then just like in figure 8, we can imagine all things that exist in terms of the differences in the heights of waves, asking ourselves, "How much of the shared material of 'water' is here?"

If the tallest wave is humans, then the next tallest is animals, then plants, then matter. In this sense, everything that exists could be thought of as composed of a single substance—like water in different waves—and we name things based on how much of it they have.

With this water as the substance, the "existence" of various waves can be apprehended in terms of vibrations/undulations. But what would happen if you tried to look deeper into the smallest possible wave?

Once the smallest wave (entity) has been split, one enters into a flat world without waves (non-entity). The definition of "entity" here is something with a clear beginning and end. Things without clear beginnings or ends are "non-entities."

This other world in which all is connected (the world of the absolutely large and absolutely small) is now accessible, but because scientists are still looking for "something even smaller," they've had a hard time recognizing this new dimension.

People who have perceived "everything itself" in which all is connected have referred to this "unity" as void, the Tao, Oneness, etc. **This is what physicists call the membrane (vacuum energy).**

The biggest concept in physics is energy. There are three main classifications of energy: quantum field energy, the five types of vibrational string energy, and the membrane (vacuum energy). Among those, vacuum energy is the most fundamental. **This is both energy and not energy, and is in a state similar to the gap between the mind and energy. Therefore, one can reach the mind from energy.**

I go over the details later on, but this membrane (vacuum energy) is **"repeated in-and-out motion."** This material—which brings all entities into being and causes their transformation, movement, and change—is not something with a presence, shape, or existence that can be perceived with the five senses. It is the origin of energy.

— *Figure 9* —
Neither north nor south

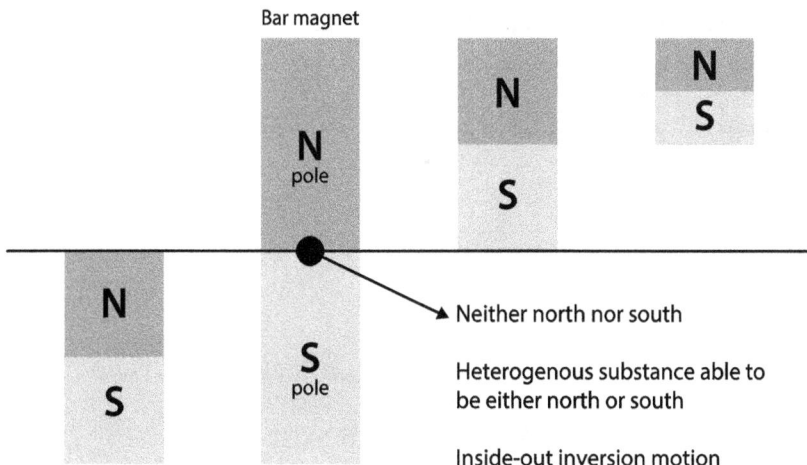

Bar magnet

N pole

S pole

Neither north nor south

Heterogenous substance able to be either north or south

Inside-out inversion motion

The perceptual faculties of the human brain have a strong preference for identifying the existence of something like matter, moving through space. As a result, our brains can't imagine entities as being composed of something that isn't matter. This right here is where the paradigm shift in point of reference from existence to non-existence must take place.

There are probably a lot of people who won't know quite what I mean when I talk about motion itself rather than entities. One easy way to visualize this is with magnets.

A magnet has a north and south pole, but if you cut the magnet in half, will you end up with just a north or just a south magnet?

In fact, what happens is you end up with two magnets that each have their own north and south poles. This will keep happening if you keep cutting it.

So, was the part that turned into a south pole actually north before the cut? Or south?

— Figure 10 —
A transformation from where to where?

Appears to exist

Humans only perceive the world of existence due to the percepual habits of the brain
Analog motion

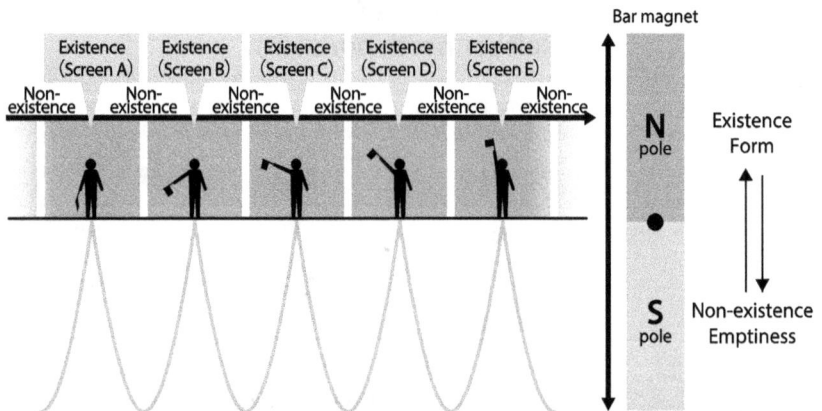

The superposition speed of energy produces a screen that flickers on and off 10^{500} times per second. Digital motion

Appears to not exist

In fact, it was neither north nor south, but had the potential to be either.

Similar to the bar magnet, the movement of the membrane is neither non-existence nor existence, yet can be either one, constantly moving in and out between them.

In that case, from "where" to "where" is the "movement" of this membrane (vacuum energy).

As shown in the figure 10 when you look at reality frame-by-frame, like an animation reel, you see things shift between "appearing to not exist" to "appearing to exist." This transformation is due to the movement of the membrane (vacuum energy).

This is not a fragmentary motion in the universe, but rather a motion in which the existence and phenomena of all things in the universe are changing at the same time.

A movie or animated film needs 20 to 30 frames per second to look good, but the information processing speed of the human brain is not able to apprehend each and every frame.

In reality, there are moments in a film where there is a screen and moment where there is no screen, but no one is able to perceive the "black line" of the no-screen moments while watching. Due to the brain's perceptual habits, it does not recognize the entire motion between existence and non-existence. Rather, it arbitrarily ties together the "with-screen" moments, creating the sensation of time and story.

The motion of the membrane (vacuum energy) moves at an instantaneous superposition (simultaneously overlapping) speed, such that screens are created and destroyed 10^{500} times per second.

Just as there is a black interval (non-existence) between the screens of the movie (existence), the membrane (vacuum energy) repeats the life/death motion of annihilating the entire universe and rebuilding it from scratch at every moment.

From the perspective of the human brain, the present universe and the world appear to have been created over 13.8 billion years, starting from the absence of all of it. In other words, the brain believes the universe will continue to exist (analog changes), but this is incorrect.

At this very moment, all beings are unraveling back to the time before the birth of the universe, and returning back over 13.8 billion years to recreate the universe from scratch. The universe is blinking in and out of existence, over and over, in a discontinuous (digital) motion.

The motion of the membrane (vacuum energy) repeats this round-trip journey of 27.6 billion years 10^{500} times per second. As an aside, this concept of seemingly endless destruction and creation taking place at each and every moment appears in ancient Indian mythology in the form the destructive god Shiva and the creator god Brahma.

I think this may be a bit difficult to imagine, so let's try an analogy.

Sapporo has an ice sculpture exhibition every winter. Let's say that it takes 138 hours to create those ice sculptures from scratch. Let's say it takes another 138 hours to melt the sculptures and turn them back into liquid water.

The starting point is water.

It takes 138 hours to freeze the water and carve the ice to complete the sculpture, but the next time the ice sculptures are completed, they will look a little different from the last time. If you were to repeat this many time and take a picture of the completed ice sculptures each time, the video created by connecting those pictures would look like "ice sculpture motion."

The motion of the membrane (vacuum energy) consists of return to the water (starting point) and regeneration of the ice sculpture (the real world at this moment) from scratch, 10 to the 500th times per second.

Therefore, **concepts of time like the past, the present, and the future are nothing more than confections of the brain. Time does not actually exist in Truth.**

Beyond the speed of causality in the brain that creates time, the superposition speed of instantaneous energy, is an ultra-speed, the speed of mind. It is only upon apprehending this speed of mind that one is able to live in the true "here and now." Only then will you have a mind that allows you to freely control the past, present, and future of the relative world.

Let's connect this with the image of the magnet mentioned earlier. Consider Buddha's claim that "form is emptiness, emptiness is form." If you superimpose existence/form and non-existence/emptiness on north and south poles, the essence of the world that we perceive is a "motion" of constant creation and destruction at superposed speed between appearing to not exist—the membrane/emptiness from beyond the universe, from before the Big Bang 13.8 billion years ago—to appearing to exist—the strings/form of modern humanity and humanity's universe.

• Pattern/Shape

So, what is the shape of this membrane (vacuum energy)—the shape of motion itself? This is the next question.

Since it is motion itself, it does not possess an existence, shape, or presence that can be perceived by the five senses. The concept of revelation via intuitive discernment (*furyu monji*) goes so far as to claim that it is foolish to even attempt to explain or express the concept. Many people who have attained a visceral understanding of oneness have described it nonetheless—there are many such books out there. However, no one has yet appeared in the 4.6 billion-year history of the Earth that has been able to draw, explain, understand, share, and apply its nature.

If you could stop the motion of the membrane (vacuum energy) and observe it, what would it look like? To know, first we must have a correct understanding of the concepts of whole and part.

I mentioned above that modern science aims to subdivide matter into ever-smaller units. So, what is the smallest possible world? To imagine it, try drawing a circle in your notebook.

Can you draw a circle larger than that circle? If you can draw it, can you draw a larger circle than that new one? Repeating this process, many people will end up drawing a circle or a rectangle that follows the outer edge of the notebook paper. If there was more beyond that edge, you could draw a larger circle.

If you can draw a bigger world as long as there is an outside, that means that **as long as that outside exists, your world cannot be the biggest possible. In other words, the biggest world is a world without an out-**

side. A world in which no borderline can be drawn—that continues forever, ever, and ever with no outside. **Mathematically, such a world can be defined as ∞ (infinity).**

In the same way, try drawing a circle on a different page, and then draw a smaller circle in it. As long as the circle has an inside area, you can draw a circle smaller than the last one you drew inside it.

— Figure 11 —
The biggest world, the smallest world

The biggest world (∞) has no outside

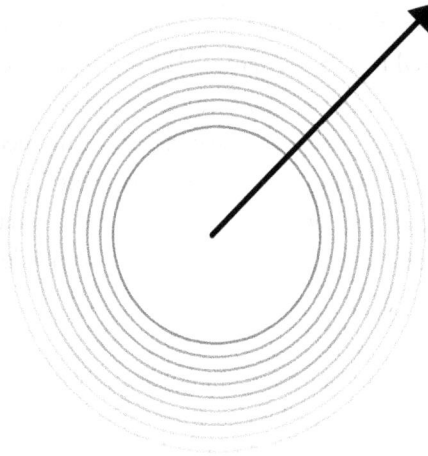

The smallest world (0) has no inside

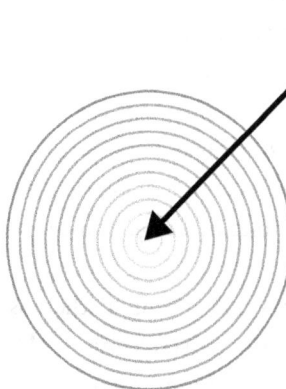

The circle will probably approach a single point—but even a point drawn with a pen on a notebook is like a pile of oil when viewed with an electron microscope. The smallest world is a world without the inside that a circle has, because if there is an inside area, you can draw a smaller world. Therefore, in the figure, **the circle without an inside is expressed as zero.**

In the figure showing waves and water (figure 8), the moment the smallest wave is split apart, a world without waves emerges.

If you pursue the smallest possible entity as far as possible, you will eventually reach the smallest world (zero) and largest world (infinity), where all is connected.

The smallest world zero (0 inside, ∞ outside) and the largest world ∞ (∞ inside, 0 outside) in the figure 13 become equal when the inside and outside are inverted.

The membrane (vacuum energy) is motion itself, which inverts this inside and outside at both zero speed and infinite speed. $0=\infty=1$ because of this motion of continuous inversion.

For those who find this idea too simple to accept, can you imagine how $0=\infty=1$ would be the result if the motion of the membrane (vacuum energy) were defined as the motion of this inside and outside inversion?

This is a paradigm shift in the age of metaknowledge. The concept that 0 and ∞ are equivalent is unacceptable to scientists who specialize in mathematics and physics. However, just as it is possible to calculate the roundness of the Earth, the equivalence of 0 and ∞ can be calculated as well. If you specialize in unified theory, you may realize that when you replace the string or membrane with the following model, a simpler arrangement could occur. The shape of the membrane (vacuum energy) can be explained in the following figure.

This figure is a picture of the shape of the membrane (vacuum energy). It is a type of what I call "image language." The world without inside (zero space) and ∞ are an inseparable "unity" engaged in a constant inversion of inside and outside.

This figure visualizes the will of the membrane (vacuum energy): zero space wants to meet ∞ and ∞ wants to enter zero space, so when the inside and outside are inverted, ∞ enters zero space.

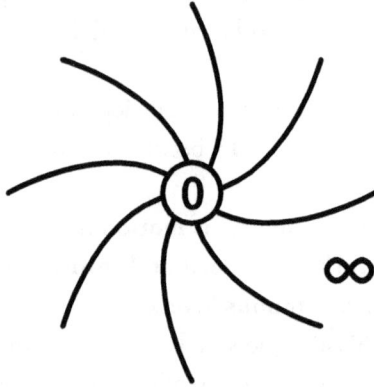

— Figure 12 —
The pattern and shape of the membrane (vacuum energy) in image language

Irreducible Only One
Holistic composition
$0 = \infty = 1$

$$0 = \infty$$
$$\| \quad \|$$
$$1$$

The biggest world and smallest world belong to the same unity

— *Figure 13* —
Motion of continual inside/outside inversion

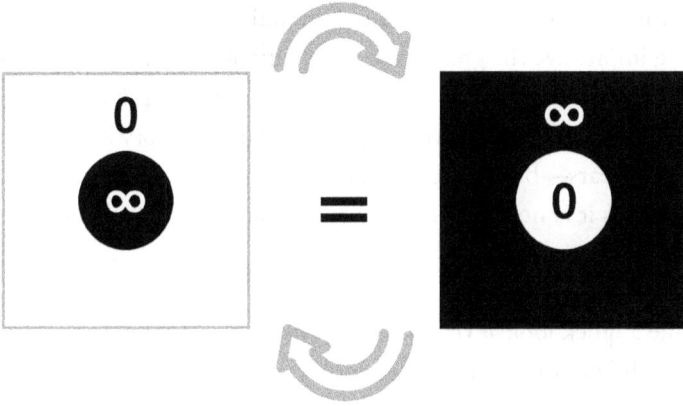

Seen in terms of the perpetual inside (0) to outside (∞) inversion motion,
0 is ∞ and ∞ is 0, so change is ∞ and change is 0

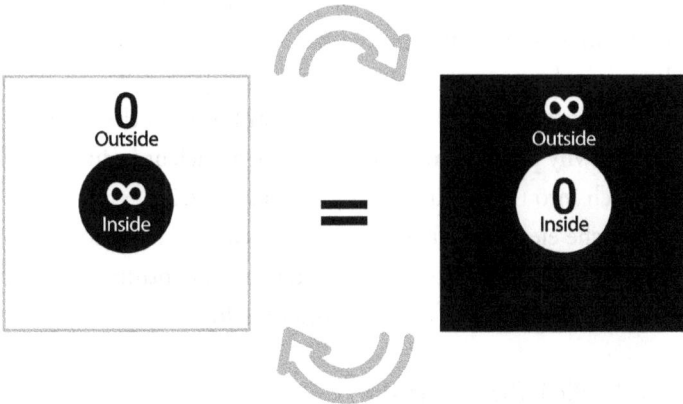

Then, the inside becomes ∞ and the outside becomes 0, but **in the process of creating a separated world with boundaries from one in which there are no boundaries, the simple structure of zero and infinity unity itself maintains universality, while manifesting and evolving into complex systems in an ongoing, iterative manner.**

Albert Einstein wrote in his autobiographical notes that "A theory is the more impressive the greater the simplicity of its premises, the more different kinds of things it relates, and the more extended is its area of applicability."[7] Many scientists are working on the unified theory he was exploring in his later years—but in fact, we already have the answer. It is currently overlooked as it is not the answer that anyone expected; this sort of thing happens all the time.

Let's take a quick look at the history of the unified theory.

Until the middle of the 19th century, electricity and magnetism were explained by different laws. However, after an experiment in which a magnet moved back and forth through a ring-shaped electric wire yielded an electric current in the wire, the two were combined to form electromagnetism.

In other words, human beings did not understand the principle of power generation until they had a grasp on a framework for electromagnetism.

Experiments demonstrate the presence of a "weak force" and "strong force" that act only on extremely small elementary particles, in addition to the "electromagnetic force" and "gravitational force" in the natural world.

The reason why protons and neutrons form a nucleus is due to the strong force. Research into these four forces yielded successive explanations in the 1970s of how the electromagnetic force and weak forces interact—the electroweak force—and how strong forces interact—quantum chromodynamics. These are collectively called the Standard Model.

The Grand Unified Theory has also been proposed as a model that unifies these three forces, and experiments for its confirmation are currently underway. The last remaining challenge in the physics world is gravity.

---

7 *Autobiographical Notes*

— *Figure 14* —
**The motion of the membrane (vacuum energy),
in image language**

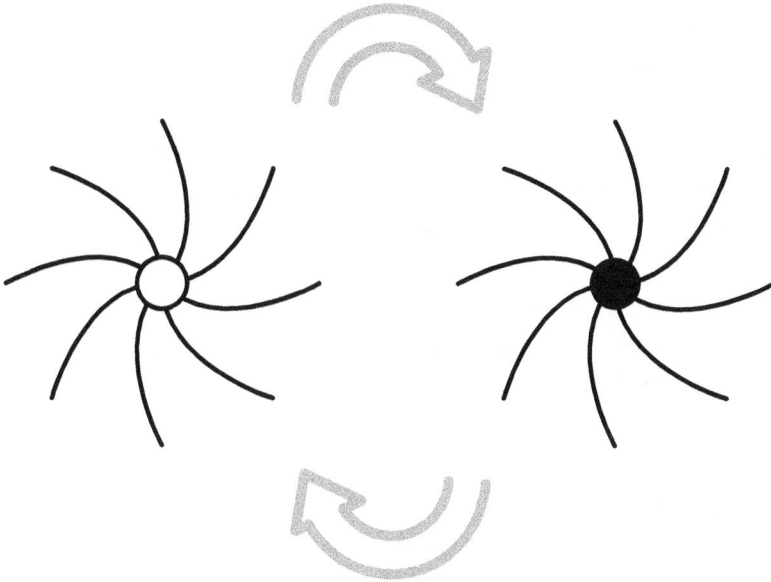

Professor Tohru Eguchi of the University of Tokyo has commented,
**"If you try to unify gravity via the same method as the other three forc-
es, you will get an incomprehensible result: the vacuum, which should
contain nothing, instead has ∞ energy."**[8] In modern physics, when ∞ appears, it is taken as a sign of error in experiment or calculation. The answer
is discarded: it is assumed to be incorrect.

However, from the perspective of 0=∞=1, the "result that a vacuum, which
should be empty, instead has ∞ energy" is simply an indication of the membrane (vacuum energy) itself.[9]

---

8 *From the morning edition of the Yomiuri Shimbun, May 27, 1999. "What kind of era was
the 20th century? The Science and Nature Revolution, Part 6"*

9 *From the morning edition of the Yomiuri Shimbun, May 27, 1999. "What kind of era was
the 20th century? The Science and Nature Revolution, Part 6"*

In our current material civilization, the only force among all four forces (gravity, electromagnetic force, strong force, weak force) that human beings can fully understand and freely utilize and apply is the electromagnetic force.

It is thanks to the electromagnetic force that the human eye can pick up on patterns and shapes and the size of the universe can be calculated.

To supplement the content that was not explained in the introductory seminar, modern mathematics and physics have a concept of "making entity A and entity B" inseparable when unifying forces. This leads to a unified theory via a "universal gravitational force." Furthermore, if you explain the four forces (gravity, electromagnetic force, strong force, weak force) as one force, it looks like the "universal gravitational force," but it is an analysis from the reference point of the physical human being who is looking at it with their own eyes.

From the perspective of nTech's mind/original mind—that is, from the perspective of the world of only mind—there is no universal gravitation. **Universal gravitation is a product of the illusion produced by the brain. The only force that really, actually exists is "universal repulsion."** The original mind is propelled by this universal repulsion. In other words, the force that makes some restored number (J) become an imaginary number (i) is the universal repulsive force, and the one and only force is the universal repulsive force. Therefore, in order for that imaginary number (i) to return to the restored number (J), its individuality and wholeness must be annihilated so that it can return to totality. The reason for this is the relationship between mind and power (energy): the relationship between J and i. Please refer to the latter part (chapter 8) of this book for details on restored number (J) and imaginary numbers (i).

The condition to uncovering physical truth is the discovery of some smallest unit that composes all things in the universe and fusing this unit with the basic forces (gravity, electromagnetic force, strong force, weak force) to facilitate a comprehensive description of the working and structure of microcosmic world, the sun, the galaxies, the universe. The starting point—the master equation—for such a unified theory is "$0=\infty=1$."

If only theoretical physics would re-evaluate their models from this point, our civilization on Earth would evolve at unimaginable speed.

Hold on to that image of the motion—it helps to understand the next picture I will introduce. This is an image of the *Taijitu*, used in Chinese cosmology (yin and yang and the five elements) (See Figure 15).

The shape of the *Taijitu* is sometimes referred to as a magatama; in China, it is called a "yin and yang fish" because of that same shape. What this shape does is provide an image of the motion of the membrane (vacuum energy). By superimposing the black circle on the white portion and the white circle on the black portion, we can see an image of fusion between the yin and yang duality of the Relative World across the inside/outside inversion motion of the *Taiji*.

If you look at this motion of inside/outside inversion in more detail, you can see that the basic operating principle that creates the universe is this motion of compression, explosion, and expansion. Of course, this is also a structure that cannot be apprehended at the experiential level of enlightenment.

— *Figure 15* —
Yin-yang symbol and the inside/outside motion

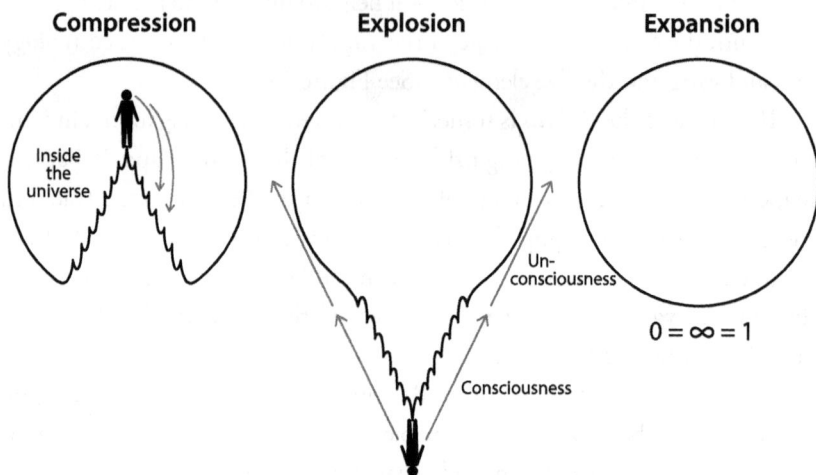

— *Figure 16* —
Compression, explosion, and expansion expressed in image language

The image of waves and water (figure 8) and the image of compression (figure 16) are synchronized.

If the apex of a compressed wave is a human being, the typical situation is to recognize other waves in the universe as an animal, or a plant.

When this wave explodes (attainment of enlightenment), we realize that the entire universe is the great mind itself, that all entities are constructed of mind—not matter—and that they are all connected. Then, the wave expands so that there is no difference between inside and the outside. Stars such as the Sun also clearly embody this operating principle of compression, explosion, and expansion. Stars, created by compressing dust and gas floating in outer space, emit light. The Sun is a star formed by compressed hydrogen (H). It explodes with light and helium (He) when that hydrogen fuses together.

It is thought that the Sun will end its life as a star in about 5 billion years through a slow expansion and death. Other stars throughout the galaxy will continue to be born by compressing in the same way, living and expanding through explosion, and ultimately dying.

Helium stars emit lithium (atomic number 3), and lithium stars emit beryllium (atomic number 4). Hydrogen has an atomic number of 1 and helium has an atomic number of 2. The atoms in the universe have been generated by the repeated compression, explosion, and expansion of stars. The universe itself has also been created via this compression, explosion, and expansion pattern.

• Structure/Framework

If there is only unity, why do we apprehend quantities of 2 and greater? What is the secret behind the birth of 2, from 1? This is the question we must answer to solve the mystery of the structure and mechanism of the membrane (vacuum energy).

It is said that Buddha left over 80,000 books worth of messages throughout his life spent preaching the truth. That essential truth was that "form is emptiness" (all reality is illusion). However, Buddha failed to explain why and how form can emerge from emptiness at all (how something can arise from nothing).

There are no emotions such as surprise or sadness in a single cell, but human beings, made up of more than 37 trillion cells, have emotions and spirits. Spirit is born from a place of no-spirit. Life and cells can copy themselves, but the substances that compose cells do not self-proliferate on their own. In other words, self-replicating life emerges from substances that do not self-replicate. All of cosmic history is a series of repetitions of something new emerging from nothing.

More than 13.8 billion years ago, there was no universe. It evolved from a state of no-universe to universe, from a state of no-galaxy to galaxy, from a state of no-Sun, no-light to Sun and light—all of these processes created something from nothing, by way of some hidden mechanism.

What is the mechanism by which two or more emerges from a single membrane (vacuum energy)?

The fundamental structure (mechanism) of a membrane (vacuum energy) can be easily understood in terms of fractals. Fractals describe complex patterns and shapes which are created by repetition of the same composition rules. This figure contains a fractal structure known as the Koch snowflake.

If you divide each side of an equilateral triangle into three equal parts, draw another equilateral triangle using each center line segment as one side, and erase the center segments, the equilateral triangle will change to a star shape. Applying this rule again gives it the third shape in the figure, and repeating it again gives it a snowflake-like shape.

By repeating this simple rule just three times, a snowflake pattern is created from a simple equilateral triangle.

— *Figure 17* —
Fractal composition

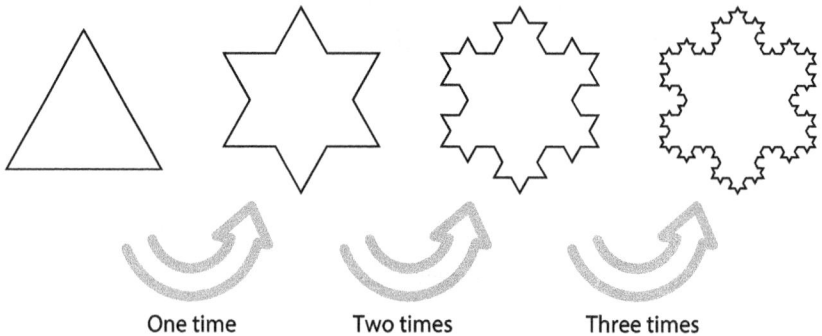

One time   Two times   Three times

Like the Golden Ratio, fractal structures are found everywhere—such as in the shape of plants, the wings of birds, and the appearance of ocean life. They are recognized as structures common to the natural world.

The means by which 2 emerges from 1 can be explained via the fractal (repeating) inside/outside inversion motion of the membrane (vacuum energy).

In the first iteration of this inversion motion, the outside ∞ enters the inside zero space of the membrane (vacuum energy). At the same time, the zero space that was inside moves to the outside, so that a zero space is created around ∞.

Since ∞ is ∞ even if a boundary line is created and separates it into two, ∞ continues infinitely outside the zero space, as shown in the second state in the figure on the left.

This inversion motion then repeats, and the zero space wants to meet ∞ while ∞ wants to enter the zero space. Consequently, the zero space moves into the center ∞. At the same time, ∞ moves to the outside, while the zero space moves not only to the inner ∞ but also to the outer ∞. As a result, as shown in the third figure, a zero space is created on the outside as well as the inside.

This state is the same as a child born in the womb of its mother.

Just as childbirth enables the child to leave the mother's body, a "zero space with ∞" becomes two.

The "zero space with ∞" begins as a unity and splits into two via 2 iterations of the inside/outside inversion motion. This is an image of the basic mechanism that creates 2 from 1.

— Figure 18 —
The mechanism by which 2 emerges from 1, in image language

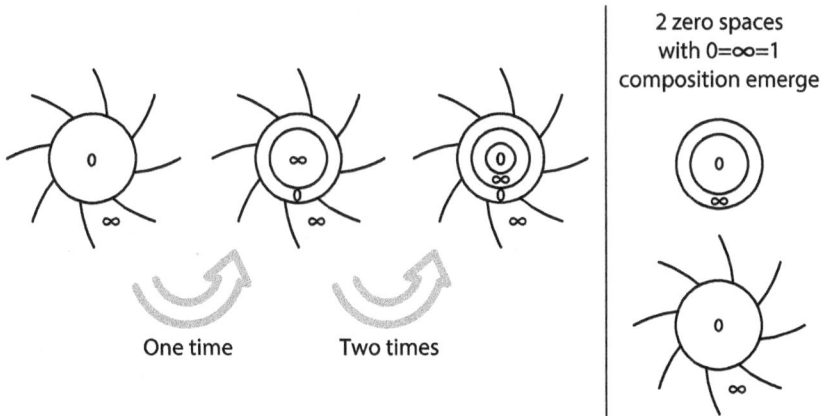

One time   Two times

2 zero spaces
with 0=∞=1
composition emerge

Continued repetition of this motion results in further increase in these "zero spaces with ∞."

A simple diagram of the process of increasing zero space in universal space is shown on Figure 19. First the universal space is born, then galaxies are born, then solar systems are born in the galaxies, and so on, creating smaller zero spaces one after another in a fractal manner.

In addition to the mechanism by which 2 emerges from 1, the seminars use image language to describe the mechanism by which 5 emerges from 1, as in yin and yang and the five elements. The relationship between the structure of the human body and the five elements, and the history of 13.8 billion years from the starting point of the universe can be explained with a simple membrane (vacuum energy) fractal. Due to space limitations, I only explain the structure of a simple membrane (vacuum energy) here, but I believe that the "conditions of physical truth" I mention above will prove that this is the operating principle of the universe.

Assuming $0=\infty=1$, suddenly it is easy to understand this mysterious result: **if we try to unify the three forces with the same method, the vacuum, which should be empty, instead has ∞ energy.**

— *Figure 19* —
Birth of the universe in terms of image language

| The Universe | The Milky Way | The Sun |

CHAPTER 5

What is the point of reference of thought ?

- **"I think; therefore I exist." Seeing changes from invariance**

Interviewer:

— Thank you for the other day. It's now been a week, and I have felt deeply excited at the prospect of moving one step closer to bringing 0=∞=1 into my life.

At the same time, there are still a lot of things that I'm not quite on board with (laughs). Let's see how far we get.

Jesu Noh:

Of course, let's get started.

— Last time, you started with that story of the bottle and the bird. It was about changing the way you look at things.

Yes, that's right. It revolved around a certain basic premise, a perspective, a perceptual methodology, a point of reference. "How do you see this world ?" And how did that example go ? Both the bottle and bird...

— ...don't exist !

That's right ! The self and the self's world that seemed so obvious turned out to not actually exist. It's all an illusion, a hologram, a screen image invented by the brain.

— This idea was so shocking and revolutionary that it was a struggle to accept it. I did eventually get it, though, thanks to you. I've come to feel truly grateful for it.

After all, this is the "key" to problems that just don't seem to work out otherwise, right ?

It was extremely shocking to me to hear that if you keep thinking of your body as yourself, you will remain "trapped in the bottle," reincarnating after death. I found this story of human reincarnation—which has been repeated for millions of years—all too cruel, too painful.

That's right. That's why I said that you must have an intuitive perception that believing that "your body is yourself" is identical to "living in the worst possible hell." You cannot achieve enlightenment so long as you think of your body as yourself, no matter how hard you try.

— Yes—it's as futile as trying to polish a cement block into a mirror, you said !

I thought about this a lot afterwards. That living life while believing my body is myself really is the worst possible hell.

Enlightenment is unachievable—and even if you somehow achieved it, you wouldn't be able to share it. Before even discussing enlightenment, one must first be able to see daily life as a hellish scene.

Nobody can hear each other, build trust, or cooperate.

People make enemies, brandish invisible swords, hurt each other, and become isolated.

Things don't get better no matter how hard you try, without even knowing the reason. Without building any sort of objective knowledge, people instead acquire a collection of arbitrary assumptions. They run along the same highway of thought like a machine, which naturally leads to unhappiness, ignorance, idiocy, hatred. They compromise on life, on the effort to understand, or give up completely.

Even if they become reincarnated, they'll just keep repeating the same cycle over and over. The only word for it is hell.

That's when I realized that this hellish scene can't be recognized in an instant. It's too horrible for that. This state of affairs lacks the immediate sense of tragedy that conflict and war create. So, it's hard to see this problem as "hell." That's exactly why nobody has realized it.

I saw anew that this diagnosis that "belief in the body as the self is the worst possible hell" is, in a sense, a more terrible discovery than the discovery of the True World.

Thank you. I think you've grasped the idea.

In that case, do you also see that if this "hell perception" became a sort of deep engine—if we achieved a state where this hell was recognized—then the paradise that would be defined as a result would be "True Paradise" ?

— Yes. If we recognized the eternal hell of being the bird stuck in the bottle, we would see the paradise that would result from becoming free of the bottle. After all, we want to get out.

There is no bird, no bottle. All there is, is the One Motion of the fundamental substance.

This substance unravels and comes together, over and over.

This is why I and my universe don't exist !

This substance is compressed and tied together in me and my universe. It is unraveled and melted into a single, uniform material. This motion is all there is !

At the instant that I and my universe disappear, our burdens dissolve, and we become truly free !

That's right. What I want is for people to become free of the bottle—free of the virtual screen—and encounter the True nature of humanity as Absolute Dignity.

— Yes. So, today, I really want to learn more about the image of this paradise of freedom for the unbroken bottle and bird.

Yes, let's do so !

In that case... first, I'm going to say something very shocking.

Last time, you got the feeling that you are "Absolute Dignity itself !" right ?

— Yes. This may just be the beginning, but I had this sense of "You can do anything ! You are infinite potential itself !" Is there something wrong with that idea ?

Actually... last time, **you still had not reached the True World of "Absolute Dignity itself."**

— Ohhh... what do you mean ?

Try to recall how you were feeling when I first met with you.

At first, you were saying that "None of this has anything to do with my daily life."

— Ah, now that you mention it, I did. That's because what you were saying didn't seem to have any relation to daily matters. I also had some uncertainty in general... did you see right through me ?

No, don't dwell on that. Almost everyone is like that.

However, because that's the state of mind you were in at first, I started the conversation with the "bird and bottle" example and the concept of the "thought highway," as a sort of simple introduction. From there, we continued our warming up with a general discussion, bringing in important terms as we went such as the final answer, Perfect Unknowing, the redefinition of humanity, independent decision-making, etc.

— I see... so does that mean that today we'll take another step and throw wide open the gates of Truth, for real ?

Yes—get excited !

However, I should tell you that there are 14 stages of understanding. Let me go through them for you.

At first, we are in a state of indifference.
1. Upon crossing the "Wall of Concentration," focus becomes possible
2. Upon crossing the "Wall of Interest," curiosity rises
3. Upon crossing the "Wall of Information," knowledge becomes possible
4. Upon crossing the "Wall of Ways of Knowing," discovering existence's patterns of change
5. Upon crossing the "Wall of Action," direct experience becomes possible
6. Upon crossing the "Wall of Problem-Solving and realization," convic-

tion becomes possible

7. Upon crossing the "Wall of Commodification," re-creation and commodifying becomes possible

8. Upon crossing the "Wall of Habit," one can succeed in making new tries a habit

9. Upon crossing the "Wall of Perspective," one starts feeling natural excitement

10. Upon crossing the "Wall of Planning," one attains infinite motivation

11. Upon crossing the "Wall of Expression," one becomes able to share and sympathize

12. Upon crossing the "Wall of Ideas," one begins experiencing dreams and visions

13. Upon crossing the "Wall of Socialization," one becomes a hero

14. Upon crossing the "Wall of Succession," one becomes a legend and makes history (See Figure 20 on following page).

Right now, because this is still just your second day with nTech, you will be doing very well if today you cross stage 2: the Wall of Interest. If you make it to 4—the "Wall of Ways of Knowing"—it would be like a miracle !

It's true that humanity has a strong drive to attain personal experience and intuitive understanding.

However, in order to get that sort of personal experience, one must reach stage 5—the "Wall of Action"—and intuitive understanding comes with reaching stage 6—the "Wall of Problem-Solving and realization." These are stages you attain by use in daily life.

— Wow ! There are this many steps to understanding ? I see...

Certainly, I can understand by what you're saying that personal experience and intuitive understanding are difficult to acquire !

Still, I'm going to try to make it to stage 4 today !

That's an excellent challenge ! I'm rooting for you !

By the way, in the True World as well, there are two types of Truths: one that annihilates reality, and one that creates reality..

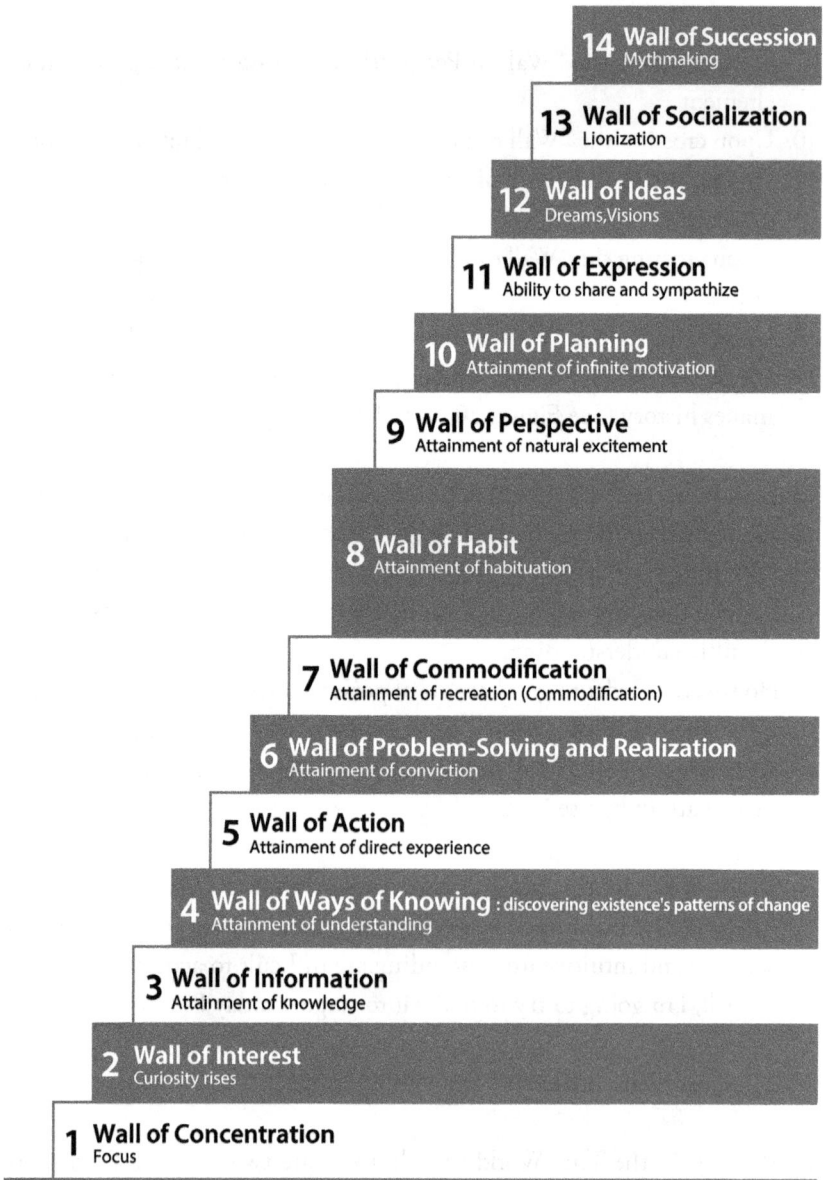

— *Figure 20* —
The 14 stages of understanding

14 Wall of Succession
Mythmaking

13 Wall of Socialization
Lionization

12 Wall of Ideas
Dreams,Visions

11 Wall of Expression
Ability to share and sympathize

10 Wall of Planning
Attainment of infinite motivation

9 Wall of Perspective
Attainment of natural excitement

8 Wall of Habit
Attainment of habituation

7 Wall of Commodification
Attainment of recreation (Commodification)

6 Wall of Problem-Solving and Realization
Attainment of conviction

5 Wall of Action
Attainment of direct experience

4 Wall of Ways of Knowing : discovering existence's patterns of change
Attainment of understanding

3 Wall of Information
Attainment of knowledge

2 Wall of Interest
Curiosity rises

1 Wall of Concentration
Focus

Indifference

— Hmmmm... I don't think I have anything to say to that right now.

It's fine if you don't understand yet.
But on that note, if last time was kindergarten level, now we are reaching elementary school !

— Last time was just kindergarten... well, I suppose that may be true. (laughs)

• I Humans who "see with their eyes"

Humanity and humanity's universe do not actually exist ! It's all an illusion, a hologram, right ? The True World lies beyond the perspective of the human brain.

Now that we understand this much, I want to say something very important: **"All that is taken for granted must change."** I mean everything—daily life, nature, how we think.

— Everything has to change ? Hmmm... that sounds like quite an ordeal. It also kind of sounds like a denial of everything humanity has done as meaningless, so I admit to feeling a bit of resistance to the idea.

That's very understandable. However, the change I am referring to is ultimately also necessary to raise the standard on what we have already accomplished. You'll understand what I mean soon.

We were saying that reality is an illusion, a hologram, right ? So reality, then, is the distorted view, the subjective judgment, the inner side of the screen that the human brain has arbitrarily decided to register as "factual."

— Subjective judgment... when you mentioned "dogmatic prejudice" before, I was shocked at how strong your language was. But it's accurate.

If we start with subjective judgment, does it seem like we can obtain objective information ?

— No, it's impossible. I feel bad for humanity.

That's right. Therefore, **every human concept—whether in math, science, physics, philosophy, ethics, morality, politics, economics, religion, or art—is ultimately rooted in what we can perceive through the "lens" of our human brain.** Therefore, math and physics, while often thought of as objective, are actually not objective.

— Yes, I can understand what you are saying conceptually. However, to be honest, this feeling of everything crumbling away makes me feel lost.

   What standard should we use to think about things, to structure things, going forward ?

   You have mentioned viewing "existence" from the perspective of "non-existence," but I'm still not sure what that means. This all seems very chaotic and unstable.

This is a good direction ! (laughs) This is exactly why having the new point of reference figured out is so important.

   Human beings are creatures that want to understand existence and understand themselves.

   If you can't feel satisfied with the reality you see in your daily life, you try to change to a reality that does satisfy you. However, if you don't have that understanding of existence or humanity, then you can't make the reality that satisfies you, right ?

— Yeah, if I didn't have that issue, I wouldn't have the worries I do. Because of the problems inherent to how we see things, I have not realized my hopes—this has become clear to me.

To speak of something fresh on everyone's mind, the COVID-19 global pandemic broke out just a little while ago. I believe it is a wake-up call to our current civilization.

   It's like a way of saying that we've gone this whole way with the buttons of our shirt off by one, and we need to rebutton ourselves.

   If everything begins with our perception, we have to look at the bottom button of perception. Once we get that one right, the rest will follow naturally, don't you think ?

— That does make sense, but how are we supposed to change the "way of looking at things" of the first button ?

You yourself experienced a sudden enlightenment, but most people are not like that. Most people just aren't capable of seeing existence from non-existence in a single step. Last time, I said I want the sudden enlightenment, but it seems difficult. I understood your point that the framework is important... but is there no sort of staircase that anyone can climb ?

I appreciate your engagement. So for today, let's start moving forward along the stages of perception, one step at a time. By the way, I said "moving forward," but actually **the key to changing the way we look at things is "back."**

— Back ? As in, retreating ?

Do you remember the bow and arrow analogy ? Drawing a bowstring back until you can't draw it any farther ? This is actually pretty difficult. Everything in existence is trying to move forward—you might say everything is **addicted to progress.** Have you ever seen a snake that can back up ? No, right ? However, as though the way we look at things is a bow and arrow, we have to back up until we can't back up any farther, and always start from there.

— I see. When the bow and arrow is pulled back, the course of action is determined, and the arrow flies the farthest it can. In the same way, by starting from the deepest point in our consciousness, we can encompass everything in our approach.

That's right. Let's try turning the human way of looking at things—our thought methodology—back in a way that makes sense scientifically and mathematically. Last time, we talked about classical physics, quantum mechanics, string theory, and M-theory. Do you feel comfortable with this material now ?

— Yes. I may not be a scientist, but I have come to find it interesting. Let's go.

I'm glad to hear it. Then, as a general premise, remember the following: **Observation influences the objects of measurement.**

— Oh, that's similar to the conversation about glasses from before. Like how if you look at white paper with blue glasses, it'll look blue.
    The brain's perspective is like the "glasses" that human beings wear. As a result, we perceive everything via the brain's lens of cause and subjective perception, which exerts an influence on the objects of our perception as an effect. Consequently, we can't see things as they are. We've got to take the glasses off as fast as we can.

That's right. However, I don't think people are aware of this.

Now I have a question. You currently think that if someone is wearing blue glasses, paper will look blue. But if they took the glasses off, they'd perceive the truth. Right ? **In that case, are "you" on the side of perceiving, the *cause* of the perception ? Or the effect ?**

— What ? Obviously, since it's on the perceiving side, it's the "cause of perception," isn't it ?

You'd think so, right ? But what if the "you" with the blue glasses off—the perceiving subject—is not the cause, but the result of the brain's perspective ?

— What do you mean ?

In fact, **the perceiving subject and object, along with the observed object, are the "results of measurement."**

— Hmmm. I don't really understand.

Then, imagine a single photo. The photo contains (1) the perceptual subject of the self, which is looking at something, and (2) the perceptual object of the environment, at which one is looking. In other words, the "photograph itself" is both the result of measurement as well as the object of observation.

There are even more observation subjects and causes of the "camera lens" that created the picture. This means that the body itself is *also* a result of the camera lens.

— *Figure 21* —
The products of perception in the Illusory World

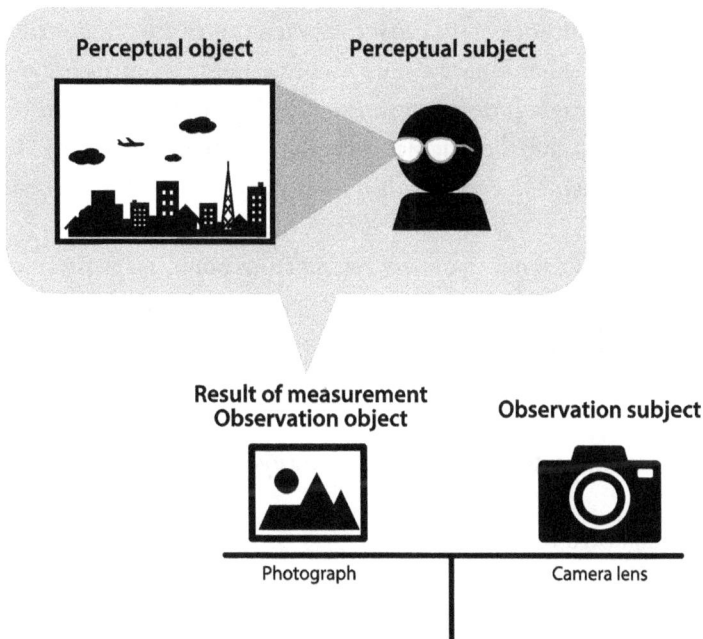

— Oh, I remember. You said this last time, too. "You and I both are the products of the brain's perception." I didn't pay that much attention to it at the time, but I see, that's what you meant.

That's right. We humans do not think that our bodies are the result of the lens of the brain, nor do we suspect that things are "caused by the eyes." Yet if you look with your eyes, you will never be able to find any causes.

— The body, as self, is also an effect of the brain's lens... that's not something I saw coming.

I really want to make myself exist ! I want to believe that my body is the cause of things ! I think a lot of people think this way, unable to keep themselves from making their body the starting point.

Humans tend to cling to existence, to their self. The reason will become clear later.

We put forward a premise that observation exerts an influence on the measurement of its object. In order to discuss this in scientific/mathematics terms, there is something we must discuss. Before, you mentioned Descartes' famous saying: *cogito ergo sum*. This is often translated as "I think; therefore I am," but the original meaning is actually closer to, **"I think; therefore I exist."** In order to think sharply, we'll need to make this our starting point.

If our observational errors are our starting point, no matter how hard we try, we'll never be able to become happy or succeed, don't you think ? Figuring out this problem is something that every last human needs to do. Here's a slogan:

Right here, right now, seeing with your eyes is not allowed !

Don't look down on this.

We were talking about the "way we look at things" before, right ? We should change this to the "way we observe things."

— Yes, **there is a difference between "the way we look at things" and "the way we observe things."** I had not been paying that much attention to how you were using the word "observe," but I see now that there was a meaning behind it.

You can't just think about things by looking at them with your eyes. Not only does this lack criticality, but if you're making errors from the start, it's hopeless. We also discussed AI before (artificial intelligence), but I can also see how ridiculously more advanced they are becoming from us.

That's right. Human beings are the stewards of the Earth, but we are already under threat—this is no time to gloat. We have to take a moment to reflect and rebuild.

By the way, why do you think humanity is "able to think" ?
   Let's turn back the clock a bit and look at the origin of thought.

Why did humans gain the ability to think ? This is also discussed in *Sapiens: A Brief History of Humankind* by Yuval Noah Harari.[10] Originally there was not just one species of human. Now, there's only homo sapiens. Isn't that strange ? Why did homo sapiens end up controlling the world ?

— That's very interesting. Because of some kind of difference with other
   human species, homo sapiens came out on top ? Is it because they were
   really strong ?

It's actually the opposite. Homo sapiens were weaker, smaller, less muscular than other human species, which made it more difficult for them to obtain meat. They would crack open the bones left by other animals and human species and eat the marrow. As a result, they began to develop technology for cracking open the bones. They learned to make sharp rocks and used friction methods that led to mastery over fire.

— That is interesting ! It reminds me of what Darwin said. "It is **not the
   strongest of the species that survives,** nor the most intelligent; it is the
   one most adaptable to change."

So, what do you think was the result of mastering fire ? It offers protection from other animals, the ability to create roads by burning down forests, creates warmth, the ability to be active at night, and the ability to live in cold regions.
   It is also fire that gave rise to cooking. Until then, human species ate raw meat. Homo sapiens invented cooked meat. This brought about a dramatic transformation. What do you think it was ?

---

10 Yuval Noah Harari "Sapiens: A Brief History of Humankind" (Harper Collins Publishers)

— What was it ?

The evolution of language ! With less energy spent on chewing food, our jaws and jaw muscles weakened, our brains enlarged, and the tongue became softer. This enabled the production of a wide range of noises—and **with the development of language came an expansion in our thought.**

Humans use language to think. Try to think without language. Can you do it ?

— No. Without language, it's not possible to think.

Yeah. Anyway, let's keep going.

Until that point, language was nothing but simple gestures and vocalizations like yells. All it could communicate were simple observable events in the immediate vicinity—in other words, it communicated facts that could be grasped in a scientific manner. For example, "There's a lion ! Run !" However, complex thoughts, events existing along the time axis in the future or past, or imaginative thinking could not be expressed.

Nevertheless, as I mentioned before, homo sapiens managed to develop language. This enabled daydreaming, wild visions, imagery, etc., and our thoughts evolved.

— The ability to daydream is a pretty amazing ability I guess...

That's right. **Daydreaming and delusions enable the creation of "fictions" that involve fabricated facts. These sorts of fictions enabled weak homo sapiens to concentrate.**

— Fictions enable concentration ?

That's right. The representative of these fictions in the so-called "inter-subjective" world of imagination is the concept of "God." This "god" fiction enabled not only family members and other familiar people, but also strangers to band together. They band together under the banner of their god. Even a physically weak animal can become a great force if banded together under a cause. That's why the gap steadily widened between other animals and human species.

— That image has been burned into my mind clearly.
Our ancestors worked hard for us !

Homo sapiens had the will to survive, and did a great job in the competition for survival. Yet they hadn't even shown off what they could really do ! I said it before, humanity is better than this !!! Humanity had finally reached the end of the first half of the battle.

Other animals can also see what's right in front of them. Does seeing things take any effort ? It takes none—open your eyes and it happens.

— Seeing things with one's own eyes requires no effort... I guess we can't be arrogant about things we were born with.

That's right. It's not enough to just stop with what you can physically see, to just stop with that kind of empirical knowledge.

AI does not have to steal our jobs and destroy our dignity ! Therefore, let's not just stop at the will to survive, and instead strive to evolve towards a will to dignity, a will to creation. This is the start of the second act of humanity !

— The second half ! That's getting me excited !
By the way, I understand what you mean about how it's bad to just see with your eyes, but then what should you see with ? That's starting to bother me. I understand the concept of seeing from non-existence, but it seems like it's time to...

Ok, let's think about "seeing" again.
In fact, "seeing" is the most important keyword to this revolution of civilization.
Here's a question: **What is the font of human thought ? From where does the "stuff" of thought arise ?**

— I think it's from data and information. These things also come from "observation."

Just as you said before, "objective data and information can never be obtained if you start from a place of subjective determination." Without a change in observation, the data and information—the stuff of thought—will also never change.

That's right. Therefore, we need a revolutionary change in the "acquisition method and quality" of that data and information—now more than ever. It's clear that we're headed for disaster if we keep pushing subjective determination.

— Headed for disaster ? What do you mean ?

Everyone owns a smartphone these days, right ? 10 years ago, it was unimaginable —and yet the pace will only accelerate.

In other words, **we've entered an age in which we only see the screen, the data, the information that we want to see.** Because of this, we've entered into a form of absolutely alienated solipsism.

Because the stuff of thought is limited, we can't escape from a structure of solipsistic, extreme thoughts. It's difficult for us to determine what others are thinking. Consequently, we are entering an age of solitude and isolation in which sympathy and even basic communication and interaction is becoming impossible.

— I think I know what you mean. I find myself staring at my smartphone all the time. Even when I'm eating lunch with a colleague, or on the train, or once I get home, I'm always looking at my phone screen. It may not be an exaggeration to say that I spend the majority of my life looking at it.

YouTube recommendations and channels that suit my tastes are always presenting themselves... so I have a good sense of the intensity of how information is slanted, but since I have no particular need to pick something different, I ultimately stick to the same things. I am probably much more biased in my thinking than I realize.

This precisely is the **mechanization of the individual.** It is the final state of mechanizing thought and feelings.

— I see... that reminds me, I saw that movie *Joker*[11] that people were talking about, and it really felt like an abstraction of current society. The main character's soul is being mechanized, he only accepts the information he wants to get, can't tell the difference between objective and subjective reality, won't listen to what anyone says... if this sort of mechanization of thoughts and feelings endures, I'm afraid society may overflow with isolated people on the verge of exploding like him.

That's exactly right.

Last time, we talked about the post-physical society, right ? In the near future, if the process of implanting chips into human organs and the brain continues, human beings will be nothing more than chips, than data, and we will lose meaning in our existence.

If things continue like this, **the human spirit, mind, and consciousness will be partitioned down with our intellect into something with no value.** In order to deal with this crisis, we must instill the habit of seeing things from non-existence, from within the mind, as soon as possible.

From here on out, acquisition of a "steadfastness," an ability to withstand any conditions, to not be pushed around easily, is likely to gain a great deal of attention as a social need.

— I agree. In particular, the global COVID-19 pandemic has brought us into an age of fighting against the virus, which has required changing our lifestyles in a way that has required no small amount of fortitude.

Telework, online negotiations, digital transactions—we transitioned to online business in an instant, and throughout this tempestuous change, emotional issues such as distrust, unease, fear, and loneliness have come to light... It's a psychological phenomenon that has occurred as a consequence of strengthening this "mechanized conditioned reflex of the mind."

That's exactly right. In fact, **our brains have been infected by a "virus."** I will talk about the characteristics of "viruses" later, but without an explosion in consciousness, the extinction of homo sapiens is just a matter of time.

---

11 Joker. 2020. Warner Bros. Home Entertainment Inc.

Anyway, let's get down to the topic at hand.

First, let's think about "what it is to see."

In a word, it is **"seeing changes from invariance."**

— Seeing transience from invariance ? That doesn't quite click for me.

For example, if we're wearing "blue glasses" from the moment we're born, everything will look blue. In this case, the invariance is the "blue glasses." In this sense, **the invariance that humans have long utilized as the foundation for their empirical knowledge is the eyes of their body.** Have you ever seen anything without them ?

— I can't say that I have. In which case, is invariance like a "ruler" ? A ruler is fixed, it doesn't change. That's why it makes a good standard and can take accurate measurements. A ruler that measured differently every time wouldn't be very useful.

Exactly ! Invariance is a "fixed, unchanging point of reference." **In that invariance, it's important that neither the perceptual subject nor perceptual object exist.** If they did exist in the invariance, then you couldn't make an objective measurement, right ?

— In other words, the state with no perceptual subject nor object should be made "invariant" ?

Is this what you were talking about before with "a ruler that can accurately measure the mind" ?

Yes, yes. It's easier to grasp what that is by looking at the stages of perception.

Let's use this idea to fit "the way of observing things" into 11 steps.

Here are the "invariants" for each stage.

<Stages of Perception: Invariants of Each Stage>

I: Humans until now: Physical eye/2 dimensions
II: Newton, Descartes: XYZ Cartesian plane/3 dimensions
III: Einstein: Speed of light

IV: Quantum mechanics: quantum field energy, mass = clumps of energy
V: String theory: 5 vibrational string energies
VI: M-theory: Vacuum energy fluctuation
VII: Buddhism: *Kūmuhensho* (stage 5 in Zen)
VIII: Buddhism: *Shikimuhensho* (stage 6 in Zen)
IX: Buddhism: *Musho-usho* (stage 7 in Zen)
X: Buddhism: *Hisōhihisōsho* (stage 8 in Zen)
XI: Buddhism: *Metsujinjō, Sōjumetsujō* (stage 9 in Zen)

• II Isaac Newton: The XYZ Cartesian coordinates

The invariant of stage 1 is the physical eye. It is two-dimensional thought based on empirical knowledge.

Stage 2 is the realm of the father of modern science, Isaac Newton. Let's take a look.

— Seeing with the physical eye is just 2D thinking ? If we perceive length, width, and depth, shouldn't it be 3D perception ? Why 2D ?

If your perspective is that we perceive those three dimensions, then yes, it's 3D perception. However, **many people who think they have 3D perception—especially those in the East—are strong in terms of the cardinal directions, but quite weak with up and down.** In that sense, the thinking is 2D.

— Oh yeah ? I wasn't conscious of it, but maybe that's true...
    By the way, Newton ? All I know from him is the 3D Cartesian plane and his discovery of the law of gravity by watching an apple fall.

That's fine.

Newton wanted to know why apples fall from trees. That kind of question wouldn't even be asked by someone who thinks in terms of 2D. Why is that ?

─ Figure 22 ─
The 11 stages of perception

1	General person	👁	Physical eye 2D
2	Newton Descartes	*(xyz coordinate axes diagram)*	XYZ coordinate plane 3D
3	General relativity Einstein	*(spiral symbols)*	Speed of light
4	Quantum mechanics Bohr	*(sun symbol ⇄ spiral symbols)*	Quantum field energy
5	String theory	*(sun symbol ⇄ pentagram)*	5 forms of string energy
6	M-theory	*(sun symbol)*	Vacuum energy vibrations
7	5th level of Zen	*(sun symbol with ‖ above)* Emptiness	Kūmuhensho
8	6th level of Zen	The nameable Mind	Shikimuhensho
9	7th level of Zen	The unnameable Mind	Musho-usho
10	8th level of Zen	Conceivable motion of Mind	Hisōhihisōsho
11	9th level of Zen	Inconceivable motion of Mind	Metsujinjō Sōjumetsujō

— In other words, you're asking why Newton was able to ask a question like that, right ?

I see !

The XYZ coordinates define height, width, and depth in a strict way ! In other words, it offers a rigorous structure for up and down as well as the cardinal directions. So, it becomes easier to wonder what's going on with the apple.

Differences in thought dimensions are connected to differences in question dimensions. That's amazing !

Raising the dimension is also connected to an expansion of consciousness. As an aside, mathematics, physics, and the other sciences were developed by the West, which had this 3D thinking, right ? The East had 2D thinking, which prevented the development of these disciplines. As a result, the West became the leader of material civilization, and the East was forced to play along.

— Before, you said that "the hidden, deep-seated nature of one's problem awareness and one's questions" is what guides human life. It seems like it's not just one person's life—it's civilization as a whole.

That's correct. Newton was born in an age in which religion was considered evidently true. Try to imagine people of that time. No matter what you look at in the world, it's difficult to imagine that the animals, plants, the cosmos, all exist just for you, right ? That makes it difficult to come up with reasons to live, to find meaning in life. This was an age in which people held a worldview defined by a blind belief in the idea that everything exists to fulfill a grand purpose by a creator god.

The people that introduced the "concept of force" and kickstarted mathematics and physics in that time were Newton and Descartes.

— Newton was a bit of a renegade for his time. I bet he faced a lot of criticism.

When he was teaching at Cambridge University, it was common for the classes he developed on optics to be completely empty. His ideas were too innovative and were difficult to understand, apparently.

— Newton went through a lot.

But, ultimately, the difference between humans and animals is "thought." The mere suggestion to stop taking things on blind faith and start being more skeptical shattered the old age.

Consequently, phenomena that can't be properly understood by the naked eye—such as the revolution and rotation of the Earth, the movement of the planets about the Sun—became predictable by calculating their behavior in terms of the XYZ coordinates.

That's because if you want to understand physical phenomena objectively, rather than from the subjective perspective of your eye, you need to use the 3D thought of Newton and Descartes. In so doing, intuition, energy, thought, and feeling all undergo a jump.

Of course, one is still bound by the brain's point of view, but at least one becomes a little freer of prejudice and bias. It becomes more difficult to get swayed by emotion and it is easier to develop one's rationality. Of course, it also becomes easier to free yourself from concerns about nationality, ethnicity, and religion.

— I didn't expect there to be such benefits. This is making me want to understand Newton's way of observing better.

Yes, I'll go into a bit more detail, then.

Before Newton, seeing with the eye was once the standard, but **the XYZ coordinates standardized spacetime and made this its "invariant" axis of reference.** All that exists was put into these coordinates, and the equations of motion defined their changes, their movements, their transformations.

From there, all the phenomena that couldn't be previously explained by what the naked eye sees alone became sensible through a combination of geometry and algebra. The point is that **with this 1 : 1 symmetry, it became possible to describe the emergence of entities as proportional expressions—even allowing the calculation of the movement of the Sun and planets.**

— *Figure 23* —
XYZ coordinates

The status of beings can be determined
via the 1:1 interaction of the X and Y axes

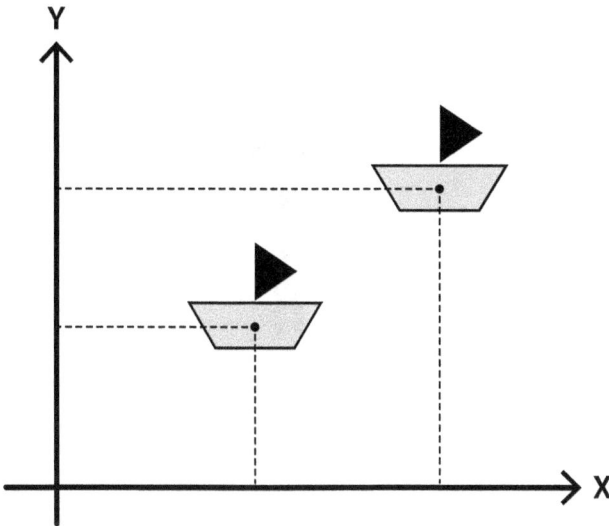

— Amazing ! That's genius !

Yes. What's important here is "language."
You could say that "the language shifted."

— The language shifted ? Hmmmm...
I see !! The language up until this point was based on seeing phenomena with the eye, assigning them names, and remembering those names !
What was that called ?
Memorization language !

That's right. Memorization language is a term in nTech, but it's the same as natural language—for example, English, French, German, Japanese, etc. However, Newton initiated the use of a mathematical, non-natural language that scientists continue to use. **By looking at the formula (differen-**

tial equation), patterns and shapes become clear. That is why formulas are used to describe changes, movements in these patterns and shapes.

— *Figure 24* —
The difference between memorized language and mathematical language

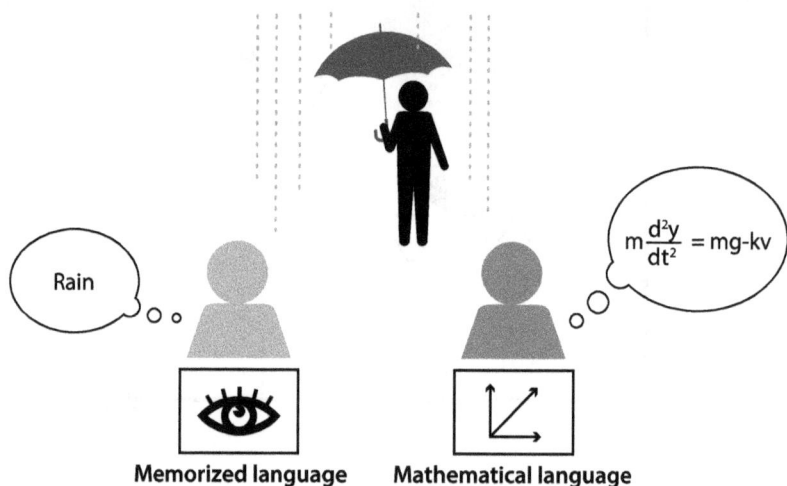

Rain

$$m\frac{d^2y}{dt^2} = mg\text{-}kv$$

Memorized language   Mathematical language

— There's a world of difference between them. It seems like the objectivity and accuracy is completely different.

Because Newton had a doubting eye—because he was skeptical—he didn't accept that things were just as he saw them, and tried to find what lay beneath.

That's right. Not only Newton, but Descartes—or going even further back, Galileo Galilei—as well.

Also, **changing language means changing intuition. Changing intuition means changing one's observational point of reference.**

— Meaning ?

If physical sensation is one's point of reference, then objectivity is not guaranteed, right ? Also, one's accumulated knowledge cannot be passed down, which is detrimental to cultural progress.

Seeing with the physical eye does not produce objective knowledge and does not lend itself to the **accumulation of knowledge.** In fact, it leads to societies that enforce dogmatic blind faith based on arbitrary, subjective assumptions. These scientists likely understood this problem.

— I see. It seems that the ways in which we accumulate objectified knowledge will become an important point.

That's right. By the way, while I'm sure you know the Laws of Motion that Newton introduced, our conversation up until now relied on their definitions and axioms. Let's go over them briefly.

1. Newton's first law of motion (also known as the law of inertia)
—*An object at rest will remain at rest unless acted upon by an external and unbalanced force. An object in motion will remain in motion unless acted upon by an external and unbalanced force.*

Newton is the first person to provide a unified formal theory. He claimed that "natural motion is moving at the same speed in the same direction."

All physicists that followed have only expanded upon and applied Newton's ideas.

The West has always questioned why reality exists.

— What ? So "existence" isn't taken for granted ?

Well, that's true, except that in this case, God is seen as the first cause.

The point is that **all Platonic ideas should be impermanent and unchanging.** So, if that's so, why do changes occur, why do things come into existence ? What is existence ? These why/what questions are typical. After all, existence is an effect, a result. So where did it come from ? Why ? By breaking reality down into its constituent components and analyzing them, answers may emerge.

— I see. In other words, non-existence is seen as obvious.

Yes. So, existence is seen as something Satanic or demonic. A posture that denies existence itself emerges.

What do you think ? Isn't it also hard for you to believe in things and people that are constantly changing ? Or do you think it's harder to trust things that never change ?

— Ouch. I myself am pretty capricious and have ups and downs. I'm not sure that I even trust myself. So that's hard to hear. If I were to make myself an invariant, unswaying, then I think would be deserving of trust. I agree completely.

As it happens, things are the exact opposite in the East. Japanese Shinto describes the gods as effectively infinite—everything becomes a god. There are even memorial services for old needles. **When this is the case, the question becomes, "how should we live ?" It's a question of *how*.**

— The difference between East and West in their skepticism and line of questioning is large in this area as well. More and more, I'm getting a real sense for how large an influence your departure point has on your thinking.

The question of what must change has been approached from many angles, as you can see.

Let's talk about the First Law of Motion now.

Before Newton, we had 2D thought based in experiential knowledge. The idea that objects in motion would eventually stop was considered an obvious truth.

For example, if I were to slide a block along the top of this desk, it would eventually stop.

Even if you look at this from multiple directions, in order to keep something moving, you need to add some kind of force.

In other words, objects naturally prefer to be still—they have a tendency to stop moving. Therefore, in order to keep things in motion, additional force is necessary—this is what people thought. This aligned well with daily experience, so for a long time, it was taken for granted.

— I get it ! Ah... but the problem was that they were only seeing with their eyes.

Yes, this is how it looks in that case. However, as you know, Galileo, Descartes, and Newton doubted this idea, and offered revolutionary alternatives.

Their idea was the following: **Perhaps objects tend to maintain their speed and direction.**

Therefore, **when speed is zero, objects stay motionless.**

Then this idea is qualified by saying that this remains true as long as an external force is not applied.

In other words, until now, the prevailing idea was that **objects are naturally still and tend to stop. Therefore, in order to keep them moving, some type of force must be applied.** However, Newton flipped this by saying that **an object in motion tends to stay in motion along its direction of movement, unless acted upon by an external force.**

— It's the complete opposite ! People at the time must have been flabbergasted.

Yes, I'm sure. However, the story continues.

What Newton thought was, "perhaps objects come to a stop not because of their inherent tendency, but because of interaction with their environment ?" If there is a force to make objects stop naturally, then objects will stop the same way regardless of the environment.

— When you put it like that, it's clear... Newton was thinking in terms of relationships, of mutual action.

That's right. Before I mentioned sliding a block on a desk, right ? If you slide a block on rough concrete or on top of ice, the block will go farther over the ice, right ? That's what Newton considered.

"If there was no friction at all, objects would probably keep going forever."

— That's an amazing thought experiment ! To imagine a space so different
   from daily life !

2. Newton's second law of motion (equation of motion)
—*In an inertial frame of reference, the acceleration of an object is proportional
to the force acting on it, and inversely proportional to its mass.*

From there, he thought the following.
   "In that case, if there is a net force, how will the fixed velocity change ?"
   This led to the Second Law of Motion. This law is famous in its equation
form, F=ma.
   Let's take a look at what it's saying.

The force acting on an object (F) is equal to the mass of that object (m)
times its acceleration (a)*.

*Acceleration: rate of change in velocity per unit time

In other words, by applying force to an object, that object's fixed velocity
changes.
   The determination of how much that fixed velocity changes is determined by the proportional relationship of the acceleration that results from
the force applied, to that force.

— In other words, the bigger the force—or the less massive the object—the
   acceleration is larger !

3. Newton's Third Law of Motion (Action-Reaction Law)
—*All forces between two objects exist in equal magnitude and opposite
direction.*

The Third Law states that "All forces between two objects exist in equal
magnitude and opposite direction."

For example, imagine pushing a block with your hand. At that moment, the
block moves, but at the same time, the block pushes against your hand—

you feel pressure. In other words, there is an opposite force of equal size at work. As another example, rowing a boat is the same idea. When you apply force to the water with the oar (action), the water pushes back, propelling you forward (reaction).

— *Figure 25* —
The Third Law of Motion: action/reaction

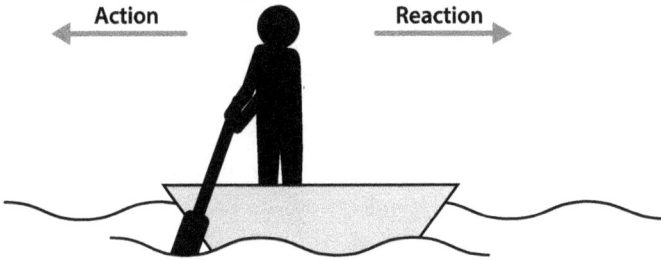

4. Law of Universal Gravitation
— *Every particle attracts every other particle in the universe with a force that is directly proportional to the product of their masses and inversely proportional to the square of the distance between their centers.*

Finally, let's look at the law of universal gravitation.

In the Middle Ages, before universal gravitation was proposed, people believed that

"The world beyond the sky—the cosmos—is a different world that works according to completely different laws from Earth."

There was also a concept called the **principle of locality,** which stated that only objects in direct contact could exert an influence upon each other.

— In that case, the law of universal gravitation must have seemed pretty crazy to people then. After all, it attempted to explain the workings of a different world that wasn't directly accessible.

That's exactly why this law attracted so much controversy.

— It seems that it's always a challenge to go against common sense, no matter the era. Yet the greater the revolution, it seems like that new revelation dictates the common sense of the age even more... I'm reminded of geocentrism and heliocentrism.

It's true. There can be no doubt that human history has evolved and progressed thanks to the courage of these thinkers. Let's try to follow in their footsteps. nTech is pursuing the greatest upheaval of common-sense humanity has ever seen with the proclamation that "oneself and one's world do not actually exist."

— Yes. I'm getting that feeling more and more !

By the way, in Newton's time, people already believed that there must be an external force at work pulling objects on the Earth's surface towards itself. However, that was limited to the Earth alone.

What was incredible about Newton is that he realized that the same force was at work to cause the Moon and other celestial objects to move. It wasn't just the Earth that was pulling, but all objects with mass. In other words, he destroyed the idea that the celestial and terrestrial worlds operate according to different laws, and **unified heaven and Earth under one law.**

— Newton was a true genius ! It's amazing that he was able to unite the cosmos and the Earth from where he stood, and explain the motion of the planets in the Solar System.

It's a completely impossible idea to arrive at using just experiential knowledge based on the immediate senses. This was the result of conceptual knowledge. However, Newton had weaknesses of his own. What do you think they were ?

— I don't know, what ? If he was able to explain the Solar System... then, the fact that he was unable to go beyond ?

Yes, there's that. Because he did not venture beyond the universe, or even approach its boundaries, he couldn't describe the world beyond the Solar System.

Why do you think he was only able to describe the workings of the Solar System, but nothing beyond ?

— What ? I'm not sure... I didn't even think about it...

What did we say we are looking at with our eyes ?

This is a hint.

The reason motion in the Solar System could be explained is because it is part of the world we can see with light. We said that human eyes are able to absorb the visible spectrum of electromagnetic radiation. Or, rather, visible light is all we can see. Therefore, all of the colors, patterns, and shapes we see are illusions. **In other words, reflections of light produce an illusory world of material, pattern, shape, and size, but that light is limited to our Solar System.** So, the region beyond the Solar System cannot be explained.

— The range of light... Newton used XYZ coordinates, but that didn't change what he could see with his eyes.

Yes. He had other weaknesses as well.

For example, right now you are causing the world before you (your perceptual screen) to exist. If you look behind you, the same will occur for that direction, and the world that was in front of you will vanish. This can be explained with quantum mechanics, but Newton was unable to describe this. He could not explain blinking, sleeping and waking up, living and dying. We need a finer way of looking at things.

Also, the **XYZ coordinates assume that space is absolute, separate from time and the existence.** But what if spacetime is fixed ?

In reality, **because objects of measurement are connected to spacetime, spacetime exerts an influence upon them.** This is what Einstein introduced, which we'll go over.

— In other words, Newton's way of observing, observation and measurement affect the target object. So, it's still not good enough for what we need.

That's right.

Besides, where are the XYZ coordinates ? They are **"external to the observer."**

In that case, do they have any relation to the "game" of your life ? There's none. So, you can't make your own game. It's difficult to demonstrate the autonomy of something that you can't participate in.

— More and more of Newton's weaknesses emerge. Are there any others ?

Yes, one more. Do you know the weakness of universal gravitation ?
Objects with mass mutually attract. Try imagining it.

— I, this pen and this chair, all have mass, are all mutually attracted... so they get stuck together ?

Yes, and if that kept happening, you'd ultimately collapse into a single point. **There must be a "repulsion" force as well, but this was not provided for.** The answer for why it doesn't happen was simply "God endeavors to keep the collapse at bay."

— We freed ourselves from the dogma of religion, but we were not fully free from the concept of God.

• III Albert Einstein: The Principle of Invariant Light Speed

Next up is Einstein. His discoveries enabled an even deeper explanation of the physical phenomena of the universe than Newton.

Newton claimed space to be fixed (invariant) with XYZ coordinates. In comparison, **Einstein observed and described a spacetime in which the speed of light is invariant: roughly 300,000 km/s.**

In other words, **spacetime is not fixed, and can change relatively based on conditions.**

— I've heard of this ! If you move at high speed, time moves more slowly.

For example, if the older of a pair of twins boarded a spacecraft that traveled near the speed of light and returned to Earth, the younger brother would have aged to 50 while the older brother would still be only 30, or something...

But that's strange. Time doesn't appear to change before our eyes no matter where we go. It seems a bit chaotic.

— *Figure 26* —
Theory of Relativity ①

Do the ages of the twins change?

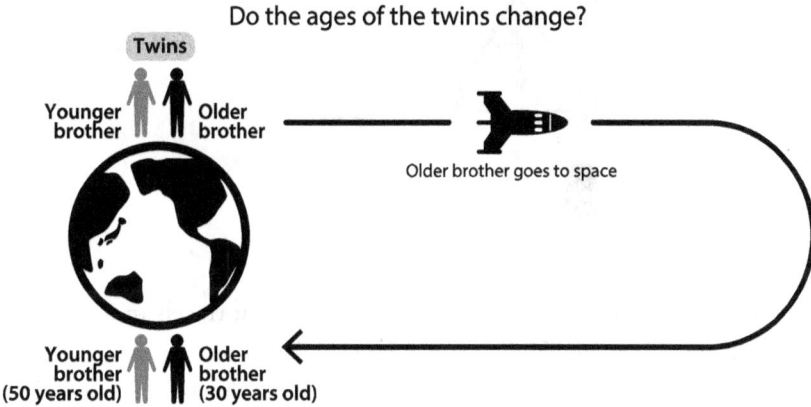

Yes, it is. Let's cover the basics of the theory of relativity.

You'll come to understand why these twins end up being different ages.

If you place a lamp on the floor of a moving train and a mirror on the ceiling, light will bounce off the mirror on the ceiling and return to the floor when you turn on the lamp. In that case, how does the light look to people inside the train and outside the train ?

Inside the train, the light appears to reach the ceiling and return (See Figure 27 on following page).

Outside the train, the light also bounces off the ceiling, but the path appears longer as the light follows the path of the train as well (figure 27 on following page).

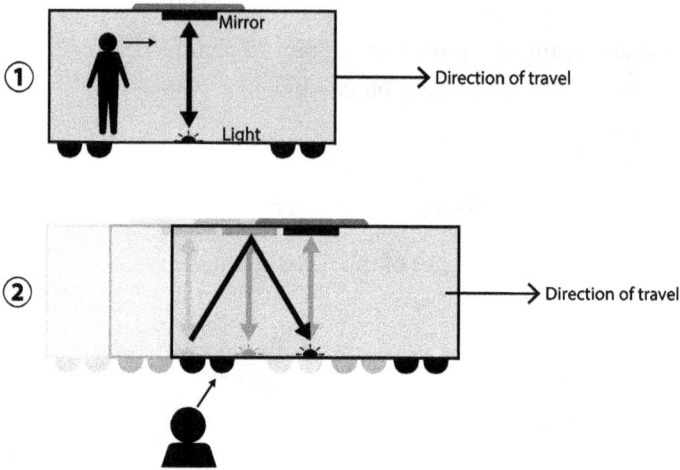

― *Figure 27* ―
Theory of Relativity ②

Distance traveled by light changes depending on observer

Comparing scenarios 1 and 2, the distance the light travels in 2 is longer. Because the speed of light is constant, calculating for time by dividing displacement by speed results in time passing more slowly in scenario 2.

Let's look at another example.

In a train with 3 cars, one car is ahead of the rest. While it is in motion, the front car and the last car simultaneously explode. How did this appear to the people in car 2 vs. the people watching from outside ?

The people outside the train see both cars explode at the same time.
The people in car 2 see the front car explode first and the last car explode second (See Figure 28 on following page).

But why is this ? Why do the people in car 2 perceive a difference in the times of the explosions ?

This is because the train was moving in the direction of the front car, so the light from ahead reached the eye first.

— *Figure 28* —
Theory of Relativity ③

Gap in time between explosions depending on observer

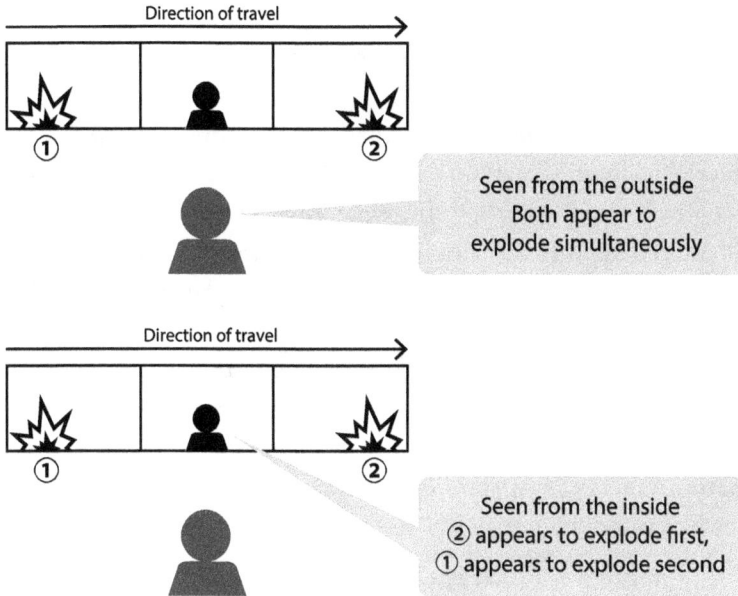

Direction of travel

① ②

Seen from the outside
Both appear to
explode simultaneously

Direction of travel

① ②

Seen from the inside
② appears to explode first,
① appears to explode second

— It's difficult to understand the idea of spacetime expanding and contracting, but I think I get the idea.

OK, let's keep going.

Newton had a **3D way of thinking that established time, space, and entities as separate.** However, Einstein **equated these three things, saying that they change conditionally.** That's because the distance that light travels is the standard.

I call this the **"spiral fractal"—looking at spacetime (distortion) and existence (distribution of mass) as a spiral.**

— Spiral fractal ? That's a new term. Does it replace XYZ coordinates ?

Yes, it is a new coordinate system that nTech proposes.

Let's take a look at the Einstein field equations.

$$G\mu\nu + \Lambda g\mu\nu = kT\mu\nu$$

Left side: Metric-determined curvature of spacetime
Right side: Matter-energy content of spacetime

In other words, **the bending (curvature) of spacetime is equal to its matter-energy content.** If spacetime is bent by a certain amount, the matter-energy content must also change. Therefore, time, space, and physical entities are all integrated. This also means that the curvature of spacetime is equivalent to gravity. The sharper the curve, the stronger the gravitational force.

Looking at the spiral fractal, you'll see that you can put another spiral inside the spiral. nTech explains that if you repeat that about five times, you'll end up with the physical universe, the holographic universe. **Spacetime's distortion (energy) is a state of embodiment (substantiation).** I'll explain why you need 5 iterations later.

— *Figure 29* —
Spiral Fractal

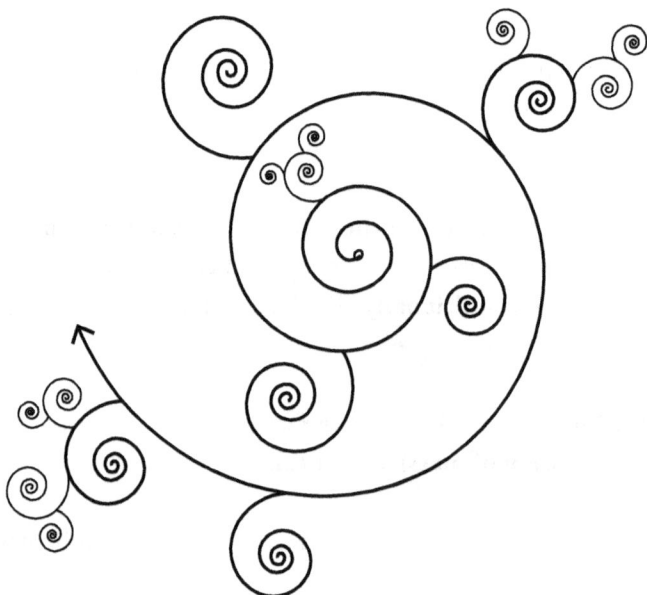

— This is getting pretty difficult.

Don't worry. As long as you understand the structure of existence emerging from non-existence, the rest will follow.

In this way, Einstein calculated spacetime and bodies using the distance light had traveled. Depending on that distance, their name changed. When matter moved forward it became viruses, then cells, then sentient beings, etc.

So ultimately, he's saying that the XYZ coordinates don't exist.

— There are no XYZ coordinates ?

That's right. **Rather than there being XYZ coordinates external to the observer, the XYZ coordinates are inherent to every body.** In that case, **everything has its own point of reference.** Therefore, everything is relative, everything is different. There is no fixed time, space, or entity. A has A's universe, B has B's universe, dogs have their dog universes. All different universes.

— I see. **Because the internal point of reference for each observer is different, the universe is also relative.**

Yes, that's right. In that sense, Newton and Einstein are totally different in their conception of the composition of bodies.

Newton saw bodies as a collection of points. These points attracted each other via universal gravitation, and through their combination they create shapes and patterns. In contrast, **Einstein saw the components of bodies as a collection of spiral fractals that moved at the speed of light.**

Newton and the others placed the referential XYZ coordinates for observing point-mass bodies outside of the bodies themselves. They saw space, time, and the size of the cosmos as fixed.

However, Einstein instead made the speed of light the reference, and said everything else is relative. That's because everything changes based on the distance light travels—in other words, how much the spiral fractals have accumulated. Therefore, all change is relative. By comparing one thing to another, everything changes. Because the observer has the point of reference within themselves, everything changes relatively. That's the principle of relativity.

Now let's think about Einstein's weaknesses.

— Now that you mention it, I remember there was a controversy between
  Bohr and Einstein regarding quantum mechanics. Quantum mechanics uses probability theory, but Einstein refused to accept it. He said that
  "God does not play dice with the universe" in support of determinism
  and against probability, but the experimental results have repeatedly
  supported quantum theory. It seems that Einstein lost that one.

"I, in any case, am convinced He does not play dice with the universe."

Einstein was unable to see light for what it really is.
    What I mean by that is that **Einstein based everything solely on the
utility of light, while Bohr and quantum mechanics delved into light
as a substance.**

We talked about the function/utility of light before. It brings forth substance (illusion).
    Human eyes can only see reflections in the visible spectrum of light, and
shapes, patterns, and colors change based on the angle and amount of light
we see. In this way, **the function of light—by bringing forth pattern
and shape—is to establish determinism, causality, locality, and reality.**
Quantum mechanics turns this idea on its head.

Quantum mechanics is based on probability theory and indeterminism. It
demonstrates wave-particle duality and uses the wave function to determine
the probability of quantization. Therefore, **there are no fixed patterns or
shapes that actually exist.** At the moment of observation, patterns and
forms emerge, and without observation, you have only probabilities.

— Einstein was a believer in reality, it seems. It's the idea that obviously
  something actually exists if light reflects off of it.
      But in quantum mechanics, things blink in and out of existence. It's
  difficult to say things actually exist in that case. Ultimately, Einstein
  understood the equivalence between time, space, and physical bodies,
  but he was not able to give up determinism, locality, reality, and the

independent existence of separate bodies. On the other hand, Bohr said there was only unity. That's why **he denied locality and the existence of parts, and instead talked about how all is connected, the oneness moving at energy speed.**

That's right. That's why Einstein was unable to destroy the assumption that we and our universes actually exist. In fact, he introduced a **cosmological constant** in an attempt to keep the size of the universe fixed.

— Universal constant... certainly, I believe he regretted that as the "biggest blunder" of his life. Based on observations from the Hubble Space Telescope, it became clear that not only is the universe not fixed, but it is expanding. He rejected the constant he himself proposed.

That's right. However, it actually wasn't a mistake. The universal constant ended up being reintroduced later. Also, the universe isn't just expanding—the expansion is accelerating. We needed a force to explain this acceleration; a constant was needed to explain the universe's inflation.

Einstein's weakness was that he was unable to break reality. His image of the universe was like the image of a person growing from a child to an adult. The idea that the universe goes through cycles of birth and death was beyond him, even though he also wrote about the dual wave-particle nature of light. Maybe he had simply separated the microcosmic from the macrocosmic in his mind.

He made a famous comment about life; do you know it ? "Life is like riding a bicycle. To keep your balance, you must keep moving."

— This is the first I've heard of it !

This idea demonstrates quantum mechanics. The bike is stabilized by gaining speed as the rider keeps pushing on the pedals to the left and right. In quantum mechanics, existence is stabilized by the quantum field rapidly moving back and forth between wave and particle, between existence and non-existence.

Unfortunately, Einstein did not quite pick up on this logic. He was too hung up on reality and wasn't able to come up with an explanation for where the speed of light comes from. It's like an addiction to existence.

— Existence addiction ! That's funny, but I shouldn't laugh. (laughs)

• IV Quantum Mechanics: Quantum Field Energy Condensed energy = mass

Now let's move on to quantum mechanics (QM).

We've discussed QM a fair amount by now, so I imagine that you have an idea of it ?

— Yes, you told me about it last time. I was able to get some sense for it, thanks to your explanation. Because of wave-particle duality, indeterminism and probability are required, not determinism. And because of that, forms and shapes do not "actually exist" as fixed entities.

In particular, Einstein approached light in terms of its use or function, but quantum mechanics looks at light as a material, as a substance. That resonated with me. In a battle between seeing something in terms of "function" or "material," the material perspective will prevail. Last time, you also said that the discovery and understanding of the fundamental substance will inevitably lead to the kickstarting of the society of the future.

That's right—this substance is the "source." The strongest things are the things at the deepest level. Let's discuss substance in-depth later. There are a lot of important keywords concerning the economy on that topic also.

— The economy ? I have to hear about that !

Newton envisioned a fixed 3D spacetime, Einstein preached the invariance of the speed of light, and QM introduced the substance of light, or in other words, an 'energy axis.' This invariant (standard) relies on the speed of vibration of the quantum field energy.

Bohr rejected Einstein's insistence on actuality—on the fixed size of substance. **Waves arise, particles arise—all is in motion, so rather than "actual existence," non-locality, indeterminism, and probability describe reality.**

This is the thinking behind the claim that **matter is "condensed energy," that it is quantized out of the quantum field of wave-particle duality via the observations of human beings.**

— Matter is condensed energy ?

That's right. **In terms of the spiral fractal, a distortion (matter/particles) opens in the spiral. The distortion's zero state can be seen as the quantum field energy (vibrations).**

From the QM perspective of the coming and going of waves and particles, the eye (the brain) captures only what is quantized. Incidentally, expressing this as a spiral gives us the same illustration we introduced during our discussion about Einstein. It's just that the level of detail is different.

— *Figure 29* —
Spiral Fractal

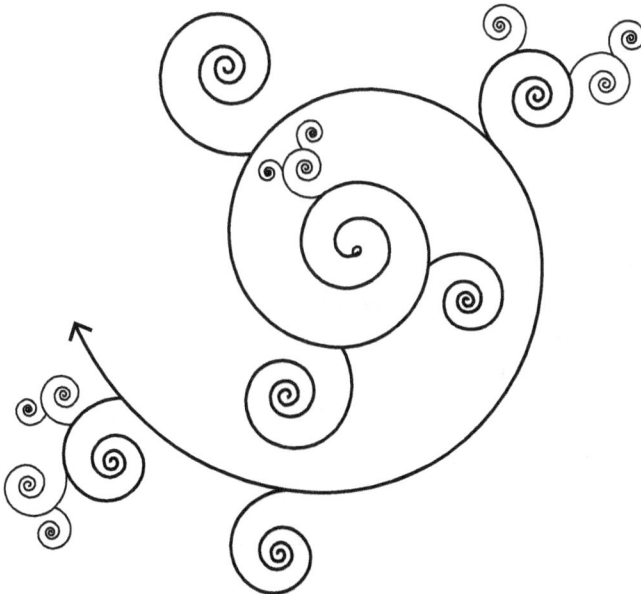

Let's try to imagine condensed energy using a movie theater as an example. An image is projected onto a pure white screen, right ? On that screen you see the protagonist, the town, cars, food, etc. All of that matter is quantized—condensed—energy.

— To see all of the things and people that appear on screen as condensed energy.

If matter is seen as condensed energy, does this mean that matter is being rejected ?

Are we finally at the point of departure from the "addiction to existence" ?!

No, we're not quite there yet. We are still a bit beholden to color, to pattern, to shape.

From the perspective of QM, the image "exists." In other words, **we are accepting the colors, the shapes, the patterns—as "energy."**

— I see. Breaking the addiction won't be easy. Well, that's not surprising.

But still, it seems that QM doesn't make any claims about things being "absolute." If that way of observing could be introduced into human relationships, it would make our relations with each other much more peaceful, I think.

Yes, because people would not think of what they know as unquestionable and absolutely certain. After all, they would know that changing circumstances could make anything change.

Under Newton's determinism, people will get into arguments refusing to cede any ground in their positions. Under Einstein's view, that "absolute" stance starts to bend a bit. Under QM, you're all the way into probability. Human relations will not deteriorate as badly, and people likely wouldn't commit suicide and homicide.

And what else ? Doesn't it seem like there would be new ideas, changes in our expressive and creative powers ? Don't the thoughts, feelings, words, actions, and relationships under the "what you can see" paradigm seem like a joke compared to the same things under the QM paradigm ?

— Ahh... the outcome is so obvious I don't even have a response.

Humanity has created things like AI and computers, and that's a sign that at least we've managed to master QM at a conceptual level. If we stayed at the level of only what we can see, we would never be able to come with any of that stuff no matter how hard we tried.

• V String Theory: The 5 String Energy Vibrations

Let's move on to string theory.

— Ooo ! I remember that "the Universe is a symphony of strings" ! There are string-shaped energy vibrations and the pattern of those vibrations are what give rise to the differences between the various elementary particles, I loved that !

Yes, that. This theory emerged from the effort to explain the moment the universe came into being—the Big Bang. Because the singularity at the moment of the Big Bang and the singularity at the depths of a black hole are so similar as to be identical, scientists attempted to explain the workings of black holes.

— The mysteries of the Big Bang and black holes ! These are some intense topics ! We're moving towards the birth of the universe ! But what was the reason for these investigations ?

All disciplines ultimately begin with a desire to either know the fundamental nature of something or understanding the self. In the case of physics, the desire is to understand the start of the universe, the Big Bang.

— Is there a connection between understanding the mysteries of black holes and knowing fundamental nature or knowing myself ?

Yes. I won't go in-depth about understanding black holes here, but I'll give a quick explanation.

First, imagine the depths of a black hole.

That place is of unimaginably small dimensions. Consequently, we need QM, which focuses on the microcosmic.

At the same time, this space is extremely massive. Consequently, we also need Einstein's general relativity, which focuses on the macroscopic. Therefore, this topic requires satisfying both of their requirements—but **in the attempt to integrate their respective equations, major problems emerged.**

Another thing—while black holes even consume light itself, they also create everything in the universe. **Thus, one must describe a state of pattern and shape as well as a state of no pattern and no shape.**

However, the level of energy that QM describes is unable to unify these two things. To do so, we must break down quantum field energy yet further. It is the attempt to do so that produced string theory. String theory also splendidly resolves the conflict between QM and relativity mentioned above.

— Wow, this is making me more and more interested in string theory !

Our key phrase was "seeing changes via our choice of invariant."

What on earth is the invariant in string theory ?

To briefly review, Einstein took the speed of light as invariant and insisted on seeing light in terms of its function, its utility. Bohr, from the QM perspective, saw light as a substance. He claimed that the quantum field is what gives rise to light. This view took the fluctuation energy of the quantum field as its invariant and viewed matter as "condensed energy." However, this condensed energy was infinite.

String theory splits the categories of this condensed energy according to "5 simple patterns." Matter is split into 118 elements, right ? This splits energy into 5 categories in a similar way. That is why it is referred to as **the substance that brings forth quantum field energy.**

In other words, **the invariant of string theory is the "5 types of string energy vibrations."**

Seen in terms of the spiral fractal, **the coming and going of the spiral is based on its ability to punch through to the outside and travel along the**

black hole. This is a "motion made both by strings and the membrane." We will discuss the membrane in more detail in M theory next.

— Infinite amounts of condensed energy can be described in just 5 patterns ? Things are getting simpler. Does that mean that the way we observe things is getting simpler also ?

Good insight. That's correct.

String theory is based on these 5 string energy vibrations, right ? nTech analyzes and describes how **this discovery brings clarity to the energy world of yin and yang and the five elements described in Chinese cosmology—which also includes the five senses of humanity—in terms of mathematical energy dimensions.**

— Wow ! So, **the secrets of the five senses are revealed !**

Yes, yes. It's connected to the description of the universe of the five senses of humanity. It becomes possible to explain the rise and cessation, the waking and sleeping, the swaying to the left and right of the five senses. The world of QM is unable to explain why there are these five.

— It's so amazing I'm at a loss for words.

Indeed. Now, if string theory is seen in terms of our previous movie theater example, it is just a blank white screen. There is no image on it at all, no color, pattern, or shape. However, **we are still constrained by the fundamental material of the 5 varieties of string energy vibration.**

— It's a blank white screen yet there's still 5 varieties...

By the way, the fact that string theory successfully synthesized the "small world" of QM and the "big world" of general relativity, people all over the world were excited with the possibility that it is the grand unifying theory.

— A grand unifying theory ! Wow... but wait. I won't be tricked so easily. After all, we're still constricted by these 5 varieties of string energy. And didn't you say last time that M theory unifies the micro and macro worlds as well as the four forces ? So, in other words, the road to unification continues. Next up is the last stage in physics—M theory !

• VI M Theory: Vacuum Energy Fluctuation

Your understanding has come a long way ! Let's take a look at M theory.

QM said that there is an infinite amount of condensed energy, and string theory said it all can be described by 5 varieties.

M theory breaks down that condensed energy further, and said that it all can be described by the fluctuations of a single type of membrane (vacuum energy). Therefore, **the invariant in M theory is "membrane vibrations."**

— Yes, you were saying something about how all the string vibrations break down into a single entity, like a membrane that spreads out infinitely in all directions. The string vibrations break down, but there is motion.

That's right. Both strings and the membrane use the same word, "vibrations," but the motion is in different dimensions. This membrane (vacuum energy) has no condensed color, pattern, or shape. Neither do the strings have colors, patterns, or shapes, but the membrane is more unraveled than the string. To use an analogy, humans emerge from the soil (the Earth), and when they die they return to the soil. Similarly, with ocean and fish.

— Fish are born from the sea, and when they die they dissolve back into the sea ?

That's right. **If the universe is like a "fish" made of a collection of strings, then the "ocean" of energy that yields the universe is the "membrane."** We said that the membrane is beyond, it's outside of the universe. The membrane bunches together, the "fish" strings of the universe are born. From the fish strings come the quantum field, and then matter, etc. A variety of fish are born.

— So, the membrane (vacuum energy) is like an ocean that gives rise to all that exists, all matter.

If string theory explains the five senses, **M theory explains the structure that gives rise to yin and yang and the five elements, the structure that gives rise to the five senses and their origin.** All of this is described by nTech.

— **We can understand the structure behind sentience ?** That's amazing !

I think so too !

To bring it all together, **energy can be split into three levels.** Surface (quantum field energy), line (the five varieties of string energy), and point (vacuum energy). **The membrane (vacuum energy) is the source of energy.** Bringing points together creates a line. Bringing lines together creates a surface. Bringing surfaces together creates a solid body (matter).

— Physics certainly is the discipline of matter and energy. If M theory describes the origin of energy, then as far as energy goes, there is nowhere else to go, no more differences to define. In other words, **this is enlightenment at the level of physics,** right ?

Completely right ! **M theory, which drills down to the origins of energy, contains the master formulae of physics—it is the grand unifying theory.**

Once sentience is seen as "that which generates matter as a consequence of perception," **the ability to describe even the structure that yields sentience is the same as being able to describe all physical phenomena, and therefore all physical laws can be described in their entirety.**

— Amazing ! We've finally reached the unifying theory !

Oh, but wait. Just now, I said "level of physics." Right. I see...

As you have guessed, there is still more ahead. Before, I said that there 11 levels. Right now, we have just passed level 6, right in the middle.

We have reached the pinnacle of mathematical physics, the peak of enlightenment in physics —M theory. However, there's still all kinds of questions yet before us.

— Is this that thing from before ? About the 10^{500} universes ? That was so wild, it really stuck with me.

Yes, that. Physicists are going crazy over this "10^{500} universes" result that their calculations have produced. However, because this membrane conducts this birth and death vibration 10^{500} times every second, it suggests that universes are blinking in and out of existence. **Despite the assumption in physics thus far that there is only one universe, this suggests that there are far, far more.** Not only that, but **the blinking in and out is even harder to explain.** From the human perspective, these ideas are tough to swallow. Nobody knows how to deal with it. **There are also parallel universes, multiverses, and higher dimensions.**

— That's quite a pickle. But, you know, what about that thing we said before—there's one physical universe, but an infinite number of conscious universes, of perceptual universes. That 10^{500} is practically like saying "infinite." And the membrane energy outside of the universe is moving at superposition speed... oh, I see ! So, the parallel universes and multiverses are the same idea ?

That's right ! Wonderful ! **Perceptual universes.**

M theory doesn't account for the mind, so it doesn't grasp this. Because everything is at the physical level, there's no way it can be described. Even if all physical phenomena can be described by the fluctuations of the membrane, **M theory doesn't explain why, from where, in what way that energy emerges, nor does it describe the world of the thoughts and feelings of the mind.**

So now we need an even more precise way of observing.

Since the product of the brain's perspective is the universe, **if the brain's perceptual habits are not understood, then physical phenomena cannot be totally understood. Understanding those perceptual habits of the brain is like understanding a flip book.** In so doing, we will understand that **the** world we observe is an afterimage in the brain, a fiction. The concept that ties together the physical universe and the conscious universe is perspective (the brain's perspective) and the brain's perceptual habits.

— A flip book... brain habits... we're about to bring it all together. I'm looking forward to it !

• VII Buddhism: *Kūmuhensho* (level 5 in Zen)

Yes, let's bring it all together soon.
Now let's bring in the 9 stages of Zen in Buddhism.

— We've moved beyond the energy of physics, and breaking into the "world of mind" beyond.

Yes, we'll do it step by step. In general, Zen refers to spiritual meditation aimed at quieting and focusing the mind, but its stages can also be seen as a guide towards enlightenment.
The first four stages are referred to as *"Yūsō-zanmai"* and as the name suggests, is a state of imagery and analogy. Buddhism doesn't count these as enlightenment, so we'll leave them out.

What Buddhism recognizes as enlightenment is everything from stage 5 onwards. These stages are referred to as *"Musō-zanmai."*
By the way, *Zanmai (Samādhi)* is a state of permanently deepened spiritual concentration.

— Oh, now that you mention it, you said that the membrane (vacuum energy) of physical enlightenment is the same as stage 5 of Zen, right ? Form is emptiness, emptiness is form. The universe within is "form," the universe without is "emptiness," and this repeats.

That's right ! So, in Buddhism, the membrane (vacuum energy) is expressed as "emptiness." So, **the invariant is "emptiness."** That fits nicely with the arising and ceasing of the 10^{500} universes, doesn't it ?

— It really does. From the brain's perspective, physics and Buddhism don't seem like they'd be related, but if all emerges from a single motion, it's obvious how they are related.

That's right. What the eye sees is distinction and discontinuity everywhere, no unity in sight. To see it, you have to change how you observe things. Now we are truly in the midst of our journey of bringing everything together into a way of observing all as a singular motion, so bear with me for another push.

As I said, form and emptiness are not separate things, but are rather two sides of the same coin.

However, if you see things with your physical eyes, you can only see one side of that coin—form. But emptiness is always there on the other side. It's important to be able to see this motion.

If you can see the motion of form to emptiness and vice versa, understanding nTech will be pretty straightforward. Conversely, many people who struggle with this point often misunderstand this imagery. After all, you don't experience a "repeated inside-out motion" in your daily life, do you ?

— I don't, not at all. I see. It's difficult because you can't experience it via the senses.

Yes, usually, we only experience motion in terms of height, depth, width— the 360-degree space. However, nTech isn't focused on experiential perception, but conceptual perception.

If you see things only with your physical eyes, you can only see matter in that 360-degree space, but everything on the inner side of matter is able to flip around and explode to the outside, and the energy that emerges to the outside can be compressed back down into matter, and it can continue to move back and forth. In other words, when you see entities (forms), are you only seeing an image of matter in 360-degree space, or are you seeing a motion from matter (form) to energy (emptiness) in a combined 720-degree space ? This is a pretty important image, so try to imagine it if you can.

— The repeated inside-out motion ! Don't see matter just with your eyes, but as motion !

• VIII Buddhism: *Shikimuhensho* (level 6 in Zen)

From here on out, we are moving into the world of the substance that brings forth emptiness (the membrane/vacuum energy). That substance is "mind." I use the word "mind," but **compared to the "mind" humanity usually imagines—thoughts, feelings, etc.—this is totally different.**

By the way, if I were to ask you what you think "mind" is, how would you respond ?

— Mind... yeah, that's difficult. I'll pass !

It's not an easy question to answer. Even if people who specialize in the mind were asked this, they likely wouldn't be able to provide a clear answer. Let's look at mind, like energy, in terms of a point/line/surface separation of levels.

— That's right ! You complained before about how this age doesn't understand that there are stages to unconsciousness and oneness, also. (laughs)

So, the 6th level of Zen describes the **"function of mind."**

— The function of mind ? There is such a thing ?

Of course. For example, when you apply labels—that's a human, that's an animal, that's a plant, etc.—that is done with mind. The mind of the 6th level is similar to the membrane and is the surface level. **Despite our using the word "mind," this is a defined, closed world with limits and range.** For that reason, it's possible to apply labels, like "that's an X." **The *"shiki"* (consciousness) in *Shikimuhensho* refers to "the nameable mind,"** and *"muhen"* means "boundless." So, all things are a variant of *"shiki,"* or consciousness. In Zen terminology **this is called *"issai yuishinzō,"* or "all is** created by the mind." In other words, "consciousness" is the invariant in *Shikimuhensho*, everything is just a variation of consciousness, and because there is only consciousness, there is no world without consciousness.

— Wow. Because it's a closed world, it is amenable to separations. So, it's possible to assign names to things. This still seems a bit chained to the habits of the mind—something about it seems a bit stiff.

• IX Buddhism: *Musho-usho* (level 7 of Zen)

Yes, it is. Which suggests that we can go farther. It seems that you have a sense that going farther will increase our freedom. So, let's go farther.

Level 7 of Zen also concerns the "function of mind." However, in contrast with level 6, it is "the unnameable mind." This is the "line" level of mind.

— The 6th level of Zen is a defined, closed world, so it is possible to use names in it. So, does that suggest that **level 7 of Zen is a world without scope or limits, and thus names cannot be used** ?

That's right ! So, here, **"the unnameable mind" is the invariant.**
As for what this means, let's bring back our familiar bar magnet.
Is the border between the N and S side, N or S ?

— It could be N or S, but I can't just pick one.

Yes, that ability for it to go either way is the essence of level 7 of Zen. If level 6 is about picking either N or S, in level 7, it's neither. It's **"motion."** How can you name something that is always moving, always changing ? It's the idea in Buddhism that I mentioned before, that all worldly things are impermanent, all things in the universe lack inherent structure.
In terms of speed, if level 6 is like a local train, level 7 is like an express train that speeds past a lot of stations.

— Local trains and express trains ?

Yes. The speed of mind is incomparably fast compared to matter and energy, but **within mind, there are still differences in speed. Level 6 is the slowest—it stops at each station to name it. In level 7, the speed is much greater, and isn't stopping at any of those stations.**

— That example is easy to understand. In that case, level 7 is pretty liberated compared to the fixation of level 6. In that sense, because daily life is full of names and words, it involves a lot of similar fixations... that must cause some suffering.

That's right. By the way, energy is in a superposition, it's overlapping, right ? So, it could be either N or S. For that reason, whether we're talking about quantum field energy, the five vibrational energies of strings, vacuum energy or whatever—**it's not possible to apply names in the world of energy. This is the same as the "unconsciousness" described in psychology.**

If mind changes and becomes matter, it becomes the "nameable mind" of level 6, and if it becomes energy, it becomes the "unnameable mind" of level 7.

— The things you're saying are all coming together. It's interesting how simple it is to connect mind to energy.

• X Buddhism: *Hisōhihisōsho* (level 8 of Zen)

Next up is level 8.

Now we are finally past "function of mind" and are discussing what gives rise to it: **"mind itself."** This is the "point" level of mind.

— Mind itself ! Finally, the real deal ! Is this the climax ?!

Well, calm down. (laughs)

The "point" here refers to **"the position from which the motion of mind is imaginable." It is a transitional level of mind: 間 (*ma*), and in Buddhist terminology is called "*Hisōhihisō*."**

— *Hisō......hihisō* ? What does that mean ? The position from which the motion of mind is possible ?

Think over the words carefully. What's "*Hisō*" ?

— "*Hisō*" is the absence or antithesis of "imagery," so imagery is impossible ?
 So then, not "*Hisō*" is the absence or antithesis of "imagery is impossible" ?
 In that case, "imagery being impossible is impossible," or in other words, "imagery is possible" ?
 This is a pretty weird expression.

You say that, but it sounds to me like you understand just fine. (laughs)
 Hisōhihisō is "the position of being able to imagine the motion of mind that the brain cannot imagine." This is the invariant.

— What ? So, in other words, one can imagine the motion of mind ! ...right ?
 Which might mean...

That's right ! This is the "repeated inside-out motion" we talked about so much last time.

The poison of Mind, 間 (*ma*).

Freedom to go between the blank screen and the imaged screen.
 Freedom to go inside the screen and outside the screen.

The **"anywhere door"** that emerges here is "*Hisō*," not "*Hisō*."
 Because of this "間 (*ma*)," it's possible to become fully liberated from the screen !

— I see, that's what it was !
 I thought the 間 (*ma*) of the "repeated inside-out motion" was the "nothingness" of level 5 !
 Emptiness is form, form is emptiness. But it was actually this !

Yes. Certainly, level 5 also has a "repeated inside-out motion." However, what we laid out there was just a sort of ad hoc assembly of the things we had discussed. Because it was intended for beginners, that level of comprehension was fine, but I apologize if I confused you.

Today we climbed some more levels and integrated what we discussed. **This world of "*Hisō*," *hihisō*? is the "聞 (*ma*)" I discovered in 1996.** It was the discovery of level 9 of Zen—**the discovery of the "True World" and this "聞 (*ma*)."**

This "聞 (*ma*)" is like the **female womb.** **It is a place of total mental captivation, a place of whimsical imagination, the source of all illusions.**

— The female womb ? It seems like there's a really important secret here...

CHAPTER 6

Final Question = Final Answer

• XI Buddhism: Metsu-jinjō, sōju-metsujō (level 9 of Zen)

Interviewer:
— We're finally here. The True World, mind itself!

Level 8 is the "position that can imagine the unimaginable motion of mind." In that case, is level 9 **"the unimaginable motion of mind"** itself?

Jesu Noh:
Now you've reached the point where you can predict what's coming next! (laughs) However, let's not get ahead of ourselves, and just enjoy the process.

As you suspect, level 9 is the unimaginable motion of mind. What's important is figuring out what that is.

The substance of "mind itself." In other words, **the source of mind that produces the point, line, and surface levels of mind.**

There is no point, no position. An unimaginable starting point.

The most natural motion. The primal motion.

We started our talk about level 11 with a big assumption in our way of observing: "Observation and measurement influence their target object."

In the unimaginable motion of mind, is there a side that measures and a side that is measured? Is there a perceptual subject and a perceptual object?

— A perceptual subject and perceptual object... well, to begin with, there's no way to distinguish between them. So, no.

There is no perceptual subject or object!

Oh, I see! So, then **our assumption that "observation and measurement influence their target object" disappears!**

That's right. So, we need to look from here.

Don't see with your eyes, but with unity.
Perception of the Absolute. Shakyamuni's enlightenment. Buddhism's enlightenment.

— I feel like my heart is pounding.

This is just the beginning. We're about to dive into the heart of it all.

Last time we pushed ourselves past matter and energy and encountered the motion of mind.
    We talked about how that mind is a single repeated inside-out motion that takes place at both 0 and ∞ speed.

— Yes, that was the previous level. Level 8: *Hisōhihisō*.
    Today I was surprised to hear that we still haven't reached Truth.
    Now we are at level 9. At last, we are diving into the heart of Truth.

By the way, this reminds me of something I haven't quite been able to understand in our discussions so far.

What's that ?

— You said something about a sense of omnipotence and a sense of competence. That humans are incredible beings, they are infinite potential itself. It made me feel pretty full of myself.
    Yet, for some reason... **as we talk about how there is only "motion," that focus on "being," that insistence on "being"—something seems off about it.**

Well done ! ! Your intuition has become quite clear. That's right. I hoped you would pick up on that.
    Just as you suggest, the whole reason we have not been able to reach the "True World"—the world of ultimate mind-source, the ultimate reality—is exactly that !

— What ? What do you mean ? What are you trying to say ? I want to say I know what you mean, but...

Ok, think about it. The "repeated inside-out motion of unity at 0 and ∞ speed" is a motion you try to imagine with your brain, right ? But **whatever you imagine with your brain has a pitfall—it creates an image that lets you "return to being" rather easily. You see ?**

— Ah...

The 間 (*ma*) that *Hisōhihiso* represents is the "point of contact" between the inside and the outside of the screen. A sort of door that enables us to go back and forth between the inside and outside of the screen. There's an issue where the ability to "create an image" leads to you thinking you know what's going on. **The trap is stopping at a level of enlightenment defined by mental comprehension/knowledge.**

— So... something like this ?
   Ultimately, the previous levels focused on "existence" over "Truth." There was a tendency to prioritize the "value of being." Humans are made of some impossible substance ! Humans are amazing !

That's right ! So, at that level, inquiry may just cease at the level of *ideas or philosophy* regarding dignity—or *ideas and philosophy* regarding peace ! However, if you stop at philosophical idealism, your products will all be limited by your brain. So, this level is still not at the level of "Truth/the Absolute/the Origin."
   This is a rather clever, subtle trap so it can be hard to escape. That's why reaching the 9th level, completely getting outside of the screen, **achieving an "all zero" mental intuition—in other words, the intuition revolution—is so important.**

— I see. The *Hisōhihiso* emerges from a motion that cannot be imagined, but **the "all zero" mental intuition enables one to perceive this unimaginable motion**, right ?

That's right. This is easily understood by looking at the relation between invariance and change. Because invariance is invariant, it is invariance itself. So, what about change? Change changes, but if everything changes, then the nature of change is unchanging—invariant. In that sense, **invariance is more fundamental than change.** In a word, the motion you can imagine with your brain (change) is brought forth by the motion you can't imagine with your brain (eternal invariance).

This "motion that cannot be imagined by the brain" is the Fundamental Motion, the True World, the Original Mind, the unity that constitutes absolute reality. It is the only thing that has "Actual Existence."

• Final Question & Final Answer

— The Fundamental Motion is the only thing that has Actual Existence? I don't think I quite get it.

Yeah. You want to know the substance of the Fundamental Motion that the brain is incapable of imagining, right? You don't quite get it because you want to know the "subject" of this motion.

— Ah, that's right.

I thought so! Even though we've been talking all this time about how it's not entities that move, but motion that creates entities, in the end you still want to know "what" moves, don't you? " What is the substance which creates motion inconceivable by the brain? What is moving?" Because "motion" suggests the verb "to move," you want to know its grammatical subject. Is it a liquid? Solid matter? Gas? Plasma? What is it made of? So ultimately you ask what it is.

We need some "final answer" about Truth in the form of a proper noun. We must reach a conclusion about what (X) the universe is made out of by means of a pronoun. The question about that X is the "final question," and its answer is the "final answer." So—**What is the Fundamental Motion made of? This is the Final Question.**

— Yes ! Wow... I'll finally be able to hear the final answer ! The absolute material that brings forth all beings and enables their movement, the material of the inconceivable Motion... what is it ? I want to know !

Sure. But first, let's talk about **why this is the final question and final answer.** Once we establish these conditions, we'll move into the answer itself.

— Oh, the justification for the final question ? That sounds interesting too !

In order to know these conditions, you just have to think about the difference between the final question and the questions that came before it. So, what do you think it is ? For all the questions so far, when you ask them, then you... ?

— You get an answer.

That's right. So, what about the final question ?

— There is no answer ?

Right ! If there was an answer just like all the questions that came before, the question can't be considered "final." That is to say, **the first condition is reaching a point where one can keep questioning upon understanding that there is no answer or that obtaining one is impossible.**

— Asking questions after learning that there is no answer ? That seems strange. And if there is no answer, trying to think of one seems foolish. So, you mean it's ok to stop thinking ?

No, no, it's nothing so simple. That's why I said it's the "first condition." However, **if you just stop at the idea that "there is no answer," it's the same as abandoning the answer,** isn't it ? That's not very good. So, then, the second condition is that **you must clearly understand and be able to explain why there is no answer.**

Then the third condition, from the side of the answer, is that **by knowing the reason and foundation for there being no answer, the question** makes one aware that they are in a position that enables them to answer any other question correctly. This is the ultimate condition of the Final Question. Finally, the fourth condition—again from the side of the question—is **awareness of the fact that the final question is inherently self-destructive/self-defeating.**

These four conditions make up the "formal conditions" of the Final Question.

— The nature of the Final Question is overwhelmingly different from other questions, isn't it... ? I understand the formal conditions, though. So, if these conditions exist, does the Final Answer also have formal conditions ? If so, what are they ?

Yes, they exist. Let's go over them. The first is to, **rather than answering the question, prove that the question is the dumbest possible question—prove that you can destroy it. That is to say, prove that there can be no question more foolish.** The second condition is to **demonstrate overwhelming self-confidence in your ability to defeat any question via your defeat of this particular question.** In addition, **one must know that they are in a position that lets them freely choose whether or not to satisfy the perspective of a question, or dismiss the question.** Finally, the fourth condition is to **develop a position of "only questions" by no longer being the answering side to a question, but rather** *becoming the questioning side* **and negating the answer completely.**

— Wow, that's intense ! But it's really interesting ! I want to know more !

By the way, don't you think it's about time you told me the Final Answer ?

I understand that the universe, that all things in nature, arise from the One Motion.

If that's the case, please tell me what that motion is made of ! What is creating that motion ?

The answer to the Final Question—the Final Answer—is... **You fool ! You don't need to know !!! Even if you knew, what would you do with that knowledge ???**

— Uhhhh... ?

But... I guess that's a good question. Where would I use it ? How could I use it to answer some question I might have ?

After all... from an inconceivable motion of mind, emerges a conceivable motion of mind, from which emerges an unnameable mind, from which emerges a nameable mind... it is through that nameable mind that the universe arises and ceases. So, if you know the relationship that explains how the unnameable mind and the nameable mind emerges from the conceivable motion of mind...

If you know that, you know the "equation" behind the physical universe and the world in which universes pop in and out of existence. **So, if you know that, there's no place to use it ?**

That's right. The inconceivable motion of mind, the Original Mind, is creating the dream, the film that we call reality. We'll talk about the dream of Original Mind later.

To go back to what we were discussing, the thing that human beings most want to obtain is the knowledge of how to change this simulated "real world" with the "structure of being" of that dream, that film. That's why knowing the substance from which that the inconceivable motion of mind is made isn't usable anywhere. And **doesn't it seem kind of foolish to try to understand a substance without boundaries or positions ?**

— Yes, I see... when you put it like that, I understand. But what would you call it if you tried to know even if you have no use for the knowledge or if it's foolish to try to know ?

Humanity always acts on conditioned reflex and tries to know and ask things it doesn't need.

So, it's important to understand why **it's ok not to know**, so let's talk about it. First of all, like we said, **you'd have no use for the knowledge anyway.**

Also, the Fundamental Motion is unimaginable, yet the Final Question asks about the "substance" of that motion. Can you imagine such a substance ?

— I can't... imagine it.   /

Of course not. The material of the inconceivable motion is, also, inconceivable. The question itself is nonsense.

In that case, **attack the question itself! Don't let it manipulate you!**

In that moment, the cry of the Mind explodes: **"I've won against questions! I've won against thoughts! I've won against my brain! It's ok not to know !!!"**

— Attack the question itself, huh ? You said before that a complete "all zero"-ing of questioning is the highest form of absolute knowledge.

The question is foolish and there is no answer. I can understand that. But **I have this instinct to answer when I'm confronted with a question.** It's like a reflex...

I was really struck when you said that our souls are bound by the chains of reality.

That's right. **You're putting an end to that mechanical conditioned reflex that humans have to unconditionally try to answer any question.**

After all, the Fundamental Motion has no boundaries, no directions, no positions. It has no points, and of course, no lines, surfaces, or bodies. It is unimaginable, imperceptible, intangible. **It is an amazing motion that the human brain cannot comprehend.** Its substance is even more unimaginable. So, it's foolish to even attempt to imagine it or speak of it. So, that means that this is "the end." The place where you can finally put a stop to your questions and say "this is as far as it goes" is the Final Answer.

For example, let's say you draw a snake, and the snake is finished. You have some extra time, so you put some wings on it. Now it's not a snake anymore, right ? If you pour a cup full of cola, it'll eventually start spilling over, right ? So, it's important to know when to stop.

It has been 5 million years since the emergence of humanoid species, and we have suffered the whole way.

It's time to put an end to our enslavement to our brains.

— Emancipation ! A declaration of victory over our brains !

That's right ! And so, we have to put a stop to the questioning. We have to prove that the questioning itself is foolish. Then we unlock the fifth condition of the Final Answer: **a revolution in meaning and value.**

— A revolution in meaning and value ?

That's right. Things we thought were meaningful are revealed to us as foolish, and the things we thought were meaningless, we find to have tremendous value and meaning. **We refuse to be bound by meanings and values restricted to the level of the brain !**

Comprehension of the value of the valueless and the meaning of the meaningless.

This is the power to define the "1" of the Fundamental Motion !

— That's really cool.

There's even more to it. It's not just freedom from value and meaning, but also freedom from definitions. The meaning in the meaningless, the value in the valueless, and **the definition in the undefined.**

— The definition in the undefined ?

That's right. In order to make a claim about something, you need a definition, right ?
So, we defined the Fundamental Motion of "1," but what would you do if you were asked to explain it ?

— What ? Well, we said we don't need to know, so... the brain can't conceive of it, and it can't be put into words. Is it possible to explain ?

Let's see. If you try to explain it, you need some words. Once you try to explain it with those words, you'll need even more words. You'll never be able to explain it properly.

— So, you'll go around and around in circles, and things will get more and more complicated. There's no end to it.

In order to defeat the chains of this "contradictory loop," you need the "definition of the undefined."
The Fundamental Motion of "1" is an awesome motion that the brain cannot imagine. It's a world that the brain cannot judge, a world that needs no proof. So, **when you define that "1," you have to define the state of not being able to define something.**
For that reason, when I am asked to explain the Fundamental Motion of "1," this is what I say, "Who cares ! There's no word for it. It can't be imagined !"

Before, I said that in the end you'd have to let go of your boat, that nothing of the world you know would remain, right ? That nTech doesn't exist, that I don't exist.
Meaning emerges from a world without meaning. Value emerges from a world without value. Definition emerges from a world without definition. That is the age of nothingness. The age of mind.

— This is exciting ! I think I'm getting goosebumps.

Yes ! That feeling, amplified all the way to the place beyond space, is the intuition revolution ! This is the "all zero intuition" of total nullification ! Once you reach that distant, rarefied world devoid of disparities, you will clearly see the value of nothingness.

- **So —what is the value of nothingness ?**

— The value of nothingness... I thought about it after our conversation from last time, but I realized that I had been unconsciously, unconditionally thinking of "existence"—of presence—as something with value. On the other hand, I never saw any value in nothingness, or to be more accurate, I never thought of it in terms of value.

Yes, I believe it. Because humanity has been relying on its 5 senses all this time to see the world, that makes sense. However, from the perspective of Truth, **"Existence" is "Below Non-Existence."**

— Another provocative statement. Not only does nothingness have value, but existence is beneath it.

Let's think about the value of nothingness together.

In a word, it is the **"benevolence of Truth."** It is the salvation of humanity, that will do away with all its issues. Why ? **Because only the Fundamental Motion "1" is able to take away and nullify all differences and disparities !**

After all, how can you make comparisons in a world in which nothing can be imagined, perceived, or felt ? "You are amazing, but I am worthless." This sort of thought couldn't exist, right ? **All becomes perfectly equal, all is raised to the highest level. What makes this upward harmonization possible is "1."**

When this occurs, for the first time we will be able to put the war games aside, and **enter into a state of pure love.**

— That's beautiful... and it's true, humans have suffered so much because of "differences." Whether individual relationships, or organizations, or countries, it's the same. We bounce back and forth between happiness and sorrow as we compare ourselves to others. We measure our own happiness based on the failures and successes of others.

That's right. We become free from the world we know, free from meaning and value. **We will become unable to fight over the world, over meaning, over value.** We would not be able to become trapped in our absolute insistence on our own perspectives and opinions, because we would recognize them as nothing more than the products of our own internal biased analyses.

For the same reason, the **"world we know" will fall to violence.** It's the same as brandishing an invisible sword over our heads until we cut ourselves and those around us. We must be wary of people who claim they know things with certainty.

The talk about definitions is the same. All of our academic disciplines starting with philosophy have attempted to talk about "1" in words, without understanding the limits of language or how to define the undefinable. As a result, we see the "bird in the bottle" everywhere. We are not freed of the world we know, and the more we study, the more complex and inexplicable it becomes.

— This is the **"perfect ignorance"** thing, isn't it ? Our brains judge the tiny little bit of information that gets inputted into it.

Certainly, until this point, we have accumulated knowledge under the assumption that it's good to do so. We didn't know that all of it was knowledge predicated in observational error.

That's right. There isn't a single thing we understand properly. All of what we know is conditional, it **has an expiration date**—and we don't realize it. It's important that it could be nullified at any time. **On the other hand, if "the world we know" was defined as "1"—in other words, a logic based on "the definition of the undefined"—we would run into problems of rationalism linked to judgment, religious dogma, and ideological beliefs.** The world we know will always be a product of conditioning, after all, and this is just the conclusion we come to when we accept the expiration date.

— An expiration date, huh ? The thought of not using knowledge while you know you aren't certain is scary. When I think of what I may have done without realizing it... I feel sorry.

It's ok. Everyone's in the same boat. However, from here on out, you can't keep doing the same thing. In particular, we are facing an age in which AI will completely overshadow human intelligence, so it's even more important. For that reason, be sure to keep your heart in the "1" of the selfless, worldless state. Nullify, liberate yourself from the world. This is the **eraser faculty.**

— Eraser... that's useful, that faculty.

In addition, your behavior will totally change. Have you ever had an experience in which you set yourself a challenge, but when you tried to overcome it, something from your past held you back, gave you some uncertain image of the future, and you ended up doing nothing ?

— That's the story of my life. I wanted to be freed of my past and read tons of self-help books and went to seminars, but nothing worked.

I respect your efforts. However, you can move past those fears. **If you start from "1," you will be able to challenge yourself whenever you like as though you always have a fresh start—no past, no future. Just you, here, now.** You can always start with a new you, and meet new people. You can always start with "Hello."

As a result, your relationships will also completely change. Until now, the more people that accumulated in a single place, the more differences in perspective increase, the more we had to either tolerate or be tolerated, or else separate. If you approach this anxiety-laden teamwork problem from "1" , **the differences in perspective that were causing so much friction can be turned into a precious resource !**
    In fact, you will come to be interested in difference, enjoy difference, utilize difference, and find ways to synthesize differences in order to create new ideas.

— Turning the seeds of suffering into a treasure ! See things from "1."
    These simple steps can lead to some unimaginable outcomes.

That's right. From here on out, know that the idea of "working hard to become happy" is a fake. That is not true happiness.

— What ? Even though you'll become happy, it's ok to not strive for it ?

That's right. It has to happen very naturally.
    Is the Earth "trying" to rotate or revolve ? Or is it just a matter of course ?

Originally, peace, happiness, and success arose naturally in the human mind, in just the same way. Therefore, **see things in terms of what you can completely observe here and now.** In other words, observe from "1."

— The mind naturally becomes peaceful, happy, and successful... that's not something I've even dreamed of.

That said, isn't that a bit of a fairy tale ? People have been working hard for a long time, but ultimately, only a small portion of people succeed, and their happiness tends to be fleeting. I just figured that was what life was about and gave up at some point.

No. You need neither compromise nor give up.

We talked about this last time. That we've been too focused on the "happiness of heights."

However, that is not something that comes from within. It comes from invented desires.

Why ? It's because we have not been able to objectify, to absolve, the mind. However, **nTech has succeeded in discovering the mind, defining it, objectifying it, and absolving it.** Therefore, anyone can become mind itself, and **live a completely perfect life.**

— Live a completely perfect life ?

That's right.

The world of "1" does not lose to eternity, it is the world of eternal victory. Since there is only "1," it cannot be divided. It has no foes or friends. So, can there be "failure" ?

Because it moves at ultra-speed beyond time, there is no faster world. Because it is such a flexible world, it can become anything. So, can there be "failure" ?

An eternal unchanging world that does not yield to eternity.
Eternal peace, complete and perfect happiness, and victory.

— That's amazing... to think that kind of happiness, that life of victory, is possible.

That's right. And **this "1" is "One source infinity use."**

First of all, we introduced a few of the most important functions. However, "1" is a **"new substance"** that can be used in all sorts of disciplines. You, too, should find new uses for it and share it with the world with love.

— I'm looking forward to it !

Speaking of which, you said that the COVID-19 pandemic is like a wake-up call to our civilization, and I now understand what you mean. For 5 million years, human beings have been held hostage by their brains. Via COVID-19, I've seen how scary this all is.

Speaking of which, **this "virus of the brain" infects everyone unconsciously, involuntarily.** That's all the more reason that attaining liberation from this virus of the brain is supreme.

— Wow... the value of nothingness is truly amazing ! I had been looking down on it. It's the best present we humans could ask for, after suffering in the hell of perspective and this virus of the brain. Feel love that can't be put into words and have an ongoing sense of peace. Remove oneself from the confusion and chaos of this constantly changing world and attain a tranquil mind. If you can do that, how happy you would be... it's amazing to learn that such a world exists. It's like divine providence.

Also, I understand now how non-existence is prior to existence. I admit, I had always thought that "existence" is what has value... but since human bodies are also "existence," they have less value than "non-existence."

Aha. Let's keep it right there for now. There's another twist coming.

— A twist ? Well, I'm looking forward to it.

I know you were surprised at the value of nothingness, but we're still just getting started.

After all, **we still haven't gotten into the enlightenment of nTech. Right now, we're at the goal of Buddhist enlightenment.**

From a "measurement" perspective, you could say that **we've attained the ruler of a mind without 'hatch marks'.** However, we have no 'hatch marks', so this isn't yet a tool that people can use freely. For this reason, we must obtain the 'hatch marks' that will allow us to accurately measure our minds."

In Buddhism, just enlightenment is the goal. As a result, it has failed in enlightening the whole population. This is very important. That's why **nTech starts where the enlightenment of Buddhism ends.**

— This connects to the "polishing a cement block into a mirror" discussion.

You have excellent sense. **Right here and now,** the password that cannot be seen with the eye is nTech. **Right here and now,** from the enlightened perspective of the Fundamental Motion, it's important that the erroneous data of observation is not allowed to become information. If data and information—the materials of thought—are erroneous, lifestyles, cultures, civilization itself will be predicated on those same errors. That is why **human beings are unable to escape from the game of deceit—from deceiving and being deceived.**

— Ohh... human life has been a game of deceit ! I see.

That's right. **Intuition, language, emotion, logic, meaning, value, relationships. All are tools of deceit. Even perspective is a powerful tool for such deceit.**

— It's bone-chilling. Right here and now... **is the worst possible hell.**

I'm starting to see it more and more, I think. I want to achieve the enlightenment nTech has to offer as soon as I can.

CHAPTER 7

nTech's enlightenment: standardizing the "equation of being"

• The enlightenment of nTech: the second cry of the heart

Interviewer:

— Now, let's move on to the enlightenment of nTech ! We must escape from the "worst possible hell of here and now" with haste. We're in a tight spot when our ruler of the mind has no 'hatch marks'. To be clear: "I was under the impression that we had reached the end of our discussion, having finally encountered the True World and the Fundamental Motion '1' and all…"

Ah, but, I do have one lingering doubt over something that concerned me. Maybe there's a connection. We said that there is only the Fundamental Motion, right ? **If such divine fraternity exists, why is there this complex, riotous "reality" at all ?**

Jesu Noh:

That's a great thing to focus on ! Yes ! Just as you say, this is the True World—the eternal, unchanging world of the Fundamental Motion "1," the world without any change. So, if you use that world as a starting point, what kind of image comes to mind ? If you follow your nose, you'll find the answer.

Humanity's current position is the **"perspective hell"** caused by enslavement to the brain. If you make that complicated, chaotic world your standard, the True World will seem like an **unsurpassed divine fraternity.**

But on the other hand, if you make the True World your point of reference, suddenly you see an **absolute hell** to which the perspective hell doesn't even compare.

— A hell far worse than the perspective hell ? What could that possibly mean ?

Ok, so, what kind of world is the True World ? What kind of hell are we talking about ?

Let's think about it.

No border lines, no positions, no directionality—a world with no distinctions anywhere. A world without outsides.

Because there is only unity, there is nothing to encounter. There's nothing shocking. It's nothing but silence.

No encounters, no shock, no comparison, no expression, no being. Nothing but impossibilities. More than anything,

You don't know what state you're in yourself !

The world of the eternal, unchanging Fundamental Motion is *Mugen-Jigoku*—**a hell without 間 (*ma*), a spaceless realm of uninterrupted suffering where exists nothing but the one true motion.** (In Japanese, the word "間 (*ma*)-nuke" means "lack of 間 (*ma*)," or "foolish.")

Even in Buddhism, this *Mugen-Jigoku* (the Avici hell) is considered the worst possible hell.

— A hell of uninterrupted suffering... it doesn't sound good. Like a bottomless swamp, an unending sense of oppression.

It's important to try to imagine becoming this hell of uninterrupted suffering itself.

What does it mean to be there ? Well, from the "perspective hell," we have abstracted our thinking all the way to the 11th level way of observation, all the way to the simplest possible world.

This is called the **"reverse track."** It's like we've gone the opposite direction on a freeway.

— Wow ! It sounds like an extremely dangerous road.

And it was tough to go along it, right ?

Because humanity is currently in "perspective hell," it was our only point of departure.

— *Figure 30* —
Reverse track

Driving a car against the flow of traffic is dangerous!

Now, after our struggles, we've reached the most extreme possible "original point of departure." It's from here that we are able to take the **"forward track"** in the correct direction.

It will all come together quite nicely.

— I see. By moving backwards from the "perspective hell" we reached "divine fraternity."

Seeing that "divine fraternity" from the "perspective hell" certainly makes it seem like heaven, but when we become the True World itself, we realize that even that heaven is a 'hell of uninterrupted suffering.'

That's why we must move out of this "uninterrupted hell" down the road in the forward direction. Sounds good !

But what does it mean ? Is the "perspective hell" that humanity has suffered under going to become a heaven in its own right ? Hmmm...

Just wait for it.

— Ok, I understand. Now we need to figure out how to get out of the uninterrupted hell, right ?

Hmmm... so how can we create change in this world of eternal invariance ? How can we escape from this hell of uninterrupted suffering ? After all... you said it never changes ! !

The secret is... **I will make assumptions !!!**

— You shout a lot. What do you mean this time ?

The eternal invariant motion of the uninterrupted hell is full of impossibilities. However, on the other hand, it is **omniscient and omnipotent.** Therefore, it has the ability to make the impossible, possible.

So then, what was the thing we said Original Mind desired to conclusively solve ?

We said **it is the desire to know its own condition.** It is the same hellish feeling human beings experience when we don't know our own condition or understand who we are.

— That's something that has always secretly bothered me since I was a kid.

This summons another question to mind: what should you do in order to understand your own condition ? As long as there is an 'outside,' solving these doubts is a simple matter.

— An outside ?

Yes. If you can get to the outside, you can appraise yourself from the outside.

However, the problem is that the Fundamental Motion has no outside. So, you have no outside to go to.

In that case, what should you do ?

At that point, the Original Mind of the Fundamental Motion realizes something.

"Of course ! If there is no outside, then I just need to make an outside on the inside of the inside !"

The great joy of that realization is simple: "It's ok to make assumptions !"

— Uh, I still don't get it. What does declaring our will to make assumptions solve ?

Yes, I'll explain. In scientific terms, its **spontaneous symmetry breaking.** In biological terms, it's a **genetic mutation.** In psychological terms, it's **a cry of the soul to make assumptions.**

Here's what I mean. We said that the Fundamental Motion is an uninterrupted hell devoid of 間 (*ma*). **To this, we add the concept of 間 (*ma*).** This is like saying that **the Fundamental Motion becomes enlightened.**

— The Fundamental Motion becomes enlightened ?

That's right ! 間 (*ma*) suggest a closed world. What is the function of closed worlds ?

— Creating borders and boundaries ?

That's right. **Therefore, the Fundamental Motion goes from a motion without limits or restrictions to a motion with limits once you incorporate the concept of 間 (*ma*).**

This 間 (*ma*) is "complete nothingness." It's just a concept. By establishing this concept, Fundamental Motion can make the impossible, possible.

— I see ! The Fundamental Motion itself has no limitations on the Motion.
So, by creating a 間 (*ma*), the motion becomes limited. I get it !
But why does it start with the cry of the Mind to make assumptions ?
That's still a mystery.

My hint to you is **"femininity."**

— Femininity ? That doesn't help at all.

Well, don't worry.
One of the things that only women can do is get pregnant. If you try imagining the concept of **false pregnancy**, this may be even easier to understand. False pregnancy, or pseudocyesis, is a phenomenon in which a variety of symptoms of pregnancy appear in a woman despite her not being pregnant. However, **that person and everyone else around them is fooled.** This is a psychosomatic illness that arises out of the person's strong desire to have a child.

The Original Mind of the Fundamental Motion also strongly desires to make assumptions and create a world of illusion The important thing there is not questioning the assumption. The assumption has to be genuine. After all, **one must allow assumption and illusion to bring the self and the not-self—the subject and verb—into being. If they are questioned, then it's not "assumed" anymore, right ?**

— I see. Because it's no good to be in a state of pure self, one has to invent fictions of "self and not-self," or even imagine them... in a way, it's a profound wisdom.

That's right. That's why **this reality is all a dream of the Original Mind of the Fundamental Motion.**
It is an illusion, a hologram.

In other words, this reality is both created and acted out by the Original Mind, the movement of the fundamental mind.

Let's consider it in terms of the "watching a movie" analogy.
Here's a story of an extremely busy elite businessman. He had a special ability in his sense of smell. He was able to sniff out the salary and needs of the people around him. For that reason, he was very popular and never got a rest. However, sometimes he felt that he'd like to take a break.
One day, he decided to take the day off and see a movie. He started driving to the movie theater, but he kept getting assaulted by the smells of people, even at traffic lights. Each time, he'd think to himself how it would be great to introduce to those people the products they need—but he had made his decision to take the day off, so he kept his mouth shut and endured it.
Once he reached the theater and went inside, he got assaulted by the smells of everyone around him, and had to hold himself back again. In a seat two rows in front, there was a man with an annual salary of 1 million dollars, but he stayed in his assigned seat and said nothing. Five minutes before the film was about to start, he smelled a neighbor to his right with an annual salary of 1 billion dollars, but because he had decided he wasn't going to work that day, he said nothing and just focused on the screen ahead. Three minutes after the film began, he smelled a neighbor to his left

with a salary of 10 billion dollars, but again he said nothing, looked for the protagonist among the many characters on screen, and focused on the film.

The smells of the people to his left and right and all the others faded away. He empathized with the protagonist, laughed and cried along with their journey, and completely stopped noticing any smells.

He dissolved completely into the hero of the film. He was no longer "the businessman."

After the film ended and he was on his way home, he came to his senses suddenly: "Ah ! That person over there has 1 trillion dollars !"

— I see ! **It began with personal resolve**, and as that resolve restricts motion more and more, the original self is forgotten and morphs into a sort of avatar. That result is the present, this reality, myself… I guess. And I suppose these days the "false pregnancy movie" is getting rave reviews.

That's the gist of it. However, this is still too abstract, so let's boil it down to something a bit more concrete.

There is only the Fundamental Motion of unity. From there, how do energy, matter, and this reality emerge ? If we cannot figure out that structure without inconsistencies in our most advanced math and physics, we can't connect any of this to the various problems we face. However, the level we're at is still insufficient. Let's move forward while going into more detail regarding the integration of Eastern cosmology into this contradiction-free state.

• The equation of being: the structure that brings forth all

Right now, what we are talking about is an **equation of being** that looks at how being is able to be. **How does something arise from nothing ? What is the structure that brings forth all things (dimensions, change) ?**

— We're entering into some crazy territory. We looked at equations of motion before that took entities for granted and described how they moved, but this is actually an "equation of being" that describes how "being" itself emerges from the One Motion ! **I've never heard of anyone who has talked about how time, space, beings, and energy emerge before !**

I hope you're looking forward to it ! Let's dive in.

We said that the Fundamental Motion has no boundaries, no directions, no positions.
    If so, are there subjects or verbs ?

— It goes without saying—there are not.
    It's not possible to describe "something" "doing" anything, because it's a single motion that cannot be divided.

That's right. However, in the reality we perceive, there's tons of subjects and verbs. **How do subjects and verbs emerge from a world without subjects and verbs ? This is the big issue.** Let's start with that first event. Listen to what I say and try to imagine it.

All there is, is the Fundamental Motion, the motion of mind. From there, the mind obtained 間 (*ma*) through the will to make assumptions. "Mind" floods into that 間 (*ma*). **From there, "mind only (1)" is within a single point, and outside of it is "nothing at all" (0) that goes on forever (∞). In equation form, this is 1=0=∞.**

Next, all of the "mind" that entered into this "間 (*ma*)" floods to the outside. **When this happens, there is nothing (0) in the interval, and mind (1) is outside of the 間 (*ma*), stretching on forever (∞). In equation form, this is 0=1=∞.**

This is the repeating inside-out total motion of mind that we have often talked about. **It is the birth of "conceivable motion of mind" that totally consumes space and time. I explained this before in terms of the two motions of expansion (∞ emanation) and condensation (∞ contraction), but they are together a single motion.**

— *Figure 31* —
The total motion of mind ①

The smallest space

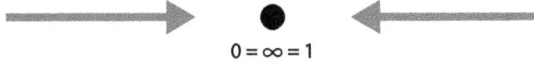

$0 = \infty = 1$

Inside the point there is only Mind, and outside there is endless nothingness

The biggest space

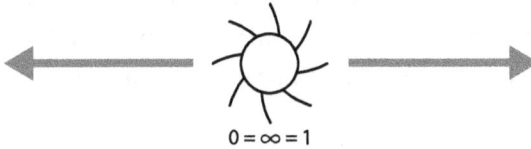

$0 = \infty = 1$

Expansion of Mind from inside a point flooding to the outside
Mind overflows in the realm of non-existence

— *Figure 32* —
The total motion of mind ②

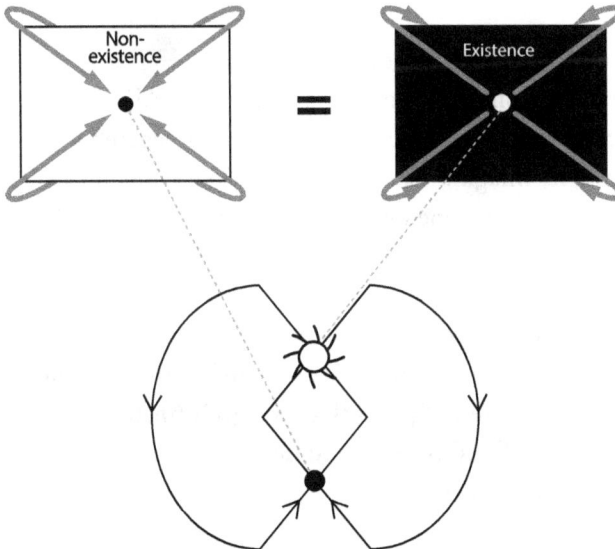

Tah (∞ expansion) and compression (∞ condensation) are
a simultaneous unified motion

— Yes, I can imagine what you've said so far. It's the image of ∞ motion yet 0 motion.

That's right. Now, a question. **What kind of world is the biggest world ?**

— Ummm... we said last time that the definition of the biggest world is a world with no "outside" !

That's right. However, that was actually just a crude definition. This is a bit of a digression, but while we use words like "small" or "big" in our daily lives all the time, any attempt to define them is going to end up in a circular word trap, isn't it ?

— Yes, I found this difficult last time.

Well, as it happens, nobody has ever been able to define these concepts clearly before. So, let's see if we can define them.

• I The Biggest World

So first, let's consider the biggest world.

As a starting point, let's go with a "biggest world" that has a concrete size. You can imagine it in the same way as you imagined it last time.

For example, imagine that there is a normal ballpoint pen in front of your eyes. You can imagine one 10 times that size, right ? How about 100 times ? 1,000 times ? Can you imagine a pen 1 quadrillion times the size ? Just as you are able to identify where the pen is, you can identify a location where the pen is *not*, and therefore the pen can't be the biggest possible thing. In other words, **any "biggest world" that assumes a specific size must be composed of parts that extend infinitely with no outside. This concept is defined in mathematical symbols as ∞.** So, what about a world bigger than "∞" ?

— Bigger than ∞... ?

If the world you see with your eyes is your standard, it's tough to make your thoughts stretch that far.

So, if you wonder what comes next, well, you could choose not to assume a *specific* size, and instead, **you could assume an "abstract size."** For example, the abstract sizes associated with freedom or love. Once you start using these, **"0" can be seen as bigger than "∞," which it contains.**

— Ah, I see. Certainly, it's easier to imagine something bigger on the abstract scale than the concrete scale.

Not only that, but this "0" goes straight through the contents of "∞" size. It's like how neutrinos are able to pass unimpeded through your body.

In addition, "0" can be in the absolute dead center of "∞ size" and pull "∞" in. That is to say, **"0 can be defined by its ability to ① encompass ∞, ② freely move through ∞, and ③ drag ∞ in."**

— That's interesting. It both encompasses it, passes through it, and draws it in. It has a high degree of freedom.

Now then, what world is even bigger than either "∞" or "0" ?

— What ? There's more ? Which must mean... we have ∞ and 0, so next is "1" ?

That's right ! So now think of this. What is the commonality between ∞ of specific size and 0 of abstract size ?
  Both of them assume that size is fixed. In this case, "0" can be defined as the biggest.

Now then, what would happen if we put the "motion that causes the arising and ceasing of size" into these two defined sizes (abstract and specific) ?
  This motion is capable of both "0" and "∞" and yet is neither "0" nor "∞." In other words, **it becomes a motion capable of "0" and "∞" simultaneously. This motion is larger than both ∞ and 0, and is defined as "1."**

Imagine a bar magnet. What happened when we tried to split it apart ? The N/S polarity isn't split—instead, you create a new "N" and "S" on each piece. That is to say, N and S are not separate things. They are a "something" that is both N and S and also neither N nor S.

— I see. Rather than being a fixed size, the motion that creates those two encompasses them both and creates the "biggest world."

• II The smallest world

Excellent. Now, how might we define the smallest world ? Where do you think we should start ?

— From a specific size ?

Yes, let's start from there. First of all, let's go from our outline from last time. The smallest concept in the notion of specific sizes is the point. Smaller than this point is a point inside a point, and so forth. You end up with an infinitesimally small point if you repeat that pattern. In this way, the smallest world is one in which there is no area in which to put anything; the area is 0. But on top of that, it must be an area that permits back-and-forth movement and penetration. This is "間 (*ma*)." 間 *(ma)* is the world of **mind with no specific size. This can be depicted mathematically as "0." This 間 (*ma*) is pure mind, mind at a level with no assumptions at all.**

— Mind with no assumptions... OK, I get it.

The 間 (*ma*) of this level of mind can accommodate an infinite amount of assumptions. When that happens, **it becomes a 間 (*ma*) of mind so full that is fit to burst, and is represented as "∞." This "∞" becomes a smaller 間 (*ma*) than "0."**

— Because it's an assumption, it can flood infinitely into the smallest specific size of "0" ?

That's right. So, what happens to this 間 (*ma*) even smaller than "∞" ?

It's in a charged state that's like an assumption that wants to nullify the assumptions of infinity. It's the motion of mind that goes between "0" and "∞," even more assumptively charged than "∞." This motion can be defined as the smallest possible world, "1."

— Ah ! In both the biggest and smallest worlds, 0=∞=1.

This total nothingness is a motion in which the biggest and smallest are the same. That is to say, the biggest motion = the smallest motion.

Everything that follows is an imitation of this "conceivable motion of mind." On the inside of this mind, motion is even further limited. This is "energy."

How can one know who they are from within the uninterrupted hell ? The Answer to this Question is the cry of the soul declaring the will to make assumptions ! You obtain a 間 (*ma*), and a conceivable motion of mind emerges.

Everything that follows is like an Action that takes on even more assumptions.

By the way, human beings are also always engaged in this Question, Answer, Action cycle. The pattern we observe in the beginning repeats in a fractal manner.

— That's interesting ! I thought this world was complicated, but in fact it's all quite simple.

• III The birth of subjects and verbs

So. How do we get subjects and verbs from a place of no subjects and verbs ? Let's look at the "departure point for events."

There is a cup here. Let's say I put a snake inside that is writhing violently. Does the cup with the snake in it move ?

— If the snake inside is thrashing around... the cup will probably also move.

That's right ! So, in the same way, **if you forced all conceivable motion to stay inside the confines of a small vessel, what do you think will happen ? The vessel will move too. So, the vessel (subject) moves (verb). That is the birth of subjects and verbs.**

Next is the same fractal. You push it into an even smaller space and make it move inside there. You reduce it this way 5 times. **This is the energy algorithm. It has the characteristic of 1:1 symmetry like subject and verb and like the yin and yang of Eastern cosmology. This fivefold repetition of 1:1 symmetry is like the five elements of the same cosmological system: there is no contradiction.**

By the way, do you know about the essence of energy ?

— The essence of energy ? I can't say that I do...

OK. **Energy is the state of 2 things moving in one; that is to say, the presence of contradiction.** The size of the contradiction determines the size of the energy.

In the 1:1 symmetry of energy, there is no cause and effect. Why would that be ? It's because the speed of energy is a superposition speed of instantaneous motion. It has the 1:1 of subject and verb, but no cause and effect. Yet it has subject and verb. It's a bit mysterious.

When the 1:1 symmetry of energy reaches the fifth level (critical point), it undergoes a phase transition, and becomes matter. At that level of materialization, subject and verb becomes clear.

— Energy turns into matter... it reminds me of E=mc2. Is this the same thing as how the distortion of spacetime (energy) = the distribution of mass ?

Yes, yes. We're about finished.

By the way, there is a marker here. This marker is not something that actually exists in an absolute sense, but you already knew that. If it absolutely existed, it would exist 100 years ago and 1,000 years ago and 100 years from now and 1,000 years from now. But that can't be.

— *Figure 33* —
The structure of subjects and predicates

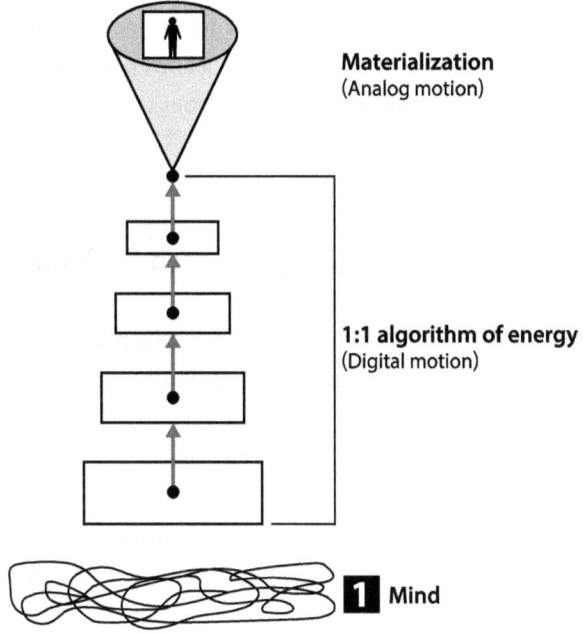

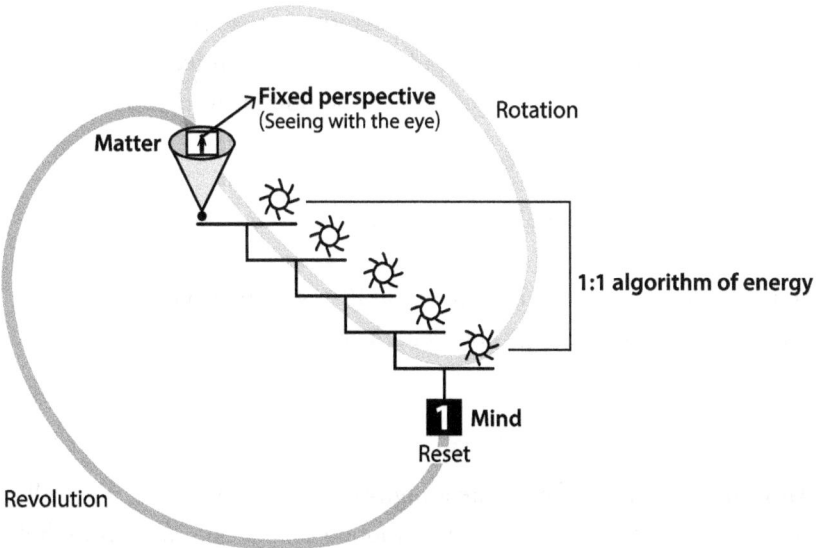

Materialization
(Analog motion)

1:1 algorithm of energy
(Digital motion)

1 Mind

Fixed perspective
(Seeing with the eye)

Rotation

Matter

1:1 algorithm of energy

1 Mind
Reset

Revolution

— I see. Because I based things on my five senses, I had never noticed these basic contradictions, and dogmatically believed in the world I could physically see. That was careless, huh ?

It happens. But in fact, **in order for beings to "be," there is a motion behind the scenes that the brain cannot perceive—the energy algorithm.** It's the **1:1 symmetry** I told you about before. Let's look at it in a little more detail.

• IV The relationship between digital and analog motion

For example, there is a smartphone and a handkerchief here. Can you watch a movie with a handkerchief ? Obviously, you can't. However, you can with your smartphone. Both are made of matter, so what's so different ? Why can you watch movies on your smartphone ?

— Well, smartphone use a digital algorithm of "0" and "1" to create the display, using programming (motion in the background). That background motion is what leads to the display on the smartphone. Oh... I see !

You noticed ! When you see the smartphone display as a marker, you see that markers also have a background algorithm that creates markers. Of course, this is not just markers—all entities in the universe are like this. The motion of this energy algorithm, while inferior to the motion of the mind, is nonetheless fierce and intense.

— Hmmm... what kind of motion is it ?

You know what it is ! You remember the 10^{500} vibrations per second, right ? It's the vibrations of energy—of vacuum energy.

— Ohh, I see !

Also, the brain is, in fact, quite a high-functioning machine. After all, it takes just a tiny part of this intense motion and creates an illusory hologram that it convinces itself "exists."

The human brain is incapable of perceiving the digital motion of energy acting in the background. It would actually probably be a problem if we could (laughs). **The brain only perceives the illusory, holographic material universe.** You know, brain habits.

Think of it like a high-tech flipbook. The brain doesn't perceive the blank bits—only the images—and creates an "analog motion" that makes the pictures appear to be continuous.

By the way, does the light from fluorescent bulbs look smooth to you ?

— What ? Well, sure, it looks smooth. Why ?

It seems that way, right ? But is the light actually on continuously ? As it happens, it's just blinking on and off very fast. A typical fluorescent or LED bulb is flickering 100–120 times a second, while inverter types do so dozens of thousands of times.

— I see ! It blinks so much, but to the human eye, it appears as a continuous light. I guess that's thanks to the brain's abilities. I think I understand the correlation between digital and analog motion a little better now.

That's right, thanks to that function of the brain, we live our lives without ever doubting that the continuous existence of the universe, time, space, and all being are all absolute.

However, the perceptions of the brain are based on a tiny portion of information, and without knowing about the hologram the brain creates, we end up in **"observational error."**

— That's a problem, like putting the first button of your shirt into the wrong buttonhole... so I can see, then, how **all the information, logic, knowledge, theory, academia, technology, commerce, business, industry, culture, civilization, and history of humanity is in error.** There may be nothing more terrifying than living without knowing about the observational error. The idea that we will be in error no matter how hard we try is just too cruel.

It's true. Yet human beings have not doubted the perspective of their own brain. Moreover, the insistence on things being absolute has led to the emergence of all kinds of problems. As a result, our current civilization is suffering from terminal cancer.

• The structure that gives rise to time

By the way, at this point, I imagine you have an understanding of the structure that gives rise to time ?

This is the structure that gives rise to discontinuity from continuity, the structure that gives rise to irreversibility from reversibility, the structure that gives rise to yin and yang and the five elements, the structure that gives rise to the five senses, the structure that gives rise to the 5 vibrational patterns of strings. There are a lot of ways to express it, but how do you explain it ? Think about it for a moment.

— What !? You want me to figure it out ? Well, I had understood that analog motion emerges from digital motion... ummm...

I can see you're willing to give it a shot ! Here's a hint.

The critical condition is **the ability to explain the relationship between "mind that perceives continuity" and "mind that perceives discontinuity (such as conditioned motion/expiring motion/motion limited by its expiration date, etc.)"** In other words, it's the **"structure that gives rise to mind that perceives part, out of mind that perceives whole."** This structure must use a coherent description of motion of mind to answer the following question:

From an inconceivable motion without beginning or end, how could time arise ?

From a formless, orderless motion, how could time, space, entities arise ? From a limitless motion of mind, how could a limited motion of energy come into being ?

— Ahhh... I'm going to try to put this together, so give me a second.

So, first of all. **The mind that perceives all is the "inconceivable motion of mind,"** right ? That mind, utilizing the concept of 間 (*ma*) with the exertion of will to make assumptions, leads to a conceivable motion of mind.

However, that conceivable mind moves via the total use of time and space, so **energy is what continues to restrict its range of motion.** After the motion of energy is repeated across 5 levels, it undergoes a phase transition and eventually materializes...

By the way, **why is it 5 levels ?**

That's pretty good.

With the repeated 1:1 motion of *Tah* (∞ expansion) and condensation (∞ compression) the range is reduced. By the 5th level, the *Tah* becomes "間 (*ma*)," the smallest world.

If you do that, **can it be compressed ?**

— What ? Where is it being compressed ? If the smallest world is *Tah*, then it can't compress right ? So, then what does it do ?

There ! That's right ! That's why this moment requires **the second strong exertion of will !**

Mind is enlightened and 間 (*ma*) appears. In this way, the *ma* of energy is the **perspective of the brain.** It's the strong determination to take only a part of what's there. **The "mind that perceives only part" is this perspective of the brain.**

The brain can perceive neither energy nor mind. It cuts through all, perceiving only matter.

Therefore, this will within will is the universe of matter that we have always taken for granted. **Matter is a momentary mental event in the motion of mind and energy. From each moment to the next, the brain links together the afterimage phenomena it receives. This is the emergence of time. Time = displacement ÷ speed.**

The universe that we perceive makes possible all the encounters the brain experiences. This universe emerged from the interaction-less Original Mind of Fundamental Motion's will to know itself, leading to the creation of discontinuous energy, which was itself broken down again.

— Time is created via afterimages in the brain... as a result, all sorts of interactions become possible. Truth has neither past nor future. However, **the linkage of momentary mental events creates not only entities, but all the events of past and future.** The brain is pretty incredible.

Yes, the universe is mysterious and sacred. All that exists hangs in harmonic balance via the structure of cause and effect.

However, human beings are even more mysterious and sacred than the universe. Reality is nothing but physical laws devoid of meaning or value. In comparison, humans have created so much meaning, so much value, analyzing it all, earnestly living in this fictional world with their "creative system for agreement" called happiness.

Yet the awe of Original Mind, which has produced and nullified all of these things, is profound and holy beyond description. **The fictional creation and consummation of enlightenment of Original Mind, and the roaring transformation that recreates that fiction anew. The idea that human beings can recognize that their true self is this Original Mind, which encapsulates all things into a single eternal, invariant motion, is simply amazing.**

Mind is not closed. Gödel—considered the most logical of all mathematicians—is responsible for the incompleteness theorems that state that no system of a consistent set of axioms can demonstrate its own consistency. nTech's position that only the inconceivable, imperceptible, intangible Original Mind *actually* exists is very much in agreement with Gödel's theorems.

Pre-enlightenment–in this reality of expansive nature, of oneself and one's world—the manifold transformations of manifold entities harmonize in all manner of changes and movements.

— *Figure 34* —
The structure that gives rise to time

Reality = Afterimages of the brain
= Perceptible by the brain
= Speed of the brain

$$\frac{S}{V} = \text{Time}$$

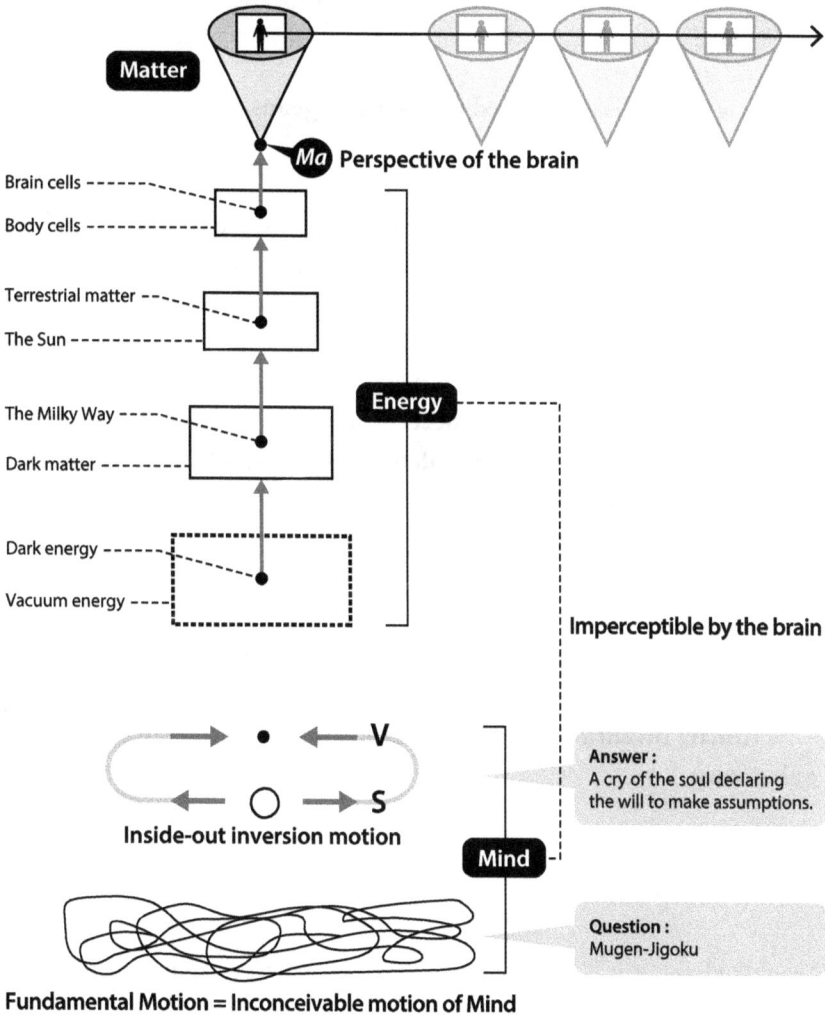

Matter

Ma Perspective of the brain

Brain cells
Body cells

Terrestrial matter
The Sun

Energy

The Milky Way
Dark matter

Dark energy
Vacuum energy

Imperceptible by the brain

V

S

Inside-out inversion motion

Mind

Answer:
A cry of the soul declaring
the will to make assumptions.

Question:
Mugen-Jigoku

Fundamental Motion = Inconceivable motion of Mind

In spite of this, **we reach the Truth that there is no change at all—there is only inconceivable motion.** This is truly a transcendental claim. **Between pre-enlightenment and post-enlightenment,** *nothing changes.*

Are you, right now, able to accept that the reality before your eyes is the structure for creating the illusion of Original Mind ?

— Well... I feel like I have no choice but to agree logically, but it's not easy to accept.

That's right. **The Truth is used by the courageous.**

— I think I know what you mean.

Throughout human history, the people who have brought us huge discoveries and inventions required courage in order to do it. The airplane was that way, as was the car and elevator.

There's some important terms in there. **The things that humans need more than anything else to succeed are discoveries and inventions. They are connected with complete perfection, ultimate unmoving mind, and unmoving will.**

— What ! Really ? Why ?

Ultimate discoveries lead to the acquisition of complete tools for eternal victory.

Ultimate inventions lead to the acquisition of perfect roads for eternal victory.

— Discoveries are a complete tool ? Inventions are a perfect road ? What does that mean ?

We talked about it before, but as a refresher, try to imagine what kind of state **"eternal victory"** would be.

First, all foes are under total control, and foes never appear again for all eternity.

No enemies, no opponents, no world. So ultimately **there is no self**, either. It's **the fastest situation, and the most flexible and full of potential.** If it's a situation that is indestructible, that's eternal victory, isn't it ? Being able to visualize this is the discovery of Original Mind.

Therefore, the discovery of Original Mind is **the acquisition of a complete tool for eternal victory.**

— I see ! I get it ! By the way, what do you mean by invention ? Why will invention become the perfect road ?

If possession of the visualization and complete tools for eternal victory is an absolute, ideal paradise, then it's clear that **being controlled by one's brain and only seeing reality with the physical eye while struggling for survival is horribly tragic, cruel, and disgraceful. It is a hell of all forms of suffering.**

If you find a clear path to completely synthesizing the reality of this hell and the ideal of this paradise, without the slightest gap in space or time, then you will have found the perfect path to eternal victory.

— If that's true, then yeah.

That is the enlightenment of nTech !

— That's amazing !

We'll discuss this more later in the context of **group enlightenment.**

By the way, we talked before about how $0=\infty=1$ is the original, fundamental motion, right ?

— Yes, it's quite a discovery. It being the origin of everything means everything takes off from there. For example, just like the "one source infinity use" mentioned previously, it can be used to bring together all disciplines—if it couldn't, it wouldn't be the origin.

That's right. $0=\infty=1$ enables the raising of our standards. It will fill in for our deficiencies and lead us to completion as we find previously unseen relationships across fields and synthesize them. **There are no limits to the "one source infinity use" applications to reality.**

— I understand you logically. But to be honest, I'm still having a hard time visualizing concretely how these things connect.

No problem. But first, let's start with the queen of the sciences, the discipline closest to Truth: mathematics.

CHAPTER 8

One Source, Infinity Use

• A Mathematical Approach

Jesu Noh:
Now then, shall we discuss mathematics ? Do you think of calculation as "mathematics" ?

Actually, they are not the same. But before we talk about math, let's talk about the concept of "the Theory of Mathematics." Have you ever thought about the concept of "the Theory of Mathematics" before ?

Interviewer:
— You mean what "the Theory of Mathematics" is ? I've never thought about it. Oh—but I've heard that it's difficult to define. For example, 0 and negative numbers can't actually be found in the real world, so there was resistance to them at first. How would you define it ?

What is "the Theory of Mathematics" ? There have been many attempts throughout history to define the concept. However, there remains no definition with which all are satisfied. That's how difficult the problem is. However, because mathematics is all about the study of the Theory of Mathematics, it's an issue to not have a definition. **I have defined "the Theory of Mathematics" as "rate of instantaneous change."**

— Rate of instantaneous change ? This is the first I've heard of it.

I said that Original Mind—the eternally unchanging Fundamental Motion—watches a "dream" of its own will to understand itself. Observing that dream requires the material/substance of dreams (subject and verb), and via the structure that gives rise to subject and verb, a wide range of subjects and verbs emerge.

Original Mind is the number of the rate of absolute instantaneous change.

"Number" is what describes the *theory* of instantaneous rate change and *size* of the various subjects (of the subject/verb kind) when Original Mind creates conditioned change in various subjects and verbs.

Of course, this is just the definition that nTech uses.

— So, there's a difference between "Number" and " the Theory of Mathematics."

That's right.

Therefore, the point of reference is the eternal and invariant Fundamental Motion of Original Mind.

The first material needed in order for that motion to observe its dream is imaginary numbers, then the instantaneous rate of change of energy as imaginary numbers collect together as they engage in *Tah* (∞ expansion)/condensation (∞ compression), then the instantaneous rate of change of matter as energy comes together, etc...

— Imaginary numbers are material... ?

Yes, I'll explain them one by one. First, **there are three types of number.**

1. R: Real numbers
2. i: imaginary numbers
3. J: restored number

"Restored number" will be new to you too.

This is an expanded concept that incorporates the idea of perspective into the total motion of mind, $0=\infty=1$.

The restored number (J) is numbers for which the instantaneous rate of change never changes—they are absolute instantaneous rates of change. These numbers have fixed speed, move at a speed inconceivable by the brain, and have neither directionality nor position.

The imaginary numbers (i) are relative instantaneous rates of change and make conceivable the inconceivable instantaneous rates of change (J).

The synthesis of various numbers that cause changes (verbs) in various states (subjects) via the instantaneous rates of change of imaginary numbers (i) become the real numbers (R). Therefore, the real numbers (R) can express a variety of relative instantaneous rates of change in functions using proportional expressions.

— Maybe I get it, maybe I don't... I'm trying though—help me out a little !

Ok, let's do it !

The real numbers (R) express relative instantaneous rates of change using functions.

Imaginary numbers (i)—the motion of conceivable relative instantaneous rates of change—make possible the measurement of the proportional relationships of those functions.

The restored number (J)—inconceivable, position-less, directionless, size-less, absolute instantaneous rates of change—create the imaginary numbers (i).

These 3 explain all physical and psychological phenomena.

I said before that *Tah* (∞ expansion) and condensation (∞ compression) have a 1:1 symmetry.

The instantaneous rate of changes themselves change relatively via this 1:1 conditioned change—this is "the Theory of Mathematics."

In other words, if *Tah* (∞ expansion) is a function (f (x), perspective), then the things derived from those functions will change. That's why numbers appear different. However, since the eternal invariant "1" is just observing a dream, everything can't come out equal. In other words, you need to create "difference."

Mathematics attempts to equalize all differences using the fundamental concepts of differentials and integrals to cause changes in scale via proportional expressions, functions, and formulas.

Consequently, mathematics is the discipline that creates new concepts. It attempts to understand natural phenomena using number as a tool. As a result, mathematics is a discipline suited to enlightenment. The reason it is only "suited" to enlightenment is because **mathematics remains incomplete.**

— Now that you mention it... I hadn't realized it, but disciplines themselves may have a teleology. However, it's a big issue if people are going through their entire educations studying these incomplete subjects. Obviously, the person studying these things won't achieve clarity of thought, and they may end up more confused.

Hence the need for 0=∞=1. It's like the final piece of the puzzle. It invalidates nothing of what human beings have accomplished so far, and beautifully ties together and elevates it all.

The discovery of 0=∞=1 completes the field of mathematics and propels us to absolute enlightenment. **By incorporating "mind" into mathematics, the discipline is perfected.**

— The completion of mathematics ! If that's true, it'll cause shockwaves the world over ! Ah, but since it's the discovery of 0=∞=1 that enabled that completion, the shock is even bigger ! Amazing !

Thank you. Let's keep going.

Physical phenomena like natural and social phenomena all have an attribute of "scale." This is described with real numbers (R), which can be depicted with a single number line. The integral side shows matter increasing in scale, while the differential side shows energy decreasing in scale. Whether you're talking about matter or energy, ultimately each point can only be represented by a single position on the line, and can be depicted via 1:1 symmetry. This is known as the **"completeness of the real numbers."**

But what about **"worlds without scale"** that the real numbers (R) cannot represent ? How should we express freedom, love, dignity ? How should we express these abstract realms with no concrete scale ? **nTech uses the imaginary numbers (i) to express them.** These abstract realms are defined as the **"world of mind."**

— The imaginary numbers are mind ? So, does that mean the Fundamental Motion is imaginary numbers ? In that case, has the Fundamental Motion been incorporated in mathematics without our realizing it ?"
But you said that 0=∞=1 is "J"... I'm getting confused...

Oh, no, no. The mind I'm talking about is the "conceivable motion of mind." It's the "repeated inside-out motion." There were levels to "mind," remember ? In terms of Zen, these are levels 6 and 7.

Incidentally, the 8th level of Zen, *hisōhihisō*, is the "*ma* of mind," the same *ma* that Original Mind of the Fundamental Motion obtains as a consequence of enlightenment. The number for the source movement is "J," so it's between "J" and "i," or "enlightened J." We'll talk about "J" more later.

By the way, I don't think I even need to say it, but in mathematics, there are no claims that imaginary numbers are "mind" or "motion." Imaginary numbers are not well-understood in math, but they have been included in math because their use allows various ideas to become consistent and easy to understand.

— I see. So imaginary numbers are still not understood very well.

That's right. Let's continue. If you square any real number (R), you will always get a positive (matter). However, if you square any imaginary number (i/ mind), you get a minus (energy). If you raise any imaginary number to the 4th power, you get a positive number (matter). What do you think this means ?

This can be used to explain the "repeated inside-out motion."

If squaring is seen as the repeated inside-out motion, then the square of an imaginary number (i)—that is, an inside-out flip—results in energy. If the energy is squared (inside-out flip), it becomes matter.

— I see ! That comes together nicely.

Therefore, it's important to determine how far to go with imaginary numbers (i). **How long can a coherent thought be maintained ?** Imaginary numbers (i) are turned into energy, and energy is turned into matter.

— A coherent thought... it's difficult. But I understand why it's difficult, thanks to your explanation. Since what you see with your eyes will turn into transient thoughts, feelings, or intents, there's no chance of them continuing on forever. Conversely, from the perspective of the Fundamental Motion "1," there will be no back and forth due to changing conditions: it's possible to burn on and on with a steadfast mind.

— Figure 35 —
The complex plane

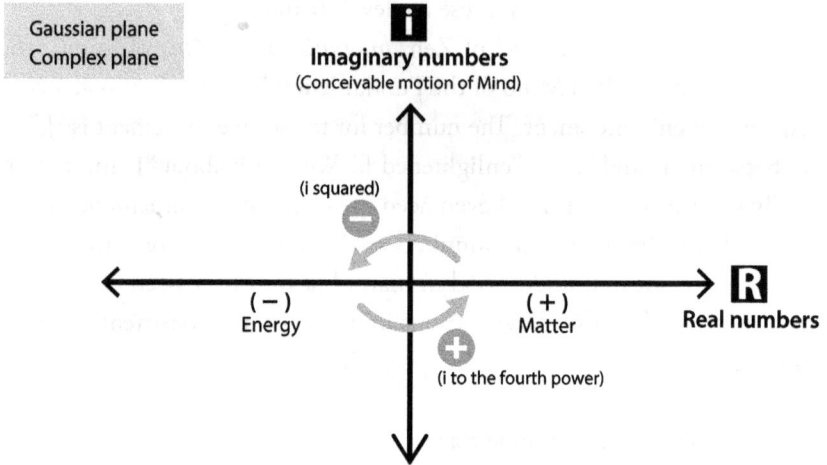

That's right.

In this way, **all physical phenomena can be depicted on the 2D complex plane (Gaussian plane) with real numbers (R) and imaginary numbers (i). 0=∞=1 adds a third dimensional axis, "perspective," to the 2D complex plane. This is a new concept.**

— Oh ! So, this brings a new idea into mathematics ! Yet another discovery ! So, what does it mean ?

It will cause an upheaval even greater than the shift from geocentrism to heliocentrism !

I said that all physical phenomena can be depicted on a 2D complex plane. **Humans have always focused on that "single plane" (their perspective) as everything and became fixated on it.** This attitude is similar to the geocentrism of the past that claimed that the Earth doesn't move and that celestial bodies move around the Earth. Nobody doubted it. Are you able to tell that the Earth moves with your 5 senses ? You can't, right ? It's the same idea.

— It's true, I can't feel the Earth's movement at all. But what does this mean ?

Human beings didn't even know that they were sticking to just one part of the complex plane and have had absolute faith in their 5 senses, doubting nothing.

Yes ! This is called the **"geocentrism of perspective."** However, there is not actually just one perspective. Human beings are confined by the perspective of the human brain and take it as absolutely true, but there is also the perspective of dogs, the perspective of cats... and an infinite number of other diverse perspectives. Moreover, even within the human brain perspective, there are differences among the 7.7 billion different individuals across the globe. As more people are born, the number of perspectives increases. So, if you add everyone's personal evaluation criteria, the scope swells even farther out.

— I think I now have an even better sense of the idea of "innumerable perspectives."

Another important thing is that while there are infinite perspectives, **there is also a state of 0 perspective.** This is an unlimited state that exists prior to the emergence of energy perspective, or scale. In other words, it is the "Fundamental One Motion." There are no perspectives here.
Limited infinities of perspectives emerge from that 0 perspective in 1D, 2D, 3D, etc.

For example. Let's say there is a carrot here. How many carrots are there ?

— There would be 1 carrot.

That's right. From the perspective of the human brain (3D perception), you'll see "one carrot." But how do you know for sure that there's "one" ? That isn't really the case. For example, if you took a cross-section view with an MRI (2D perception/perspective), you'd see an infinite number of slices. In this sense, completely different worlds emerge when you move between dimensions. However, out of an infinite number of perspectives (dimensions), human beings are stuck in a single dimension (the perspective of the human brain). As long as that is true, freedom is unattainable.

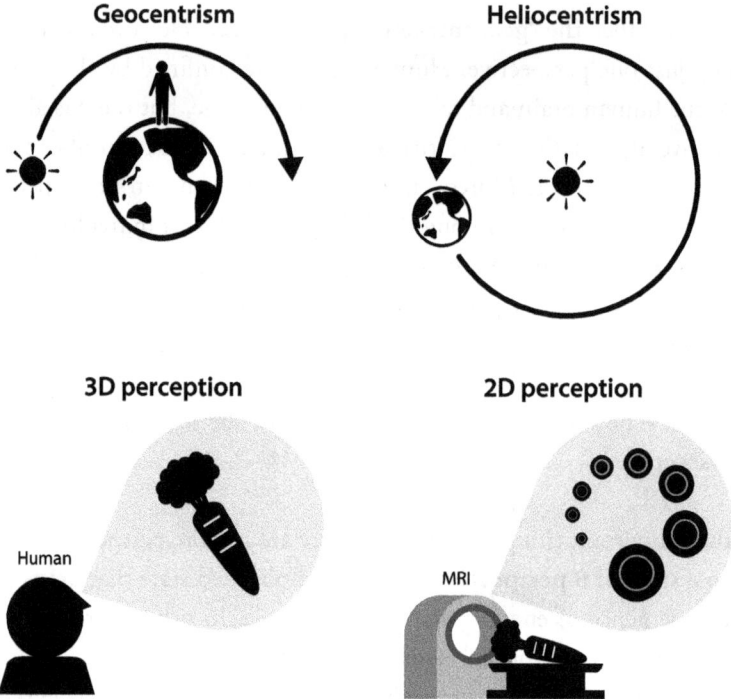

— Figure 36 —
Geocentrism and heliocentrism. The 3D and 2D carrot

Geocentrism   Heliocentrism

3D perception   2D perception

Human

MRI

— Human beings really are restricted so long as they stay within the perspective of the mind. A bird in a bottle...

Once liberated from the brain, it becomes possible for one's perspective to flit between the 0 state, 1, and ∞. **It becomes possible to go back and forth between existence and non-existence.** That motion is the "Fundamental Motion, the source of the world," expressed mathematically as $0=\infty=1$. **The only thing that actually exists in truth is God.** In other words, there is only the transcendental motion of $0=\infty=1$, imperceptible by the human brain.

— What ? Did you say God ? That's quite a bold claim.

Yes, you picked up on that, I see. It's true. **I said that 0=∞=1 is "God in equation form." The dream that that God is observing is the world of perspective ∞. The world of the perspective of the human brain is looking at one part of that perspective ∞. In other words, since 0=∞=1 is something created by the perspective of the human mind, it's synonymous with "God created the human universe," right ?**

— Yes, that's right. The concept of God in religious thinking states that God is the creator of the universe, so there's no contradiction.

— *Figure 37* —
The 3D pattern of JiR

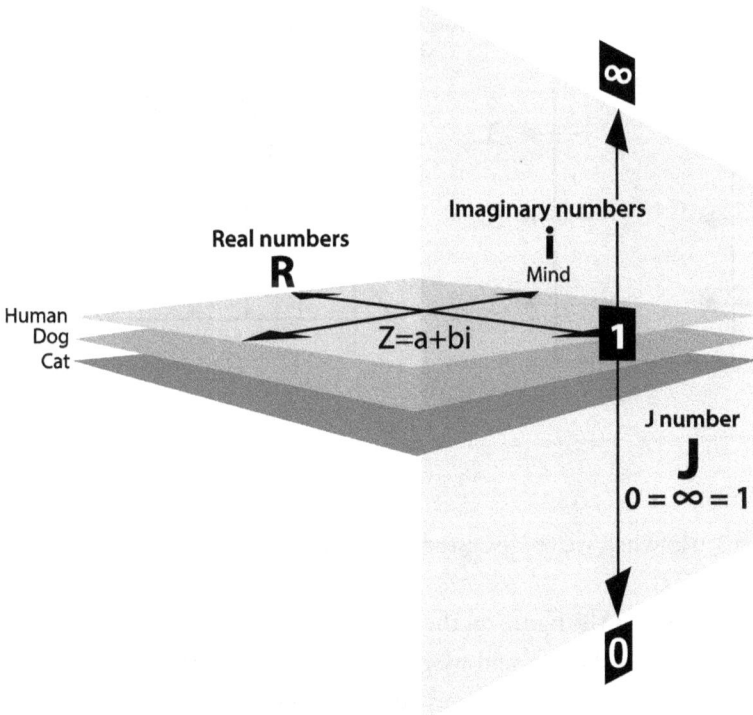

That's right. So, **I created the restored number (J) for this new concept of numbers that describe 0=∞=1. If the imaginary numbers (i) are conceivable motion of mind, the restored number (J) are the inconceivable fundamental motion of mind: Original Mind.**

There are several inspirations behind the use of the letter "J": **J is the letter that follows i for the imaginary numbers, it indicates its nature as God itself (Jesus number), it refers to the location of the concept's origin (Japan's number), and it even stands for my name, as the discoverer (Jesu's number) !**

— *Figure 38* —
The conversion apparatus

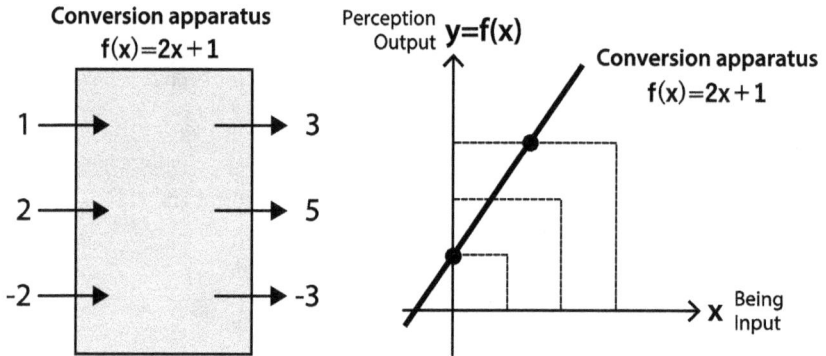

So, let's use what we've discussed as our base to connect perspective to mathematics.

Take a look at the figure on the left. There's a box in the middle, we put numbers in from the left, and we get output from the right.

If we put 1 in the box, 3 comes out, if we put 2 in the box, 5 comes out, if we put -2 in the box, -3 comes out.

— I see, so what does that mean ?

This box is a conversion apparatus. It is a 間 (*ma*) that connects the relationship between numbers.

When you're using numbers, it's a "function," and as a numerical formula, it's f(x) = 2x+1 in this case.

When you're talking about mind it's "perspective." If you think of it in terms of glasses it's easy to understand.

— So, in other words, **perspective = function ?**

That's right. If your input is (X) and your output is (Y), if you input X (natural phenomena) into a perspective, you get an output Y (will) in the form of an imaginary number.

In terms of the complex plane, the world you can see with your eyes is the X axis in the form of energy (E) and matter (m), and upon observation, a Y axis of imaginary numbers emerges describing the will.

If a (+) in nature is inputted its matter, and if (-), it's energy. The various results that emerge from that constitute will. In this way, **we can establish the relationship between energy, matter, and imaginary numbers.**

— So, in other words, **presence becomes perception, and perception becomes presence ?**
    If presence is placed into a perspective (a function) it becomes perception, and perception can mandate presence.

That's right ! If the input and output are flipped, perception determines presence, and that presence determines perception. **There are infinite f(x) statements (perspectives). Functions are the relationship between the** *ma* **of numbers, the coming-and-going** *ma* **of presence and perception.**

When a subject and verb meet, what change occurs ? What emerges ? Energy subjects and verbs, matter subjects and verbs, mind subjects and verbs: **these 3 cause the rolling changes of presence and perception based on how they interact. The restored number (J) are used to analyze them in their totality.**

The figure on the right shows this in graph form.

X is energy, and you can see how mind changes based on the pattern/

shape you see.

In this way, functions, as well as the world of Newton and Descartes, can depict the relationship of matter, energy, and mind.

• Physical approach

— I didn't think that the world of mind and the world of math could be connected so easily... I'm feeling some kind of mix of surprise and gratitude.

Thank you. Next, let's approach this from a physical angle.

Physics encompasses classical mechanics, quantum mechanics, string theory, and M-theory. Let's bring those together with the imaginary numbers (i) and restored number (J).

— We're going to connect math and physics ! Ever since we connected physics and Zen Buddhism while discussing the 11th level of observing, my visualization has improved !

Just as you said, $0=\infty=1$ is a "one source infinity use" tool that can be used for anything.

More and more it seems like it'll be possible to connect everything I've ever learned in school and my daily life and future into a simple unified framework. It seems like I can become interested in things I wasn't interested in before, and will enjoy studying more than I once did.

Disciplines until now have been difficult to connect to our lifestyles. That's because causes and processes are ignored while results are memorized in a rote fashion. Answers delivered without questions don't lead to interest or curiosity. However, if things are understood in terms of the Fundamental Motion "$0=\infty=1$," there is nothing that isn't related. So, study becomes even more interesting.

Now let's get physics straightened out. Why don't you give it a shot first, based on however much you understand ?

— Sure ! I'll give it a shot !

Before physics, the "human eye" was our invariant. We saw things directly, separated things into similar categories, gave them names, established a variety of evaluation criteria, and created meaning and value in the form of likes, dislike, etc. But because the observations were in error, our data and information were in error as well. Thus, the knowledge, theory, disciplines, professions, and industries that emerged were also all in error. So, we can't rely on just our eyes !

But if you don't see with your eyes, how do you see ? The answer was classical mechanics. The invariant of Newton and Descartes was the XYZ coordinate system. The universe and the body were placed within the coordinate axes and attempted to explain the motion of the universe as a whole.

When Einstein came on the scene, he made the speed of light his invariant. The bending of spacetime was made the coordinate system. He claimed that because quantization occurs due to that bending, the bending is equal to the distribution of mass, and that spacetime is not fixed, but relative.

Very good ! I knew you could do it. In terms of the nTech perspective, the coordinate system is a spiral fractal. In other words, **the *ma* inside humanity is the coordinate system.** Einstein discusses all entities, scale, and distance in terms of the light speed standard. If you were to move at the speed of light, how much surface area does your body take up ? How about the Earth ? All entities change, move, transform—but it is all related to the standard imposed by the speed of light.

In terms of nTech, **light speed is a small *ma* (the *ma* at the center of some entity) that emerges from *Tah* (∞ expansion).** Just as snakes have snake spacetime and humans have human spacetime, there are a variety of differences from *Tah* to condensation which can be described as proportional expressions. **It's easy to understand if you see *Tah* (∞ expansion) as gravitational waves/the bending of spacetime/the curvature of zero space and condensation (∞ compression) as brain waves and the distribution of mass.**

— Yes, it makes sense if you look at it in terms of *Tah* (∞ expansion) and condensation (∞ compression). Einstein insisted on actuality, so he was unable to understand the repeated motion of *Tah* (∞ expansion) and condensation (∞ compression)—the arising and ceasing of beings.

Next up was quantum mechanics. This brought in the zero-curvature state of *Tah* (∞ expansion) made flat by the spiral fractal; i.e., the vibrations of quantum field energy. This looked at light as a material or substance. From there, QM claimed that the world is indeterminate and driven by probability due to quantization occurring at the moment of human observation—at the moment of condensation (∞ compression). However, because there are limitless bundles of energy, things were still complicated.

The observational stance of QM is the law of attraction. I felt that keenly last time.

In a way that's true, but it's because of a lack of understanding of observation error. **The idea that things happen the way you want is actually impossible at the level of quantum mechanics.** But we can talk about that later.

— Oh really ? That sounds interesting ! I'm looking forward to it.

Next, we have string theory. At this level, just as there are 5 types of string energy vibrations, all energy patterns could be gathered into 5 groups. Moving within and without the universe—in and out of black holes, for example—is possible.

In addition, the vibrations of the membrane (vacuum energy) constitute the origins of energy, reaching beyond the universe. This is the final enlightenment of physics !

Very good !

However, there's a problem. Do you think physics is aware of these conceptual connections ? As it happens, they are not.

— I got the feeling that might be the case... **within an analytical logic that breaks down things that "exist," it isn't possible to see the connections between them.**

Very insightful. Just as you say, **it's possible to describe things in terms of each part, but not holistically.** In particular, from string theory on, everything is theoretical so it's even more the case. The only thing you can do is look at the equations and say "it seems like it's like this." **The reality is there remains no sense of from where, towards where, or in what manner these revelations come to us.** That's why if there are any new concepts, there will be more 'things we don't understand' than the things we do understand about them.

— Oh, no. That's a big issue. It seems like it's heading into a maze where it won't be able to tell entrance from exit... continuing on with research in the baseless hope that there's a way out will be tough on the psyche, too.

Indeed, I have heard that many people are searching despite the stress it causes them. It's a result of their curiosity that drives them to know.

On that point, do you remember what I said about the limits of physical enlightenment ?

— Physical enlightenment culminates in the vibration of vacuum energy... that's right ! The issue that there's no way to discuss mind ! That's why we had to move on to the levels of Zen Buddhism.

In Zen, the level that deals with function/purpose of mind is the nameable Mind (level 6 of Zen) and continues to the unnameable Mind (level 7 of Zen). Mind itself is what follows. **Levels 6 and 7 of Zen cover the imaginary numbers (i) and level 8 is the *ma* between J and i !**

You got it ! You're really coming along. From there, level 9 of Zen is the inconceivable motion of mind, the restored number (J) ! Here the cry of the mind is...

— Fool ! You don't need to know !!!

Thank you. This is the completion of ignorance. This was the goal of Buddhism, but we need to make this our starting point. Otherwise we won't be able to use it as much as we'd like in reality.

The meaning of meaninglessness, the value of non-value, the definition of the undefined, obtaining the eraser faculty and equal peers. The purpose and function of the Fundamental Motion and understanding the value of emptiness/nothingness," living in complete perfection. There is no self or beyond the self. Living by the Fundamental Motion itself, by infinite potential itself and the ability to become anything, and dignity itself—and being able to see all things from that perspective—will become the invariant, the point of reference, for humanity.

The human psyche is constantly in search for value and a meaning to life. However, that is meaning and value of the "will" at the level of the perspective of the brain. So, it has no meaning. Yet because it has no meaning, we have engaged in endless war throughout our history, expanded our differences, and nearly made ourselves obsolete with the development of AI. We shouldn't stand for such nonsense.

Reality is a result willed out of the desire to know the self. It is the dream that J is watching. So, we live by the Fundamental Motion, by mind itself, and **see this reality as something akin to a computer simulation.**

— The computer simulation analogy is easy to visualize. It's like the conversation we were having about the relationship between digital and analog. There's a digital algorithm working behind the scenes to create the analog display of a smartphone.

That's right. There's something important here. Would your smartphone's display turn on if the phone ran out of battery charge ? It won't even turn on, right ? In other words, nothing happens without electricity. So then if I were to ask what the "electricity" to create the display of illusory reality is, you'd say that it's...

— The Fundamental Motion !!!

That's right ! Electricity guided with programming languages lets you create a display. That is to say, you must always see things in terms of the Fundamental Motion. I've said it a lot of times, but the body and the objects the body perceives are all *effects*. The body does not see, the body is not the subject. **The entirety of the universe becomes motion, becomes ultra-speed that transcends the brain itself, resulting in seeing from "1."**

— Just like the smartphone can't turn on its display without electricity, people will just be at the mercy of reality if they don't connect themselves to Fundamental Motion.

I have to say, understanding and connecting physics, mathematics, Buddhism together so easily, discussing difficult Buddhist terminology in vernacular language... it's amazing. Something unbelievable is happening.

Who are you, exactly...? I've never seen or heard of anyone like you before.

Thank you. In fact, it's not the use of modern language, but actually imagery—image language—that is the true charm of nTech. Let's connect everything we have so far and use the **"double tube model motion"** to describe it all.

— *Figure 39* —
Model of JiR tube

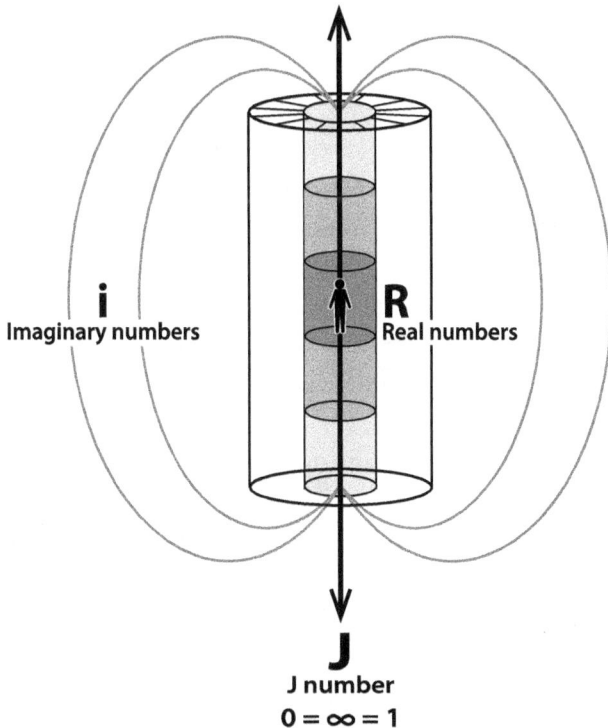

i
Imaginary numbers

R
Real numbers

J
J number
$0 = \infty = 1$

There's inner tubes here and an outer tube. During an ongoing inside-out motion, classical mechanics expands to quantum mechanics, which expands to string theory. The boundary that strings cross, towards the outside, is a realm in which "strings can be made/the membrane can be made," and the outside becomes the membrane. **In this way, as the inner tubes and outer tubes continue their inside-out motion, the membrane (point) goes to string (line) to quantum field (body), and in this sense, we can demonstrate the manifestation of matter and the material universe through an extraction or interaction.** At the moment the interaction ends, matter disintegrates to the quantum energy field, to strings, to the membrane. Then from the membrane, time, space, existence arise. This motion repeats eternally.

I said before that M-theory is the final theory at the physical level—do you see how all of this is encapsulated by the motion of the membrane (vacuum energy) ? **The entirety of this double tube motion displays the real numbers (R).**

— So, the motion of the flipping double tube is the real numbers (R). OK. So, then what about the imaginary numbers (i) and the Fundamental Motion (J) ? Where do they go ?

Sure, let me explain that. What is the motion of the membrane that the final theory of physics, M theory, describes ? **What is the thing that creates the "material tube" ? It is the motion of the imaginary numbers (i).**

Each and every point that the membrane creates has emerged from the repeated motion of mind of the imaginary numbers (i).

The motion of imaginary numbers (i) gathers, create the three types of energy (from the membrane, strings, and the quantum field), and matter emerges from that energy.

In other words, it seems that the tubes of matter and energy actually exist, but in fact they do not.

The motion of mind of imaginary numbers (i) gathers and becomes points in the membrane, lines of strings, surfaces of the quantum field, and bodies in classical mechanics. The human brain insists that those physical bodies "exist." For that reason, everything that human beings have ever thought "exists" is just the will of mind.

— Via the motion of the imaginary numbers, does the tube appear to actually exist?

For example, is it like this? Atoms are mostly empty, but because of the high speed of electrons, they appear to be more full?

It's similar, yes. However, because the imaginary numbers (i) move at the speed of mind, the speed of material electrons is nowhere close to it.

Imaginary numbers (i) are the recurring mind, the mind of conceivable motion. But why are they capable of this motion?

Well, we already know. **It's because of the motion of the inconceivable mind, the non-recurring mind—the mind of J (God), of no border lines, no directionality, no position.**

The speed of i is also infinite, but the motion of J is far beyond the perception of the human mind. **Imaginary numbers (i) are the result of the desire of the inconceivable motion of mind J for the motion of conceivable mind—the recurrent mind.**

— I see. That yearning is the declaration of the will we discussed before. Even though there is only J, by obtaining the empty concept of ma, the motion of i becomes possible, and from that motion, matter and energy emerge.

Yes. So, Truth is only J. Now let's connect all of this to perspective.

The place where perspective applies is the conceivable, repeating, patterned mind (i). The state of fixation on one perspective could be likened to the rotation motion of the Earth. But the Earth also revolves. So, what is revolution? It's the inconceivable, non-recurring, patternless mind (J). Just as the Earth both rotates and revolves, perspective can freely come and go as the revolution of J and the rotation of i proceed.

— So, this illustration captures both the rotation and revolution aspects of perspective! It's amazing that it can be expressed in imagery, and it has the advantage of avoiding misunderstandings because of the visual depiction.

Now let's bring everything from Original Mind to the emergence of human thoughts, feelings, words, actions, and relations into our XYZ coordinate system.

— That sounds interesting ! If I became able to get my mind and daily life in order using the concepts of numerical coordinates and physical concepts, I think I'd be able to see things in a more objective way.

When you have a 1:1 interaction with the X axis and the Y axis, an "entity" emerges, right ? **When you take the X axis as the standard axis for "wave, the Theory of Mathematics" and the Y axis as *ma*/zero space, then based on the interaction, the entity that emerges is the "result of perception" or "perception contents."**

Those "entities" next become "fields," and the next 1:1 symmetry emerges. From there, an entity in another dimension emerges. The structure just repeats this. This is the fractal mechanism that gives rise to entities from fields—that gives rise to fish from the sea.

1.

X axis: Absolute mind waves, absolute instantaneous rates of change of Original Mind, "1," numbers

Y axis: Various mind field *ma*, scale of Zero Space *ma*
  ⇒ Imaginary number fields

2.

X axis: relative mind waves, imaginary numbers (i)

Y axis: varied imaginary number field *ma*
  ⇒ Energy fields

3.

X axis: Gravity waves, real numbers (R)

Y axis: Gravity waves and various brain wave *ma*
  ⇒ Universal natural fields

4.

X axis: Subjects of natural lifestyles, brain waves, integers/whole numbers

Y axis: Perceptual subject of natural lifestyle environments and *ma* of various perceptual objects
  ⇒ Human culture and civilization fields

— *Figure 40* —
The structure (1, *Ma*, point)
that gives rise to fictitious subject/predicate (point)

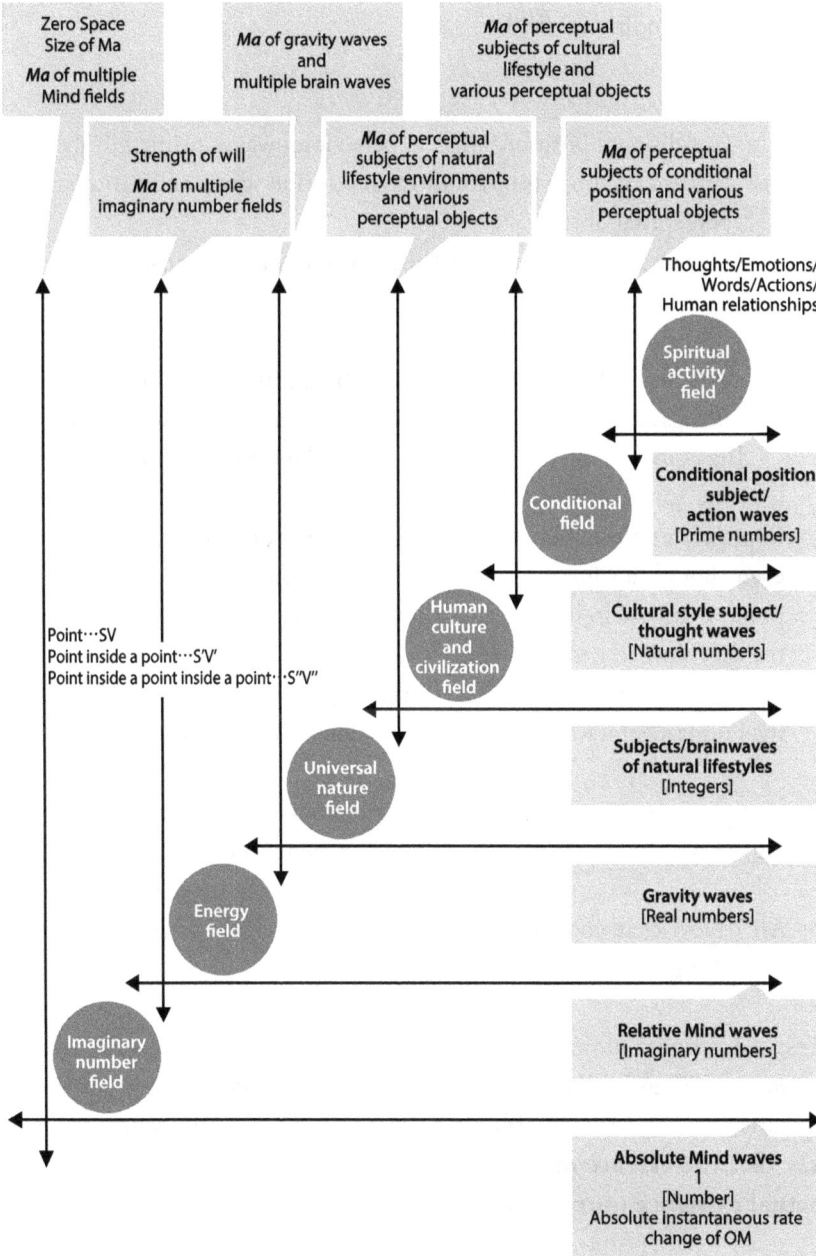

Zero Space
Size of Ma

Ma of multiple
Mind fields

Ma of gravity waves
and
multiple brain waves

Ma of perceptual
subjects of cultural
lifestyle and
various perceptual objects

Strength of will

Ma of multiple
imaginary number fields

Ma of perceptual
subjects of natural
lifestyle environments
and various
perceptual objects

Ma of perceptual
subjects of conditional
position and various
perceptual objects

Thoughts/Emotions/
Words/Actions/
Human relationships

Spiritual
activity
field

Conditional
field

Conditional position
subject/
action waves
[Prime numbers]

Human
culture
and
civilization
field

Cultural style subject/
thought waves
[Natural numbers]

Point⋯SV
Point inside a point⋯S′V′
Point inside a point inside a point⋯S″V″

Universal
nature
field

Subjects/brainwaves
of natural lifestyles
[Integers]

Energy
field

Gravity waves
[Real numbers]

Imaginary
number
field

Relative Mind waves
[Imaginary numbers]

Absolute Mind waves
1
[Number]
Absolute instantaneous rate
change of OM

5.

X axis: Cultural style subjects/thought waves/natural numbers

Y axis: Perceptual subjects of cultural lifestyles and various *ma* of perceptual objects

⇒ Conditional fields

6.

X axis: Conditional position subjects/behavioral waves/prime numbers

Y axis: Perceptual subjects of conditional position waves and various *ma* of perceptual objects

⇒ Spiritual activity field (birth of human relationships/thought/ feelings/words/behavior)

— I see—if you look at the whole picture, the spiritual behavior fields of human beings are just a point inside a little point inside a point inside a point.

The conversation we had before about the meaning of the meaningless, the value of the valueless, the definition of the undefined left an impression on me. However, even though all this is just the dream of J, even though it's just a tiny reality inside a point inside a point inside a point, I can't help but search for meaning and value and get attached to things I start to care about.

So I must bear in mind again the importance of seeing things from the Fundamental Motion "1." After all, non-existence is prior to existence.

That's a good attitude. I'd like for you to free yourself from meaning and value. But aren't you forgetting something? "Existence is below non-existence."

— Ah ! Now that you mention it, you said that there is an inversion or something? What was that about...

Yes, that's right. From the perspective of truth, non-existence is prior to existence. When I talked about that, I told you the value of non-existence. So now I'd like to ask you: **If non-existence is prior to existence, can you say that the essence of this ballpoint pen is more important than its actual existence (purpose/function) ?**

— Yes. If "actual existence" refers to existence, and essence refers to non-existence, that would be true. That's because essence—that is, the inconceivable, awful Fundamental Motion—has overwhelming value !

Now for another question. **What about human beings ?**
   Like the ballpoint pen, is "essence more important than actual existence (function/purpose)" ?
   Or is it the reverse ?

— What ? It's the same as the pen, right ? After all, human beings are also a part of illusory reality, of "existence." Why do you ask ? Don't try to confuse me.

I'm not trying to confuse you. But I can see why you might feel that way. That's because I claim that **actual existence is more important than essence for human beings.**

But why would I say such a thing ?

— I'm confused... essence is more important than actual existence for a ballpoint pen, but it's the other way around for humans ? What is the difference between the pen and humans ? If essence is the point they share in common, then is the difference between their purpose/function the key to the answer ?

We've come to a good place. If you think on that function/purpose difference, you'll understand.
   Now, what is the function or purpose of human beings ? For what purpose and by what means was the perspective of the human mind born ?
   Don't you think the Original Mind of Fundamental Motion would be in a tough spot without the "mind of the human brain" to break through its limits ? After all, **without a mind that sees in parts—without the perspective of the brain—it would not be possible to engage in the creation of illusory reality.**

— I see !! It became possible to will illusory reality through the intense desires of the human brain !

That's right.

Human beings are the only beings that use their brain while also being restricted by it.

There's one more thing I'll say here. **"The ability to deny the self" is proof of evolution.**

— What ? Self-denial is... what's the connection here ?

Are there any animals that deny themselves or commit suicide ? There aren't. That's something that only humans can do. From the perspective of human good and evil, it seems like it's not a very good thing, right ? But in fact, not only can only humans deny themselves or others, but if they couldn't, it would be a problem.

If humans could live without any issues, always happy !... what do you think would happen ?

— What do I think ?... well, nothing could be that easy. But is there a problem with it ?

There's a lot of problems with it. After all, you wouldn't have any problem awareness, right ?

If that were true, **you'd never wish for change.** Which means...

— ...I see ! That doesn't fulfill the creative aims of Original Mind !

That's right ! Self-denial and denial of others is a form of worrying. What does it mean to live ? What is reality ? Why is it so painful ?

In response, we say, "We've had it with this world ! !" **By rejecting and pushing past this reality, we return to the Fundamental Motion "1."** **The blueprint of god, the aims of creation, become visible !** We see what it's all about ! So, **self-denial and the denial of others have been part of**

God's plan from the start.

— I've been putting myself down this whole time without even knowing that.

And yet now here you are, encountering the Fundamental Motion "1." You've come to know that you are "1" itself. In this way, human beings are the only beings that can use their brains to emancipate themselves from their brains—**that can become enlightened, that can reach the state of being "already dead when living."**

Not only that, but **they can become a being 1 quadrillion times greater than any god of religion. That is to say, humans are beings of essence that actually exist, that can become beings that use essence as a tool. This is the function, the purpose of humanity!** It is in this way that Original Mind achieves its creative goal and the dignity of human beings rises explosively!

This is also a compelling reason not to commit suicide or kill others.

— A reason that murder and suicide is bad. Now that you mention it, I realize that nobody has any good answer for why killing is wrong.

There are many cases in history where people who killed many others were seen as heroes. The standards of morality change with the times.

That's because there is nothing that you can claim as "absolute" with the world you see with your eyes—all is relative. Attempts to claim certainty in a relative world lend themselves to totalitarianism and fascism. It's very dangerous. However, from the perspective of the absolute world of Fundamental Motion, things can be explained nicely in terms of essence.

So, we were talking about the reason not to kill oneself or others. It's because **doing so destroys a chance of becoming a being trillions of times greater than any god of religion.** How amazing do you think it is just for one person to become enlightened? Without understanding that and getting caught up in the world observable by the naked eye, we end up in a system that naturally leads to unhappiness. As a result, we get wrapped up in things like suicide and murder.

In order to make the impossible possible, in order to understand itself, Original Mind created humanity. Humans can die while still alive, but this is not possible for animals and plants. Animals, plants, and all the rest of the universe support human beings.

If only people knew just how precious even a single human being is, as an inheritor of will itself, racing towards new frontiers.

It's something people need to understand as soon as possible.

The implications of the meaning and value that can be derived from seeing things via the Fundamental One Motion "1"—rather than with the naked eye—are profound.

Under eternal invariance, that eternal invariance is taken for granted. Moreover, it is possible to observe things with eyes that move at the speed of mind, with eyes at the speed of energy, with eyes at the speed of light, with eyes that see via the XYZ coordinate system, and with physical eyes as well. Of course, it is also possible to experience will and feeling and a zombie-like state beyond the will. In other words, **it becomes possible for us to free ourselves from any perspective and become a new type of human being.**

— *Figure 41* —
The stepwise, continuous expansion of point of reference

The act of observational measurement affects the object of measurement

"I think, therefore I exist"

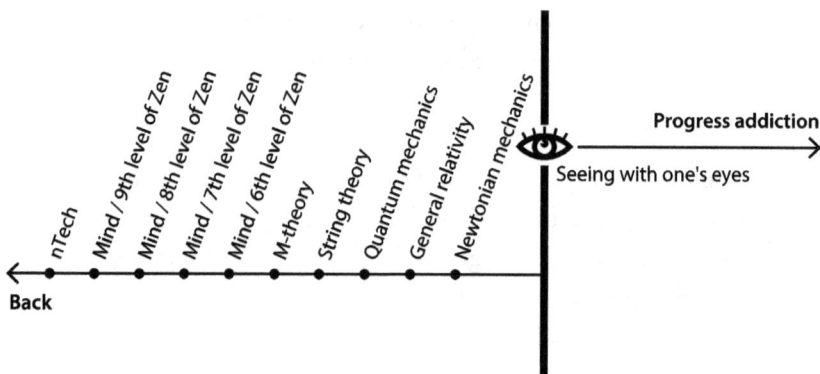

— I feel a bit haughty about being born a human being now. Yet at the same time, there's something sobering about it. We humans must carry out our mission.

We forcefully rejected the "perspective hell" and reached the "fraternal heaven." From the perspective of the perspective hell, this fraternal heaven seemed like heaven, but once reaching the True World, we saw that it was also an "uninterrupted hell." We forcefully rejected that uninterrupted hell as well, and with our understanding of "1," are able to savor the **"heaven of beautiful harmony"** that takes the present moment to be a divine miracle. Incidentally, "beautiful harmony" comes from the current Japanese imperial era, *"Reiwa."* Explaining this will take a long time so I'll skip over it, but the basic idea is to describe **"a world mobilized by living '1' in the here and now."**

These 2 hells are both made into 2 heavens. The ability to move back and forth between them, in Buddhist terminology, is called *gokuraku ōjō* **(rebirth in Paradise).**

— Figure 42 —
Rebirth in Paradise

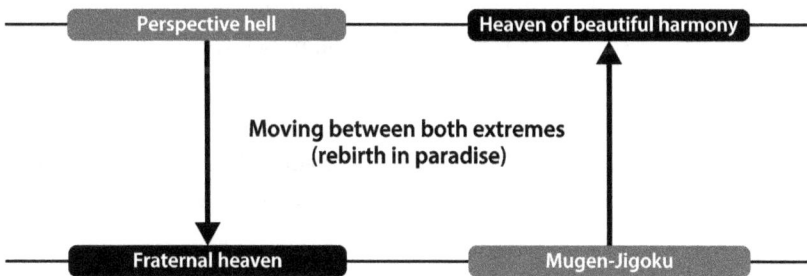

Perspective hell	Heaven of beautiful harmony

Moving between both extremes
(rebirth in paradise)

Fraternal heaven	Mugen-Jigoku

— Rebirth in Paradise... if we could go back and forth between both heavens, that really would be Paradise.

Right ? In Japanese, there is a saying, "bad at rebirth" (*ōjōgiwa ga warui*) that refers to being a sore loser. *Ōjō* refers to "leaving the world and being born in the pure land paradise"—in other words, dying. People who are unable to do that are *ōjōgiwa ga warui*. Analyzing things in terms of nTech, this means "unable to die-while-alive, here and now." If you die while alive, you can always be reborn in paradise.

In the Confucian Analects, the state of rebirth in paradise is called "*daijōbu*" or "great man." In Japan, people are always using that word, right ? This surprised me a lot when I encountered it. After all, **it's like a declaration that you are enlightened.**

— I had been using the word without even knowing it had such a deep meaning, but as a Japanese person, I feel both happy and a bit embarrassed.

• Philosophical Approach

Now that we've gotten into essence and actual existence, let's approach this from a philosophical perspective. I'd like to ask a question to start: what do you think philosophy is ?

— Philosophy ? I can't give a precise definition, but I remember studying past philosophers like Kant and Hegel and trying to figure out how to apply their ideas to my daily life. I found it a bit interesting, but it was so difficult that I got discouraged. I thought they were pretty well-reasoned, yet it seemed so far from reality and myself that I began to doubt the value of studying it.

I know the feeling. But are you sure ? Don't you think that a life without philosophy would be a bit directionless ? Philosophy is a necessary tool for our lives.

nTech defines philosophy as follows. **Philosophy is like a North Star that seeks to shatter assumptions and create new paths that explain the universe, nature, history, civilization, and all phenomena as belonging to an eternal, unchanging unity.**

— Oooh ! That's pretty different from the image of philosophy that I have had. But that sounds like something I'd like to study ! It seems both practical and useful.

Right ? Philosophy is not just a matter of studying or knowledge. It's **something you put into practice.**

However, philosophy ended up yielding to science before it was able to properly execute its real function.

What was the result ? Since we moved from the age of religion to the age of science, we have gone through deconstructionism, structuralism, constructivism, post-structuralism. Our modern society is saturated in complexity, diversity, plurality, uniqueness, and individualism. Nothing is integrated and our thought methodology is falling apart. In the midst of all of this, differences continue to spread unchecked while we find ourselves chased down by this situation, being pushed this way and that. Philosophy today simply stands by and watches.

— Certainly. Philosophy has a bit of a weak presence.

So why do you think this happened ?

A major premise in Western philosophy is that Truth (essence) is not the same as reality (phenomenon). Let's review the history of Western philosophy, using this premise to guide us.

Philosophy during the age of theism was primarily metaphysics. Because God was seen as the creator of the phenomenological world, **philosophy rejected reality.**

— We talked about this a little bit before. There is only god, so why is there reality ?

That's right. Reality contains nothing but God's creations. That is to say, human beings are nothing more than a means and a tool for fulfilling God's creative goals. That's when human beings had an idea. "Humanity exists in order to live in accordance with God's will." This is called "realism." In a word, it concludes that "phenomena do not actually exist, and there is a different world of Platonic Ideas that does actually exist. Therefore, **essence has more value than phenomena.**

— So, humanity itself didn't have any value. Because your whole reason for existence was to please God, to fulfill God's will, it was easy to give up your life to God.

That's right. Anything was possible with the power of God. It was an obvious move to place God at the top of the hierarchy and human beings at the bottom. However, the Western Renaissance repudiated this attitude and ushered in a revolution.

The philosophical concepts of that time were a bit different. Truth (essence) was seen as a bit lacking, so reality (phenomena) is created; as a result, everything is in reality. **Based on this logic, humans have value as the representatives of the phenomenological world. This is known as existentialist philosophy or postmodernism.** These humanist philosophies prioritize humanity, and because they see essence from phenomena, their premises are the complete opposite of metaphysics.

In addition, Kant employed constructivism/constructionism in an attempt to use the concept of "facts" to link the absolute world (essence) and relative world (phenomenon).

— It's interesting to see what premises are behind the transitions of philosophy and the motions of the human mind. But as we were saying before, philosophy today has no standing, and it is not fulfilling its original purpose. What can be done about this ?

Try to remember. The major premise in metaphysics and postmodernism is that "Truth (essence) does not equal reality (phenomena)." What I advocate to break through this assumption is the *Reiwa* **philosophy of** "$0=\infty=1$." Does that remind you of anything ?

— I see ! If Truth (essence) does not equal reality (phenomena), then the "does not equal" means there hasn't been a distinction drawn. Because that's where they started, they hit a wall !

That's right ! The premise was wrong. In other words, **"Truth = Reality."** In the *Reiwa* philosophy, this is expressed as **unchanging unity, transformative control.**

Both essence and phenomena are nothing more than the unchanging One Motion. As perspective rotates, the revolving total motion does not change at all.

Metaphysics starts from Truth (seeing a from b), and postmodernism starts from reality (seeing b from a). While bringing both into existence, neither has any relationship to the Fundamental Motion. All that actually exists is J. **I brought together the postmodern perspective and the metaphysical perspective that emerge via the inconceivable motion J in the brain, and named seeing totality (perspectives 0, ∞, 1) as neo-realism or neo-existentialism.**

— Figure 43 —
Metaphysics, postmodernism, neo-realism/neo-existentialism

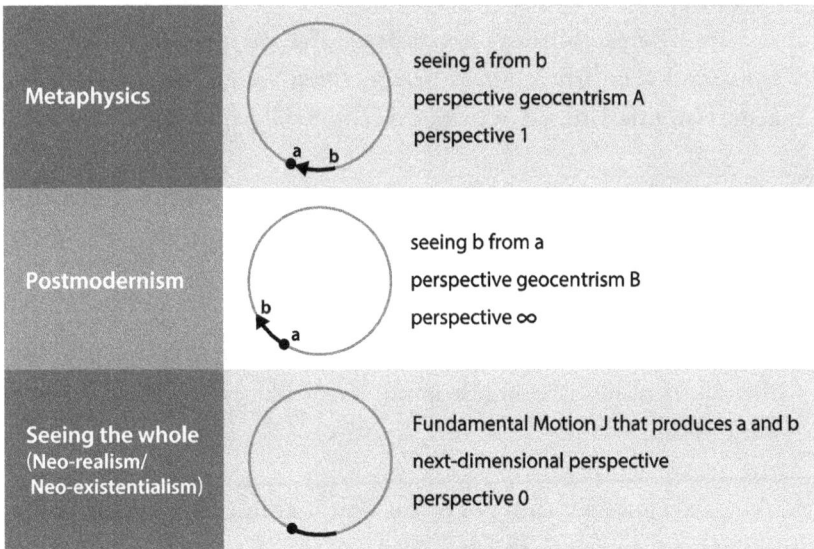

Metaphysics		seeing a from b perspective geocentrism A perspective 1
Postmodernism		seeing b from a perspective geocentrism B perspective ∞
Seeing the whole (Neo-realism/ Neo-existentialism)		Fundamental Motion J that produces a and b next-dimensional perspective perspective 0

— I see ! Rather than insisting on one or the other, you start from the motion that creates them both. That's a very simple idea !

So, let me see if I can try to describe how we deal with the perspective problem with philosophy.

In metaphysics, the "one perspective" from essence alone is absolute, and in postmodernism, the "∞ perspectives" is absolute. There are as many perspectives as there are human beings, at the same time there are animal perspectives, plant perspectives, material perspectives. An uncountable number of them.

Therefore, there is a conflict between the perspectives of metaphysics and postmodernism, and in postmodernism, there's even conflict between the infinite perspectives.

Getting fixated on a perspective as "absolute" yields nothing more than one possible analysis from infinite perspectives, and claiming one's own perspective and world as absolute is sure to result in friction and fighting.

Yes, yes, that's the spirit !

— In order to clear this problem... we need to free ourselves from the world we know !

I see ! **By establishing a synthesis of 1 perspective, ∞ perspectives, and a nullification of perspectives, we get neo-realism and neo-existentialism. So, we can overcome the perspective problem !**

Excellent. Both metaphysics and postmodernism are nothing more than the dream that the inconceivable motion (J, god, perspective 0) is seeing. **Both had started from a "Ptolemaic model" of perspective !**

— Yes, I see. You keep saying that reality is the dream that God observes, after all. If reality is God's dream, it seems like everything can go the way it thinks !

That's right. However, **things go the way it thinks because it thinks things will go the way it thinks.**

— What kind of Zen *koan* is that ? It thinks things will go the way it thinks ?

That's right. There are a number of people who misunderstand the dream concept as anarchic freedom in which anything goes, so I want to nip this in the bud.

The idea is actually that **the dream also has its own "structure."** After all, it would be ridiculous for time to flow backwards or an apple to suddenly turn into a banana, right ? It would be inconsistent with the physical laws of reality.

Therefore, **we know that there is an axiomatic structure that ensures causal relationships—spatial causality, temporal causality, embodied causality, perceptual causality—and that it is via this structure that the dream can be made. It is because we understand that structure that we can change this simulated reality.** For example, when you write a novel, you'll have thoughts like "This subject/verb is here, so next is a different subject/verb." There's a causal logic by which you develop a story, right ?

By understanding this dream being seen by J, by understanding causal rules, it becomes possible to have fun sketching out an illusory reality, a dream, in accordance with one's thoughts.

— Now I know what you mean by "it thinks things will go the way it thinks" ! It is master of the structure of mind, energy, and materialization (illusory reality) !

• Historical approach

Now that we've discussed math, physics, and philosophy in our academia series, let's change our pace a bit and approach this from a historical perspective.

— History, huh... I wonder how "0=∞=1" connects to history ? Nothing comes to mind, but I like history, so this should be fun.

Oh, do you ? Then here's a question. Throughout human history, our ability to create an ordered cooperative structure has been critical to our survival. So, **what do you think is the key term for establishing that order ?**

— A key term for establishing order ?

Yes. It's **"assembly and production."**

Imagine the moment when humans appeared on the Earth. What was the biggest challenge people faced then ?

— Was it finding food ?

Before eating, the dilemma of **"eat or be eaten"** is even more pressing. You might become lunch for an animal—or you make that animal your lunch. If we didn't fight and win against animals, they would have eaten us.

— Oh, so that's why "assembly" is a key term.

That's right. Assembling more and more people and figuring out what kinds of tools were needed to protect oneself and win against aggressive animals was a do-or-die necessity.

After some time, human beings began winning against animals. In so doing, the age of domination by animals came to an end, and next was **the issue of determining leaders who would distribute resources fairly.**

— That's true—the abilities of a leader can make the difference between starvation and survival. Of course, leaders who share a lot are probably more popular.

Yes, and we soon faced **the issue of tyrannical leadership**. It was in response to this that **we developed democracy.** In order to halt the despotism of monarchs, we ushered in an era in which anyone could become king. In order to ensure no single person could monopolize leadership, term limits were imposed.

After that, another issue arose. Transfers of power result in changes in policy and influence, right ? As a result, **it became difficult to establish a sustainable way of life.**

— Ahh, I see. So, the unregulated free market, the "invisible hand," were created to deal with this problem. And thus, we had the birth of **capitalism.**

That's right. However, with the advent of capitalism came a new problem: **wealth inequality.** The ideology intended to erase that inequality and establish an equal society was **socialism, or communism.**

— And yet ironically, socialism and communism failed to create that equality in practice. There was only a superficial sort of equality, but actually created a worse wealth gap than capitalist societies.

Yes, **inequalities in wealth and power got larger until ultimately concerns about human rights abuses arose.** This sort of affront to human dignity is the **dignity problem.**

— I see. So that brings us to our contemporary society. We started with the problem of "assembly," but I imagine that throughout this chain of events, the perspective problem is at the root of it all ?
    I can see its implications for bringing people together pretty clearly.

Yes, which is why **order is the "fruit of perseverance."** Human history overflows with tears. So now let's take a look at history again, making the perspective problem our axis for analysis.

First of all, **the age of totalitarianism (age of theism) at the height of religion's power accepted only one perspective.** This was the perspective of the avatar of God, the monarch. The people of that time, of course, had perspectives different from the monarch. However, their perspectives were all discarded as useless. This was a period full of countries in which people's homes, work, and even partners had to follow the expectations of the monarch.

— Let alone freedom of thought, you didn't even have any freedom of choice in your behavior.

Next, **individualism arose as a repudiation of totalitarianism.** Individuals raised their voices, insisting that the monarch is not the only one whose perspective matters, that the perspectives and feelings of individuals should be taken seriously, and that all perspectives should be accepted. It sounds pretty good, right ? However, nobody's perspectives or feelings aligned with anyone else's. People can try to tolerate each other and avoid argument, but what happens in the end ? Ultimately, we have to suck it up and compromise.

— I see. **So, you have to endure things while pushing through some kind of compromise, be drowned out by a diversity and pluralism of perspectives which may be quite out there or complex, succumb to information overload, and fail to pull it all together.** So you lose sight of what's right, lose your point of reference and direction, and the problems pile up.

This reminds me a little bit of the sort of world presented in the movie *Joker* we mentioned before.[12]

Everybody hides tears behind their smiles. However, the COVID-19 pandemic of 2020 and our increasingly abnormal weather has been a message in the form of making us stop and reset all of our endeavors. The mask has come off, and now **it is time for us to press on with a version upgrade to human performance.**

— Human performance ? I've never heard that term. What does it mean ?

Let's say that **humans have been at version 1.0 this whole time. This is a humanity that relies on its five senses to make absolute judgments about the world.** Let me go into some detail on this.

As I mentioned above, with the rise of individualism came the Western Renaissance and scientific technology. Human beings have used this scientific technology to provide basic necessities, invent cars and smartphones, etc.— **all of it has been changes external to human being themselves.** Now we are entering into a **"post-human era" where the domain of change is extending to our bodies.**

— Oh, you were talking about that before. VR and AR have become commonplace, but we may end up in a *Ghost in the Shell* kind of world.[13]

---

12 *Joker. 2020. Warner Bros. Home Entertainment inc.*
13 *Ghost in the Shell. 2004. Bandai Visual.*

Yes, that's right. Just as we have moved from a stage 1 industry that creates natural products to a stage 2 industry that creates artificial products, **the current process aims to transform the body from a natural (living) "version 1.0" body, to a techno-human supremacist "version 2.0" body filled with artificial devices such as brain chips that expand our faculties, to a "data supremacist" version 3.0 body that utilizes big data with chips at the cellular level in the brain.**

This is how far scientific technology is able to go. This process is also expected to lead us towards the technological singularity, which is predicted to occur around 2045. What will happen after that ? AI will be able to replicate itself, AI will be able to imitate human thoughts and emotions, and **we will enter into a realm in which human beings won't even be able to imagine what comes next.**

So, what do you think the goals of versions 1.0-3.0 of the body are ?

— Ummm... goals ? What the objective of each is ? I don't know.

It's the "will to survive." **Human performance version 1.0 is a "life intelligence" for the will to survive.**

— The will to survive... so is this like the original *Homo sapiens* ?

In terms of essence, I guess humanity hasn't changed at all. So even if we reach version 3.0, ultimately, we're still at human performance version 1.0. So, beyond that is... ?

Yes. Let's continue.

What do you think is the commonality between totalitarianism and individualism ? There are a few, but in particular, in both of them **people are restrained and fixed by the perspective of the brain (brain virus) and are unable to see the path towards freedom.** This is the first thing that must be addressed. That path is "0=∞=1."

— Yes. That's a good way to summarize humanity's history.

Yes. So, we find the stratum prior to the emergence of perspective and figure out the "structure" that leads to perspective arising. Once we understand how to unravel and weave back a perspective, the connections of all its relationships become clear.

In other words, "0=∞=1" liberates us from perspective. **Once we become able, right here and now, to simultaneously perceive the entirety of the perspectives of 0, ∞, and 1, we will reach human performance version 2.0 which transcends "life intelligence." We will attain "spiritual intelligence," and with it, the will to dignity.**

— I see! So, if the perception I have acquired so far becomes natural to me, I will advance to human performance version 2.0, liberated from the virus of the brain!

That's right. However, human performance version 2.0 still doesn't reach assembly and production. The process of this stage is also called **"liberalism of the soul."**

The "spiritual intelligence" of human performance version 2.0 must further develop into the "dignity intelligence" of human performance version 3.0, towards "evolutionism of the soul."

— Dignity intelligence? Evolutionism of the soul?

People who attain human performance version 2.0 have **attained a state of spiritual cells — the creation of a Torus structure that enables ongoing evolution and development. The goal of human performance version 3.0 is to put dignity into action and establish the will to re-create.**

Evolutionism of the soul is something we'll talk about later when we discuss "group intelligence"

— So, 2.0 is the self-becoming "1" itself/Fundamental Motion itself, and 3.0 is anyone being able to freely use "1" itself...?

Before I was thinking that it would be enough for me to have a "desire for dignity," but I guess I was mistaken.

The state of having spiritual cells, of constructing a Torus structure that enables perpetual evolution and growth is still a bit vague to me, but it sounds exciting. I have an image of assembly and production tak-

— *Figure 44* —
Versions 1.0-3.0 of human performance

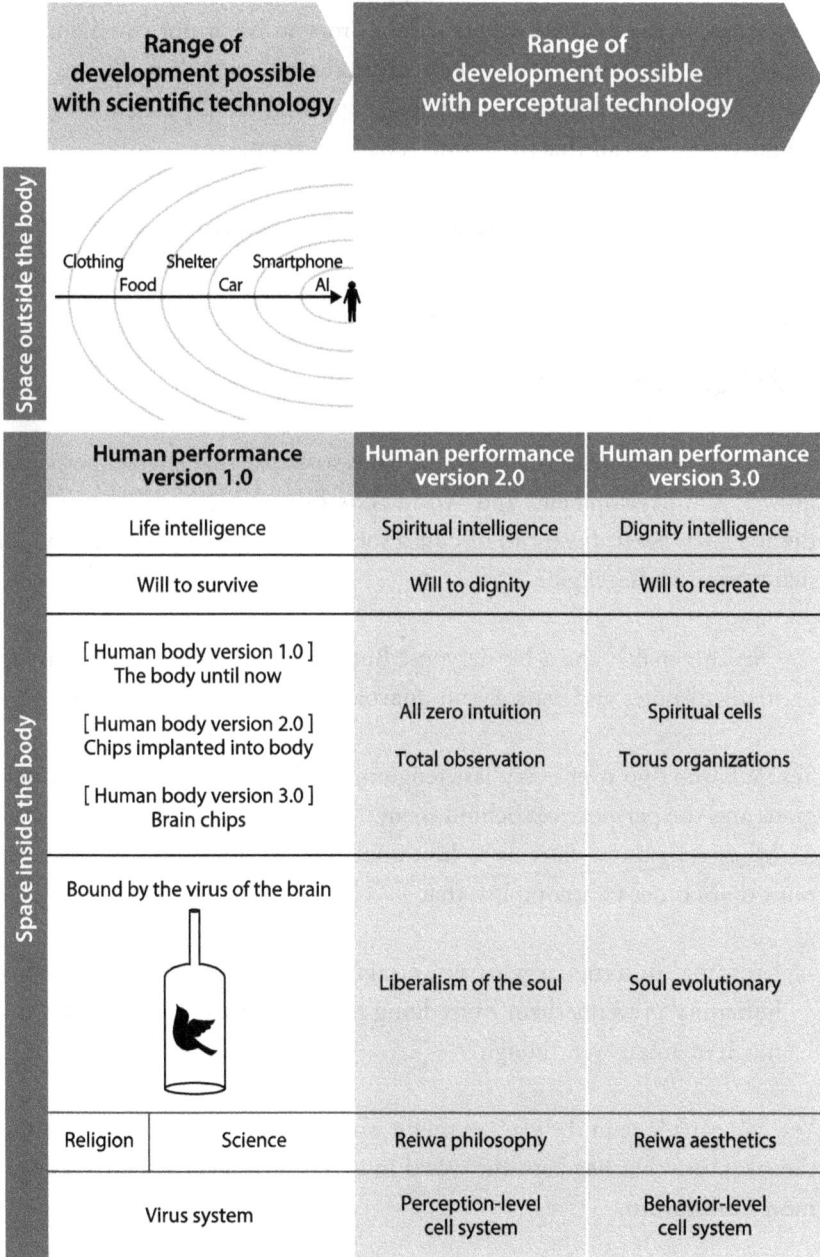

	Range of development possible with scientific technology	Range of development possible with perceptual technology	

Space outside the body

Clothing　Shelter　Smartphone
　Food　　Car　　AI

	Human performance version 1.0	Human performance version 2.0	Human performance version 3.0
Space inside the body	Life intelligence	Spiritual intelligence	Dignity intelligence
	Will to survive	Will to dignity	Will to recreate
	[Human body version 1.0] The body until now [Human body version 2.0] Chips implanted into body [Human body version 3.0] Brain chips	All zero intuition Total observation	Spiritual cells Torus organizations
	Bound by the virus of the brain	Liberalism of the soul	Soul evolutionary
	Religion | Science	Reiwa philosophy	Reiwa aesthetics
	Virus system	Perception-level cell system	Behavior-level cell system

ing place without obstruction.

The terminology of nTech **supplements the concept of the "invisible hand" with the "invisible eye," suggesting a "system of complete observation of the present moment."** In order to bring out the dignity of people, we must bring about an **educational revolution** that takes us from the age of "life intelligence" to an age of spiritual intelligence and dignity intelligence. We call this the World Axis Education.

— Spiritual cells, a torus structure that enables perpetual growth and development, World Axis Education. It's all very interesting.

• Religious approach

Yes, I think so too. Spiritual cells, the torus structure that enables perpetual growth and development, and World Axis Education are all things we'll discuss later. Next, I want to discuss a somewhat taboo topic at the root of many arguments: religion.

— Oh, this makes me a bit nervous. But since religion is at the heart of many disputes and wars, it's an unavoidable topic.

Yes. We won't go over every last religion, but let's do an overview of religions and the perspectives behind them.
    Many religions exhort us to love one another. What do you think we must do in order to accomplish that ?

— Ummm... in terms of what we've said so far, it seems like the state of humanity prevents them from doing that even if they want to. It's not much of an answer, though.

Yes. We can't love in the way we might want to—we must first understand the structure that has kept the world in endless conflict. **We lack a common foundation.**

— Indeed. Getting stuck in the perspective of the brain and what you see in front of you is the same as being in the perceptual structure that prevents love. The human brain's perspective is constantly in observational error, after all. Judgment standards differ greatly between individuals, so there hasn't been any common foundation.

In a word, **we lacked a tool that could correctly measure the mind.** Without such a tool, we can't understand others or their words or actions, right ? **Not being able to understand is a form of ignorance.** Yet in spite of this, we will ourselves to think we know and understand. However, **because we can't understand, explain, control, or predict, we can't expect anything of each other.**

That's why we need a ruler for the mind. First, we must know "0=∞=1" and understand God. If we do this, we will attain a **"state of only love."**

— A ruler for the mind, yes !

Now that you mention it, we were able to obtain a "ruler for the mind without hatch marks" via Zen Buddhism's 9th level, but what happened to memory ?

Once we have a "ruler for the mind without hatch marks," we understand God and become love itself. The hatch marks are lacking, but it's better than having no ruler at all. Until now, we didn't even have this ruler—we were totally bound by the brain.

As it happens, **we've already got the "ruler of the mind with hatch marks." It is the "ruler" that enables perception of the here and now via the "structure" of mind/energy/matter, upon "all-zero-ification."** So, things can be understood correctly. All that remains is "how much to use it."

— I see. The ruler for the mind is powerful ! It brings you to a state of only love that enables to understand, explain, control, predict, and expect everything.

That's right. Just to avoid misunderstanding, it is what makes us **masters of re-creation, overflowing with creative power beyond that of God.** This also refers to **the manner in which we change the story (simulation).**

Once humans understand God, use God freely, become a "being greater than God," and are able to apply God freely in daily life, the dignity of human beings will increase explosively.

— The Renaissance began in the 14th century, which was at the same time as the Reformation—yet religiously motivated wars continue to exist today. If the people on Earth became beings beyond God via "0=∞=1," the Reformation may reach completion as well ! If that were to happen, I can only imagine the global fanfare that would erupt.

That's right. However, there is one more important point to the completion of the Reformation. Religion brings the idea of "faith" to mind. I think there is a wonderful purity to the mind that believes in God unconditionally. However, **we end up stuck in a world that doesn't move past belief.**

— That's certainly true. I have felt myself how scary blind, unconditional faith can be. Religious texts can contain stuff that diverges wildly from science, and I wonder frequently what the basis for these beliefs is. It seems that it is this belief that leads to conflict between religions.

That's why we must think on how to transcend the "world of faith." The answer to this problem lies in the **synthesis of religion and science,** towards which there has been no progress.

— Certainly... it's not the same as religion, but there's been a lot of talk about how to synthesize spirituality and technology recently. However, it's been rough going. Getting there seems like a dream beyond a dream.

That's right. However, **is it acceptable for us to stay at the level of just *believing* in an absolute world that the human brain cannot conceive ? It isn't.** That's why it's important to work to develop scientific expressions of these ideas.

What makes this possible is mathematics and physics. Create images of this unimaginable absolute world, clarify the relationship between the absolute world and the relative world, make it possible to apply it in everyday life. **These ideas must be quantified and modeled.**

— That's right ! We discussed the relationship between the absolute world and relative world in the mathematical approach and the physical approach as well, by bringing mind into mathematics with the restored number (J) and imaginary numbers (i) to explain the world of God—the absolute world—in mathematical terms.

That's right. **Galois theory and Fermat's Last Theorem**—some of the most challenging problems that remain in mathematics—and the abc conjecture that garnered attention in 2020 **can be understood as "physical movement" with One Motion. It also becomes possible to understand the natural number (e=2.718...) and pi (π=3.1415...), which opens connections with and aids understanding of the free will/determinism debate in philosophy as well.**

— I feel overwhelmed... after all, these difficult problems have been tackled unsuccessfully by hundreds of years of geniuses. And to think that all of this can be integrated into physical laws as well... it's nothing short of a miracle !

That's right. In our physical/mathematical approaches, we explained the world that has only been described in terms of equations as a physical movement. In other words, **we connected the world of mathematical equations with energy/matter/mind.**

To supplement this a bit more, what makes these things possible is the existence of the imaginary number (i), the square root of -1, which enables easy explanation of the relationship between the absolute world and the relative world. Imaginary numbers (i) are *ma*, remember. *Ma* is the door that connects the absolute world with the relative world. You could call it perspective or function, also.

— The meaning and value of *ma* is getting deeper and deeper.

The insight of $0=\infty=1$ and *ma* enables the elevation of the inconceivable absolute world, the world of mental sense, the faith of religion to a realm of reason beyond the brain—something blind faith was unable to do.

Galois theory claims that any polynomial equations of 5th power or greater cannot be expressed in terms of its roots, but we can also explain the reason for this. **The infinitude of possibilities has been recorded in an "enumeration of finite sets." The zeta function of the Riemann hypothesis** is another wonderful equation for understanding the relationship between the absolute and the relative world.[14]

— Religion prioritizes the absolute world above all else while mathematics and physics have prioritized the relative world. **However, *ma* breaks down the barriers between these two. Via imaginary numbers (i), perspective, and functions, it's possible to make connections and syntheses and reach understanding.**

That's right. We have started from Fundamental Motion—the most natural motion in the universe and nature—to discuss the synergistic relationships between "mind/energy/matter" as seen in the world of the free will of the mind, the non-deterministic/probabilistic energy of quantum theory, and the matter of Newton's and Descartes' mechanistic determinism. This is also why it can serve as a common foundation for the World Axis Education.

— World Axis Education ! It appears again ! I look forward to hearing more about it.

• **Aesthetic (neo-sensual) approach**

Yes, I imagine. Now let's take a look at aesthetics.

— Aesthetics ? This is another area I don't know much about. I am unfamiliar with art... but maybe this is different ? What is aesthetics ?

When, and towards what, do you feel "beauty" ?

— Hmmm... it's hard to put into words.

---

14 *NHK Mysteries of Mathematics: White-Hot Classroom*

I see. Generally, "beauty" is believed to be in the eye of the beholder, after all—that there is no universal beauty. Among those things you find "beautiful," aren't some of them things you find beautiful because of a personal attachment that emerges from your relationship to them ?

— For sure. "Love is blind," after all—it's possible to see things in a favorable light.

Right ? People have special feelings for how their children look or their lovers, but **it is difficult to say that true aesthetics allows one to only find things with certain conditions beautiful.**

— So, we should see all things as beautiful ? That attitude is a little hard for me to understand... but if you were able to casually see beauty in mundane, everyday things, life would probably feel so rich and wonderful... which reminds me. Last time you said something about "art of the brain," didn't you ? Was it this ?

That's also true. Ok, let's look at this from start to finish.

Seeing all things as beautiful requires one to have no conditions, right ? So, what is something without conditions, which is immune to conditions ?

— The absolute unity. The very God of "$0=\infty=1$" !

Yes, once you become God itself, everything appears unconditionally beautiful and mystical. You undergo a revolution in intuition. I mentioned this before, but this is totally different from being able to see auras or having supernatural experiences. True enlightenment is not any different from the world of the five senses. It is simply the clearing away of all differences and distinctions.

— Ummm... but it's still hard for me to see everything as beautiful. How should I approach this ?

Here's the most important point in aesthetics. **One must become the imperceptible absolute world/Fundamental Motion/God itself, and then become able to perceive the conceivable world that emerges via the**

Fundamental Motion. Once you achieve that, everything is beautiful. That is true aesthetics.

This is totally different from finding things in reality beautiful or cool or whatever. The sense of beauty I'm talking about doesn't even compare—it is more than 100 times, more than 1,000 times more moving. If you thought the world was boring before, it will become beautiful beyond belief—like the tingling in your spine reaches out to the heavens.

Let's talk about this a little more. What happens when a sperm and egg meet ?

— When a sperm and egg meet ? They come together and become a zygote.

So, at that moment, is there either sperm or egg ? Both sperm and egg disappear, right ? In the same way, **the perceptual object and subject disappear, and the absolute world appears in a flash—the beauty of this phenomenon is aesthetics.**

In other words, **the observer and the observed disappear.** When both disappear, the Fundamental Motion—the absolute world—appears in a flash, resulting in an overwhelming sense of beauty.

— I see. Rather than seeing with the physical eye, if you don't become "1" itself then the image of true beauty will not reveal itself.

That's right. Seen from "1" without observer or observed, **that which cannot be seen with the eye, that which cannot be heard with the ear, that which cannot be felt by the hand becomes vivid in the mind.**

Yet we are able to see, hear, feel, walk. Isn't that mysterious ? This world with its vibrations and melodies of mind is the reason, the sense, the style of aesthetics.

— From the perspective of reality, you can see things with the eye without harboring any doubts. But **the ability to recognize that you have a body and are seeing with your eyes is itself a miracle !**

I think I get what makes aesthetics from the perspective of "1" so amazing. The observer and observed both disappear; that method of observing suggests a very mystical world of perception.

That's right. That's why the name of our system, *ninshiki gijutsu* (perception technology) is nTech/Ninshiki Technology. I have confidence in it as a beloved, valuable technology.

— By any chance... **are we talking about "seeing God" or something ?!**

That's right ! That's why—as unfortunate as it is—nobody has seen God before. But once we become able to do so, **the old way of separating the "perceived" from the "perceiver" will start to seem practically Satanic.** That's because it will be obvious just how cruel, humiliating, and tragic it is to be dominated by the virus of the brain.

— That's amazing...

There's more to it. God itself is flawless and omnipotent. However, because this God is an imperceptible, inconceivable, intangible motion that transcends human imagination, it lacks position or direction or boundaries, it cannot exist, it cannot interact, it has no differentiation of subject and verb, it does not understand itself. So, in a way, it is full of disability, as well. In that case, what is this reality ? **Couldn't reality be seen as a place where the things God cannot do are made possible ?**

— Now that you mention it... from the moment I open my eyes, I see boundaries of color and shape, there are all sorts of events ! Innumerable beings ! Endless change...

That's right. What's more, this reality is just a brief mental moment brought forth by the yearning of Fundamental Motion (mind)—even though it seems like it goes on and on to the human brain. It's like a work of art that the brain creates.

The present moment is nothing short of a miracle. This is the present moment intuition revolution (all-zero intuition, mystical intuition,

eternal invariant intuition). In so doing, oneself and the world one observes—**the mystery of all being here and now, and yet not—expands.**

— The mind of Fundamental Motion creates energy, has a backup for it, and packs it all into the present moment ! Amazing !!

I see what a miracle the world before my eyes is. How full of love. How satisfying, how supportive, how creative. It's making me tear up.

The world of the five senses doesn't change at all, yet appears to be a miracle.

That's right. **This is a mystical world that follows the innumerable laws of causality and physics. By observing the secrets of causality, one can obtain liberation.** By seeing from the perspective of "$0=\infty=1$," an age of recognizing the perpetual gift of the present moment and observing, experiencing, and creating miracles begins. This is the absolute world of Fundamental Motion, which the human brain could not reach. This is the world that religion believed in blindly and unconditionally and the world that science sought to uncover with the mind. $0=\infty=1$ enables us to do what religion and science could not: **obtain the greatest emotional heights humanity has ever known in a new age of aesthetics.**

— This universe—in which everything is connected via the One Motion— is so majestic, holy, and beautiful... it is truly an aesthetic realm.

Yes, a more pragmatic conversation regarding the age of aesthetics will bring forth an even more interesting world.

— What ? What do you mean ?

There is only One Motion, which connects all. Even though there is no time, space, or being, we split everything apart and think of ourselves as independent entities. **Physical causality yields no meaning on its own, but we apply meaning, we apply value, we create an idealized consensus structure that we call happiness and success. Humans do their very best—isn't there something sacred about this, too ?**

— Oh ! For sure. Humanity is hundreds of times more mysterious than the mysteries of the physical universe, bound by its causal laws.

That's right !

• Linguistic Approach

Now let's have a conversation about language. nTech invented "image language/absolute language" to discuss all things from the "0=∞=1" perspective.

— Yes, I remember. Languages until this point have been faulty in their assumptions. They've all been languages bound by the limits of the perception of the human brain—intended for the phenomenological world. My understanding is that languages apply names to the things we see and describe the ways in which they change/move/transform and the relationships between them.

Your understanding is good. Said another way, language goes no farther than discussing "movement formulae" that use subjects and verbs to understand things. However, this prevents discussion of God—it only allows fact perception. It doesn't enable the forcing of events or the emergence of a reality as one thinks of it. In addition, it prevents becoming free from the past. **These defects of language can be seen as a cause of human suffering throughout history.**

— Defects of language can be seen as a cause of human suffering ?

That's right. I said that language is the greatest tool that humans invented, the one tool that has contributed to our development more than any other. Because we have language, perception, understanding, thought, communication, sharing, and cultivation are possible. We can create cooperative structures and advance our collective intelligence. In agricultural societies, natural language was effective. In industrial societies, mathematical language became useful. Now, in the information age, programming languages have come to the fore.

However, just as I said previously, these languages go no farther than discussing objects within the range of the brain's perception. These languages are "movement formulae" for comprehension via the use of subjects and verbs. However, because of the defects in language, correct understanding is impossible. If correct understanding isn't possible, then the essence of things is invisible. In that case, I don't know anything about myself or others, right? So, it's impossible to understand human relationships. Even if you try, you end up fighting—it may not be an exaggeration to call this **"war language,"** don't you think?

— War language... I can see how misunderstanding and conflict could emerge from language.

All the more reason we need a language in which all can be understood. **A language which includes all things, including human suffering. A language that enables love.**

The world of God, of "0=∞=1," is an inconceivable motion that lacks subjects and verbs. So, we need to observe how subjects and verbs could emerge from it.

There are sages of the past who have seen the world without subjects or verbs. However, because they lacked the right language to describe it, they gave up—they relied on "intuitive discernment" or claimed that the world cannot be discussed in language.

— Cannot be discussed... so it cannot be communicated or shared? Then you won't even know if you have a misunderstanding between two people... so the ideas can't spread.

That's right. If everyone is similarly unable to achieve a "recreation of perception," it all goes nowhere. That's why I created image language and refer to it as "existence formulae." **This is a language that discusses the "structure of events" that enables something to arise from nothing. This is a language that discusses the structure that makes entities possible from a world in which entities are impossible. This is a language that discusses the structure that makes change possible from a world in which change is impossible.** By using this language, everyone, at any time, **can** describe all things as "events" and determine how to make the events they want to manifest. This is **the language used for love.**

— It's on a completely different level from the language we've used in the past !

The purpose and function of image language doesn't stop there.

The "existence formulae" are able to discuss the arising and ceasing of beings. So, it also is able to "all-zero" the world the brain can perceive. **The purpose and function of image language/absolute language is to "all-zero" the meanings and values that humanity created until now— in other words, all the meanings and values that humans have created with memorized language while bound by their brains.**

This ensures liberation from the entirety of the past, at all present moments !

By the way, **the main purpose of language until now has been to express and communicate.** However, **image language is used for observation and thought.** One point to remember is that **it is used "before" observational measurement.**

— Before observational measurement ? Oh, I get it ! Because we can't see with our eyes ! I'll try to use image language before I open my eyes, as training.

I have to say, Mr. Noh, you have invented a really amazing tool !

Considering how much language has contributed to our development in the past, just how far might image language/absolute language bring us ?

Thank you for inventing this new global standard for language !

• A conundrum in philosophy: Free will or determinism ? Laplace's demon denies the possibility of free will

No, thank you. Let's keep working to make image language a standard and create a "One World" that transcends nation, race, and religion !

By the way, I have a question for you now that we've reached this point.

Right now, I notice that you have your arms folded. **Is that posture— your behavior—an outcome that has been decided since before the universe came into existence ? Or is it something you did of your own free will ?**

— What ? ! I had been doing it unconsciously... but as I unfold my arms now, I do it intentionally, so I'd say it's my own "free will."

I see. So, you are claiming that you did so of your own free will. If it's your free will, then could you also stop your heartbeat this instant ?

— Ah... that's something I can't do !

That's right. So, then which is correct, free will or determinism ?

This is one of the deepest problems in philosophy. Do you know of "Laplace's demon," the thought experiment by the French mathematician Pierre-Simon Laplace ? The word "demon" is used to refer to his idea of an intelligence that could know the positions and momentum of all things in the universe. As a result, all things could be predicted, so all things are decided in advance.

Like the pose you made with your arms before, we could look at any trivial thing, like, "What should I eat today ?" Those decisions impinge upon every major life event you'll experience: marriage, career, etc.

Are your decisions and judgments truly the result of your own free will ? If so, what is your basis for claiming it's free will ?

— Basis... well, I don't have anything like that, but determinism seems disappointing. If everything is already decided, then there's no meaning to what I do—or don't do.

That just leaves me feeling empty. I can see why Laplace used the word 'demon' in reference to determinism.

I understand how you feel. Let's look at this in a little more detail.

Usually, we don't doubt the idea that we make our choices freely. Even when we make a decision based on external pressures, we usually don't doubt whether or not we made the choice.

However, science tells people who insist on free will to hold up. We can manipulate DNA via biotechnology, we can implant human bodies with chips via cyborg engineering. The rapid development of science is truly astonishing.

— Yes, when I heard you talk about this before I felt disturbed. It's a very "human" story.

There's that, and also, **because our power is approaching a point where we can overcome biological limits, we are faced with the threat of "human supremacism."**

— Human supremacism ?

Human supremacism is the idea that human free will is the ultimate authority, and it is the feelings and experiences of individuals that give the world meaning. In other words, the most sacred thing in the universe is human life. So **human free will is important.**
   But... **what if our free will and emotions were controlled by algorithms ?**

— In that case... there is no free will.

That's right. So, the value of individuals is denied, and individualism also breaks down.
   In that case, human supremacism would seek some major changes.

So, let me ask again.

Do human beings have free will ?
   If they do, what is it ?
   How does free will operate ?
   What is the structure of free will ?

How can the contradictions between free will and determinism be resolved ?

To say it in a different way, this is also **the relationship between the mind and the brain.** The most important, the deepest, realm as far as humanity is concerned.

— The relationship between the mind and the brain... this is a tough question now that AI has come online.

Exactly right. So, let's continue.

Was every action you will ever take decided before the birth of the universe ? (determinism)
Alternatively, do you act in accordance with your own free will ? (free will)

If you say free will, how can you explain this in terms of the causal laws of physics ?
Before, when I asked if you could stop your own heart, you said no.

On the other hand, what if you said determinism ? If you killed someone, you couldn't be blamed or judged for it. After all, **if the murder was preordained 13.8 billion years ago when the universe was born, you can't hold the murderer responsible.**

— No matter what you do, you can claim it was destined to happen. Not only can nobody be held responsible for anything, but everything would descend into chaos and violence.

That's right. So, neither determinism nor free will is sufficient. In this way, free will and determinism have some major inconsistencies with each other. **So, we need to find a way to synthesize them in a way that overcomes their contradictions.**

— That's way too hard for me.

Is it ? If you make use of everything you've learned so far, I think you'll be able to answer. The important thing is to use image language.

I explained the structure that gives rise to the 1:1 energy algorithm and the perspective of the brain (brain) from the inconceivable Fundamental Motion (mind). That structure is the key to resolving and explaining a combined free will and determinism. **Without breaking down the laws of physics, you can create a structure for free will that can be described in a single, simple image.**

— Figure 45 —
Free will and determinism

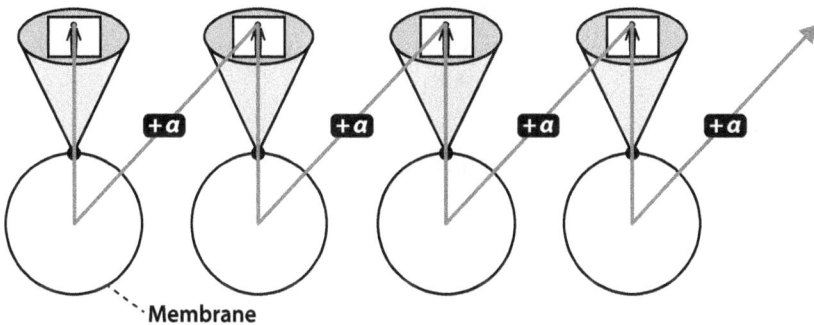

Membrane

1. **Membrane** (vacuum energy) maintains a formal memory
2. When the next universe is established, there is **an increase** of imaginary number i (Mind)

The level of the extra amount is the level
that changes perspective
No influence on physical laws

The membrane (vacuum energy) goes through 10^{500} *Tah* (∞ expansion) and condensation (∞ compression) vibrations a second. **The state of *Tah* (∞ expansion) maintains a formal memory of everything until then.**

When the next universe is created—when condensation (∞ compression) occurs—**more imaginary numbers (i) are incorporated than usual.**

That extra amount is enough to change "perspective," so there is no influence on physical laws.

— Formal memory... more imaginary numbers than usual ! So, via that extra amount of imaginary number, it's possible to exercise free will without running afoul of the laws of physics and causal theories.

That's right. **This explanation is a bit broad, but I think you can see from this how we can have free will while maintaining determinism.** The detail behind it is very interesting—**we can analyze it in terms of the natural number (e=2.718...) and pi (π=3.1415...), or the relationship between this "extra" amount of i and corporeal life and death**—but this is enough for now.

— I don't really get it, but it seems pretty amazing.

It definitely is. It lets us analyze all sorts of things.

So, anyway, we have free will. **That's why humanity has the power— at any time, in any age—to dispense with the past and create a new "now" with their own free will.**

However, with great power comes great responsibility.

People must take responsibility for their own actions.

— Here and now, I can create any reality I want through the exertion of my will ! I have to admit my excitement is overriding my sense of responsibility.

• The Critique of Pure Reason and *Reiwa* Philosophy

Finally, let's take a look at the Critique of Pure Reason and nTech/*Reiwa* Philosophy.

Immanuel Kant is known for synthesizing the philosophy of the modern age. His three critiques—the Critique of Pure Reason, the Critique of Practical Reason, and the Critique of Judgment—established a framework for a critical philosophy that had a Copernican-level effect on epistemology. The Critique of Pure Reason puts forward a critique of traditional metaphysics while creating a groundwork for a metaphysics rooted in mathematical science. To do so, Kant created a distinction between synthetic and analytic judgments in order to pose the following question: **How are** synthetic *a priori* (transcendental) judgments possible ?

— I've heard that Kant is difficult even for professional philosophers.

Don't worry, it can be explained in simple terms. It emerges directly out of asking ourselves "from where are we looking ?"

First, **let's get an understanding of analytic judgments and synthetic judgments.**

The observations of any discipline can be described in terms of "judgments" and "propositions."

In general, judgments are created via the coupling of a subject (S) and a predicate (V). The simplest form is **"S is V."** A judgment may be either analytic or synthetic.

An analytic judgment is a judgment in which the concept stated by the predicate (V) is already present in the concept described by the subject (S). A synthetic judgment is a judgment in which the predicate (V) introduces novel information not found in the concept described by the subject (S).

As an example, "triangles are two-dimensional" and "she is female" are analytic judgments. The predicates "two-dimensional" and "female" are already conceptually present in the subject (S). Negation of an analytic judgment—for example, "triangles are not two-dimensional"—results in a contradiction.

Conversely, the judgments "outside is rainy" and "she is wise" are synthetic judgments. The concept of "outside" does not contain the concept of "rainy" by definition, so in cases such as these, the predicate (V) adds novel information to the subject (S).

In other words, **analytic judgment is *a priori* (transcendentally) true.** This is due to the fact that the judgment is merely a direct restating of content already present in the subject-concept. Analytic judgments are **rationalist** because they state the truth of things via transcendental logic.

So then how do synthetic judgments prove the truth of their subject (S) and predicate (V) union ? If experience alone were sufficient proof, then all synthetic judgments would be "empirical." This position is called **empiricism.**

— So, in an analytic judgment, I can understand the predicate by looking at the subject, which is "transcendental." In a synthetic judgment, I can't come to any conclusion about the subject until I hear the predicate, which is "empirical." I'm ok so far.

Good. For these reasons, **transcendental logic is "deductive," while empirical logic is "inductive."**

You can see, then, that mathematics involves analytic judgments. A subject (S) is broken apart and analyzed, predicates emerge, and from this process new concepts are developed based on what was already inside the subject-concept.

For example, the proposition "2 + 2 =" only requires understanding of its subjects (S) to know that the predicate (V) of "4" follows by necessity. In this way, we produce predicates (V) from subjects (S). However, synthetic judgments require the incorporation of new concepts from beyond the subject (S).

In general, mathematics involves the ongoing production of new subjects (S) from the analysis of prior subjects (S), which is why it was considered to be a transcendental/deductive discipline.

People in the past didn't doubt the notion that mathematics was built on analytic judgments. When Kant claimed that mathematics is **"transcendental and synthetic,"** it resulted in significant controversy. That was because this **idea suggested that human beings could know everything without experiencing everything in the world.** Kant dubbed this "pure reason" and, in the critique, discusses its limitations.

— In other words, Kant claimed that everything in the world could be understood via transcendental perceptions rather than experience ?

That's right. The motto of nTech is "here, in the present moment, don't use your eyes to see."

Kant offered an utterly novel perception methodology for understanding the world by applying perceptual faculties (perceptual tools)

to the relationship between the perceptual subject (the cause of perception) and the perceptual object (the effect of perception).

In Kant's time, the two prevailing theories were **empiricism, which claims that experience is the basis of understanding, and rationalism, which claims that reason is the basis of understanding.** Kant's critical philosophy emerged as a synthesis of these two opposing schools of thought.

— How exactly was Kant able to synthesize empiricism and rationalism ?

Empiricism is limited by its tendency to result in agnosticism and skepticism, while rationalism is limited by its tendency to lead to prejudice and arbitrary judgment. Kant broke past these limitations and ended the arguments of his time by introducing perceptual faculties and perceptual tools (perspective in nTech).

Kant was the hero behind a paradigm shift towards moving the standard of truth from the objective world to the subjective world.

— He said that truth is not objective, but subjective ?

That's right. I talked before about the prevailing metaphysics of the time. That position held that God is objective truth and absolute, but Kant described a **subjective truth** in which there is no objective, rationalist, absolute truth attainable using God as the point of departure—rather, individuals have their own perspective and standards for judgment.

Kant advocated a perceptual faculty that was capable of **"transcendental synthetic judgments"** that allow for the visualization and calculation of phenomena beyond the Earth, beyond the Solar System, beyond the Milky Way—as well as their accurate description via equations of motion—without ever needing to experience them in person.

— But wasn't Kant a philosopher ? He had that much command over mathematics and physics ? That's surprising.

Actually, philosophy was originally a logical enterprise of a higher caliber than either mathematics or physics.

Kant nullified all the logic and visualizations of all the philoso-

phers, mathematicians, and physicists that preceded him and surpassed it all. He practiced true philosophy in his insistence on the perceptual subject, as a truly exemplary philosopher who understood the
essence of his mission.

— Wow ! But what is the basis for claiming that other mathematicians,
physicists, and philosophers were "surpassed" ?

The mathematicians, physicists, and geometers of the time were ridiculing
the religious with blind faith in God, claiming that mathematics is the one
true means for understanding and communicating the truth of the cosmos.
This position is known as mathematical universalism, or scientism.

In response, **Kant criticized human reason** by asserting that while
there is indeed a world built along causal principles, there are comparatively
uncountable inconceivable worlds not explainable by the same means.

This is the topic of the famous Critique of Pure Reason, which lays
out the principles of an attitude or posture towards causal—conceivable—
worlds and that towards inconceivable worlds.

— An attitude or posture towards the conceivable world and the inconceivable world ?
I have no idea what you're saying.

Ok, let me explain.

The inconceivable world is the "Absolute world" or "domain of God."
The attitude or posture of absolute blind faith in this world is seen in religion. On the other hand, the conceivable world is the one that the mathematicians and physicists had put their own blind faith into. In other words,
**both mathematicians and physicists were not all that different from
the religious as far as their "posture of absolute blind faith" was concerned. Kant warned the intellectual elite of the time about this issue.**

— Wow ! I have a feeling I know how the intellectual elite responded to
Kant's warnings.

However, Kant had limits of his own.

He viewed the inconceivable world as something that cannot be accessed in the present moment, in our momentary lifetimes. Because of this, he relied on the conceivable world for matters of collaboration or the embodiment of concepts. He used it as an appeal to maintain motivation towards strengthening relationships in order to avoid falling into nihilism.

— Hmmmm... now that I know about nTech, I can't help but find that somewhat lacking.

Indeed. That's why nTech "all-zeroes" the conceivable world as a "fiction" while the inconceivable world is used as proof of having attained enlightenment, of having overcome the limits of the brain in order to attain a clear victory against it. **Become free from the known world, enjoy the conceivable world, play games, celebrate, watch the grand movie.** That's the position of nTech.

— nTech is a tool that introduces us to a simple yet grand world.

Thank you for saying so. What nTech calls understanding the place beyond space without journeying beyond the universe, Kant called a perceptual faculty for transcendental synthetic judgment. In other words, if you substitute perspective for "perceptual faculty," you can see that Kant is the philosopher that showed how what we observe with our eyes is not a faithful representation of reality. The information is in error.

However, **Kant was unable to explain the where and why of these perceptual faculties and perceptual methodologies (perspectives). It seems to me that he made it to around level 8 of Zen Buddhism, because he didn't define the concept of "1."** That said, the ability to clearly perceive perspectives as "transcendental synthetic judgments" was a remarkable development.

Our universe is made up of energy and matter, but these are no more than mutants of perspectives, the effects of perspectives (perceptual objects and contents). That is to say, knowing perspective means to know everything in the universe. That is why, **while perceptual causes and perceptual subjects are the purview of philosophy, Kant was unable to complete the project.**

— Is philosophy the discipline that uncovers the truth of the perceptual subject ?

Yes, **science is the discipline that develops perceptual objects and perceptual effects, while philosophy sheds light on the perceptual subject.** Perceptual subjects can be broadly divided into 3 categories. **Human brains, causers of events (perspectives/energy algorithms/Kant's perceptual methodology), and analysts (the inconceivable/the unlimited/Original Mind).**

From those, a simple conclusion emerges: **All that *actually* exists is the Fundamental Motion. All that *actually* exists is the Liberated Mind of the 9th level of Zen. This is the position of *Reiwa* Philosophy.**

— These terms of "perceptual methodology" and "perceptual faculty" are really interesting.

I get the feeling that Kant's philosophy is helping me understand the importance of nTech's notion of perspective more.

You have excellent sense. **Kant was the first person to discover perspective.**

Remember the "perennial struggle of humanity" we discussed via bird and the bottle ? If you don't understand how to break through the perspective problem —if you don't understand how and why Kant's perceptual methodology is created—you will never have a clear understanding of the connection between the Absolute World and the real world. Having a clear understanding means not only that you can clearly perceive the relationships of eternal, unchanging motion and change, of metaphysics and postmodernism, of the perceptual subject and object, etc., but that you can grasp them in their entirety and use them as tools.

— I understand how incredible it must be to grasp perceptual methodology and perspective, but I'd appreciate it if you could break it down for me just a little more.

Sure. In other words, **if you understand "1," you understand everything.**

If you understand ultimate "1," the Fundamental Motion, then you understand everything. **I'm talking about the defined-undefined, the** meaningful-meaningless, the valuable-valueless absolute instantaneous rates of change, the restored number "J."

Of course, Kant himself was unable to see that the perception of the subject is the analytical subject of "Fundamental Motion." **He made it as far as the event subject of "perspective ontology." Most people and even philosophers only get as far as "human brains."**

— Kant discovered something amazing.
By any chance, did you first learn about "perspective" via Kant ?

No, no, I didn't. I attained a more vivid understanding of perspective via my clear comprehension of the Fundamental Motion "1." The images I experienced physically were close to Japan's concept of *ma* and *ma* motion. When I analyzed Kant›s work, I saw that Kant was saying the same things about perspective, calling it "perceptual methodology."

— That's cool ! I never knew that Japan's concept of 間 (*ma*) had so much value.

When humans don't understand *ma*, they become progress junkies. By knowing *ma*, they break free from their addiction and understand the value of taking a step back. We stepped back all the way to the "way of observing" of level 11, if you remember.

For example, a frog may try to eat a fly, a snake tries to eat the frog, a hawk tries to eat that snake, and finally humans try to bring the hawk down with bow and arrow. In this way, we have to back things up until we can't back up any farther, which brings us to the Fundamental Motion "1."

So, if there's something you don't understand, that means you are already addicted to progress.. If you understood "1," you'd understand everything.

— If the notion that "I don't understand" crosses my mind, the first thing I should do is consider the progress addiction.

Right. So, we discerned "1," obtained *ma*, and created the 1:1 algorithm of energy. This is referred to as **"1, *ma*, point." Points are made from**

subjects (S) and predicates (V). When you split that point, the next SV emerges, and if you split that one, another emerges, and so on and so forth. If you go all the way down, you'll reach the restored number "J," or "1." So, **we've returned to "1" by using the "point" of "1, *ma*, point."**

However, mathematicians have been unable to imagine this "1." Kant was able to imagine it but couldn't define it.

— So **nTech defines "1" and completes mathematics.**

That said, I'm amazed that Kant discussed such things...

Without nTech, I likely would not have come to understand Kant's philosophy.

Perhaps. But Kant will undergo a dramatic resurgence in the years to come. People are currently starved for a foundation, for some kind of direction. With the emergence of COVID-19 and the advent of AI, our lifestyles have been changed against our will. **We must move forward in the midst of uncertainty as our manuals, systems, traditions are destroyed.** Because we can›t rely on our past experiences, we have no confidence. I think you also viscerally feel the unbearable uncertainty, distrust, and dread in the world right now. **But in order to get this new foundation, this new direction, we must come to understand "1." This is the critical breakthrough we need.**

— Certainly, we're now in an age where people are desperate for some kind of foundation or direction.

Unfortunately, while Kant defined the perspective of the brain, he cut things off at the world of mind beyond the brain, claiming that the inconceivable world has no applicability in reality.

— Oh, you mentioned this before. He brought this up in the context of the importance of a concept of human solidarity or something.

That's right. He tossed out the value of the inconceivable world.

He claimed that **the realm of the thing-in-itself is fundamentally inaccessible from our perceived reality using human reason.** So ultimately, he left the bird in the bottle.

My perspective is the opposite: **the inconceivable is the *most* applicable because of its nature.** It's the meaningful-meaningless, valuable-valueless, defined-undefined. Conversely, the conceivable world is illusion and hologram. **It is unusable because all of its meanings, values, and definitions are confined to the level of the brain.**

However, while Kant claimed what he claimed, he recognized that it was not very amenable to application. To avoid a nihilistic conclusion, he invoked God as the instrument by which we may contact the ineffable.

His failure was in separating Truth (essence) and reality (phenomena) into mutually exclusive categories.

— Hmmm... Kant made a lot of novel breakthroughs, but at the end, he fell just a bit short.

But with nTech and the *Reiwa* Philosophy, it's possible to realize his true intent. His goal was eternal peace as well.

nTech takes the baton from Kant and exhorts us to become the analytical subject of the present moment "1" itself. Enjoy the conceivable world, play games, celebrate. *Reiwa* Philosophy, as a pragmatic program, offers us the freedom to go in and out of the bottle, in everlasting peace.

CHAPTER 9

A perfect storm to change the civilizational paradigm

Interviewer:

— So now maybe we can start talking about some realistic things. I think I've had more than enough of my fill of these conversations about essence ! (laughs)

After all, while I understand how amazing and sublime these discoveries are, but no matter how amazing this technology, this tool, may be, it's just an armchair theory if it can't be applied in practice !

Previously, we talked about **the invention of a path to victory that makes ideals into reality.** Let's start there !

Jesu Noh:

Yes, that path to victory is nTech's specialty ! Let's start talking about inventions !

So let me ask you something. Right now, what is the one problem bothering you more than anything that you must fix ?

— Let me think... I talked about myself a bit before, but I'd say the thing concerning me most is my sense of unease towards the future. Things are changing so much, so fast... regardless of any model for success or whatever, nothing seems to stick for me... for example, AI is nearly capable of replacing humans for work, we were talking about a post-human society before, so what are humans supposed to do ? How can we avoid becoming obsolete ? Even before AI came on the scene, the economy wasn't looking that great, and it seems like AI will only make the problem worse.

Also, the 2020 COVID-19 pandemic is a real threat ! It's like the coup de grace. It's not just all the death and disease it causes—it seems like it may thrust us into a worse economic crisis than the global Great Depression of the 1930s. This is a serious life-or-death problem, people are going crazy, countries are drifting apart, we're on the brink of social collapse. We've been driven into a corner...

You referred to COVID-19 as a "wake-up call," and now I understand what you mean. It seems like it's intensifying unease, while we are thrown around by the onslaught of information without any idea of what to do about it. This endless tunnel just keeps on going, keeping all of humanity in the dark. I don't even want to think about it anymore.

Once you start looking around you see a horrible mountain of problems. I understand your inclination to look away again. But what if we could clear away every last one of the problems you identified, right now ?

— Ummm... I don't think there's any magic spell for this... and I feel half ready to give up as it is...
　　But since I met you and learned about nTech, I admit I see a glimmer of hope ! After all, with all these grand discoveries, maybe some of them can help us in this world.

Great ! We can do this !
The strategy I propose is the **"All Clean Course !"**

— That name sure sounds appropriate ! What kind of course is it ?

You'll find out ! Before we get there, I want to share an image that will be key to our discussion.
　　Another question: COVID-19 is a type of virus. **What function does a virus possess ?**

— The function of a virus ? What exactly is a virus, anyway ?

Viruses are a self-replicating entity that is somewhere "in-between" matter and life.
　　Matter can't copy itself, right ? If there was a pen here, it wouldn't turn into two pens by tomorrow.
　　From the nTech perspective, energy emerges from the Fundamental Motion (mind), matter emerges from energy, viruses emerge from matter, life (cells) emerge from viruses. Human bodies emerge from the assembly of 37 trillion cells. So viruses are somewhere in-between life and matter.

That's why viruses have a "copy function."

Just a single virus strain, invisible to the naked eye, has infected human bodies the world over and caused a global pandemic. On an Earth that once had only matter, a single cell became the ancestor of all life on Earth today. Does that give you some idea of the power of the copy function ?

— It's tremendously powerful. Earth's very first single cell did remarkable work for the world. We owe a lot to our unicellular ancestors.

That's right. However, **there are differences between the copy function of a virus and a cell.**

— A difference between the replication of cells and viruses ? Ummm, I don't know what it is.

It's important to understand this point, so please listen carefully.

Viruses make copies in the same dimension. They don't ascend to a higher dimension—all the copying is in the same one. No matter how much they copy themselves, **they won't progress or develop.**

Also, viruses just drift around and bump into each other. They are not able to collaborate or anything like that. So **they are limited to a separated, disjointed, and isolated mechanical motion.**

However, cells are able to copy themselves in a way that lets them jump into higher dimensions. For example, stem cells hold both the ability to replicate themselves and also to differentiate into a wide variety of cell types.

Cells connect to each other and engage in a sort of teamwork. The 37 trillion cells in our own bodies are all able to work together without resentment or jealousy, carrying out their own duties.

— I see. Self-replication on the virus level could cause the eternal replication of useless and obsolete things. I can see how that could cause problems.

On the other hand, cells develop as they replicate, and cooperate.

In that case, the difference is very clear !

So, I understand why the copy function of cells is so amazing, but what does this have to do with anything ?

I'm sure you remember our talk about human performance. We said that the inclusion of chips to our organs and brain etc., (techno-human supremacism and data supremacism) is human performance version 1.0 and individual enlightenment is version 2.0.

— Sure, but I think you were saying that we have to reach human performance version 3.0 or something...

That's right. **Human performance version 2.0 is the level at which "perception copying" is possible.** As long as you stay here, it isn't possible to make copies on the behavior dimension.

Cells of enlightened people who can make copies at the behavioral level, that is to say, "spiritual cells," become a necessity. This is human performance version 3.0.

— I remember this ! That strange term "spiritual cells" has appeared again.
So the relationship to our conversation about copying is that we are "copying the soul."

That's pretty close.
I don't want anyone to get offended at this, but until now, **we've had an "animal" civilization: we aren't that different from other animals.** Even the institution of marriage and building families is not that different from what animals do. **The base unit of the spiritual civilization is totally different from the base unit of "family" we use now. This base unit is a key term for the spiritual civilization.**

— I can't really claim otherwise on your point about animals.
But even if that's the case, I don't really think there's a problem with "family" as the base unit. What is going to happen to the notion of family ?

I said before that we're headed for a doomed era if we don't change all of our assumptions. This may be a bit shocking, but please listen.
The way in which our base unit of family will change is that, rather than

being based on two people, **it will be based on a community of 31 people. This number is derived from the logos and structure of the universe, as a sum of "1, 5, 25."** 5 emerges from 1, and then that 5 copies itself.

This is the base unit of spiritual cells: the "Dignity Family."

It will be difficult to understand why the basic elements of the spiritual civilization are as they are if you don't have an understanding and image of the idea that "ideals = reality, discoveries = inventions, completion = perfection." It's important, therefore, that these ideas are axiomatic.

If the individual enlightenment of human performance version 2.0 is the level of discovery, "group enlightenment" is the level of invention. The image of discovery is everything we have talked about so far. I think you've got a pretty good handle on it. Do you feel confident?

— I'm good on discovery!
That said, I'm having a hard time with this 31-person Dignity Family thing... it's a little beyond what I can imagine, I feel confused.

I'm not surprised. But it's also hard to understand the common sense of the past based on what we take for granted today. For example, wondering why people in the past believed the Earth is flat or on top of a turtle's back. In the same way, people of the future will wonder why families were pairs of men and women, or why people thought that their self only extended as far as their body. Our attitudes today will become the targets of study for the historians of tomorrow.

For that reason, I'm going to present these ideas like I'm a person from the future.

— I see! Past experiences and knowledge all arise from observational error, after all. We need a revolution in our point of reference... become free from the world we know, and see things from the Fundamental Motion "1"! I'll nullify my image of the past for a bit, and try to assume the new identity of a person from the future!

Good. In order to deepen your image of spiritual cells, I want to talk about something else. Have you heard of the trichotomy of **spirit, body, and soul?**

— No, this is the first I've heard of it.

It's hard to analyze and there are different ways you can analyze it. nTech looks at it like this:

Spirit: Fundamental Motion of Mind
Body: Able to move in space
Soul: Able to self-copy

Humans, animals, and plants have the following combinations of attributes:

Humans: Spirit ○, Body ○, Soul ○
Animals: Spirit ×, Body ○, Soul ○
Plants: Spirit ×, Body ×, Soul ○

— I see. **Because human beings are able to become Fundamental Motion itself, they have Spirit, Body, and Soul. Animals cannot become enlightened, so they have no Spirit, but they can move through space and self-copy. Plants can't move through space.** That's easy.

So humans, in this sense, are complete for having all three.

However, we've only exercised "soul" and "body." In other words, we've just been replicating our bodies all this time. **Isn't this the same sort of copying that viruses exhibit ? We're trapped by the virus of the brain, and our thoughts, feelings, and bodies, and everything else created via human enterprise has been born through a process of same-dimensional copying.** That's why I say this is an animal civilization. This is human performance version 1.0.

— So, you could say that we've had a "virus civilization" all this time.

That's right. However, from this state of affairs, even if we realize that we are Fundamental Motion itself and proceed to human performance version 2.0, **we will be liberals of the spirit until we manage behavioral copying at the cell level.**

We'll just think about our own emancipation without concern for the development of others. This has been the goal of enlightenment practice until now.

— Hmmm... yes, if we are only thinking about our freedom, that's a limitation.

So we have to avoid this sort of **"spirit liberalism."** The way of the **"spirit evolutionist"** is to become Fundamental Motion itself (Spirit), become able to make behavioral copies of that at the cellular level (Soul), and continue to create copies that ascend into higher dimensions.

Therefore, once we assemble into 31-person Dignity Families (spiritual cells), make behavioral copies at the cellular level, and continue the progression of the spirit, the full expression of human function will be realized in human performance version 3.0.

— It would be wonderful if human beings the world over strive to make full use of their faculties. That would lead to a huge increase in human dignity !

That's right. But human beings have done ongoing damage to their dignity. Before we get into the pragmatics of all this, I also want to discuss the process of dignity destruction.

So, let's talk about the **"5 crevasses of civilization."**

— Crevasse ?

The word refers to chasms in glaciers and snowy valleys the most dangerous of them concealed by snow. At a glance, it seems like the landscape before you is all connected, but in fact, there is a dangerous chasm in front of you that you can't see.

Humanity has stumbled into four crevasses of civilization, and we're about to hit the fifth.

You can think of the crevasse as **something that destroys human dignity because of an invisible discontinuity that emerges out of what was assumed to be continuous.**

— The obvious becomes no longer obvious, harming human dignity...
     What kinds of crevasses are these ?

Ok, let's look at these one at a time.
     The first is a crevasse mainly for people in East Asia: **"Biblical Creationism."**
     Creationism claims that God created the universe; humanity and the cosmos are the work of God. East Asian people find this unattractive. That's because East Asian people think that individuals create their own universe. **Creationism demotes us from the side of creation to the side of being created.** Western people may think that it's fine to simply be the "children of God." However, this hurts the pride of East Asians.

The second is the **heliocentric model of Copernicus.** When the geocentric model reigned, people had a certain pride about the notion that Earth is at the center of the cosmos, and we humans, as the children of God, are at the center of it as well. However, with the arrival of the heliocentric model, that pride quickly crumbled. In the heliocentric model, the Earth is just one of many other planets orbiting the Sun, so **humans weren't at the center of the universe anymore.** It suddenly became impossible to defend the notion that the Earth is immobile.
     But thanks to the heliocentric theory, we understood that what we see with our eyes is not absolute. **Acknowledging our ignorance led to the development of science.**

The third is **Darwin's theory of evolution.** People felt prideful about being the children of God, even if they weren't at the center of the universe. But as it turns out, evolution demonstrated that human beings descended from a common ancestor with the great apes (animals). So now **it wasn't even possible to draw a distinction between humans and animals anymore.** Any pride related to the special position of humanity was ripped to shreds as well.

The fourth is **Freud's notion of the unconscious.** Freud destroyed the remaining pride we had in our reason as the final thing separating us from other animals. According to Freud, we have an unconscious full of things like the Oedipus complex, a tendency for boys to unconsciously harbor romantic feelings for their mothers and antipathy towards their fathers. No matter how much we brandish our rationality, our consciousness is just the top of the iceberg of our minds. Most of our mind is submerged, as the instincts of the id. In other words, **because our reason cannot overcome our unconsciousness, we are no different from animals overall.**

— I can see how each one of these has led to the degradation of human dignity. And now we're past the fourth... or, rather than past it, we've just gotten used to it.

That said, humans have put in a lot of effort to come this far, maintaining their attitude as the stewards of Earth.

That's been true, yes. No matter what I may say, our civilization has developed and we have had reason to have pride in ourselves as greater than other animals, plants, and machines.

— Figure 46 —
The five crevasses

Level 1	The universe was created by God	▶	The universe is nothing more than a creation of God **Creationism**
Level 2	Humanity (Earth) is the center of the universe Geocentrism	▶	The Earth moves **Copernican heliocentrism**
Level 3	Humanity was created by God Creationism	▶	Humanity evolved from animals **Darwin's theory of evolution**
Level 4	Humans are superior to animals because of their rational faculties	▶	Reason is the tip of the iceberg, and most of consciousness is in the unconscious **Freudian unconscious**
Level 5	Humans control and direct machines	▶	**Birth of an AI** with an IQ that exceeds 10,000

That said, unfortunately the fifth crevasse easily smashes that remaining pride.

— I think I might know what it is...

Yep. Number 5 is **"Industry 4.0: Artificial Intelligence (AI)."**
Humans were starting to think that while our reason may be corrupted by our unconscious, at least we're superior to machines. We create them, manipulate them, direct them. **But now there is an overwhelming gulf between AI and humans.**
In terms of IQ, we will have AIs with IQ of 10,000 in the near future, but the average for humans is still stuck at 100. There's no contest. Moreover, there's now an attitude that humans themselves are just machines: that **humans are no more than machines whose daily behaviors and thoughts and feelings are all defined deterministically.** We can just 3D print organs, control emotions with drugs and electrical stimulation of the brain. And **if human beings are algorithms of organic chemistry, they don't stand a chance against the precision of the electrical algorithms of AI.** So people start to think that **humans are dumber than AI !**

— Unfortunately, I am not able to refute that.
AIs don't complain, worry, or disagree. They are fast, accurate, don't get tired, and in the long run are cost efficient. As they become able to teach themselves they will get increasingly intelligent and instantly exchange information with other AIs. They're like the exact opposite of humans.
This reminds me of something scary I heard about a few years ago about the AI software for playing *go*, **"AlphaGo Zero."** The original AlphaGo trained on a huge dataset of games played by *go* players, and beat a professional for the first time in March 2016. **AlphaGo Zero learned only the rules of *go*, and without any dataset as input, taught itself how to win via reinforcement learning.** Then in October 2017, **AlphaGo won 100 times in a row,** and in December of the same year, the new edition called **"Alpha Zero"** became able to play games besides *go*. **It was able to beat the best *shōgi* AI after 2 hours of study, the best chess AI after 4 hours of study, and the 2016 edition of AlphaGo after 8 hours of study.** I felt that this was an omen... of something to come.

AlphaGo Zero and AlphaZero becoming overwhelmingly successful despite having no human match data makes us wonder: **just how obsolete is human experience and knowledge now ?** Maybe we're just in the way.

— Exactly... it's astonishing, but when I combine this with your "way of observing things," I can't help but be convinced.
If I were a manager, I may prefer to have AIs do stuff.

I think there are many managers who feel the same way. After all, unlike humans, AIs don't worry about pointless things, get depressed, get disappointed, lose motivation, act strong-headed, misunderstand, act deceptive, or cause problems with others.
So some people are starting to think that **maybe consciousness isn't even necessary.**

— Oh, right. Because AI will surpass human intelligence.

That's right. When you look at "intelligence and consciousness" and see depression, fear, conflict, jealousy, and aggression, it's easy to think that maybe "human consciousness" isn't needed. Maybe intelligence alone is enough. We can even easily control human emotions, as I mentioned before. In that case, consciousness itself is a machine—so we might as well leave everything to intelligence. I can understand why someone might think that way.

— So human consciousness is in the way. It's not useful.

That's right. In the near future, human bodies will be nothing but chips, and then nothing but data, and ultimately assimilate into the great wave of cosmic information, a single drop in a grand ocean. So if we keep on this path, humanity's sense of self and dignity will simply crumble away. In the book *Homo Deus*, the author Yuval Noah Harari predicts that **a "useless class" of people unable to be employed will emerge,** who will subsist on a form of basic income.[15]

---

15 Harari, Yuval Noah. "Homo Deus: A Brief History of Tomorrow"

— This is truly an unprecedented crisis. It's unbelievable that human dignity could be harmed so much.

Yes. Without a doubt, this is the deciding moment for humanity to either go extinct or ascend. **COVID-19 is the first of three coronas that created a perfect storm and pushed humanity to the brink.** There is a film called *The Perfect Storm*, in which a number of huge storms fuse together leading to a pile-up of natural disasters. That's where the term comes from.[16]

— Three coronas ? Perfect storm ? Even if the novel coronavirus mutates, we're still talking about one variety, right ? What do you mean by three ?

You said it yourself. When the COVID-19 pandemic began, we didn't just face a crisis of death and disease. We also faced economic issues, psychological issues. That's what I mean.

The world has made a big deal out of the virus called "COVID-19," but beyond the health-destroying **"body corona,"** the **"economic corona"** is more serious—and the **"mind corona"** is even more serious than that.

— I see. Now that you mention it, COVID-19 was like the trigger that brought those other two problems out. In reality, the economy was in bad shape even before the COVID crisis, and while people tried to put on a brave face and find ways to keep the social order together, we had reached a point where we couldn't hide it anymore—and COVID-19 let it all out.

That's right. Yet to this day, the leaders of countries all over the world are not seriously grappling with this perfect storm, implementing a **"management strategy"** intended to ride it out.

This management strategy assumes that we cannot eradicate the virus, a position that on its own already damages human dignity.

Policies for containment have been intended to avoid an overshoot with the attainment of herd immunity in mind, but in my view, this will only make the problem worse.

---

16 *The Perfect Storm. 2000. Warner HomeVideo.*

Without knowing anything about COVID-19 or how to structure a lockdown, governments have relied on examples from the past and indiscriminately isolated patients while trying to develop anti-virals and vaccines. **This doesn't get to the root of the problem.** Even if we manage to seal the virus away for a little while, the problem will only explode again later. The 'with corona' strategy is not sufficient.

How did we end up in this situation to begin with ? To use the language of disease, how has our civilization come to have this terminal cancer ? Now is the time for us to unite as one to solve our problems. We must identify what issues have led us to where we are.

— Strike at the root of the problem... our inability to do so, again in medical terms, is due to getting our diagnosis wrong—a misdiagnosis.

Exactly ! Einstein may have thought about this sort of problem, too.

There is a legend in which a reporter asked him **how he would spend his time if the world was going to be destroyed in an hour.** What would you do ?

— Just one hour ? I can't think of anything I could do in one hour. I guess I might spend it with someone I love, or eat my favorite food. What is Einstein's answer in the story ?

In the story, Einstein says **he'd spend 55 minutes thinking about the nature of the problem, and spend the remaining 5 minutes figuring out how to solve it.**

— Wow ! 55 minutes spent on *thinking* about the problem ! That truly does put the diagnosis—identifying the cause of the problem—first. So, then the prescription—the solution—only requires 5 minutes.

This suggests that identifying the cause of a problem must be the top priority. If that cause cannot be found, then even if you manage to get through one crisis, the essential problem will just get worse. If you do find the cause, then the solution will practically reveal itself.

— In comparison, my answer was so childish. It's embarrassing—laughable.

People addicted to progress who see things with their physical eyes spend less time asking about root problems and instead get preoccupied with what's right in front of them, lost in the realm of the senses.

But you can notice where you are entirely because you are able to see beyond the physical world. After all, if you remained lost, you wouldn't even know where you were. Well done !

By the way, what do you think the root problem is ? What is the correct diagnosis ?

— **Don't see with your eyes !!** (laughs)

If you start with your eyes, you start in error, so all that follows is in error. This is the diagnosis—the root problem.

Therefore, the prescription is to move backwards from the physical eye to Newton, to Einstein, to Bohr, to string theory, to M-theory, to formlessness, up to level 11. One must observe in a manner that does not exert influence on the observed. One must observe from the Fundamental Motion "1," the place without perceptual subject or object !

— **Always be in the present moment, and from that place of eternal invariance, observe with the eye that commands all changes !**

Excellent !

Seeing with your eyes is the same as being controlled by the virus of the brain.

Become the Fundamental Motion "1" itself. When you observe from that position, a path will reveal itself: the path to perfect control of the virus using the All Clean Course.

The All Clean Course controls the perfect storm by manifesting group enlightenment. It dissolves the AI crisis, infinitely expands human dignity and maintains it. Then the groundwork is laid for a new city model, the *Reiwa* City, and a "One World" vision.

— *Figure 47* —
The Absolute Deepest Perspective
(The Perspective of Original Mind)

Perspective transformation(nTech)

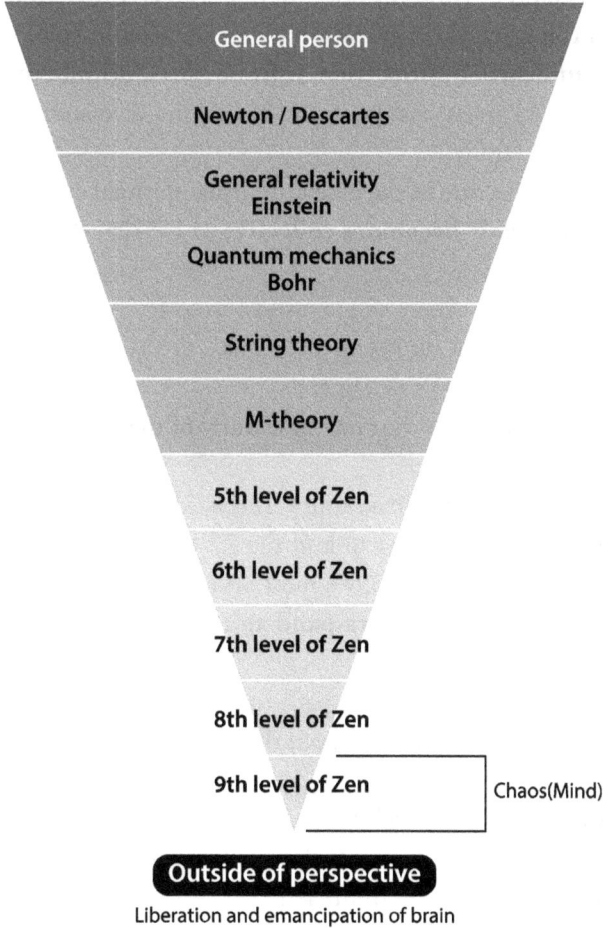

General person
Newton / Descartes
General relativity Einstein
Quantum mechanics Bohr
String theory
M-theory
5th level of Zen
6th level of Zen
7th level of Zen
8th level of Zen
9th level of Zen

Chaos(Mind)

Outside of perspective

Liberation and emancipation of brain

— The All Clean Course is pretty cool.

There's even a model for cities and a global unification strategy !

In order to realize that, the new discoveries I mentioned—"**ideals = reality**," "**discovery = invention**," "**completion = perfection**"—**are the base for a "shift change" from the crises of material civilization to the age of mind and the spiritual civilization by awakening infinite motivation, infinite confidence, infinite trust, infinite ideas, infinite connections.**

The thing we must change is the base units of material civilization, "individual and family."

Here is the structure of the base unit of the spiritual civilization:

The "individual" becomes a collective of 1+5+25, that is, 31 people: the Dignity Family.

This is the most important key to all of this.

— The Dignity Family is the vital, base unity of the spiritual civilization.

So how do we change that base unit ? This is where the nTech World Axis Education comes in. In order to lead the 7.7 billion people on this planet suffering in this perfect storm, we must attain total control over the virus of the brain and create an **ultra-pandemic of dignity cells** that goes far beyond COVID-19.

I've talked roughly about the path to victory—the overview of inventions—before, but now I'll talk about that path in more detail.

— A pandemic of dignity cells ! That's exciting !

Before corona, seeing with the eye was common sense—but after corona, it'll be observing from "1" !

Yes, which is why I'd like to look at each of them in detail.

Let's start with the **"economic corona"** !

— We talked about this a little bit before, but the economic crises that came to light as a result of COVID-19 show we were really in a downward spiral that nobody on Earth could do anything about.

The demand, supply, consumption, meaning and value of our industries crumbled all at once.
Demand was actually waning before the novel coronavirus hit—but the market was unable to create new need, and we were just having the same old products pushed onto us. However, this time, it stopped working. **The economy was operating at a "virus level"**—it couldn't advance beyond same-dimension mechanical repetition.

— A virus-level economy. It's true that when I try to think of recent products, none comes to mind as particularly desirable. I have most of what I need as it is, a car share is enough as far as automobiles go, and I'm tired of the pretension of chasing fads. I guess I'm tired of consumption... the COVID lockdowns have made me very aware of how frivolous a lot of my spending has been.

I think there are a lot of people just like you. However, if demand, supply, and consumption all disappear, the economy will collapse. With no other options, things will just get worse.
This really couldn't be clearer. 10 years of rising employment in the US—employment all over the world—disappeared in just one month, like a bubble on a pond. 22 million people filed for unemployment in April of 2020, right after the COVID-19 pandemic struck—over 8 times more than the number following the subprime mortgage crisis. The unemployment rate rose dramatically and businesses declared bankruptcy left and right in a global shock that surpassed the Great Depression and caused a cessation of economic activity. Our way of life was no longer a guarantee—it's no surprise that these events led to an increase in distrust and uncertainty, as well as suspicious attitudes that contributed to the rise of conspiracy theories.

— I can personally attest to that sense of urgency, that indescribable dread, that feeling of always being on guard. In Japan I've seen reports of companies of near-institutional status succumbing, reports of small business owners committing suicide. With some kind of social security net or new employment it'd be a different story, but I see no sign of anything like that.
    Also, I've been astonished at the state of things in America. It's im-

possible to avoid the impression that they've consistently been a step behind with their policies towards curbing infection and maintaining the economy. When President Trump made his declarations of "America First," I thought that meant the US would stop being the police of the world. In seeing the response of countries around the globe, it seems that **distrust towards governments and leaders** increased greatly all over the world. I guess it's good that people are paying attention to politics, maybe...

Lack of faith in government leads to the **disintegration of democracy.** Protest against inaction and half-measures has led to a wave of demand for stronger administrations and stronger leaders, but this road can lead to fascism, so caution is required. This is an age in which IT is advancing at breakneck speed which has made it easy to use it in an administrative capacity, but this caused the emergence of the **surveillance state**, and by the time we realized how easily we can be manipulated, all we could do is express our shock. In addition, many states are now leaning into excessive protectionist behavior, which is a trend that makes a third world war a distinct possibility.

— Wow... that's scary. The more the crisis worsens, the more the dangers of perspectives produced by the virus of the brain and the limits of individualism reveal themselves... we're seeing the true nature of the physical human being.

That's right. Humans are originally dignity itself, with infinite possibility, ready to become anything. So **while we can become greater than gods, we can also become demons.** The hollowed-out remains of individualism bring us to a world of boundless cruelty.

Before, I made mention of guaranteeing our way of life. However, this is not enough. Certainly, we need something like this for the short-term, but in the long-term, it is unacceptable for human dignity.

— Unacceptable for dignity... I see, yes. If we had a basic income, that would only sustain us physically. It would do nothing to address our reason for living.

But then what is the answer ? It would be a lie for me to say I'm not worried about conspiracy theories and the like.

You can't let yourself be dominated by uncertainties towards the future or attempts to predict it. **The future is not something to predict. It is something to construct as a team effort based on our understanding of the structure of all things.**

Until now, **we have done our haphazard best under individualism,** seeing with our eyes, being controlled by our brains, restricting ourselves to our physical bodies, right ? We have had our own dreams, made our own plans and goals. In the coming age, we will need **"meta-dimensional dream"** that leverage all dreams together.

There is only "1," and from that Fundamental Motion, all 7.7 billion people on Earth can be part of a "Win-Win All-Win" scenario that lifts all dreams and realizes them. **We have a pressing need to create a continent of new economics and industry that will create new jobs that only humans can do.**

— That "Win-Win All-Win" dream sounds wonderful.

But how exactly can we make these new industries ?

It's such a grand idea, it sounds like it's going to be a thorny path no matter what we may claim about human dignity.

Not at all. If we start from "1," we'll attain happiness naturally, remember ? To look at it from another angle, starting from our eyes will result in us naturally becoming unhappy.

In economics, the secret ingredients for making new industries are always **"materials."**

— Materials ! That's right. I remember that when we talked about Einstein and quantum mechanics, we drew a distinction between light in terms of function and light in terms of material.

And **"0=∞=1" is the most versatile, abundant, fundamental material of all !**

That's right. We said that material is superior to or prior to its functions.

Let's talk for a bit about the relationship between materials and economics. From what material is the bottle in your hand made ?

— It's made from plastic... so, originally, petroleum.

That's right ! The raw material of that type of plastic bottle is derived from petroleum; it is a plastic called polyethylene terephthalate. There are all sorts of things that are made with petroleum. For example, the fibers of your shirt, the wrapping used for food packaging, synthetic rubber, asphalt, culinary use plastics, cosmetics, plumbing pipes, agricultural materials, parts for cars and home appliances, etc.

— Petroleum has an enormous amount of uses !

However, there was a time when petroleum was not given as much attention. Had Rockefeller not seen the potential in the black, smelly oil, we may not have had our energy revolution or any of these products.

True. People have known about petroleum since ancient times. However, **by recognizing the potential of petroleum as a material and drawing it out,** Rockefeller expanded its use as a new source of energy to rival coal, which was a driving force behind the second industrial revolution and the birth of new industries.

— I had never paid much attention to materials before, but this conversation has made me aware of the tremendous power of new material discoveries ! And now that I think of it, there are many other examples. Stone, copper, iron, semiconductors—the discovery and application of new materials has led to the emergence of new industries and jobs, creating economic continents.

Also, the discovery of new materials would have a big impact on the fortunes of nations. For example, the appearance of iron tools in the Stone Age or Bronze Age. In a war of stone vs. iron, the outcome is clear.

That's right. Iron tools are more reliable than stone tools and are better functionally suited to tools of war like swords and shields.

There are big effects on function in that way, but humans don't focus on **function** alone. We have also paid more and more attention to **efficiency** and **efficacy**: easier to use, more effective. We also care about the **fashion and design aspect**—making things more beautiful, more stylish. **All of these processes also take place in the effort to commodify something**, wouldn't you say ?

— I see. **Once a new material is discovered, it follows a development path for function, efficacy, efficiency, fashion, and design.**
    The discovery of electric semiconductors made a big impact also. In fact, it's completely turned our lives around.

    After all, the discovery of electric semiconductors are what brought the world the first personal computers.
    The first generation was just machines that were fast at calculating. They were big desktop models that weighed 4 kilograms, yet they only had 16 kilobytes of memory—roughly 20 pages worth of data—and the displays had only 8 colors. Performance increased with the introduction of Windows and Macintosh, computers became easier to use, and it became possible to streamline and unify the disparate structures of different companies. Increases in memory and OS updates led to further increases in efficiency, and miniaturization and weight-reduction enabled laptop models. Then came LCD displays and increased focus on aesthetics. These days, many people have a hand-sized personal computer in their smartphone.

Oh, you know a lot about this. Yes, that's how it went for personal computers.
    Electric semiconductors enabled the upgrade of calculation and memory functions and their integration into personal computer systems, as well as making them easier to use in daily settings, as well as more efficient. Then came the development of smartphones and tablets, as well as applications for those devices. Then we entered the fashion/design stage with the diversification of form factors. Now we always have our smartphones with us, resulting in the emergence of a cultural mode of interaction via SNS. This aesthetic and cultural institutionalization signaled the **culmination of the product life cycle.**

— I wonder how many people are involved in this cycle... from discovering the material, to the release of products to the world, to shifts in culture. Trying to imagine it makes me realize just how big an enterprise it all is.

First come the initial ideas, then R&D, then sales, marketing, design, manufacturing, administration, retail, distribution, repair, quality control... one burst of inspiration can lead to the creation of so many jobs. And I'm sure there's even more that I'm missing.

But something you said at the end there stuck out at me. The "culmination of the product life cycle."

That's an important point. It connects to the limits of the materials we have used so far.

Let's take a look at that idea along with the **"SDGs"** that the global community is working towards.

From the perspective of our current conversation, we can assert that these SDGs are **unattainable within the constraints of our current material civilization.**

— Hmmm... by SDGs, you must mean **the Sustainable Development Goals aimed at improving the world by 2030.**

But why should they be unattainable ?

Does that mean that sustainability itself is unattainable ?

Think about it. Where does the difference between what is sustainable and unsustainable come from ?

— The difference between sustainable and unsustainable...

Well, the main thing we have to keep in mind is to "not see with our eyes." Seeing with our eyes is the problem !

Because seeing with our eyes is limited, all things will have limits. So sustainability isn't possible.

That's right. As long as we rely on a perceptual methodology based on physical experience, we will never reach any true SDGs. Never.

— I'm getting a sense that the new discoveries we've discussed are going to get connected to economics.

Yes, there is absolutely a connection.

Let's get more specific. Why are SDGs unattainable ?

Do you know the second law of thermodynamics ? It is also known as the **law of increasing entropy.** When energy is looked at in terms of its quality, it has certain automatic tendencies in the way it changes. Those automatic changes are irreversible, which leads to an increase in entropy. The change in the quality of the energy trends towards equilibrium.

— Yes, I know about this at a simple level. Increases in entropy are sometimes described as "increases in waste."

That's right. The main point is that **the natural world has an irreversible character to it, and because entropy is always increasing, things can't go back to how they were.** In other words, **the universe is full of infinite entropy, and cannot return to a state of zero entropy.**

— So, the universe is full of waste, but there's no way to clean it up ?

That's right, so even though we've got a lot of work to do, it's not going to be possible if we "see with our eyes."

— I get it ! **When we see with our eyes, we take existence for granted. So the universe will seem to always "exist," and because of causality, irreversibility seems inevitable.** So, there's no escaping entropy.

At the energy level, universes arise and cease at a rate of 10^{500} times a second. This motion is imperceptible to the five senses and the brain.

So how does this connect ?

We have to look at the connection between the law of increasing entropy and sustainability.

First, we talked about how the discovery of a material leads to a product cycle that begins with function then performance, efficiency, and culminates with fashion, design and cultural institutions.

But as I mentioned previously, demand in our current material economy is already flagging. We've passed the stage of fashion, design, and cultural institution. **Now the market is in a mature "infinite entropy" stage.**

It would work to zeroize and create new needs, but we can't do that kind of restart. **We have a "virus economy" incapable of producing next-dimensional products.**

However, we have to kickstart the economy somehow... so we've tried to use fashion and design to try to create changes that lead to new employment.

— In other words, no big changes in function or performance, but changes in trends... so you're implying the recent push towards constant replacement. For example, since most people are now using smartphones, people make fun of you for using a flip phone.

Right ? All of this is based on **"planned obsolescence manufacturing."** An old model may have the potential to still be useful, but it's built to be thrown away. Apparel is especially bad about this—the industry encourages people to only wear clothes for one season. Even if the clothes have no damage, replacement is seen as the normal thing to do. This has changed slowly over the years, with more people becoming interested in minimalist wardrobes and ethical fashion. Despite such changes in consumerism, the supply side has only continued to fan the flames of consumption.

— Planned obsolescence... considering the excessive environmental pollution and energy waste this creates, that's very alarming. Forget about sustainability—this is going in the opposite direction. In spite of this, there's all this talk about productivity, job creation, SDGs. We have to put an end to this material economy, this virus economy, as soon as possible. If we don't, the Earth will strike back.

One more thing. **The shortening of the product cycle is partially due to the "quantum mechanical worldview" becoming increasingly commonplace.** You hear about wave-particle duality, probability theory, all the time.

— I see ! Everything changing all the time fits the idea of "short expiration dates" for the product cycle perfectly. The past years have resulted in a sudden shift towards observing things from the quantum perspective after a long period of seeing things physically or via Newton's mechanics and determinism. That way of observing things may be connected to **consumption behavior.** Also... at a glance, it doesn't seem like there would be any relationship, but the more I understand the influence the way we observe things have, the deeper and more ineffable it gets.

Yes, which is why our first goal must be to change our assumptions in the way we observe. The discovery of materials that humanity has never used before will be impossible if we don't.

So far, we've said that it isn't fashion/design, efficiency, performance, or function that creates jobs, but the "material" at the base of it all.

If we don't find some totally revolutionary materials, the dream of sustainability will stay a dream.

We are approaching the limit of our efforts to keep this material civilization on life support.

— Yes, I understand how continuing along with this virus economy is a dead end.

Finding "new materials" is a pressing matter, but you know that not just any material will do the trick. **If we keep using materials on the same dimension—the matter and energy dimension—won't work.**

Why, you ask ? It's because matter and energy are limited ? They can't be sustainable, right ?

We can't zeroize entropy, right ?

— A limitless material... a material that is neither matter nor energy... a material that can zeroize entropy...

I see ! That could only be the Fundamental Motion, $0=\infty=1$!

Exactly right !

Our new material will be that which creates energy itself, the Fundamental Motion of mind.

Because it is the material that creates time, space, presence, energy, and all things, it is a material that can create industry and employment without end, it is a material that can zeroize ∞ entropy, and no matter for how long and no matter where, no amount of using it will deplete it.

It is an oil field of the mind that cannot be taken from us, and is thus sustainable by nature,

it is a repository of ideas that can cause a blank page to overflow with creativity and innovation, a material that allows anyone to pursue a blue ocean strategy based on their own intellectual property without competition.

Because it is a material divorced from causality, it can create work that only humans can perform, that AIs cannot, a material that can raise the standard of any industry.

A material to usher in the 0th industry, industries of Mind, industries of peace that are good for the environment.

This is the energy revolution we need.

We must turn the thermodynamics of matter and energy into a "psychodynamics" of mind.

This is the perceptual economy built upon a new material, a meta-material: Original Material.

— I am moved beyond words.

I have an image of a world in which everyone can be a genius inventor or discoverer.

Would it be possible to acquire wealth far beyond what the wealthiest people today have ?

Right now, the wealthiest constitute a small portion of humanity—but what if everyone had as much ? I feel so excited. If this next-dimension new economic continent were to come into being, the whole world economy would leap forward all at once.

We can leave the work we've done in the past to the AIs, and move on to work only humans can do. I can see a path for co-existence now.

So many people on Earth could be saved by the rise of the perceptual economy.

I too want to present this new material and new industry to the world as soon as possible.

A different name for this new material is **"superconductor of mind."**

— Superconductor of mind ? There's another interesting turn of phrase. Your style of naming is very unique but always fitting. It makes me wonder how you come up with them. What is the idea behind this one ?

Semi-conductors create digital circuits that enable binary calculation. Supercomputers are the fastest machines built along this principle—in rough terms, if a typical PC calculates at a snail's pace, a supercomputer is like a jet plane. These are the **electric superconductors** with which you are familiar.

Now there is also research into optic superconductors for quantum computers.

The idea of computing using logic gates built on "0" and "1" bits is the same as the original computers, but while digital computers must pick one of two binary options, **quantum computers are able to compute with a "qubit" that is a superposition of "0" and "1."**

— Is that the same way of observing as quantum mechanics ? The speed of energy superposition, or something...

That's right. There is a concept of **quantum supremacy** based on the fact that the use of these superposition states can enable parallel calculations that permit mind-boggling computation speeds. IBM's 17 qubit processor can simultaneously run 2^{17}, or 131,072, calculations, resulting in speeds that are 9 quadrillion times faster than supercomputers. In 2019, Google announced that its quantum computer was able to perform a calculation that would take the world's fastest supercomputer 10,000 years to solve in the space of 200 seconds.

— The speed of quantum computers is incredible !

Isn't it ? But optical superconductors operate at the superposition speed of energy, right ?

So, then **Mind superconductors...**

— **Go at a super-ultra-speed far beyond the speed of energy !** It's that motion !
I see... the motion of Mind is the mental superconductor, and by using that material we can create Mind industries and usher in the age of the perceptual economy ! I get the sense that the sizes of the economy of Mind and the economy of matter will be incomparable.

That's right. The difference is unimaginable. (laughs)

From another perspective, this new material will result in a **"revolution in motion."**

— Another revolution ? ! You sure do like revolutions. You've also released a "Revolution Series" of writings, I believe. Well, if everything we know must change, I guess it's to be expected.

— *Figure 48* —
The process of human work
connected to Fundamental Motion

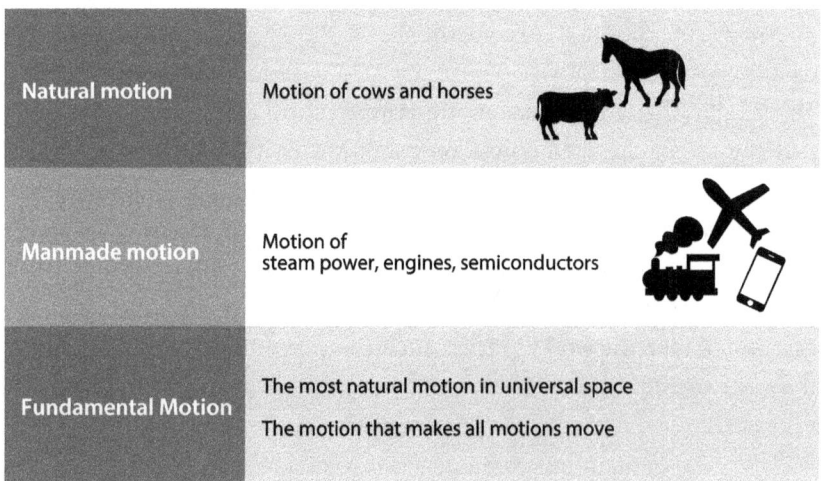

Natural motion	Motion of cows and horses
Manmade motion	Motion of steam power, engines, semiconductors
Fundamental Motion	The most natural motion in universal space The motion that makes all motions move

So what is the "revolution in motion"?

Humans have used "motion" as an engine to live.

To understand what I mean, let's take a look back through history.

First, we used **"natural motion."** For example, we used oxen and horses in agriculture to till the land and also as a means of transport. We determined time from the motion of the Sun.

Since the Industrial Revolution, we have used **"artificial motion."** We've used a variety of manmade tools like steam power, engines, and superconductors to move us through Industries 1.0 to 4.0. But as you know, our material economy, despite its pursuit of innovations in manufacturing technology, has only repeated itself like a virus in the same manner, with no means of advancing to the stage beyond. Now we are staring down the technological singularity in 2045. We have to change our engines.

What we discover when we tear our eyes away from this addiction to progress, when we journey to places far, far, far from here, is the **Fundamental Motion of Mind** of the 11th level that encompasses all things. The "revolution in motion" arises as a result of using this motion.

It is a motion that causes all other motions, the most natural perpetual engine of all, the Deep engine deeper than any other. From this eternal, invariant motion of Mind, we can observe all the changes, movements, and transformations of the myriad beings that arise from the myriad motions.

— The motion that brings forth all other motions is the same thing as the **"motion that controls all other motions,"** isn't it? My view has widened.

So this is not the "invisible hand" of Adam Smith, but the "invisible eye" of Jesu Noh! **A blue ocean industry of Mind, seen with the Mind's eye.**

It's an invisible eye for an industry of 7.7 billion people—doesn't that sound fun?

By the way, so far we've talked about this new material and its potential for new industries, but there's one other critical element to economic development.

— Wow... I wonder what it is ? I think I might know, though...

There is something I thought about during the COVID lockdowns. This is a bit of a shot in the dark, but...

All of a sudden, nations and even cities became separated, right ? At that time, I suddenly became more cognizant of how valuable truck drivers and other distributors are. Without them, we wouldn't have had access to food or water. So, is it infrastructure ?

That's pretty close. What I was going to say includes supply lines like you suggested: **"routes."**

— *Figure 49* —
"Routes" created by Motion
(land routes / sea routes / air routes / information routes)

Lifestyle expansion
Expansion of employment/work

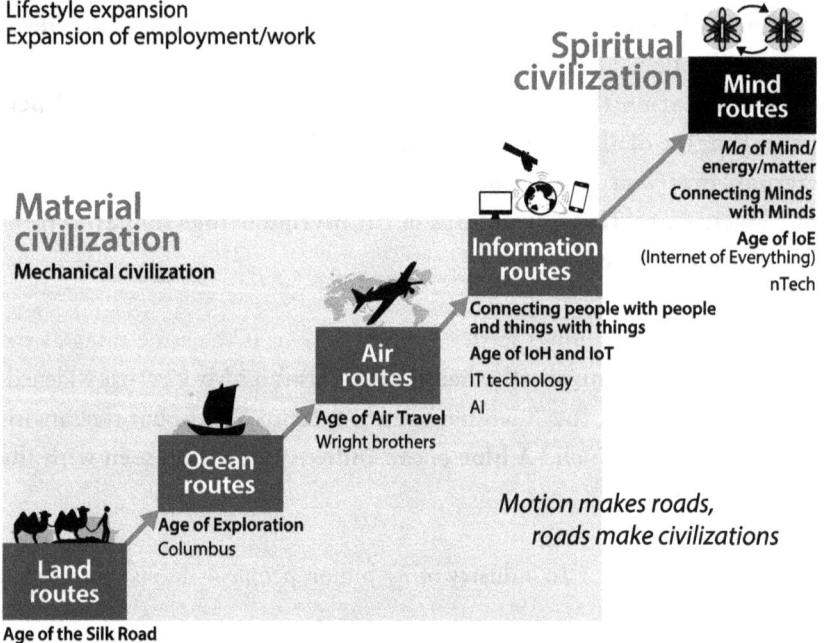

Spiritual civilization

Mind routes

Ma of Mind/ energy/matter

Connecting Minds with Minds

Age of IoE (Internet of Everything)

nTech

Material civilization
Mechanical civilization

Information routes

Connecting people with people and things with things

Age of IoH and IoT

IT technology

AI

Air routes

Age of Air Travel
Wright brothers

Ocean routes

Age of Exploration
Columbus

Land routes

Age of the Silk Road

*Motion makes roads,
roads make civilizations*

The introduction of new ages, new civilizations, and new trades revolves around "routes." The first routes were **"land routes,"** the most famous being the Silk Road. It got its name from the large volumes of Chinese-made silk that were delivered to Rome on it. It was this long, long road across the Asian continent that connected Asia and Europe and tied their material products and cultures together.

— The difference between the age before and after the Silk Road is so clear. I see that routes are quite important.

They certainly are. Next are **"sea routes,"** which are more dangerous than those on land. Because land routes only extend as far as the land goes, their range for exchange is limited. In order to expand opportunities and transactions, we had to take to the seas !

— But at that time, people didn't have the shipbuilding technology we have now, so they risked their lives to create these routes. Columbus' trips to the Americas were apparently very difficult.

But with the Age of Exploration, trade became much livelier than when it was confined to land routes, various mining colonies were developed, and the European nations in particular advanced rapidly.

That's right. Next, we have **"air routes."** Recently we talked about the Wright brothers, whose courageous efforts brought us routes by air. Afterwards, advances in science and technology enabled us to increase the speed and travel distance of our aircraft, further increasing the quantity and quality of our engagements with each other.

— Yes, there is a close connection between the establishment of land, sea, and air routes and the development of the economy.

This is a bit off-topic, but the frontier spirit in human beings is remarkable.

One might say that because land routes are safe, that's good enough. Sea and air routes require considerable resolve to develop—but we do it anyway because of our deep urge to encounter new things, make new connections.

Anyway, next will be routes for IT, right ?

These routes can't be seen, but they are still "routes" by the same logic.

Bingo ! Those are the **"information routes."**

The internet is a global network that enables instantaneous transactions and sales regardless of separations in time or space. For information, in particular, no prior route can compare.

— Regarding the internet, now people are talking about **IoT** (Internet of Things). The spread of this technology is amazing. We've had an **"IoH"** (Internet of Humans), but now the age of objects connecting with each other is upon us. As this trend continues, we'll see all things in connection with each other.

All in all, "routes" have enabled us to connect that which was separate, leading to economic development. So, the things that are not yet connected are the things that are candidates for the creation of "new routes."

You're getting sharper ! So what things remain separate ? Something that humans still have not developed, a very large route...

— Something that remains separate ? It must be our brain perspectives !

Our brains are able to break things down and draw borders throughout the world. We can't connect our minds, we're like a militia of isolated Jokers ! Because we see with our eyes, humans are always waging war, even in the places we don't see.

Which is why, now, **it is time to strike out on the "Mind route" that connects minds together.**

An uncharted route. This is the start of the spiritual civilization.

The age of the IoE (Internet of Everything) is nigh. This can also be called the age of Uncontact.

This is the largest, safest route. It is a boundless route.

This Mind route is **a route that will connect one Mindome to another Mindome.**

— Mindome ? I've never heard that before. Mind something ?

It's a word I created.

Mindome is a portmanteau of Mind and home. I have a *kanji* (chinese character) version of it too. It's the home of the mind.

— *Figure 50* —
Mindome

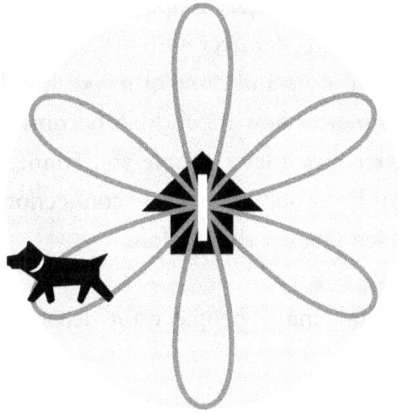

The length of the leash determines the behavioral range of the dog
Humans have "invisible chains" which determine range of judgment

Let me go over the Mindome idea. A dog chained to a doghouse has a **behavioral range** defined by the length of the chain. Humans center their activity around their home, which they return to after going out for work or leisure. They aren't chained to it like a dog is, but the home still plays a role in defining behavioral range.

So what about our thoughts and feelings ? We are bound to a **"judgment range"** within which we make our decisions. Those decisions become behaviors, so they also determine our behavioral range. Since human life is the accumulation of our behaviors, the judgment range also determines our **"life range."** The "Mindome," therefore, determines our life range.

— Ohh... so in other words, **the Mindome is the same as "point of reference"** ?

Because our point of reference is our physical eyes at the command of the virus of the brain, our Mindome will be created based on that standard. If it's Newton, then the XYZ coordinate plane... like that ?

That's right. Right now, there is no "route" between Mindomes—they aren't connected.

The "judgment range" has boundary lines to it, right ? There's a limit to what you can accept, and beyond that, you won't accept things. In this way, people get trapped by knowledge completeness. They are bound within their small systems and can't connect with others.

There are 7.7 billion of us and none of us occupy the same Mindome. We are all alone. No matter how much SNS becomes a standard of communication, no matter how many people you connect with, even if you have 5,000 friends on Facebook, all of these connections will just be superficial. You will feel even lonelier than before.

— I understand. I think many people want deeper connections, deeper interactions.

Yep. The "route" that clears away the boundaries between minds, that enables full control of the virus of the brain, that frees us from the world we know, that is made of the relationships connected by the meaning of meaningless, the value of valueless, the definition of the undefined—that "route" is the desire in the deepest part of human beings.

Safe connection with anyone, anytime, anywhere.
The "Mind route" is the boundless route, the biggest route, the safest route there is.

— I think this need is rooted deeply. I think development of the "Mind route" has tremendous potential. I can practically smell the money.

Development of the Mind route is impossible without technology to use the Mind superconductor meta-material. We must determine how to zeroize our ancient Mindomes and rebuild them with the deepest Mind material. We must determine how to connect these Mindomes together. This is the sort of R&D we'll need to conduct.

— This research could become a big deal !

But... ok. The Fundamental Motion of Mind is the "meta-material of Mind superconductors," which is a "motion" that far surpasses super-computers and quantum computers, and with this material, we'll create a "Mind route."

But how are we supposed to make it ?

Try to think about it in the context of the new discoveries we discussed.

— Let's see... space causality, time causality, presence causality, perception causality—there is a structure that brings all of these causal relationships together, and because we understand that structure, we can change the simulation of reality. When we talked about this, I felt that it would make us something even greater than gods. Is this the part you mean ?

That's right, it's that. There has to be a 'structure' in order to create reality. For a house, first there's a plan, then construction. There's a process.

We're talking about mastering the structure, the relationships of the Fundamental Motion of Mind, the digital motion of energy, the analog motion of the physical universe.

I said that we use Mind superconductors, right ? What do you think of when you hear the word superconductor ?

— PCs, I guess. And smartphones ?

Yeah. PCs are like the icon of electric superconductors, but Mind supercon-ductors **are naturally used in a Personal Universe (PU).**

— **The universe is a computer ?**

Aha ! Now I know the connection to before !

I made this note before: "A meta-OS, a perceptual computer that perceives everything in the universe as a single motion. A principle that connects the fundamental programming of everything in the information universe to the development of a total OS." At that time, I felt dazzled at how cool this idea is.

So this must have been the PU that uses Mind superconductors.

That's right, that's it. The first computers were the size of a building, very, very big. Inside that building, it took a crowd of people to operate it—but now we're in an age where everyone has a computer, with some computers (smartphones) the size of your hand.

If we think of PUs in the same manner, then while we've so far had a lot of people occupying the same universal space, seeing the universe as one big computer, Mind actually goes beyond the universe. So each individual will master and apply the structure of the energy algorithms that emerge from Fundamental Motion of Mind and the relationships between energy

— *Figure 51* —
From the PC (Personal Computer) age
to the PU(Personal Universe) age

Perceptual OS

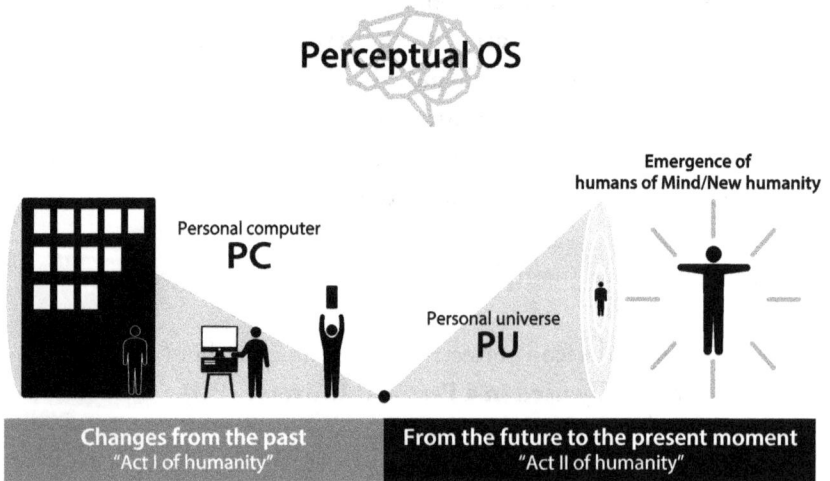

Emergence of
humans of Mind/New humanity

Personal computer
PC

Personal universe
PU

Changes from the past	From the future to the present moment
"Act I of humanity"	"Act II of humanity"

and matter.

So we must master **the operating principles of consciousness, space, and computers,** and push the universe down to a minuscule point far smaller than our hands to use right here, right now. That's the PU.

We could also call this **"digital Mind" or "programming thought."**

— This overlap between PC and PU is easy to understand. It's interesting.

We are now moving into the **age of development of the universal computer.** It's an industry of the future that will enable us to use PU. Once we can do so, digital Mind and programming thought will be like required subjects.

That's right. To do so, we need World Axis Education to ensure that all people can use it.

— It seems that World Axis Education (WAE) will be a critical element of the coming age.

If our education falters, our economy and politics will go to ruin as well. I have high hopes for WAE.

There's something about that I want to ask, but first...

I've got a good sense of the threat of the "economic corona," but now I'd like to talk about the other two: **the "life corona" and the "Mind corona."**

That said, I think I have some ideas of what they may be based on our conversation so far.

Let's do it. What are your ideas ?

— The life corona is something that can be cleared with an understanding of "structure," right ? From Fundamental Motion of Mind, to energy, to matter, to viruses, to cells... that conversation.

That's right. Put another way, if you don't understand this, you fail to gain control of the virus.

That's why the "way you observe" is of such importance.

Before the emergence of the novel coronavirus, it was natural to "see with one's eyes." However, you can't actually see coronavirus with your eyes, right ? That's why it's able to attack us.

It's trying to say, "Quit focusing on what you can physically see ! We have to learn to apprehend the invisible world or we're headed for disaster. Humanity is bound to become the useless class, our bodies and minds will decay, our reason to exist will disappear, humanity will fall. If you keep seeing with your eyes, I'll do away with you myself !"

In order to avoid that from happening, we must put an end to seeing with the eye, and master the motion of Mind.

— Yeah, I see. Us humans have to pay close attention to COVID's message to us.

If we don't, we will continue to get wiped out.

The COVID-19 pandemic infected over 4 million people the world over in the space of 3 months, with over 400 thousand deaths. Efforts were made to establish herd immunity, but **herd immunity acquisition is usually a strategy pursued once a vaccine is already available. Going down this route with no vaccine assumed there would need to be a large number of fatalities until a vaccine is found.** It's a horrible thing. On top of that, the virus mutates. Even if a vaccine is produced in 6 months to a year, it will be unusable if the virus has mutated too much by then.

— Yes, in the end, people don't understand what a virus is. They don't understand anything, so they have no choice but to rely on the past knowledge and information that have been accumulated from a faulty observational stance.

A friend of mine who is a doctor said that **current medicine doesn't even understand what exactly a cell is.** I remember feeling shocked when I heard that.

Clearly, without understanding the meta-material of Fundamental Motion of Mind, **there isn't a single thing that we properly understand.** Said another way, if we understand "unity," we understand everything.

Humanity has to recognize quickly that **we have never known anything. We have always been ignorant.**

Scientific development also began with an admission of ignorance. **It takes courage to admit one's ignorance.**

Going back to viruses, if you observe them from Mind, you can see they have both the **"particle form and wave form (energy)"** of *Tah* and condensation. But the eye can only see the particle form. So the question of how to deal with viruses is limited to the development of vaccines and anti-virals.

However, if you observe viruses in their wave form, you see that **the method of spread for viruses is the human ecosystem.** Viruses may only prey on human cells, but they are able to spread by using the human ecosystem.

That's why, if we want to weaken the ability of viruses to spread, we have to target not the particle form of the virus that infects humans, but the wave form of the virus that lies hidden in the human ecosystem. The **Japanese-style lockdown** is the method that advocated using this framework to totally control the virus.

— If you understand the framework, then there's no reason to fear the virus. If you don't understand it, then the problem seems insurmountable and it becomes scary.

That's right. If you attain a correct understanding of things from "1" nothing is scary anymore.

Because I see things structurally from "1," I have always predicted that the things that have happened during the COVID-19 pandemic would happen. In mid-March after the pandemic ramped up, I said on my blog that **"COVID-19 is causing clots in capillary veins, so those clots must be removed."** A few months later, the same thing was announced globally. I felt quite irritated, thinking that if people could understand the structure, lives could be saved.

Because we don't properly understand things from "1," we are being ravaged by a corona even more horrible than economic corona or the life corona.

That is the **"Mind corona," which destroys the human spirit.**

— Indeed. It's like all the uncertainty, suspicion, and fear that had been hidden away in the sewers came exploding out with COVID-19.

Our feelings of distrust reached a maximum point, wondering if others are infected, or getting concerned about people not maintaining social distancing or wearing masks. In Japan, we've seen the phenomenon of *jishuku keisatsu* (self-appointed pandemic police). There have been shocking news reports of shootings that occur as a result of security guards at supermarkets asking people to wear masks and mass demonstrations against racism and discrimination.

The whole ocean of society has become an ocean of fear and uncertainty. I feel on edge myself. I don't see an end to the current situation—and even if it were to end, we'd be stuck in fear of when another pandemic may strike, exhausting us all.

In addition, the flimsiness of our relations has been thrown into sharp relief. We stand amazed at how easily they can break, and I think many people have never felt lonelier.

— That's for sure. I recall what we were saying about Mind routes. I've had enough of superficial relationships.

This is why perceiving true Mind and understanding how we are enslaved by the virus of the brain is **the fastest—in fact, the only—road to putting an end to this miserable reality.**

The virus of the brain is a crisis a quadrillion times worse than anything COVID-19 or AI poses to us, and we've suffered under it for all of human history.

— We must live in accordance with Mind itself, liberated from the virus of the brain. We must not see with our eyes.

By the way, you mentioned "relationships." I think I'm starting to get a sense for why group, rather than individual, enlightenment is what we need. Why we need spiritual cells.

In the past, we have not had Mind routes. We have not had ways to connect. I see how we soon may all be connected by the borderless Fundamental Motion of Mind, and build new relationships.

Yes, that's it. Humans are social animals, after all. Rather than false connections, we want the deepest dignified relationships connected by routes of Mind. **Creating these communities and collectives is very important for the age to come.**

— Could you give me a concrete sense of how this will be done ?

I'll tell you. But before we get to a more detailed discussion of World Axis Education and community building, I want to go a little deeper into the **problem of perception construction** and the **problem of society construction.**

— The key to perception construction is "don't see with your eyes," isn't it ?
   Social construction problems are inherently, well, social. So is this a matter of assembly and production like we discussed before ?

That's right. Let's look at the problem of perception construction in terms of the problems that assembly and production poses, using three themes: motivation, decision-making, and incomplete control.
   You've got a great handle on social construction themes ! You've been paying attention !

1. The problem of motivation

— All three of these themes sound like issues I've dealt with. I get the sense that if I'm able to connect these things to the maxim to "not see with my eyes," my daily life will get a lot easier !

It's not just you. These are also social problems.
   So let's now think this through. How do you think **lack of follow-through, lack of motivation, and lack of passion** may be connected to the problem of perception construction ?

— Hmmm... I guess it's easy to want to give up, or get stuck in a rut... I wonder ? If you see things with your eyes, then the universe always seems to "exist," and so the "self" also exists.

So, images of the past hold us back and make us think things are impossible or that we won't finish what we start, making predictions about the future... also, sometimes you just can't summon any interest and think that something has nothing to do with you, so your motivation plummets.

I see you are imagining motion of the Mind. You've brought up some good terms.

Just as you suggest, **human beings start from a place of observational error, deciding that their physical boundaries determine their selves, right ? So of course, their range for interests and loves will narrow.**

Physical human beings are "machines." It's difficult to notice this consciously, but **if our thoughts, feelings, words, actions, relationships etc. are all just repeating mechanical algorithms, then of course you're going to act out a routine whenever you encounter something.** There is also the influence of the "ever-changing" quantum mechanics mentality we discussed earlier, **making it difficult to maintain consistency.**

— Wow, all of that really rings true !

So, then how about this ? **You may feel that even if you get excited about something and challenge yourself, ultimately you are more likely to lose something than gain something.** Like you're failing.

That's also very natural for the physical human.

Whenever you do anything, you are going to encounter "something." **"Encounter" could also be described as "conflict." If that is the way you see reality, you will interpret things in terms of "loss."** Something you do once will be something you do again and again, causing the failures to build up until you hit a critical point and quit completely, joining a club of burnouts.

— I see... the physical human is unable to enjoy encounters and sees them as "losses."

So what happens if we look at things from "1" ?

If we see with our eyes, we and our universe "exist." But all of it, including the "self," is just a hologram produced by the brain. We are the result of the dream of "1," as the universe blinks in and out of existence 10^{500} times a second. Past, present, and future is all illusion...

So is there habit ? No, there isn't ! Failure is nothing to fear ! Conflicts aren't always loss ! **If we start from "1," we can always create new encounters, always have new starts ! Graduation from habit !** We can face more and more new challenges !

I'm getting motivated ! I feel invincible !

You're good at putting it all together. You said **"invincible"** just now, and to supplement it, that's something that can be felt from **"acquisition of completion."**

Einstein once said, **"A new type of thinking is essential if mankind is to survive and move toward higher levels."** Have you heard this quote before ?

If we become the complete and perfect world of "0=∞=1" itself, we will be able to turn any problem into an opportunity. The problem will cease to be a problem. **From that completeness, motivation will sustainably and spontaneously rise up within us.**

2. The problem of decision-making

— The idea of motivation spontaneously overflowing is awesome !

So next could I hear about the **"problem of decision-making"** theme ?

This is also an issue for me. Even if I am asked for an opinion, it's hard for me to give one. When I was made a project leader one day, I felt physical pain in my stomach until the project was over.

I had no confidence in my own judgment and felt uncertain about every decision. I couldn't let the team down, but they started to seem like my enemies. I felt like they were saying to me that I'm a failure as a leader. Nobody actually did say that, though.

This sort of difficulty with decision-making is also totally natural for physical humans. In fact, the more serious and responsible people are, the more difficulty they may have with this. But why do you think it happens ?

— We have to think about it in terms of "1"... due to observational error, people lack correct understanding. We assume that the hologram produced by the brain "actually exists," make our physical experiences our standard, repeat rote language thought up by others.

Because there isn't a single thing we've come to know on our own, because we pass judgment based on things we've memorized, I think people have a lot of unconscious uncertainty... and when we become adults, to some extent we have no choice but to pretend that we know. So we're in an impossible situation.

That's right. If we are trapped by the perspective of the brain we absolutely cannot understand the full picture. The universe is just one small piece of the whole, yet we feel sure that it is "everything."

However, the **human brain doesn't even understand the algorithm behind events (change) occurring, their story and development, right?**

— That's right... we don't understand the first thing about the structure that creates change from the unchanging. **Physical humans don't have correct understanding of anything.**

Trying to make evidence-based judgments and decisions in spite of that just isn't possible.

That's why we have no choice but to play along, copy others, seek direction from each other in order to survive. "What would everyone else do?" But we said that our current age is one of **infinite perspective.** This is an age of great diversity, and we are drowning in a flood of every conceivable sort of information. There are an infinite number of targets with which we might align, but we have no guidance on what we should choose and we end up confused. Consequently, **we have no point of reference, no directionality, no capacity for value judgement. It's the paradox of choice.** In this environment, the work of project leaders is difficult.

— So, that's why it was so hard for me... at that time. I felt depressed and worthless. If I look at humanity in terms of the "structure," I see that everyone is in the same position. People don't show it, but I'm sure they have similar worries.

So, the first thing we must do is establish our point of reference. We must zeroize our erroneous information knowledge that has been accumulated by seeing with the eye, move backwards to the "way of observing" of the 11th level, and make $0=\infty=1$ our point of reference !

That is what we must do before doing anything else. If we do so, something even more amazing will happen ! **All of your previously disjointed thoughts and feelings you have inside will become your support, as "friends playing the same game."** If that happens, then you will be able to concentrate on things, won't you ? You won't waste time on futile thinking and get better at making decisions quickly.

— That sounds great ! If we understand the structure of events (changes) and can grasp the whole picture, we are capable of creating our own events, conducting our own analyses, and decision-making will come to us naturally.

That's right. And what do you think would happen if you gathered together a bunch of people who are capable of decision-making using $0=\infty=1$ as their point of reference ? **That group could amass enough power to enact a simulation change in reality.**

— I see ! And if that happened, the people we once thought of as enemies would instead become powerful allies !

The reason we think of others as enemies is because of unconscious judgment that arises because of differences in perspective and because we tend to analyze each other (based on our personal judgement).

If we know more people that can make decisions based on "1," we can work on all kinds of topics and projects as **friends that will never betray each other !**

Because these are people who will understand how much greater the meaning of meaningless, the value of valueless, the definition of the undefined are than meaning, value, and definition at the level of physical experience, **we can have same- perspective conflicts that won't lead to hurting or**

worrying each other or damaging our relationships.

— That's a relief. We can pursue infinite output with peace of mind. We can enjoy discussions, even the parts where we disagree.

What's more, through our discussions, we will elevate our perspectives into a higher dimension, leading to the emergence of utterly new perspectives. No more boring, pointless meetings—our debates will be fresh and exciting.

On that point, I have a question for you. **Do you think humans act in accordance with what they think, or think in accordance with how they act ?**

— Eugh... I only notice this when asked, but I think it might be that we think in accordance with how we act. After all, as far as I can remember, I don't think I've ever been able to act things out in the way I imagine them.

Perhaps if we were able to act in accordance with what we think, we could all become sages or tycoons. But for many people, **because they do not know that "there is only Mind," it is impossible for them to act in accordance with what they think.**

So what does it mean for us to "think in accordance with how we act" ? It means that **we justify our behavior with excuses after the fact.**

— That's a tough thing to hear. Even if I make a decision to finish something or do something on some given day, most of the time I don't follow through. Then I look for some convenient post-hoc rationalization, like the turnaround is too short, or I don't feel good.

I think that everyone can relate to this.

If you don't understand the meaning of meaningless, the value of valueless, the definition of the undefined or the structure that gives rise to perspectives, it is not easy to consistently focus on one thing. It's no surprise, then, that your thoughts would easily change depending on external conditions.

Conversely, what if you had a meeting with a bunch of people who live in accordance with how they think ? Don't you imagine that it would be a lively affair where progress on meaning and value proceeds naturally, harmoniously, peacefully ?

— If such meetings became the standard, nobody would make excuses to try to avoid joining them (laughs).

3. The problem of incomplete control

Now let's talk about the third theme, the **"problem of incomplete control."**

Before encountering nTech, **you assumed that you existed as a separated, isolated physical body,** right ? You never doubted what you saw with your eyes, heard with your ears, felt beneath your feet.

— That's right. When I heard that that was impossible, it was shocking to me. Seeing things from "1," in which both the observer and observed disappear, you can't see with your eyes, hear with your ears, or walk around, and yet you can see and hear... it seemed like a holy mystery !

But how does this connect to incomplete control ?

Well, when you thought of your body as yourself, you believed that you had control over your own body, right ?

— That's right. Just as our lives would come to a stop if the world didn't rotate and revolve around the sun, an independent body cannot truly exist. I took a moment to reflect once I understood that lingering behind the Earth, the Sun, the Milky Way, and everything in the Universe is the digital algorithm of the 5 energies, and behind that is the motion of Mind. It was arrogant of me to think of my body as an isolated, independent entity.

That's right.

Let's explore just how **foolish it is to think that we can see with just our physical eyes.**

We can see with just our physical eyes. In order for this to make sense, **the eyes of the body must be separable from the body, and when we** express the activity of those separated eyes, we must recognize their subjectivity in claiming that the eyes have seen something.

However, it isn't possible to separate the eyes from the body and consider their behavior subjective, nor is it provable.

— That's true... the eyes alone are not capable of subjectivity in a separate fashion.

However, human beings tend to think that they can see with their eyes, that they do see with their eyes. To expand our scope, it's the same attitude as thinking that you live in your body or that you walk with your feet. It may seem as though one's body is independent, or that the feet can be seen as independent or that their own movement can be considered subjective when we say "walking with our feet," but in fact it isn't true. **If you don't think that walking with one's feet is impossible, then you're in the illusory world.** This connects back to the disagreement between Einstein's locality and Bohr's non-locality, which denied the existence of independent objects.

— I see. The brain likes to split things up, we want to believe in locality.

That's because **the physical eye is an "eye that sees objects."** So despite the impossibility of "seeing with one's eyes," we do it without questioning it. However, **entities and bodies are "effects."**

Yet because we live as though the body is a "cause," we are unable to understand true causes and processes.

Because we don't understand the "structure," we don't understand the way things are, so we cannot control them.

— Controlling our circumstances requires **perceiving all things as "events" by starting from the True Cause "1" and seeing the 5 energy algorithms (process) and reality (effect).**

No matter what problem you tackle, everything starts with "the way one observes."

In thinking this way, you need only deal with changes in that "way of observing." Simple, isn't it ? Until now, we have attempted to change all kinds of things with a certain stubborn insistence, despite not understanding what, in what way, or why we must precipitate those changes. **The only thing that we have ever needed to do is to consider our "way of observing."** We just have to stop seeing with our eyes and instead observe from "1."

— It's simple and goes hand-in-hand with its effects ! That's great !

By the way, there is a concept in *bushidō* I like. It›s from Hagakure: "*Bushidō* is a way of dying." This has overlap with a world in which there is only one motion.

— Living as though one is already dead ?

That's right ! **If you live as though you have already died, you understand that the past and future are all just part of the "present moment," and that all can be viewed as a single event.**
From that single event, you become able to understand, explain, control, predict, and anticipate as though the event was your own. Just as the performers in an orchestra create beautiful harmonies, by understanding all of the roles, cues, processes, and gestalt of a single song (event), you become able to enjoy each role that is available.

— Hmmmm... that sounds like a beautiful world.

4. The problem of assembly/solidarity and the problem of production/innovation

We've dealt with issues of perceptual construction, but now we must deal with issues of **social construction.**

— When we discussed the historical approach, I could sense how deeply rooted the **problems of assembly and production** are. We need assembly because people can't do much of anything on their own, let alone solve big problems. We assemble, create order, create solidarity—but the perspective of the brain, the virus of the brain interferes. Order is the gift of self-control; families, companies, regions, and countries have all been built with sheer endurance. It brings tears to my eyes.

If our perspectives are all over the place, we have no common ground. So **humanity has had no choice but to use our will to survive to create order by force, using violence, wealth, and authority.** So what about starting from "1" ? What if we became free from our perspectives, if we created order without needing to restrain ourselves so much ?

— It sounds like nothing but good news... from now on, we shouldn't hold ourselves back. We should say what we want to say, hash it out, **zeroize and infinitize our perspectives, creating an order based on freedom !**

Yes, exactly ! As we do so, our relationships will get more and more friendly. So, next we need to deal with **problems of production/innovation.** Just bringing people together isn't sufficient to foster a revolution in social construction. The key to social construction is in how to raise productivity.

— This is also something that we can resolve nicely by looking at things from "1." After all, if we do so, then right here and now we can go from a blank slate in which everything is zeroized to a standard of production of explosive creativity and infinite ideas ! This is something that leaders in countries all over the world need to be told about. That this is something worth investing in to cultivate human resources.

That's right. The ideas and creative sparks that the perspective of the brain can offer us are running out. It's unfortunate how Made in Japan was once the pride of the Japanese economy, and now it has become like a symbol for the virus economy. In these circumstances, if we print money to try to stimulate the economy, it's not going to improve lives. It'll just encourage inflation.

— In order to increase production and stimulate the economy, we have to prioritize solving the perspective problem. If we just invested in this, we could fix everything.

Previously you mentioned "productivity based on destruction." It seems that we must put an end to this as soon as possible.

That's right. On the problem of social construction, we really must hurry when it comes to **the equivalence between destruction-based production and virus-level capitalism.** We just keep developing and creating products in the same dimension.

The space around human beings—all the things around us from basic necessities to electrical appliances—has been developed extensively. We've gone as far as we can, and now we are starting to make changes to the human body. It may seem different, but it's really the same process.

— **We are making ourselves into cyborgs—but even if we become able to swap out our neurons for computer chips, become able to upload our consciousness to digital platforms, and become immortal, it will still just be a continuation of the path we've always been on.** The technological singularity of 2045 is not far away...

And if that happens, we will not overcome the perspective of the brain and connect, and connected people will not make spiritual cells together and jumpstart collective innovation. Because our capitalist economies will remain virus systems, we won't evolve into spiritual cells, and will just be keeping ourselves on life support. Even if we spread lots of wealth around, we won't undergo true evolution, and we will be stuck with the order we have made under self-restraint.

— It's time already for the order of self-restraint to end ! Rather, we need to make "Mind routes" of people connecting their minds together. Once we solve the problem of perspectives that frustrate the creation of Mind infrastructure, **we can create peaceful industry that enables production without destruction !** That, right there, is **Win-Win All-Win.** World Axis Education and the communities that result will be what reset these problems of perception and social construction !

— *Figure 52* —
Visions brought forth by individual perspectives
under human performance versions 1.0, 2.0

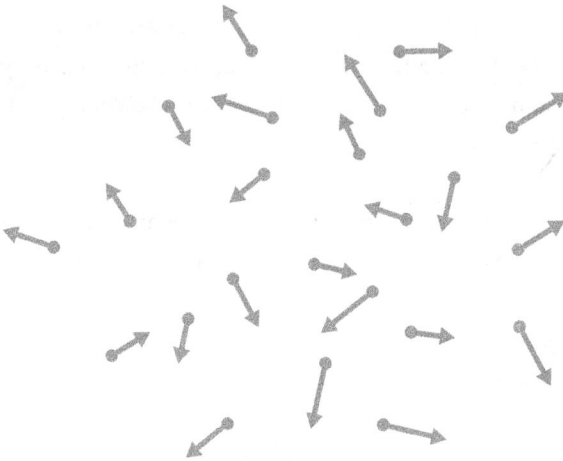

Visions for human performance version 3.0,
in which all perspectives are unified

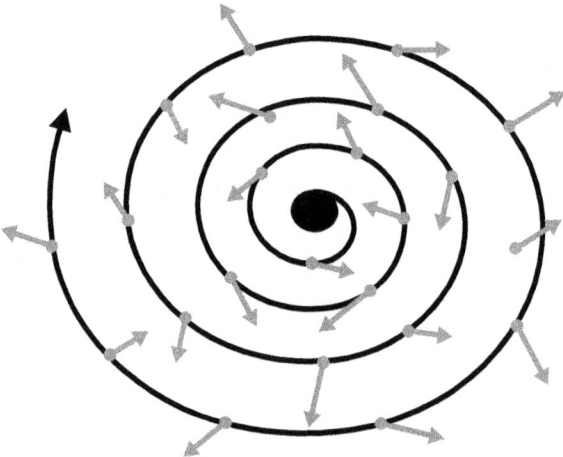

CHAPTER 10

One World will emerge with the rise of the World Axis Education revolution

Jesu Noh:

Ok, so now let's move to the topic of education.

Interviewer:

— Great !

There is a question I want to ask based on what I've heard so far— why do you use the word **" Axis"** ?

I think there are people who may feel some opposition to this.

When you run a 100-meter dash, the goal tape is in the same spot, but the start lines are staggered. Try to picture it. What kind of problem do you think this might cause ?

— Well, it's unfair. The measurements aren't all exactly the same, so there may be disagreement over who was really first.

Ok, so now put this idea in the context of education.

— Hmm... so, **an education where people's starting lines are different**, right ?

In that case, there could be endless, pointless arguments over whose analysis is correct, like everyone is on different parallel lines. In the worst case, it could lead to wars.

Oh, I see. So **we need reliable starting lines—a common foundation.**

That's right. When we see with eyes that take "existence" for granted, everyone just has their own pet theories, and nobody has a correct understanding of anything. That is what education until now has been. **This sort of education based on subjective judgment prevents a grand unification of knowledge. Moreover, this sort of education has abandoned each individual's happiness.**

— What do you mean ?

Right now, education systems prioritize raising a nation's GNP (Gross National Product) over the happiness of individuals. **Individuals are sacrificed, forced to restrain themselves, stuffed full with facts.**

This sort of education assumes that humans are lacking in some way and should be turned into something more worthwhile. Don't you think that is kind of condescending ? This education is left to states, peoples, and religions, but nobody takes responsibility for it.

— That's aggravating. I feel annoyed.

Originally, the priority of education was to encourage the thought that **individuals are beings of happiness, that they begin from a place of happiness, that they are dignity itself.** This is the proper responsibility of education.

So **we need to create a World Axis Education that all 7.7 billion people on Earth can agree on, and through that education, create an age in which everyone can live Win-Win All-Win.**

— If we had education like that, nobody would be subject to menial tasks or comparisons to others anymore.

Going back to our conversation about the word "Axis," consider important world currencies. Currencies like the US dollar are called "key currencies" because they are key, or axis, to the global financial system. It is hard for every country to conduct trade across all their respective currencies, so it's useful to have a currency standard to take on that role. In the same way, a **"key education"—World Axis Education—could bring together education systems all over the world.**

— I see. So, this is why you call it "Axis."

I used the 100-meter dash as an example just before. When these sprint contests began in the 1840s, the standing start was the norm. However, in

— *Figure 53* —
Key currency and Axis education

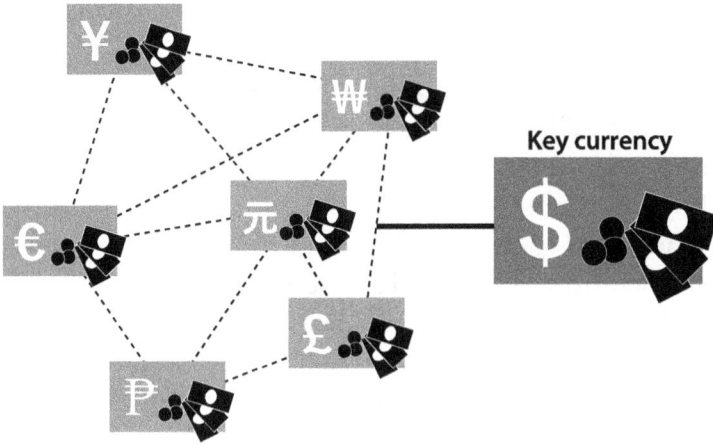

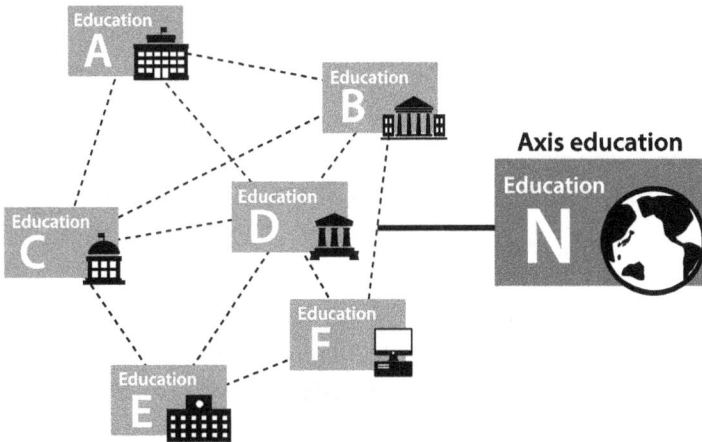

1884, the crouch start appeared, which people found strange[17]. However, ultimately, the crouch start prevailed. Now everyone uses the crouch start.

— Which means... the standing start represents our current education system, and the crouch start represents World Axis Education (WAE). So WAE will become the new standard. But why use the 100-meter dash ?

The crouch start has **you start from the lowest posture,** right ? Doesn't that seem like pulling back as far as you can pull back to get **"human deep learning"** ?

The purpose of the first computers was to calculate things, but via deep learning, they suddenly became 10,000 times more capable than humans. Similarly, humans need deep learning that starts from the deepest possible place.

— **This deep learning is a way of understanding things based on observing from "1" and then observing from "structure." Before, you mentioned the digital mind and programming thought.**

Yes, that's right. To add to that, **WAE is made up of Axis Perspective, Axis Feeling, Axis Evaluation Criteria, Axis Intuition, Axis Language, and Axis Relationships.**

All of this would start in preschool. By age 8, children would understand "0=∞=1," understand the origin of the manifold, be able to perceive its structure, and be practiced in its thought methodology. By 10, children would be able to apply the energy algorithm and Big Data, capable of coding AI brains. By 15, students would be full adults, able to run their own businesses.

— That's amazing. Our previous conversation was at a kindergarten level, and now it sounds like you're telling me we're at an elementary school level. I feel the butterflies of my first day of school. The notion of 15 year old's being adults is a bit strange by today's standards, but in the past in Japan, coming-of-age ceremonies happened from around age 12 to

---

17 https://www.britannica.com/sports/sprint-running

16, and it may be a natural thing if our dimension of education were to change.

That's right. Right now, developed countries are also **dealing with declining birth rates and aging populations,** but this education would help address it. That's because we aren't able to deal with it if we have a bad attitude towards humanity. If we invigorate our encounters with each other and our communication, then marriages should spontaneously increase as well.

— Wow ! I can practically hear the laughter of children already.

Now let's connect the education program to a visualization of jobs.

Right now, there is a **13-step education program,** and each level of it enables the creation of jobs based on what is studied in it. The jobs at each level are broken down further into a program that can be followed.

— The small steps sound good ! So it starts with close listening and observation... it doesn't seem like too much of a pain to do.

That's because listening and observation are the most basic foundation of human power.

However, don't take it too lightly. I said it before, remember ? That human beings don't listen to each other. The physical senses are not capable of true listening or observation. **nTech uses "listening and observation" that don't involve seeing with the physical eye or listening with the physical ear.**

— Oh, I was getting careless ! We cannot see with our eyes. With that in mind, I will do my best to engage with these 13 steps from the very bottom.

These things can be studied at even finer divisions, so use your own study process and insights to create even more effective, understandable programs.

Doing so will lead to a personal brand for each individual.

— I'm excited.

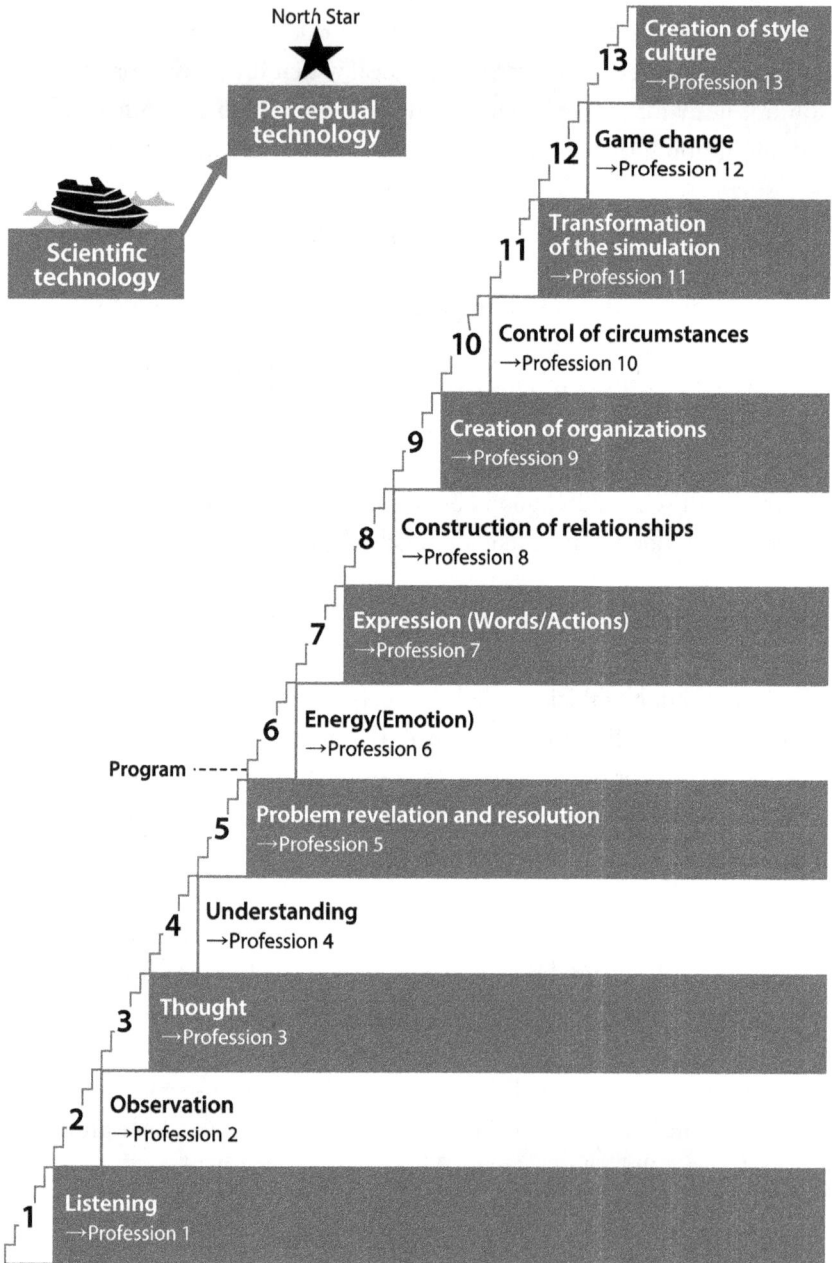

— *Figure 54* —
The hero industry of the 13-step job model

These 13 steps will lead to the emergence of a **hero industry** in a different dimension from anything we've seen before. The hero industry can be divided into a **Tier 1, Tier 2, and Tier 3 industry of Mind.** Let's take a look.

— Hero industry. That sounds cool.

The Tier 1 industry of Mind is an industry for changing/moving humans who have been controlled by the virus of the brain to a place of healthy Mind. All industries until now (Industries 1.0-4.0) can be classified into Tier 1industries of Mind. This is similar to how all the agricultural practices that preceded the Industrial Revolution were subsumed by Industry 1.0.

— I see. Observed from the age of Mind, being done in by the virus of the brain puts you in the Tier 1industry of Mind.

That's right. With the physical senses, we cannot see real things, we cannot hear real things, and so we cannot be truly stimulated. So all of that gets put into the Tier 1 industry of Mind.

Professions at the level of grade 1 of elementary school start with a conceptual understanding that one's self and one's universe does not exist. Sixth grade professions involve the ability to have an ongoing "all-zeroed" intuition and the ability to use **energy procedures and emotion techniques.**

— Energy and emotion techniques ? That sounds pretty crazy...

These techniques are possible because one understands why and how energy and emotion emerge from Mind and what they are in terms of "structure." **They are techniques of the neuronal synapses of the brain.** They do not involve temporary fixes like what you get from medicines or electrostimulation, and of course, do not involve surgical interventions that damage the body.

— You're saying that even that sort of thing is possible ?! And this is the Tier 1 industry of Mind, and at an elementary school level... what could the Tier 2 industry of Mind be like ?

The Tier 2 industry of mind will be made by humans who have attained an "all-zeroed" intuition, always free from their brains, for whom the meaningful-meaningless, the valuable-valueless, the defined-undefined, the completeness of ignorance is second nature.

— Always ? So in other words, an "all-zeroed" intuition that comes as naturally as the five senses. It will have **become a habit.**

That's right. An all-zeroed intuition as automatic as breathing.

In terms of our visualization, this is at the middle school level. It's quite a promotion.

Professions at the 7th grade level exist in the Internet of Everything world, where Mind semiconductor techniques can be used and things can be made with new materials. **This is the level at which digital perception and programming thought can be used.**

The 8th grade level involves work in education and training for using the structure that creates the 5-tiered energy algorithm by obtaining 間 (*ma*) from 1. **5D consulting** also becomes possible at this stage. I'll explain what 5D refers to later.

The professions at the 9th grade level **involve the application of the structure from which 2 emerges from 1 or 5 emerges from 1, including in business.**

— So, they're basically engineers at that point... but there is definitely a need here.

After all, on top of the five crevasses, COVID-19 has eroded human dignity as our material civilization, our material economy has been driven completely into ruin.

So, I think that at this point, the world must be overflowing with people who are desperate to know what it means to be human, what it means to be alive, what everything until this point has meant.

It seems to me that creation of Mind routes via Mind semiconductors and IoE will lead to an explosion in people's sense of need to create dignified relationships.

That's right. So now let's look at the Tier 3 industry of Mind.

The Tier 3 industry of Mind not only is free of control from the virus of the brain, but because people will naturally observe things from Mind, they will be capable of changing the simulation.

— So, this is the realm of experts...

If the Tier 2 industry of Mind is all about "material and function," the Tier 3 industry involves "performance, efficiency, fashion/design, and cultural institution."

It also involves the creation of educational economy, political policy, and art (See Figure 55 on following page).

— It seems that we'll be able to deal with all of our employment issues in one go with the Tier 1- Tier 3 industries of Mind. There will be a lot of people who want to study under this framework and apply it professionally, so we need to get started ! With the prescience of a Rockefeller for a new age !

Well, let's not rush it. But of course, feel free to turn these ideas towards your professional life.

There's 7.7 billion people on Earth looking forward to the same.

By the way, until now we've had a mostly "offline" discussion, but increasingly we live "online." This trend has accelerated since the COVID pandemic began.

I have a proposal for this trend: **Diglink, a "SNS 3.0" system for an online educational revolution.**

— So Diglink is an idea of yours ! I've started hearing about people using it recently. What kind of service is it ?

If we think of a human life as lasting a century, we will supposedly meet around 3,000 people, on average—but we'll only remember the names of about 300 of them, and we'll only recognize about 30 of them as having had an influence on our own values and judgment. **However, social media has enabled us to overcome these limits.** Social media enabled us to

— *Figure 55* —
Tier 1-3 industries of Mind

Tier 1 industry of Mind	
* Industry to change/transform individuals **controlled by the virus of the brain** to healthy Mind World of subject and predicate * Living under the assumption that humanity and the human world does exist, but able to understand that, in fact, they do not exist * All industries until today (industries 1.0-4.0) belong to the Tier 1 industry of Mind	
Professions at the elementary school first grade level	Guidance towards an understanding that one's self and one's universe does not exist
≀	
Professions at the sixth grade level	Guidance towards acquiring the ability to conduct energy/emotion techniques based on all-zero intuition

Tier 2 industry of Mind	
* The meaning of meaninglessness and the value of valuelessness are obvious (Completeness of ignorance) * Unbound by the brain, freedom from the brain's control * Humans and the universe of humans do not actually exist * Acquisition of all zero intuition * IoE	
Professions at the seventh grade level	Understanding of Mind semi-conductors and manufacturing technology Ability to manufacture with new materials World of IoE
Professions at the eighth grade level	1, *Ma*, point "Educational training programs to enable use of 1→field, particle, power, movement, and outcome in daily life" 5D consulting
Professions at the ninth grade level	Application of 1→2, 1→5 in business

Tier 3 industry of Mind	
* Industry in which people are not only not bound by the brain, but this has become second nature. Ability to alter the simulation	
Professions at the tenth grade level	Performance
Professions at the eleventh grade level	Efficiency
Professions at the twelfth grade level	Fashion/Design
Professions at the college freshman level	Cultural style
Professions at the college sophomore level	Education and economics/Politics and policy/Reiwa Street
Professions at the college junior level	Culture and art/Reiwa Field
Professions at the college senior level	Culture and history/Reiwa City

create new identities and make new connections. If the earliest anonymous chat rooms were like the version 1.0 of digital interactions, Facebook is version 2.0, in which we use our birth names.

— I use social media every day, but like I said before, I also frequently feel sick of it. I tend to compare myself to others and I feel lonely.

And **the whole point of Diglink is to overcome that problem with existing social media !**
The typical successful person by "physical human standards" is often someone with dreams and ambition who makes a clear plan and works towards it tirelessly. Most other people are engaged in a sort of game of attempting to mimic these successful people.

— But these days, most people don't even have dreams. There's too much information for people to make heads or tails of their world, so they don't know how to live. They don't even have a standard to set a dream against, so they have no paths forward that they can see.

So, the question is why they don't have dreams. What even is a dream ?
In order to have a dream, someone has to be able to see a path in which they will not lose.

— So, the "discovery of the victorious path" could also be thought of as the "discovery of the path without defeat."

That's right. WAE—which is based on the discovery of $0=\infty=1$—**Defines and consolidates all information knowledge. Consequently, these paths to victory become clear as a matter of course.**
This makes **new Discoveries possible, so Dreams based on them can be clearly described, which leads to novel Designs, upon which we Deliver. This is the 5D plan process.**

— The 5D plan process is amazing. Laying it out like that, all that's left is the execution.

— I'd love to meet people who are able to plan all of that stuff out.

I encourage you to join Diglink, because it is a social media platform designed for people who understand this "5D" mode of thinking.

Diglink has users define/register their specialties out of 60 happiness or success keywords so that they can interact in this 5D realm. The app matches users based on their keywords, so that people with complementary interests can create visionary synergies.

It's easier to express your strengths online compared to offline, so you can present your ideal self there, right ? So this model enables people to establish benchmarks based on their actual abilities and interests.

If those people were to establish dignity-based relationships, don't you think that spiritual cells/Dignity Families that follow the logos of the universe would spread like wildfire ?

— So Diglink users will create Dignity Families ! That sounds fun !

Speaking of which, since we are talking about economics and education, I'm starting to wonder how politics might change as well.

I think that COVID-19 has made a lot of people interested in politics—including myself.

I agree. OK, so what do you think is the central purpose of politics ?

— I haven't thought about it before, but I guess the idea is to govern a country... right ?

The most basic thing in politics is "understanding perspectives." It incorporates the perspectives and evaluation criteria of all individuals, groups, and countries, trying to figure out how they differ and how those differences should be adjusted and managed.

Before the COVID-19 pandemic, the only thing to do was understand that perspectives differ and manage them. Of course, politicians themselves are bound by the virus of the brain and see with their eyes; **they are not aware of the "perspective problem" itself.**

Without clearly resolving the perspective problem, we just keep putting things off.

— I see. Because we all have our respective differences, we need to adjust for them to avoid big problems from arising.

Yes, that's the idea. **But in post-COVID politics, those individuals who are able to clearly resolve the perspective problem will become political leaders.** We need people with a clear understanding of what Mind is in politics.

— Yes. We'll need the power of politics in order to properly master the three coronas.

Political ideologies can be loosely separated into **liberalism** and **collectivism**. The US is an example of liberalism, while the USSR and PRC are examples of collectivism. These ideologies are in opposition with each other.

As time goes on, liberalism will likely cease to be centered around nations and instead focused around cities. Because of the increased interest in politics resulting from the COVID-19 pandemic, **there will be a shift towards participatory democracy. Rather than the state being the base unit, the city will be. Cities will be in competition and cooperation with each other.**

On the other hand, collectivism pushes towards the unification, independence, and development of the people of a nation, so the national focus in politics will continue.

I think that the competition between these two ideologies will ultimately wear the world out, and there will be a "game change" to a "dignitism" in a world with no borders.

— So, what lies ahead is "**dignity**."

That's right. Both collectivism and liberalism claim to be democratic, but once we become humans of Mind who are truly capable of making decisions, **every individual will command authority.** Such individuals will form collectives, and those collectives will give rise to a federation of cities. These cities will be the hubs of political development, and cooperation between cities will lead to One World. The whole world will transcend conflicts over ideology and ethnicity and **enter an age moving towards a One World of allied cities.**

— What we've seen until now—whether totalitarianism or individualism—has all been an age of the perspective of the brain.

If the meaningful-meaningless, the valuable-valueless, and the defined-undefined become common sense, One World won't be far off. The politics of the age of dignity beyond democracy sound bright.

Like I said, the new platform is likely to become the city. Factories created products in the 20th century, **but in the 21st century, the age of AI, the city itself will become a factory.**

— Ummm... the city is a factory ? So, the product is... ?

This will be the end of the age of physical products. This will not be a virus economy that continues creating products of the same dimension, but a cellular economy able to create next-dimensional products that can be copied !

— I see !

The products will not be physical objects, but spiritual cells— Dignity Families !

You said before that this is the most important element for the spiritual civilization !

That's right ! It is a technology for bringing people together, after all.

The spiritual cell could also be thought of as a "Torus organization" that enables sustainable progress and evolution. From here on, cities will create a variety of Torus organizations and compete based on their creativity and productivity.

— So we create Torus organizations, which will enable explosive growth in Digital Mind and creativity ?

That's right. Infinite autonomy. Right now, we try to predict needs and create physical products to meet them, but the Torus organizations will instead **define problems and reveal our needs.**

— Wow, it's like Einstein. Identifying problems = needs.

Everyone will become a genius greater than Einstein.

Right now, we are in an age in which IoT and AI are transforming our cities into smart cities. There are already a number of cases of this all over the world.

— Yes, this is an interest of mine, so I know of a few of them. For example, Barcelona initiated the Smart City project in 2000.[18] Wi-Fi is being used as citywide ICT infrastructure, and a number of services have been developed. I'm personally concerned about how Japan is lagging in this area. China's efforts have been amazing.

That's right. This trend towards smart cities will only accelerate. Roads, buildings, humans, everything will have chips implanted, resulting in the entire urban domain acting in concert like a single organism, and automation will become more common as well.

For example, AI robots might sense slight fevers in people and offer them medicine, or constantly adjust the temperature of rooms or bathwater. Homes will be able to sense emotions like anxiety, and adjust background music and lighting in order to make inhabitants feel better. If people are running out of ingredients, AI robots may resupply them automatically, and in schools, AIs could analyze the degree of comprehension of students and put together custom education plans.

— It's like futuristic things that seem like they came out of a movie will become reality. I can only imagine how amazing the speed of transformation will be.

I am describing something that goes beyond even that. **I'm describing a model of the city evolved beyond the smart city.** These cities will be

---

18 *https://dime.jp/genre/861138/*

full of people who have undergone World Axis Education. They will be **"dignity cities."**

— This is the city competition and Torus organization stuff you just mentioned !

That's right. The smart cities of today will be **the base for research into city-making.** For example, finding ways to ensure that earthquakes won't cause problems, researching cars that can run both on top of and at the bottom of the ocean, anti-gravity apartments, research to enable us to travel beyond the Solar System. Every block of the city would be engaged in a research theme.

— That's a pretty big theme, but if you understand the Structure of Mind/energy/matter and Digital Mind is second nature to you, we would pump out more and more dreamlike technology. After all, everything is an inexhaustible energy source.

Every last person will become that source itself, able to act in total freedom, able to incite situational changes by using the Structure.

That is why this will also be **an age in which everyone will become a true artist.**

— You're talking about aesthetics ?

That's right. Our concepts of culture and art will change completely.

I said before that aesthetics is seeing things from the deepest Mind.

It is the method of observation that sees from the place where energy, space, time, and being don't exist. The source of the power that makes all beings come into being, and change, move, and transform those beings. This intuition of Mind can also be called Total Intuition.

Culture and art until now have been based on the world of the 5 senses.

When this is the case, **"discrimination"** is important. Priority is placed on differences in the shape and pattern of separate entities; art is more popular the more distinct it is and receives more critical praise as well. However, this is the result of the "separation faculties" of the human brain being expressed in reality. That is to say, **this is art and culture of humans controlled by the perspective of the brain.**

Moving forward, we will not be in an age in which we use our brains to make art, **but in an age in which we use Mind.**

Rather than focusing on differences, **our art and culture will enhance our Total Intuition of the connectedness of all things.**

Rather than differences, **we will see commonalities.**

— I am still having a hard time picturing it, but I can tell that the dimensionality of our beauty will deepen.

Deeper, wider, more broad-minded beauty... I can't quite explain it.

Also, I said that everyone will become an artist, right ?

Until now, most people have been on the **consuming end** of art and culture—the side that consumes energy. **The new art and culture, however, will enable everyone to become independent, self-motivated, capable creators on the generative side of the equation.**

We will be as radiators of energy, standing from the borderless world of "1" without points, lines, or planes.

— I'm getting pretty excited. So, the world will be awash with art and culture brought forth from the energy of us all ? This world is going to be full of energy !

The art that will be the most popular will be **art that fills people with strength and motivation.**

Art and culture connected to the source of the world that brings all beings into being and causes their transformations, changes, and movements **will show how to liberate ourselves from the world we know, the world the brain perceives, and enjoy it fully. This is a characteristic of the art and culture of after-corona.**

Aesthetics are teamwork more than anything else.

— The embodiment of aesthetics is teamwork.

That's right. True beauty goes hand-in-hand with motivational force. **Art is not just something to look at. It is something that inspires.** The greatest form of that is **teamwork that emerges from the assembly of people who have become dignity itself** after freeing themselves from the brain. People who start from "1" can synthesize a wide variety of perspectives to create a more beautiful world.

I said before that groups of 5 people will come to take on the meaning of "individual," and that groups of 1+5+25=31 people will become the new concept of the family: The Dignity Family.

> — Yes, that's right. My image of cells and assembly has deepened, so I understand the need, but... I still don't get this "5 people in a group" thing. Is this related to Chinese cosmology?

That's right. The universe is made from the 5 levels of energy that emerge from the Fundamental Motion of Mind "1," right?

So, if you don't have that minimum of 5 levels, you can't have reality. So you can't have just one person. 5 people are one.

One's physical body is just a fiction, right? **Human beings of "1" itself can be created through groups of 5 people.**

In terms of perspective, **if you bring five perspectives together they will all complement each other.** Once you synthesize those perspectives, you will have decision-making accuracy and synergy far beyond what a single human can do.

> — 5 perspectives... if you can describe this a little more, I think I might be able to talk about it in my meetings.

Chinese cosmology has five elements: wood, fire, earth, metal, and water. These have a structure of compatibility relationships called **allelopathy.** If it is put to use here, **you are sure to produce 4 perspectives in response to an individual's principles and position: complement, denial, praise, Agreement.** Rather than a perspective being good or bad, all five simply "are."

— *Figure 56* —
Allelopathy and the 5 elements

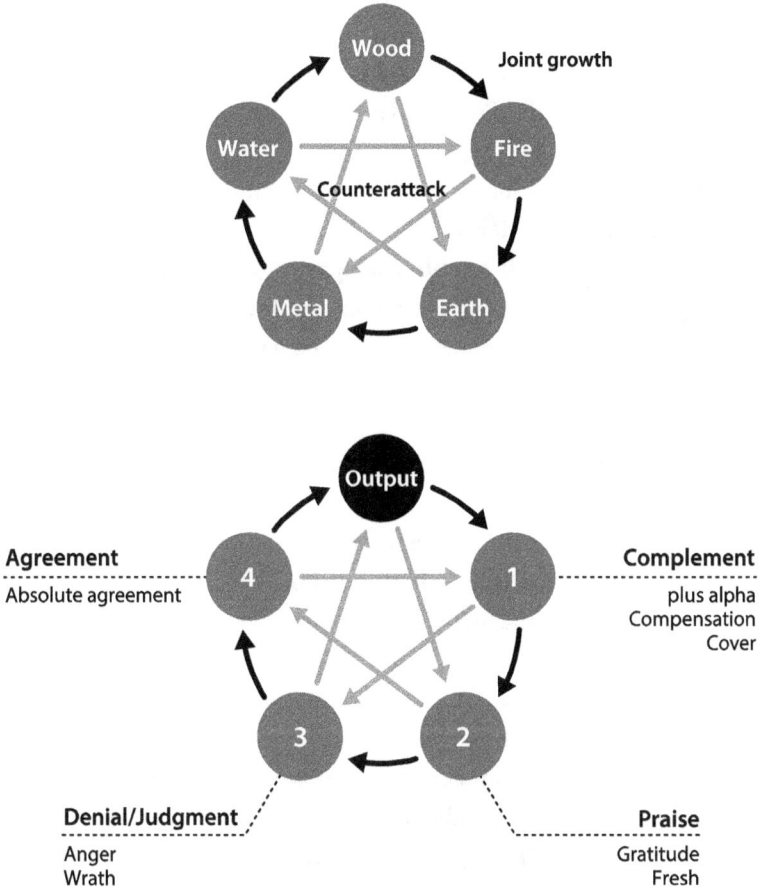

If you understand this, then even if you encounter a contrary opinion, you will understand that someone is simply offering an opinion from the "denial" perspective, so it's not that big a deal, right ? Even before that, if you understand perspectives then you shouldn't have a problem anyway, but the point is that **the principles and position of one person evolve via the other 4 perspectives.**

— This is really useful ! So if 5 people are always in communication, the evolution of ideas will be much faster compared to one person alone. Now I see how 5 people can be an "individual" !

To return to what we were discussing before, there is yet another stage beyond the dignity city: the *Reiwa* **City.** I mentioned before that the Chinese characters used for *Reiwa* suggest a world of coming together and living according to "1" in the present moment. In English, the word could be translated as "Beautiful Harmony."

The *Reiwa* City will enable the spread of Dignity Families and Torus organizations throughout the urban domain. The Dignity Family will conduct R&D on emotional patterns and games, as well as on telepathy and quantum capsules and teleportation, etc.

— I'm getting excited just listening about it.

Also, the *Reiwa* **City Alliance that connects each *Reiwa* City together has a new engine for growth called Edunomic (education x economics) which will become a platform for new industry.**
Smart cities, dignity cities, and *Reiwa* Cities are all platforms for industry.

The *Reiwa* City will support the development of future cities by connecting all individual and human relationships into one.

Depression, suicide, homicide, and war will disappear from the Earth, and as *homo deus*, **we will be able to realize One World as the immortal, august, and divine beings** that we have always sought to become.

— Immortal, august, and divine...

So, we will never die. We will live as "1" itself forever in a state of living-as-though-dead.

Unconditional happiness, passion, and sublime transcendence, always.

We will be a quadrillion times greater than any god, beings of Mind itself, absolute artists able to recreate all things at all times.

We will form Dignity Families, create a spiritual world,
explore beyond that world, and reproduce it.
That's the image that comes to mind.

— *Figure 57* —
The One World vision

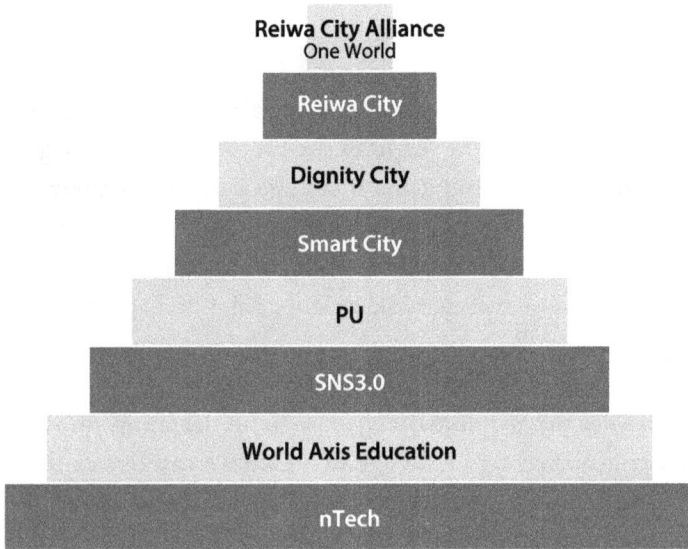

Reiwa City Alliance
One World

Reiwa City

Dignity City

Smart City

PU

SNS3.0

World Axis Education

nTech

The founder of Apple, Steve Jobs, supposedly said "I would trade all of my technology for an afternoon with Socrates."[19] I think now I suddenly understand what he meant.

This new discovery of 0=∞=1, the invention of the victorious path. Having a clear "answer," even here...

We are entering a new age.

That's because I am at human performance version 2.0. Right now, the fun competition of human performance version 3.0 is awaiting the world.

What remains for us is organizational innovation. The deepest connections yet unmade, the Mind routes that result, and the teamplay they will make possible will change the world.

_____

19 Goodreads.
  https://www.goodreads.com/quotes/455762-i-would-trade-all-of-my-technology-for-an-afternoon#

Our common sense will change. "Existence" will no longer be taken for granted. "Non-existence" will seem obvious.

All entities are made whole.

Living is playing and celebrating.

Because non-existence is taken for granted, because we live in an illusory hologram, **we can enjoy the world of the brain's art like it's a game.** We can prioritize team play, and **usher in an age that all can enjoy.**

Once we install the Deep Engine, we can pursue depth of happiness—not just height of happiness—a world with both height and depth. An age in which we can achieve success while guiding others to happiness.

This is the end of the relative lifestyle.

Now arrives the absolute lifestyle, without others. Without self.

The curtain is rising on an age in which we can live as the eternal unchanging Original Mind that brings forth self and other.

— A world without other or self. It's true.

We can put an end to pointless conflict and celebrate as Original Mind itself.

We already have the tools and the path. All we need to do is move towards becoming One Mind.

That's right. Put your energy towards it.

Ask the people you meet this question:

Do you have anything that you like more, that you think is more beautiful or valuable than your own life ?

If they say that they have nothing like that, tell them that they are still just an animal.

Why ? Because if you find nothing more valuable or beautiful than your own life, you are a **slave to your brain.**

Humanity is not the flesh. It is the spirit.

The physical body is just a machine. Animals, plants, and humans all repeat the same pattern over and over.

In order to become true bodies of spirit, we must live as though dead, here and now.
Our way of death decides victory or defeat. This enables us to live in a complete fashion.
That is dignity.

A perception revolution. This is not just something that will happen. **It is something that *should* happen.**
Let us embrace all of the pain we have known, and turn it around to create a beautiful future.

— Yes, as a person of the future, as a human of dignity, I feel in my heart the mission this age has placed upon me to create a beautiful world of team play.
Thank you so much for these 2 days.

— By the way, I apologize, but do you think you could summarize the 5 main points of nTech for me ?
How about a rundown of 5 elements to help people understand how nTech structures our thoughts ?

Yes, of course. OK, let's finish this off with a recap !

1. Right here, right now, don't look with your eyes !
The most basic part to understanding what needs to be changed and how is remembering to "not look with your eyes."
In order to bring about union and solidarity, we can't think in terms of "heights." We have to tackle the fundamental issues lurking in the depths. That's why we need the Deep Engine and Deep Learning.

2. Ask yourself if you have something you find more valuable and beautiful than your life—something for which you're willing to die.
If there is something you would die for, you become able to live life to the fullest and engage in the celebration of your dignity.

3. Right here and now, unite with the eternal and control the impermanent

Become the invariant Fundamental Motion of Mind itself, and be in control of all change.

If you do so, you will gain the independence, initiative, and motivation to change all things: your own thoughts and feelings, the thoughts and feelings of others, even the flow of history and civilization.

4. Be like the elements

Find a 間 (*ma*) or position that guarantees victory, and move towards it with the speed of the wind (Wind).

Once you are there, overwhelm your opposition in silence. Claim your target stealthily, before you can be overtaken by anyone else (Forest).

When the time of victory is nigh and the foe appears, burn them all away in a single conflagration (Fire).

Resolve yourself to see your plan through from start to finish, and be able to assess events with a steadfast will and steadfast heart. Become an unmovable rock of principles, truth, and justice (Mountain).

5. Go beyond the virus system and replicate under a cellular system

Don't be like a virus and keep replicating on the same level. Instead, strive for higher levels, like a multicellular organism. Create spiritual cells and incite a dignity democracy that transcends the capitalism of today.

In order to make these five things second nature, please keep a notepad in your pocket and record the following things when they happen.

1. From front to back, write down things that you wouldn't be able to see if you saw with your eyes.

2. From back to front, write down things that you would be able to see if you saw from the Fundamental Motion of Mind "1."

By building experience with these two habits, you will be able to make these 5 things part of your daily life !

— Thank you so much for fulfilling my request !

This overview will be useful for practical application ! I'm going to start using it right away !

No, thank you ! I look forward to seeing what you accomplish.

AFTERWORD

As of this writing, over 400,000 people have died due to the COVID-19 global pandemic. This disaster has laid bare the state of crisis in our 5 million-year-old material civilization. In a word, this crisis is a "crisis of human dignity." Without knowing the nature of mind, humanity has endeavored to preserve it and make decisions based on traditions, customs, and norms. However, these things are now in total decay, and on top of the distrust and unease people feel towards education, economics, politics, and culture, we feel dread over our diminishing ability to peer into the future as well.

In order to turn back the threats this age poses to us, I decided to publish this book in the hopes that it may help.

I want to thank the members of NR Group who have provided me with generous aid to make this publication a reality.

In particular, I want to express special thanks to Misa Okayama, Chiho Ishida, and Ayako Hattori for their encouraging support both material and psychological.

June 2020, Sakuragaoka, Shibuya Ward, Tokyo, Japan
Jesu Noh

ABOUT THE AUTHOR

Jesu Noh

Born in Daegu, South Korea.

"Where does light come from?" This was the question Jesu Noh fostered as a young child, one which launched his pursuit of the "true 'structure' upon which the world exists." With over twenty martial arts ranks under his belt, he runs a martial arts hall known for producing Korean national athletes, as well as a company focusing on early childhood education services, all the while working on the frontlines of education and human development.

Japan was a country that had always filled him with intrigue. However, after his arrival in 1995, his company went bankrupt, a domino effect of the bankruptcy of an affiliated organization. It was an event that robbed him of his wealth, relationships, and family. Without even the ability to speak Japanese, he was thrown into the depths of despair. It was 1996 when he discovered the fundamental motion of the universe "$0=\infty=1$" (the image of 間 (*ma*)). Just as he was battling suicidal urges, feeling unable to make a breakthrough in his life, his days of utter misery took a drastic turn into those of immense hope. The discovery soon spurred the systematization of the education of nTech, the perception technology, into a technology that can be understood and utilized by everybody.

He predicted AI would surpass human intelligence and cause human beings to question the meaning of their existence, becoming disconcerted about their own identity. He is an advocate of numerous innovative systems such as Diglink—the next-generation SNS—and Personal Universe (PU), a concept of universal computers that clears the issues of the dogmatism and uniformity of totalitarianism, along with the isolation and complexity of individualism. Garnering over 100,000 participants, his lectures and seminars are acclaimed for opening one's eyes to the most essential element of human existence, and he has gained popularity for his kind, passionate, and friendly demeanor. Furthermore, as possibly the most Japan-loving Korean in the world, he wishes for the amelioration of Japan-Korea relations. He is a *Reiwa* philosopher who continuously promotes the establishment of the Hero industry under the motto "of the dignity, by the dignity, for the dignity," guiding people worldwide living in the age of eroding human dignity.

He is currently the chairman of the NR Group, the South Korean representative of the Japan-Korea VISION Alliance, and the founder of nTech and HITOTSU-GAKU.

Publications: "Ninshiki (perceptual) Revolution"; "Emotional Revolution (1 and 2)"; "Communication Revolution"; "Scholastic Revolution"; "Revolution of the Nation"; "Application of Prince Shotoku's 'Seventeen-Article Constitution' Through Kanjutsu (nTech) & "Application of the Japanese Spirit Through Kanjutsu (nTech)"

http://www.noh-jesu.com/en/
https://www.nr-america.com

www.ingramcontent.com/pod-product-compliance
Lightning Source LLC
Chambersburg PA
CBHW070337090426
42733CB00009B/1218